ACTS

Also by James Montgomery Boice

Witness and Revelation in the Gospel of John

Philippians: An Expositional Commentary

The Minor Prophets: An Expositional Commentary (2 volumes)

How to Live the Christian Life (originally, *How to Really Live It Up*)

Ordinary Men Called by God (originally, *How God Can Use Nobodies*)

The Last and Future World

The Gospel of John: An Expositional Commentary (5 volumes)

The Epistles of John: An Expositional Commentary

"Galatians," in the Expositor's Bible Commentary

Can You Run Away from God?

Our Sovereign God, editor

Our Savior God: Studies on Man, Christ and the Atonement, editor

Does Inerrancy Matter?

The Foundation of Biblical Authority, editor

Making God's Word Plain, editor

The Sermon on the Mount

Genesis: An Expositional Commentary (3 volumes)

The Parables of Jesus

The Christ of Christmas

The Gospel of Matthew: An Expositional Commentary (2 volumes)

Standing on the Rock

The Christ of the Empty Tomb

Foundations of the Christian Faith (4 volumes in one)

Christ's Call to Discipleship

Transforming Our World: A Call to Action, editor

Ephesians: An Expositional Commentary

Daniel: An Expositional Commentary

Joshua: An Expositional Commentary

Nehemiah: An Expositional Commentary

The King Has Come

Romans: An Expositional Commentary (4 volumes)

Mind Renewal in a Mindless Age

The Glory of God's Grace (originally, *Amazing Grace*)

Psalms: An Expositional Commentary (3 volumes)

Sure I Believe, So What?

Hearing God When You Hurt

Foundations of God's City (originally, *Two Cities, Two Loves: Christian Responsibility in a Crumbling Culture*)

Here We Stand!: A Call from Confessing Evangelicals, editor
  with Benjamin E. Sasse

Living by the Book: The Joy of Loving and Trusting God's Word

Acts: An Expositional Commentary

The Heart of the Cross, with Philip G. Ryken

What Makes a Church Evangelical?

The Doctrines of Grace, with Philip G. Ryken

ACTS

An Expositional Commentary

JAMES MONTGOMERY BOICE

BakerBooks
Grand Rapids, Michigan

© 1997 by James Montgomery Boice

Published by Baker Books
a division of Baker Publishing Group
P.O. Box 6287, Grand Rapids, MI 49516-6287
www.bakerbooks.com

Paperback edition published in 2006
ISBN 10: 0-8010-6633-6
ISBN 978-0-8010-6633-7

Second printing, February 2007

Printed in the United States of America

The Library of Congress has cataloged the hardcover edition as follows:
Boice, James Montgomery, 1938–
    Acts : an expositional commentary / James Montgomery Boice
        p.   cm.
    Includes bibliographical references and indexes.
    ISBN 10: 0-8010-1137-X (cloth)
    ISBN 978-0-8010-1137-5 (cloth)
    1. Bible. N.T. Acts—Commentaries. 2. Bible. N.T. Acts—Homiletical use. I. Title.
BS2625.3.B58   1997
226.6'077—dc21   97-5128

To him who has called us to be his witnesses
in Jerusalem, in all Judea and Samaria,
and to the ends of the earth

Contents

Preface

In the last few years I have come across a number of disturbing books that ring a loud alarm for the church establishment known as evangelicalism. *Evangel* means "good news," or "the gospel," and the evangelical churches are those that assume they know the gospel and are defending it in a day when liberal churches are not. The books I am referring to say that this is not so, that evangelicals are actually in the process of abandoning the gospel along with many other theological convictions on which the church has been built.

One outstanding book is David F. Wells's *No Place for Truth: Or Whatever Happened to Evangelical Theology?* Michael Scott Horton edited *Power Religion: The Selling Out of the Evangelical Church.* John MacArthur has contributed *Ashamed of the Gospel: When the Church Becomes Like the World.* Those books appeared in 1992 and 1993. Now, even more recently (in 1996), we have John H. Armstrong's edited work *The Coming Evangelical Crisis* with chapters on the decline of the evangelical churches by such perceptive observers as Albert Mohler Jr., W. Robert Godfrey, R. Kent Hughes, S. Lewis Johnson, and others, including Horton and Armstrong. These authors come from a variety of denominations and represent different types of ministries. But they are united in their belief that evangelicals are in deep trouble, and what is worse, that they do not seem to know it.

As Wells sees the problem, the evangelical church is not just ill or languishing, though that would be bad enough. It is already either dead or dying, and the reason for its sad condition is that it has forgotten its theology. Today's evangelical church no longer understands the gospel it claims to uphold, and if it no longer understands the gospel, it certainly no longer proclaims it to an unbelieving world.

9

What should be done? A number of things, many of which are being done. These books are themselves attempts to clarify and work toward a solution to the problem. Some of these men, including myself, have joined together in a coalition known as the Alliance of Confessing Evangelicals, which has as its stated purpose "to call the church, amidst our dying culture, to repent of its worldliness, to recover and confess the truth of God's Word as did the Reformers, and to see that truth embodied in doctrine, worship, and life." I endorse that goal and effort wholeheartedly.

What I would like to suggest in this preface is that we might study the early church, as it is presented to us in Acts, to find what made it strong and how it made its way in the pagan culture of its time.

When I first began to study and preach on Acts nearly ten years ago I was struck by a number of things. One was the rapid, amazing growth of the early church. Humanly speaking, it had nothing going for it. It had no money, no proven leaders, no technological tools for propagating the gospel. And it faced enormous obstacles. It was utterly new. It taught truths that were incredible to the unregenerate world. It was subject to the most intense hatreds and persecutions. Yet, as Luke records its growth in this document (Acts), it spread from Jerusalem, which was an obscure corner of the world, to Rome, the world's capital, all within the lifetime of the first generation of believers. Every one of the chief characters Luke brings into the story had been living during the lifetime of the Lord.

The second thing that struck me was the concern Luke had for the actual presentation of the gospel, that is, for the early Christian preaching. His book is only twenty-eight chapters long. But in those twenty-eight chapters he has included nineteen sermons or formal addresses: many by Paul, several by Peter, the longest of all by Stephen, the first martyr.[1] In other words, the book is full of teaching. What this means is that the way the gospel spread in the first Christian century and needs to spread again in our time is by the faithful preaching and teaching of the great truths of the Bible. There is nothing today's church needs so much as to rediscover the doctrine, spirit, and commitments of the early Christian community.

As usual in my books, I want to thank the session and congregation of Tenth Presbyterian Church in Philadelphia, who from the beginning have permitted and encouraged me to spend much of my time in study and sermon preparation. I find that they have been wise, since others, laypeople as well as church staff, have done much of the other work and have done it far better than I could have, with the result that the church has grown toward a true maturity as each part has done its work (Eph. 4:11–16).

May ours become a new great day in which the gospel first preached in Jerusalem, then in Judea and Samaria and even Rome, might also go out from us to our neighborhoods, cities, countries, and the ends of the earth.

PART ONE

The Witness in Jerusalem

1

The First Forty Days

Acts 1:1-11

In my former book, Theophilus, I wrote about all that Jesus began to do and to teach until the day he was taken up to heaven, after giving instructions through the Holy Spirit to the apostles he had chosen. After his suffering, he showed himself to these men and gave many convincing proofs that he was alive. He appeared to them over a period of forty days and spoke about the kingdom of God.

Acts 1:1–3

Acts is the second volume of a two-volume history written by the companion of the apostle Paul. The first volume is the Gospel according to Luke. Sometimes scholars refer to these books as "Luke/Acts." We know they belong together, because the introductions link them. The Book of Luke begins with a dedication to a man whom he calls "most excellent Theophilus" (Luke 1:1–4), and Luke mentions Theophilus again in Acts, referring also to Luke's "former book" (Acts 1:1).

Ancient books were generally written on papyrus scrolls. It was practical to have a scroll about thirty-five feet in length. When it got any longer it got too bulky to carry around. This physical limitation has determined the length of many books of the Bible. A number of them—the Gospels (Matthew, Luke, and John especially), Acts, Romans, and some others—are about this length in ancient script. It would seem that Luke, who set out to write a history of Jesus' life and the expansion of the church up to his own age, decided to do it on two scrolls. The first scroll concerned the life of Christianity's founder and the second picked up the story and carried it to the arrival of the apostle Paul in Rome about thirty years later. Some scholars think that Luke had probably planned a third as well, dealing with Paul's release from prison and his further ministry to the western part of the Roman Empire.

A Great Historian

Acts is excellent history. It is excellent even from a secular point of view. The English scholar F. F. Bruce has written a book on the New Testament entitled *The New Testament Documents: Are They Reliable?* in which he spells out the details of Luke's extraordinary accuracy.[1] Bruce points out that to have written a history like Luke's was no easy task in those days. Today if you want to write a history of something that went on somewhere in the world, it is not at all difficult to do it because you can go to libraries and use reference works. In Luke's day that was not possible. There were very few libraries and those that existed were not accessible to the common man. Most libraries did not have reference volumes and even if they had, the events Luke was trying to chronicle had taken place—at least at the beginning—in what the people of that day would have said were remote areas of the world.

Nevertheless, as Bruce shows, not only did Luke overcome these difficulties to write his history, he also produced an exceedingly remarkable book. The titles given to the rulers of the cities to which the apostle Paul goes are accurate. The flavors of the cities are what we know them to have been from other sources. Antioch, where Paul ministered, was not at all like Jerusalem. Jerusalem was not like Rome. Ephesus also had its own flavor. Luke knew what those cities were like.

Not only can we appreciate Luke as a secular historian—that is, one who chronicles secular things well—but we also can appreciate him as the great historian of the early church.

Luke begins his book in Jerusalem, picking up his account with the closing hours of the earthly ministry of Jesus Christ. It is the period between Jesus' resurrection and ascension into heaven. Then Luke methodically records the spread of the new religion throughout the Roman world. At the beginning it is spread largely through the influence of the apostle Peter. The first half of Acts recounts this. In the second half of the book, Luke shows how Christianity spread even to Rome through the phenomenal life and ministry of the apostle Paul.

People are puzzled by history. "Does history have meaning?" they ask. Luke does not merely give us a history of the early church; he tells us that there is a plan to history. God is unfolding it. That plan does not have to do with the rise and fall of empires. It does not have to do with one race or people being more influential than another. The Bible does not even look at history as having to do primarily with individual successes or attainments. The meaning of history is in God's work: God reaching down into the mass of fallen humanity and saving some hell-bent men and women, bringing them into a new fellowship, the church, and beginning to work in them in such a way that glory is brought to Jesus Christ. That is what Luke is writing about as he unfolds these events.

Luke's history opens up and embraces the entire church age. At the beginning, we are in contact with the risen Christ and a world of miracles. This is a world we have very little contact with today. But then, as the book progresses, we have the feeling that it becomes increasingly like the kind of world we know. At the end, we find the Christians bearing witness, just as we are called to bear witness, and being persecuted, just as we are often persecuted. As we study this book we find sound principles of church growth and see the way in which temptation and trials are overcome by the grace of God.

We begin with Acts 1:1–11, verses that deal with the forty days between the resurrection of Jesus Christ and his ascension. These verses emphasize the historicity of Christianity, the presence of Christ, the missionary mandate, and the Lord's return.

Christianity: A Historical Faith

First, we find an emphasis on the historical basis of Christianity. Luke tells Theophilus that he is going to continue the history that he began in his Gospel. In that earlier book he said he had quite carefully investigated the details of the life of Jesus Christ and had written them down only after this investigation. Luke wants to continue that procedure in this volume. The things he wrote in the first book concerned "all that Jesus began to do and to teach until the day he was taken up to heaven" (Acts 1:1). These things are going to continue in the church by the power of the Holy Spirit.

"Acts" is a short name for "The Acts of the Apostles." It might more properly be called "The Acts of Jesus Christ" or, to be even more accurate, "The Acts of the Holy Spirit in the Church of Jesus Christ through God's People." The English rector John R. W. Stott suggests this title: "The Continuing Words and Deeds of Jesus by His Spirit through His Apostles."[2]

Christianity is a historical religion. It is a religion that is not based primarily on an idea or philosophy. Most of the religions of the world can exist apart from their founder. You do not have to have a historical Buddha to have Buddhism. All you have to have are Buddhist teachings. So also with many other religions. This is not the case with Christianity. If you take away the history—if you reduce it, as some have tried to do, to a religion of mere ethics or ideas—Christianity evaporates. This is because Christianity is indissolubly linked to the life and accomplishments of Christianity's founder.

Jesus taught about God, but he did not merely teach. He showed what God was like. Then, in order to achieve our salvation, he died for us, taking our place to bear the wrath of God. Without that historical basis, Christianity would pass, as have many other religions, into the trash bin of history.

But Christianity is based on proven fact. There is much skepticism about this in our day. Whenever you talk of facts or, worse yet, proven facts, people grow skeptical because they question whether ultimately anything can ever be proven or be certain. We can understand and sympathize with that skepticism because we are all fallible human beings, and we perceive things fallibly. We distort what we receive.

This distortion is pointed out in science, where in certain kinds of experiments the very presence of the observer changes what happens. In such situations scientists rightly point out that there is a barrier of observation beyond which we cannot seem to go. There are situations in which we can never really know what is going on because the very fact that we are trying to know what is going on changes what's happening.

That is true in science, but Christianity is different.

When Luke writes of Jesus' resurrection, he says that Jesus "showed himself to these men and gave *many convincing proofs* that he was alive" (v. 3, italics mine). That is a very important sentence, for it indicates that Jesus did not merely give his disciples certain ideas that they were then to carry into the world. He appeared to them as one who had risen from the dead. They knew he had died. Some of them had stood at the cross. They had heard the blow of the hammers. They had seen the nails driven and then later, when the soldiers came, had seen the spear thrust into Christ's side. They knew Jesus had died. In fact, so convinced were they of his death that they soon began to scatter and go home, because . . . well, although it was nice to have known him, he was dead now and to give one's life to the mere memory of a dead Christ would be foolishness.

But then Jesus rose and began appearing to them. His appearances were sufficient to draw them together again. They would never have come together for a philosophy or mythology. They came together because the Christ they had known and loved was alive. He had conquered death.

Thomas was the greatest of the skeptics. Even after the resurrection, when the other disciples had seen Christ and had come to Thomas to proclaim the resurrection, Thomas said, "Unless I see the nail marks in his hands and put my finger where the nails were, and put my hand into his side, I will not believe it" (John 20:25). When Jesus appeared to Thomas this alone was sufficient to dispel all this doubter's doubt. He fell before him with the confession, "My Lord and my God" (v. 28).

This and other similar experiences are what Luke had in mind when he wrote of "convincing proofs." He was saying, I am going to chart the spread of Christianity, but I want you to know at the very beginning that this is a religion based on historical facts, including even the amazing matter of the resurrection. The resurrection has been demonstrated by many convincing proofs, and it is proof of everything else that needs proving.

Here is the way the argument goes.

1. *The resurrection is a fact.* The disciples knew Jesus had been raised from the dead.

2. If the resurrection is a fact, *it proves the deity of Jesus.* Christ claimed to be divine before his crucifixion. If that was true, it was a great truth. If it was false, it was blasphemy. Moreover, Jesus said that God, his Father, was going to raise him from the dead after his crucifixion. That was a nearly impossible claim. Yet Jesus' resurrection from the dead after three days proved his deity, for it is impossible that God would have raised him from the dead if his claim to deity had been false.

3. *A divine Christ must speak truth,* because God is truthful and must speak truthfully.

4. If what Jesus says is true, then *we can trust everything he teaches.* We can trust the Bible, because Jesus taught that it was the Word of God. We can believe that God has forgiven our many sins, because Jesus taught that God would do that for all who believe in him.

The Presence of the Living Christ

There is a second thing to see about these opening verses: the dominant presence of the living Christ.

These opening verses are noteworthy for referring to each member of the Trinity. In verse 3 Jesus speaks about the "kingdom of God," a reference to God the Father. Verse 5 mentions the Holy Spirit: "John baptized with water, but in a few days you will be baptized with the Holy Spirit." Verse 6 refers to Jesus as the Lord: "Lord, are you at this time going to restore the kingdom to Israel?" References to the Trinity are not unusual for the New Testament, of course. They occur elsewhere. What is striking here is that Acts refers to the person of Jesus Christ over and over again. Every one of these first eleven verses either records Jesus speaking or refers to him.

The ending of this section is particularly important. The angels are talking about Jesus: "This same Jesus, who has been taken from you into heaven, will come back in the same way you have seen him go into heaven" (v. 11). That is important because in critical New Testament studies there has been an attempt on the part of some scholars to abandon the New Testament to discover what they choose to call the real or "historical" Jesus. The historical Jesus movement began more than one hundred years ago with the German scholar Hermann Samuel Reimarus. When he died, he left a manuscript in which he suggested that future New Testament scholarship would have to distinguish between what he called "the aim of Jesus" and "the aim of his disciples," that is, between the Jesus of history and the Christ of faith. By "Jesus of history" he meant the real Jesus, the Jesus who actually lived so many centuries ago. By "Christ of faith" he meant the Jesus of the fervent belief of the early Christians. In other words, Reimarus suggested—and later German scholarship affirmed—that the Jesus we find in the Gospels is not the true Jesus.[3]

As a result of Reimarus's work, German scholarship, in its typically thorough way, launched what became one hundred years of historical Jesus research. During these years, great German thinkers produced volume after volume purporting to tell who the historical Jesus really was. Nevertheless, toward the end of that period, Albert Schweitzer, in *The Quest of the Historical Jesus,* exposed these efforts as a critical dead-end. He said that despite their ability, these scholars only managed to create a Jesus in their own image. If the scholar was a socialist, he produced a socialist Jesus. If he was a moralist, he produced a Jesus who was a teacher of ethics. If he identified with the common man, he produced a Jesus who was a model of the common man. Schweitzer pointed out rightly and wisely that it is impossible to separate the Christ of faith from the Jesus of history.

The Christ of faith, the Christ presented to us in the pages of the New Testament, *is* the Jesus of history. There is no other. This is what Luke says as he begins both his Gospel and Acts. The Lord Jesus Christ, who is and has always been the object of the faith of Christians down through all the Christian centuries, is the Jesus who really lived, who was crucified, and who rose from the dead.

The Missionary Mandate

The third thing we notice about these introductory verses is the missionary mandate. We find it in verses 7 and 8.

The disciples who were with Jesus in the days between his resurrection and ascension still had old-fashioned ideas, and one of these, as we know from the Gospels, was that the kingdom of God was going to be established by political, earthly power. Their idea of the Messiah was a soldier like Judas Maccabeus (Judas the Hammer), who was going to be strong enough to drive out any occupying military forces. In these days, the land was occupied by Romans. So the Jews were looking for a Messiah who would expel the Romans and set up the earthly kingdom of David. The disciples expected to reign with him in this kingdom. On one occasion, the mother of James and John approached Jesus and said, "Grant that one of these two sons of mine may sit at your right and the other at your left in your kingdom" (Matt. 20:21). She was not thinking of a kingdom in some far-off future day. She thought that Jesus was going to establish his kingdom on earth right then by political means.

Even here, after the resurrection, the disciples had these warped ideas. John Stott notes, "The verb *restore* shows that they were expecting a political and territorial kingdom; the noun *Israel* that they were expecting a national kingdom; and the adverbial clause *at this time* that they were expecting its immediate establishment."[4]

We find them saying something like this: Lord, we have waited a long time. We have waited through the three long years of your ministry. You obviously considered those three years to be important. We're not sure that they were as important as all that. We wish you had gotten the kingdom going a lot sooner. But we were patient because, after all, you are the Lord, and we are only disciples. And, of course, we went through that whole nasty business of the crucifixion when you were rejected and killed. Then we experienced the resurrection, and we're sure you had your purpose in that, too. But enough is enough! Let's get down to the thing that really matters. Are you at this time—now, at last, after all this waiting on our part—going to restore the kingdom?

Jesus answered: It is not your business to know when I am going to set up my kingdom. Your job is to be my witnesses in the world. And that is what you will be. You are going to receive power when the Holy Spirit comes upon you, and you will be my witnesses in Jerusalem, in all Judea and Samaria, and to the ends of the world.

Believers in Christ have always been faced with two great temptations where this assignment is concerned. One is the temptation to idleness, to say, "Well, Jesus has saved me, my wife (or husband), and my children. I have a nice church. Everything is comfortable. I think I'll just sit around and wait for Jesus to come back. We'll be patient. We'll wait."

Jesus says to such an inactive church that they are to be filled with the Holy Spirit and when they are filled they are to go out and witness to him in all the earth. The church that is not witnessing is not obeying its Lord.

The second temptation is the one the disciples were already caught up in. It is the temptation to think that we are to do the Lord's work in the world's way. We are to establish the kingdom politically—by law, by getting Christians into high positions in government, and by imposing our vision of society on the world.

Of course, there is a proper place for a political and legal expression of the Christian world and life view. Christians should seek proper public expression of their beliefs, but they must not suppose that they can bring in the kingdom of God by imposing their views on others. Moral reform will not come by political power or power tactics. Only the Holy Spirit can take the gospel to the hearts and minds of men and women and change them into disciples of the Lord.

The Lord's Return

At the end of these verses is a fourth emphasis. It is the expectation of the return of the Lord. This is the passage that tells of Christ's ascension into heaven. During these days he had been appearing to the disciples on unanticipated occasions to teach them spiritual things. If that had continued, they might have thought, Well, that's the way it's going to be forever. Every so often, Jesus will just be here to give us the kind of instruction we need. Jesus had to teach them that this phase of his work was ending. The moment came when Jesus bade them good-bye, ascended visibly into heaven, and disappeared from sight.

Suddenly the disciples became aware that there were angels standing by them. The angels said, "Men of Galilee, why do you stand here looking up into the sky?" (v. 11). It was a way of saying, Why are you just standing here? There is work to do. Get on with it. Then the angels gave a great promise: "This same Jesus, who has been taken from you into heaven, will come back in the same way you have seen him go into heaven."

We know that the Lord Jesus Christ is returning to judge the world, because we are told about it elsewhere in the New Testament. The disciples also had been told that one day Jesus would return to render judgment. But when the disciples were told that "this same Jesus" would be coming back, they would have thought of the Jesus they loved, not a judge. It was this gentle, loving, gracious but sovereign, holy, and majestic Jesus who would come back. He would stand with them and would say, Well, brothers, how have you done? What have you accomplished during all these years that I have left you to carry out my Great Commission? Have you done the work well? Or have you been lazy? Have you let your opportunities slide? The disciples, as they thought of Jesus' return, would have been encouraged for the task at hand.

In the summer of 1986 I was in England taking part in the great Keswick convention, and one of my blessings at that convention was meeting Derrick Bingham, an Irish preacher. He has a great work in Belfast, where every Tuesday night he teaches more than one thousand young people. We spent a good bit of time together, and he shared many of his experiences with me. On one occasion he told how he was called into the ministry. His dying mother said to him, "Derrick, my boy, you have the gift of gab. But you don't know the Word. If you'd learn the Word, the Lord might be able to use you." That was how Derrick Bingham received his call to the ministry. Within three weeks of his mother's death Derrick Bingham was preaching.

Bingham was greatly impressed with the Keswick convention, as was I. One evening, as we were walking home late at night after speaking to perhaps five thousand or more people, he said, "You know, as I was sitting there on the platform I was thinking about my mother. And I was thinking that if my mother could come back from heaven for a moment and walk in here and see this great convention and me sitting there on the speaker's platform, I'd say to her, 'Look what we're doing, Mom. Here we are. We're doing what you wanted us to do all the time.'" Derrick was encouraged by that thought.

If that was an inspiration to him, if that kept him going, if that fired him for the task at hand, how much more should we be inspired by the thought that one day the Lord Jesus Christ himself is going to return. He is going to say to us, How are you doing, my brothers? How are you doing, my sisters? Have you carried out your assignment? Jesus will not be harsh, but he will come expecting that we will have carried out the task.

2

World Christians

Acts 1:7–8

He said to them: "It is not for you to know the times or dates the Father has set by his own authority. But you will receive power when the Holy Spirit comes on you; and you will be my witnesses in Jerusalem, and in all Judea and Samaria, and to the ends of the earth."

Acts 1:7–8

The introduction to Acts contains two verses that are of special importance for anyone who wants to understand this book. In them is an outline for it.

There are four geographical references in verse 8: Jerusalem, Judea, Samaria, and the ends of the earth. In the New International Version the middle terms are combined by the verse's punctuation so that there is a three-part progression: Jerusalem (comma), Judea and Samaria (comma), and the ends of the earth. This is because in the Greek text, "Samaria" does not have a definite article before it. The article occurs before "Judea," which suggests that Judea and Samaria belong together, and this makes a three-part outline for the book. Acts 1–7 deals with the preaching of the gospel in Jerusalem. In Acts 8–12 the gospel expands beyond Jerusalem into Judea and Samaria. Acts 13–28 records the expansion of the gospel throughout the Roman world.

The Great Commission

But it is not chiefly for that reason that we need to study these key verses. They are also important because they give a plan for witnessing that has made Christianity a world religion.

Each version of the Great Commission has its own emphasis. Like Acts, John's version speaks of Christians being sent into the world, but his emphasis is on the nature of the Christian's witness: "*As you sent me* into the world, I have sent them into the world" (John 17:18, italics mine). That is, the disciples were sent into the world as Jesus was sent into it. He was to be the model for their ministry. Matthew stresses the authority of Jesus on the basis of which they were to make disciples of all nations: "*All authority* in heaven and on earth has been given to me" (Matt. 28:18, italics mine). They were to call all people to Christ because the Son of God had authorized them to do so.

When we turn to the seventh and eighth verses of Acts 1, we find the emphasis on two other things. First, the disciples were to be empowered for their task by the Holy Spirit. Second, they were to be agents of a world-wide geographical expansion of Christianity. The two go together. Jesus said they would receive power from the Holy Spirit and that when that happened they were to go into the entire world with the gospel. That is, their witness was to begin at Jerusalem; then it was to expand outward like ripples on a pond, embracing Judea and Samaria, and then overflowing beyond those known communities to the farthest reaches of the Roman Empire.

I do not sense that Christians today are always fully aware of how thoroughly that plan was carried out by the first generation of the church. The entire pagan world acknowledged as fact the early Christian apologists' claim that Christianity had permeated everywhere. Tertullian, who wrote around the year 200, declared in his *Apology*, "We are but of yesterday, and we have filled every place among you—cities, islands, fortresses, towns, market places, the very camp, tribes, companies, palace, senate, forum—we have left nothing to you but the temples of your gods."[1]

Historians have asked how this first generation of Christians, who for the most part were unlearned men and women, could have propagated the gospel so rapidly. Adolf Harnack, a German church historian of the nineteenth century, knew how. He said, "We cannot hesitate to believe that the great mission of Christianity was in reality accomplished by means of informal missionaries."[2] That was the secret. Every Christian—not just a formal order of missionaries supplied by the Christians at home—considered it his or her obligation to bear witness.

A Profound Misunderstanding

Acts 1:7–8 also corrects a misconception of the Lord's plan by the disciples. Jesus told them that they would be empowered by the Holy Spirit, but the disciples were not thinking about spiritual things at this time. As we learned in chapter 1 of this study, they were thinking about earthly kingdoms.

Jesus had taught them differently, of course. He taught that his kingdom was spiritual, saying, "The kingdom of God is within you" (Luke 17:21). They did not understand that. What kind of a kingdom were they looking for?

1. *They were looking for a political kingdom.* They betrayed this by their use of the verb "restore." The disciples could have thought ahead to a new and different kind of kingdom, a kingdom that up to then had never existed on earth. But that is not what they had in mind. They wanted the restoration of something they had already known. If you had asked them, they would have said, "We want the Davidic kingdom. We want it to be like it was when David was on the throne and Israel experienced her greatest glory."

2. *They were looking for an ethnically restricted kingdom.* We know this because of the way they asked their question. They did not ask merely, "Lord, are you at this time going to restore the kingdom?" They asked, "Are you at this time going to restore the kingdom to *Israel?*" (v. 6, italics mine). They meant "to us Jews." They were not interested in a gentile kingdom. They despised the Gentiles. Of course, they would have granted that Gentiles are welcome: "God has all kinds of people that serve him. They are welcome if they wish to join our kingdom." But it was still a Jewish kingdom that they had in mind.

3. *They were looking for a geographically restricted kingdom.* If you had asked them where this kingdom was to be located, they would have answered, "There can be no question about that. This kingdom is to be in Jerusalem. Jerusalem is God's city. That is where David and Solomon reigned. That is where the Messiah will reign, too."

What about the Greeks? What about the Romans?

"They are welcome to come to Jerusalem any time they want to."

When Jesus answered them he did not say, as we might have expected, "Really now, have we come to this point and you still don't understand the nature of this kingdom? Don't you understand that there's not going to *be* an earthly kingdom?" I notice that Jesus did not say, "There will never be an earthly kingdom." He simply said that it would be in the future, in a time not known to them, though certainly known to God. He added, in effect, "In the meantime, there is another task for you." People may disagree with me here, but that is the equivalent, it seems to me, of saying that one day God *will* establish an earthly kingdom. Our present task is to go out into the world and proclaim a kingdom that Jesus established by his death and resurrection.

The Nature of the Kingdom

Against that background, notice what Jesus Christ taught about the nature of the kingdom.

A Spiritual Kingdom

Jesus emphasized the coming of the Holy Spirit because the kingdom is spiritual. He did this earlier in verse 5: "John baptized with water, but in a few days you will be baptized with the Holy Spirit." Now he does it in the context of the Great Commission itself: "You will receive power when the Holy Spirit comes on you; and you will be my witnesses. . . ."

I do not know what your reaction is when you hear someone talk about a spiritual kingdom. I suspect that many, if not all, have a reaction that says, "Oh, I see, a spiritual kingdom. Who cares about a spiritual kingdom?" We think a spiritual kingdom is not really important because no one can see it. We do not want to put a spiritual kingdom down. It may be nice that Jesus is in the business of establishing a spiritual kingdom. But we are formed by our culture, and our culture thinks that something invisible is not really that important.

If we think that way, we should notice that when Jesus spoke of the spiritual nature of his kingdom, he did not use the word "spiritual," though he could have. He could have said, It is a spiritual kingdom I have in mind. What he actually said was, The kingdom I have in mind is one that is going to be established by the Holy Spirit. The Holy Spirit is the Third Person of the Godhead, so Jesus was actually saying that this was going to be God's kingdom. What does "spiritual" mean? We use it to refer to somebody who is not in touch with life, to a person living in the clouds. Actually, "spiritual" has to do with God the Holy Spirit. What is spiritual is what the Holy Spirit does.

I was in Washington, D.C., at a meeting in which a number of us were talking about the impact of Christians upon culture. We were talking about various Christian social service agencies and what they should be doing. We mentioned the importance of having Christians involved in government. Present at that meeting was Doug Coe, a man whom God has used in a remarkable way over the years. Coe is so successful in what he does that you almost never hear of him. He works behind the scenes. He knows all the members of Congress, senators, and staff persons. He meets with them and prays with them. It is through his ministry and that of people like him that Fellowship House was established.

Doug Coe was listening to what we were saying. He was not disagreeing. But after a while, when we turned to him and said, "Doug, you've been in Washington a long time. What kind of counsel do you have for us as we try to think along these lines?" he said, "What you're saying is very important. But I want to leave this with you. Remember that it says in the Bible that the visible things pass away, but that the invisible things are eternal."

Christians believe in things that are invisible. We believe in God; God is not visible. We believe in eternal life; eternal life is not visible either. We talk about redemption, regeneration, justification. None of those are visible. Yet we believe in these things. We are committed to them. In the same way, we must be committed to the invisible spiritual kingdom that, although it is invisible, is eternal and will never pass away.

A Powerful Kingdom

The word Jesus used in verse 8 is significant. It is *dynamis*, translated "power." In some versions of this text "power" occurs twice, once in verse 7 ("It is not for you to know the times or the seasons, which the Father hath put in his own *power*" [KJV, italics mine]) and once in verse 8 ("But ye shall receive *power*" [KJV, italics mine]). This is misleading, because in Greek these are two entirely different words. The New International Version translates the first word as "authority" ("It is not for you to know the times or dates the Father has set by his own *authority*" [italics mine]), which is right, and the second word as "power" ("But you will receive *power*" [italics mine]), as most of the other versions do. Actually, it is only in the second instance that the text speaks of "power" as we understand that term.

The Greek word *dynamis* entered the English language when the Swedish chemist and engineer Alfred Bernhard Nobel (1833–96) made the discovery that became his fortune. He discovered a power stronger than anything the world had known up to that time. He asked a friend of his who was a Greek scholar what the word for "explosive power" was in Greek. His friend answered, *"Dynamis."*

Nobel said, "Well, I am going to call my discovery by that name." So he called his explosive power "dynamite."

That is the word here. And it refers not to the power one has by intrinsic or even by a delegated authority, though these are also important kinds of power, but to the explosive, life-changing dynamic of the Holy Spirit operating through the proclamation of the gospel. This is *not* political power. Political power is what the disciples wanted. They asked Jesus if he was going to set up a political machine. They could understand that kind of power, but that was not the power Jesus was talking about. He was talking about power that flows from God.

Several years ago, the French writer Jacques Ellul wrote *The Political Illusion*. It is a brilliant book because it examines and exposes the mystique of political power. Ellul calls political power an illusion created by politicians, because they want to be thought powerful, and by the media, who feed on it. This is not to say that the state is unimportant. God established the state to protect the innocent, secure the just punishment of the guilty, and defend its citizens against oppression, both from within and without. This involves power. But there is an illusion surrounding the political process, and it is this that Ellul is debunking: the illusion that because a person possesses political office, somehow he or she can control events, change things, and produce reformation in the world. Many people believe that, but it is not where true, significant power is located. Otherwise, politicians would not be so sensitive to public opinion.

Power for change comes from another source entirely.

I was speaking about that power at a meeting of the Philadelphia Conference on Reformed Theology, and Charles W. Colson was present. When I finished and he began to speak he picked up on a reference I had made to *The Political Illusion*, saying, "Ellul's *Political Illusion* is the most important political book I've ever read. When I read it, I decided to send it to every friend I had in government. But when I went to buy it, I found that it was out of print, which is an indication that even the evangelical publishers have bought into the political illusion. Today you can't get the one book that exposes the illusion for what it is."

What is it that really changes the world? If I were speaking in secular terms to a secular audience, I could say, quite rightly, that it is always the power of an idea. It is not armies that change the world. Not really! They just put different people in charge of the problems. It is not money that changes the world. Not even laws change the world. Americans should understand that very well, because we passed a law prohibiting the sale of alcohol and it did not eliminate drinking. As a matter of fact, it did the opposite, which is what Paul said laws tend to do. It encouraged people to drink, so that there was actually more traffic in liquor in those days than had existed beforehand. Laws do not change things. Only ideas change things. Changes occur when ideas possess people's minds.

In the spiritual realm, real changes come when the Holy Spirit uses the gospel to regenerate fallen men and women, causing them to repent of their sin, seek righteousness, and live for Jesus Christ. Changes follow in a big way when that happens. Then you have reformation.

A Kingdom of Truth

When Jesus stood before Pilate to be tried by him, the Lord described his kingdom with the word *truth*. He had been accused of setting himself up as a king. Pilate asked if he was a king, and Jesus answered: "My kingdom is not of this world. If it were, my servants would fight to prevent my arrest by the Jews. But now my kingdom is from another place" (John 18:36).

Pilate did not understand what this meant. So he said, no doubt in a questioning tone, "You are a king, then!"

This time Jesus answered in words Pilate could understand: "You are right in saying I am a king. In fact, for this reason I was born, and for this I came into the world, to testify to the truth. Everyone on the side of truth listens to me" (v. 37). Pilate understood that, of course, but he wasn't interested. He dismissed the notion of truth entirely.

This is what Jesus was talking about in Acts before his ascension to heaven, telling the disciples that they were to be his witnesses. Our English word *witness* comes from an old English word we do not use very much anymore but was used in Elizabethan times and afterwards. It is the word *wit*. "To wit" means "to know." A "wit" is "a knowledgeable person." So a "witness" is one who knows something and testifies to it. In the case of the disciples, these men were to be witnesses to who Jesus was and what he had done. Above all, they were to be witnesses to the truth of the resurrection. They were to advance Christ's kingdom not by coercion, but by testimony to the truth.

In the evangelical church we often think that we can advance the kingdom just by raising money. Of course, we live in a world where money generally is a necessity. I am not against money. In fact, one of the blessings promised to the people of God in the Old Testament in a general sense—not always on a personal basis, but generally—is material blessing. The problems come when we think that raising money is the way spiritual work must be done. We think if we are able to raise $100,000 for an evangelical cause one year that we can do twice as well the next year if we can only raise $200,000. When we think that way, we are falling into a trap. In fact, the more we think this way, the more dangerous our situation is.

I have always said that one reason God does not give more of us more money is that he cannot trust us with it. He knows that if he gave us more, it would ruin us.

The second mistake we make is to think that we can advance the gospel by law, which ultimately comes down to advancing it by force (see p. 24). I am not against trying to change the country's laws as part of the political process. If we have bad laws, we should certainly attempt to change them for better laws. I think there are examples of where that might be done in our country right now. But changing laws does not in itself advance the kingdom. Rather it is the other way around. Where the kingdom advances, good laws follow.

Why is it like this? God has made it like this because "law" always means force. Get a country to change its laws, and then what? Then the power of the state, which boils down to the power of the policeman with a gun, forces compliance. But even then it is only an external compliance that is achieved. Christians know, or should know, that spiritual changes, above all, can only be effected spiritually and not by force of arms.

There is another error into which some are falling today, and this is the error of thinking that the kingdom of God is advanced by the "miraculous" or by what those who argue for it sometimes call "signs and wonders." The argument is that where the Holy Spirit is active, signs and wonders follow. According to exponents of this view, we should seek healings and miraculous demonstrations of God's power in the church today. If that is what we are looking for, we are in error, because that is not what Jesus taught. Jesus taught that when we receive the power of the Holy Spirit, the result will not be miracles, signs, or healings, but witnessing.

Some years ago I studied all occurrences of the phrase "filled with the Holy Spirit" in the Book of Acts.[3] There are fourteen of them, ten of which refer to the present era. I looked at the circumstances in which these phrases occurred, and I discovered that in each case in which a person or a group of persons was filled with the Holy Spirit the people involved immediately began to witness powerfully for Jesus Christ. The one sure evidence of the power of the Holy Spirit in people's lives is that they testify to Jesus.

Revelation 12:11 speaks of the victory of the saints over the devil. This is how victory comes: "They overcame him by the blood of the Lamb and by the word of their testimony."

Do you want to be Spirit-filled? Do you want to experience the power of the Holy Spirit? Testify to Jesus Christ. You say, "But I stammer." It doesn't matter. The Holy Spirit doesn't stammer. He will speak clearly.

You say, "But I make mistakes." That is all right. The Holy Spirit does not make mistakes, and he will cause them to forget your errors.

You say, "But I don't know my Bible well enough." Work at it. But in the meantime, testify to the portions you know. If you are a believer in Jesus Christ, you understand the gospel at least, because if you did not understand it, you would not believe it. Testify to that.

You say, "But I am afraid it won't work." Really? It worked with you. Besides, how can you say it won't work when Jesus promised that the Holy Spirit will work through your testimony?

A Worldwide Kingdom

The final point is that the kingdom is worldwide. The kingdom of God must embrace all the nations and regions of this world and it is doing it.

The wonderful thing about this commission is that the disciples really understood what Jesus was talking about. They were like us, of course, awfully thick. Even after having been with Jesus for three years they still did not have the point quite in mind. Yet in the end they got it. We know because their error in Acts 1 is the last flicker of their earthbound misunderstanding. We never read about them making this mistake again. When they understood, they actually carried out the Great Commission.

What they did is what the Book of Acts is all about.

Prophecy or Command?

When Jesus said, "You will be my witnesses," were those words a prophecy (You are going to be my witnesses) or a command (Be my witnesses)? The answer, surely, is both. They are a prophecy, because the disciples *were* going to be Christ's witnesses. God had ordained it. They were going to take the gospel into all the world. The world would hear. But at the same time these words were also a command, because Jesus was telling his followers what they had to do. They were to carry the gospel everywhere.

The Great Commission is something every generation of Christians must obey. The early church obeyed it. They took the gospel to the farthest reaches of their world. We must do exactly as they did. There have been times in the history of the church when God's people have heard his voice and have taken this commission seriously. In those times the gospel has flowed far and wide, and God has blessed it. Unfortunately there have been other times when the mandate has been forgotten and suppressed. Christians have been content and preoccupied with the world's way of doing things, and they have suffered for their disobedience.

You and I must tell others who Jesus is and what the gospel of salvation by his death means for them. We must not think that this is unimportant. It is the most important thing in the world.

3

Preparing for Growth

Acts 1:12–26

Then they returned to Jerusalem from the hill called the Mount of Olives, a Sabbath day's walk from the city. When they arrived, they went upstairs to the room where they were staying. Those present were Peter, John, James and Andrew; Philip and Thomas, Bartholomew and Matthew; James son of Alphaeus and Simon the Zealot, and Judas son of James. They all joined together constantly in prayer, along with the women and Mary the mother of Jesus, and with his brothers.

Acts 1:12–14

T he second half of Acts 1 deals with the disciples' waiting period prior to the coming of the Holy Spirit. It lasted ten days. We know that it was ten days because the Holy Spirit came at Pentecost. Pentecost refers to the Feast of Weeks, which was held fifty days after Passover. Since the Lord was taken back to heaven forty days after the resurrection, which occurred at Passover, there must have been a ten-day period in which the disciples waited in Jerusalem.

When we recognize that the Holy Spirit came at Pentecost, that Pentecost was the Feast of Weeks, and that the Feast of Weeks was the time in the Jewish year when the first sheaves of the harvest were presented, we see that the timing is symbolic. The early Christians, who were Jews well-steeped in Old Testament traditions, also undoubtedly understood the symbolic timing—once it had happened. They understood that the blessing they experienced at Pentecost, when thousands of people believed and came into the church, was only the first-fruit of a much greater response that they were to see as that same gospel was preached in Jerusalem, then in Judea and Samaria, and eventually to the far reaches of the world.

But at the beginning, while they were waiting for the Spirit's coming "in a few days," all they would have known was that the Lord had been taken away from them into heaven and that they were to wait for his second coming.

A Bridge Book

Acts is similar to the Old Testament Book of Joshua in that it is a bridge book. It is a bridge between the Gospels, which describe the life and ministry of Jesus Christ, and the epistles, which unfold the life and nature of the church, just as in the Old Testament the Book of Joshua bridges the period between the time of preparation in the wilderness and the time of settling down in the land.

At the beginning of Acts we find a striking parallel to Joshua. After the Jewish people had crossed the Jordan River into Palestine, we would have thought that it was time for them immediately to move against the fortified cities of the land, when the citizens of the land were still unsettled by the Jews' unexpected passage of the Jordan. Instead we find that God told them to wait and consecrate themselves. This took four days. They crossed the Jordan on the tenth of the first month, and they waited at Gilgal—where they observed the Passover, circumcised those who were born in the wilderness, and did a number of other things—until the fourteenth. This is similar to what we find in Acts. Instead of moving directly on to Pentecost, we find a ten-day waiting period in which God worked in the disciples to accomplish several important things.

We are people of action. So we expect action—immediately. The Holy Spirit should come at once. The gospel should be preached right away. Instead, we find delay.

Sometimes we have periods like this in our lives, and they make tough going for us. These are often the hardest periods for us to live through. We want to *do* something. Or, what is even more significant, we want God to do something. When God does not do anything, we think, Things have gone wrong. Things should be happening if I really am a Christian and really am on track with God. That is not necessarily the case.

This period of waiting was not, however, a period of utter inactivity. It was a period of preparation, which is what waiting times are for. Sometimes in periods of waiting we can see the preparation. At other times we cannot. God is doing things in our lives that we cannot see or at least of which we are unaware. Perhaps he is developing our character. We seldom see that, either in others or in ourselves. The second half of Acts 1 shows the early Christians practicing obedience, fellowshiping, praying, studying the Scriptures, and choosing leaders in preparation for their ministry.

A Time to Practice Obedience

This ten-day period was a time to practice obedience. If we compare verse 12 with verse 4, we find that what the disciples did in verse 12 was a direct response to what the Lord Jesus Christ earlier told them they were to do. Earlier Jesus had said, "Do not leave Jerusalem, but wait for the gift my Father promised, which you have heard me speak about." In verse 12, we find that this is precisely what they were doing.

I do not think it was easy for them. We might say, not knowing a great deal about the situation, "Well, what else could they do? They had to wait." Actually there were many things they could have done—and had been doing before Jesus gave his commandment. After the crucifixion they had scattered each to his or her own home. When Jesus did not drive out the Romans, well, that was the end of the dream, as far as they were concerned. The Emmaus disciples were going back to Emmaus. The others were on their way back to Galilee. And why not? There was nothing there to hold them together.

Another thing they might have done was to get on about their various business obligations. Some had been fishermen. One was a tax collector. During the prior forty days some of them went back to Galilee and began to take up fishing again. The disciples could have said, "Jesus has left us. He said he is going to come back, but we don't know when that's going to be. Right now we have to get on with the business of living."

If they had been thinking along spiritual lines, they might have said, "There are people to be won. There is work to do. There are cities to be evangelized." I suppose it must have seemed utterly pointless for them to wait inactively in Jerusalem.

The situations in which we learn most about obedience are those in which we cannot see why we are called to do what we are doing. If we can give a reason for what we are doing, then we are not necessarily learning obedience, at least not simple obedience. What we are really doing is trusting our ability to reason things out. We are doing what we are doing because we think it is the best thing to do. There is nothing wrong with thinking things out, of course. But it is quite another thing to learn obedience when the proscribed course does not seem the best option.

If you are going through a period like that in your life, when you know what you should do but do not know why you need to do it, or if you are experiencing a delay in God's dealings with you and it seems that you are stuck in one spot and can't quite get off it, learn that there is valuable preparation for future work just in remaining where God has put you. The action will come later.

A Time for Fellowship

There is another way in which the disciples prepared for what was coming: they gathered together for fellowship. We read about it in verse 14: "They all joined together constantly." There were the eleven disciples mentioned in verse 13: "Peter, John, James and Andrew; Philip and Thomas, Bartholomew and Matthew; James son of Alphaeus and Simon the Zealot, and Judas son of James" (this was not Judas Iscariot. There had been two Judases in the apostolic band. Judas Iscariot had committed suicide, and this was the other one). There were also women: "the women and Mary the mother of Jesus, and his brothers."[1]

As we go on to verse 15, we find that by the time Peter stood to give his speech about the need to choose a twelfth person to fill out the apostolic band, there were 120 gathered. We do not know who the 120 were. But we can imagine whom some of them might have been. Nicodemus had shown an interest in Christ; he may have been there. Joseph of Arimathea may have been present. How about the Emmaus disciples, Cleopas and Mary? They had returned to Jerusalem earlier, according to Luke 24, and probably stayed once they knew that Jesus had been raised from the dead. What about Mary, Martha, and Lazarus of Bethany? What about people Jesus had healed? These and many others would have been present, the nucleus of the emerging church.

People need people. This need is part of what it means to be a human being. One of the worst things that can happen to a person is to be utterly isolated from other people, and the converse of this is that if we are to grow intellectually, socially, and spiritually, we need others. Christians need other Christians. When you become a Christian, you do not become a Christian in isolation. Rather, you enter into the body of those who are also Christ's disciples, and you find fellowship with them.

I have noticed that when students go away to college, the thing that seems more important than anything else in determining whether they get on in the Christian life or whether they drift away is whether in the first months of school they identify with other Christians on the campus. There are other things they need, of course. They need prayer and Bible study. They need to worship God in church. But peer contact and encouragement seem to be especially important. So I always tell students who are about to go away to college, "Get in touch with a Christian group right off. It does not make a great deal of difference what group it is. Just identify with the other Christians on the campus. God will work through those others to hold you and build you up during your days of preparation."

A Time for Constant Prayer

Verse 14 indicates a third item in the disciples' preparation. Not only did they practice obedience and fellowship by joining together in Jerusalem during these ten days; they also joined together "constantly in prayer."

What do you suppose they prayed for?

We sometimes talk about prayer in terms of the ACTS acrostic—A for adoration, C for confession, T for thanksgiving, and S for supplication. I can imagine that they did each of these four things. Certainly they gave adoration. After all, God had worked among them in a great way. God had sent the Lord Jesus Christ to die for their sins and then rise again from the dead. When they prayed in those days, they must have praised God for the wisdom, love, power, and grace by which he had accomplished such a great plan of salvation in their time.

It must have been a time of confession for them too. They were getting ready to do the work Jesus had for them. They must have been conscious of their inadequacy and sin. Peter was there. He had denied his Lord on the night of Jesus' arrest in Gethsemane. He had begun by following the Lord at a distance, then he had hung out around the campfire of Christ's enemies. One of them said to him, "You also were with Jesus of Galilee."

"I don't know what you're talking about," he said.

They noticed his accent. "Surely you are one of them, for your accent gives you away" (Matt. 26:69–73). They began to press him, but Peter denied that he was Christ's disciple, even, we are told, with oaths and cursings. As Peter gathered with the others on this occasion, he must have been confessing his sin. He must have been saying, "Lord Jesus Christ, forgive me for denying you as I did. Forgive me for denying that I was your disciple."

The others had not denied Jesus, but they had scattered. When the Lord was arrested they must have fled away from Jerusalem in the direction of Bethany, where they had been staying each night of that final week. They knew that Jesus' enemies had come from Jerusalem. He was being taken there for trial. They would not have fled toward Jerusalem. They were not even in Jerusalem when Jesus was brought to trial and crucified.

These men must have had their cowardice to confess before God. "We can hardly believe that at the crucial moment we were so fearful that we ran away to save our own skins," they must have said. The Lord had chosen them to be apostles. He had said, You are going to be my witnesses in this very city of Jerusalem to those very men who arrested and then crucified me. They must have wondered how they could be Christ's witnesses, especially since they had failed him so grievously the first time.

They must also have given thanks—thanks to the Father for what he had done and to the Lord Jesus Christ for all he had accomplished and taught them during the previous forty days. Thanks for forgiveness, restoration, work to do, each other, life, health, and other things.

They must have made abundant supplication, too, asking God for the necessary faithfulness and strength to do the task before them. They must have even prayed for the coming of the Holy Spirit, whom Jesus had told them to expect. Sometimes people get hung up on situations like this. They say, "If God is going to do something, if it is in his sovereign will for him to accomplish a certain thing, why pray for it? He is going to do it anyway." This is a bad misunderstanding of how God works. It is true that God is sovereign. God does what God wills to do. God accomplishes his purposes. The disobedience of man does not frustrate him. But when God accomplishes his purposes, he does it through means. If he is going to save someone, he usually does it by leading someone else to go to him or her with the gospel and speak about Jesus Christ. Similarly, when God sends revival, he almost always does it by leading his people to pray. Prayer is not superfluous. The disciples knew this. Jesus had taught them. So they must have prayed for the coming of the Holy Spirit and for blessing when the Holy Spirit came.

Those who have studied the history of revivals in the church point out that they have always been preceded by times of great prayer by Christian people. It has not always been a large number who have prayed, at least at the beginning. Often a small number gathered. But there was always prayer as the people of God came together to ask for God's blessing.

A Time for Study

When Peter spoke about the need to replace Judas, he began to quote Scripture: "Brothers, the Scripture had to be fulfilled which the Holy Spirit spoke long ago through the mouth of David concerning Judas" (v. 16). Later he quoted two specific passages: Psalm 69:25 ("May his place be deserted; let there be no one to dwell in it") and Psalm 109:8 ("May another take his place of leadership"). This must mean that Peter was studying the Scriptures in those days and, probably, that the other disciples had been studying them too.

Two things go together in the Christian life: prayer, in which we talk to God, and Bible study, in which God talks to us. Prayer is of great importance. But somebody once said, I think wisely, that when we're talking to God and God is talking to us, we had better let God do most of the talking. In other words, we should spend most of our time in Bible study.

What did the apostles study in those days? They began to search the Old Testament for prophecies that concerned the life, death, and resurrection of Jesus Christ. Presumably this is what Jesus himself had been sharing with them. We have a clue to what he did in the account of his ministry to the Emmaus disciples, where we are told: "And beginning with Moses and all the Prophets, he explained to them what was said in all the Scriptures concerning himself" (Luke 24:27). That is, from each of the three divisions of the Old Testament (the Law, the Prophets, and the Writings), Jesus taught what the Messiah was to do when he came. Jesus must have begun to explain this to them, and when he was taken back to heaven, perhaps they said, "That was fascinating, wasn't it? Why don't we look these things up for ourselves?" So they got out their Bibles and began to study them.

I do not think I am merely imagining this, because when Peter stood up to preach, as he did on the day of Pentecost, he instinctively spoke about the

Old Testament Scriptures. How did he get them in his mind if not from this kind of in-depth, meaningful study?

I think, too, that when Jesus sent them back to Jerusalem to wait for the outpouring of the Holy Spirit, they must have used the time to search in the Old Testament for prophecies that concerned the Holy Spirit. I say this because when the Holy Spirit did come and Peter then stood up to preach his first great sermon, he began with the most important text about the coming of the Holy Spirit in all the Old Testament: Joel 2:28–32. Peter must have said to himself, If Jesus is going to send the Holy Spirit, as he has promised, if the Holy Spirit is going to be poured out on the church, we had better find out what this is about. So he and the others went to the Old Testament to study about the Holy Spirit.

We as Christians sometimes say, "We want God to bless our church" or "We want God to bless our family" (or our Bible study or nation or whatever it might be). But if we are serious, we must learn that the way God blesses is usually through a study of the Bible—as people come to know what God has written, respond to it, believe it, and proclaim it to other people in the world. If you find yourself in what seems to be a time of waiting or inactivity, redeem the time, as these disciples did. Become a better student—a more knowledgeable student—of the Word of God.

A Time for the Recognition and Choice of Leaders

The last thing the disciples did that is mentioned in these verses is to recognize the need for leadership and take steps to supply it. In their case, it involved the election of Matthias to fill Judas's place.

Some people have been critical of the disciples at this point. They have suggested that because the disciples chose Matthias by lot—that is, as we would say, by drawing straws—they were acting like pagans, since this was a pagan way of doing things. Others have argued that since we never hear of Matthias again, he must not have been God's choice to fill the vacancy. Some have looked at Paul and have concluded that he, rather than this relatively unknown man, must have been God's choice to be the twelfth apostle.[2]

I do not think this is right. Paul was an apostle, as was Barnabas and perhaps some others too, but in a different sense than these twelve. And so far as lots are concerned, the casting of lots was actually an Old Testament tradition—and a strong one. The disciples were not just falling into pagan ways. They were following Old Testament precedent. More than that, since they had just been praying and studying the Scriptures, we must assume that they were led by the Holy Spirit to seek a qualified person to fill this place of leadership. Maybe they had been saying, "If the Holy Spirit is going to empower us to be Christ's witnesses in the world, we had better get our house in order. We are missing one apostle, so let's ask Jesus whom he wants to choose to fill the twelfth position. We should get to know and begin to work with him."

Sometimes we pray for revival. We pray sincerely, "Lord, bless the church; convict many of sin; bring them to salvation; send a revival in our time." That is very good. But I wonder, do we think what would be needed if a real revival should come? Most of us are ignorant of what happens in great movements of the Spirit of God. If you read church history, you will find out that such times are very draining—physically as well as spiritually. In times of revival people are under such conviction of sin that they press into the churches. They do not want to go home. They want instruction and help. They want their sins dealt with and their lives straightened out. What does one do in times like that? Who is going to teach and pastor such people? If we are serious about revival, we need to prepare for it now.

There is a revival going on in Argentina today, and I have been told by people who know the situation that preparation for the revival began years before it happened, when the churches began to ask what they should do to prepare for revival when God should eventually answer their prayers and send it. They asked, for example, "What are we going to do if God sends one thousand more people into our church?" They didn't have much money. So building bigger churches was no solution. They said, "The only way we can possibly handle so many people is in the believers' homes. Each home is going to have to become a miniature church. But if it is to be a good one, then the leaders of those homes have to be trained to do spiritual work." They began to train home leaders—the mothers and the fathers of their congregations—to be hosts of little churches. They did a number of similar things. After that, when the preparation was complete, God sent the prayed-for blessing.

The same thing should be true for us. Even if we are not in a time of revival now, or if a time of revival is delayed, all the things seen in the early church (in Acts 1) should be encouraged in our fellowships.

I often say at Tenth Presbyterian Church, where I pastor, that the most effective means of outreach and growth we have is our home Bible studies, which we greatly encourage. I was sitting on the platform the night I first preached this sermon, and I was looking at the evening's bulletin. I noticed that right below the subject of the sermon, "Preparing for Growth," there was an item headed: "Home Bible Studies." As I read it, I found that it described most of the items highlighted in this first chapter of Acts. It read: "Through prayer, the study of God's Word, and mutual sharing, these groups provide fellowship and support that are not found elsewhere." That is it exactly.

I look at Philadelphia and see the work that still needs to be done. I see the flight of our country into gross materialism and overt sin. I notice the church's mindless conformity to the world's culture. I say, "Lord, send a revival in our time." But I know, even as I say that, that if we are serious about wanting a revival, we must get ready for it. We must prepare. We must use these days of waiting wisely, believing that if we do, Jesus will send the blessing we desperately need.

4

That Incendiary Fellowship

Acts 2:1-13

When the day of Pentecost came, they were all together in one place. Suddenly a sound like the blowing of a violent wind came from heaven and filled the whole house where they were sitting. They saw what seemed to be tongues of fire that separated and came to rest on each of them. All of them were filled with the Holy Spirit and began to speak in other tongues as the Spirit enabled them.

Acts 2:1–4

Acts tells what the Holy Spirit did to glorify Jesus Christ in the church through the early preachers of the gospel. Acts 1 leads up to the coming of the Holy Spirit. Acts 2:1–13 tells of his coming. We should have Acts 1 in mind as we come to Acts 2, because the first chapter promised the Holy Spirit's coming. It reminds us that everything that happens in Acts is an unfolding of what God said was going to happen. John R. W. Stott writes correctly that "in the early chapters of Acts Luke refers to the promise, the gift, the baptism, the power and the fullness of the Spirit in the experience of God's people."[1]

In Acts' version of the Great Commission we have an emphasis upon the power of the Holy Spirit. The disciples were being sent into the world with the gospel. But they were not to go in their own strength. If they had gone in their own strength, nothing would have happened. At Pentecost no one would have believed if the Holy Spirit had not blessed Peter's preaching. The people would have ridiculed Peter, if they did not do something worse.

In Acts 2 we find that the event we have been waiting for happens. But what does it mean? The only way to understand what it means is by the symbols the Holy Spirit has given to help us understand it. There are two of them. One is the wind. We read in verse 2: "Suddenly a sound like the blowing of *a violent wind* came from heaven and filled the whole house where they were sitting" (italics mine). The other is fire. We read in verse 3: "They saw what seemed to be *tongues of fire* that separated and came to rest on each of them" (italics mine).

I emphasize that we ought to look at Pentecost in terms of these symbols because, if we do not, we inevitably get off the track—as, for example, by our contemporary preoccupation with the gift of speaking in tongues. If we read Acts 2 with our current interests in mind, the word that will probably jump out at us is "tongues." But that is not the emphasis of the passage itself. It is true that the disciples did speak in tongues, but the way the Holy Spirit was presented to the disciples was as wind and fire. Thus, it follows that if we want to understand what the coming of the Holy Spirit meant, these are the images by which we must do so.

The First Symbol: Wind

The importance of wind as a symbol is evident linguistically, though we have to stretch ourselves to appreciate it today, because to us "spirit" usually means nothing more than either the Holy Spirit or the human spirit. In the major ancient languages—Hebrew and Greek (in which the Old and New Testaments were written) and even Latin (which was spoken widely at this time)—the word for "spirit" was also used for "wind" or "breath." So when Acts 2:2 says that they heard "a sound like the blowing of a violent wind," "wind" also means "spirit." As a result, no one who normally thought in Hebrew, Greek, or Latin would have missed the symbolism.

The Hebrew word for "wind" or "spirit" is *ruach*. You can't say that properly without a strong sound of breath: it is pronounced *ru-aaah*. So what is true linguistically—that the word means both "breath" and "spirit"—is also conveyed sensually. It is the same with the Greek word *pneuma* and with the Latin word *spiritus*. So there is not one of these three great ancient languages in which a person could even say the word for "spirit" without an audible breath sound.

The Rich Biblical Background

At the very beginning of the Bible, Genesis 1:1–2 says, "In the beginning God created the heavens and the earth. Now the earth was formless and empty, darkness was over the surface of the deep, and the Spirit of God was hovering over the waters." In English the choice of words does not mean a whole lot. We think perhaps of the Holy Spirit as a dove somehow skimming over the waters that were covering the earth at that time. But that is not the idea at all. Rather, the Holy Spirit of God is portrayed as God's breath—as the creative, moving, dynamic breath of God. This breath—this divine, life-giving wind—is what is blowing across the waters at the beginning.

One chapter later in Genesis we have the story of the creation of Adam from the dust of the ground.[2] There we read, "The LORD God formed the man from the dust of the ground and breathed into his nostrils the breath of life, and man became a living being" (Gen. 2:7). This indicates that apart from the breath of God, man was just dead matter. He was as dead as dust. In order for him to have life, God, who is the source of life, had to breathe some of his life—some of the divine breath, or spirit—into Adam. Only then did Adam become a living being.

In the New Testament, in the third chapter of John, the Lord Jesus Christ is speaking to Nicodemus about the new birth and he picks up on this idea. He tells Nicodemus not merely that a person needs to be regenerated in some mystical way in order to have eternal life and be saved but that he or she needs to be "born again" (John 3:3, 7), using a word for "again" that actually means (1) "again, just like the first time," and (2) "from above." That is, Jesus said that a person needs to be born again from above just like the first time.

What was Jesus getting at? Nicodemus did not know. He hadn't the faintest idea. He said, "How can a man be born when he is old? Surely he cannot enter a second time into his mother's womb to be born!" (v. 4). But Jesus explained, saying,

> I tell you the truth, no one can enter the kingdom of God unless he is born of water and the Spirit. Flesh gives birth to flesh, but the Spirit gives birth to spirit. You should not be surprised at my saying, "You must be born again." The wind blows wherever it pleases. You hear its sound, but you cannot tell where it comes from or where it is going. So it is with everyone born of the Spirit.
>
> John 3:5–8

Nicodemus did not understand Jesus. But we can, if we put these things together. Think of what is said of the creation of Adam at the beginning of Genesis. God breathed into Adam so that he became a living being. His Spirit (which we remember means "breath" or "wind") was the vehicle. Now we find Jesus saying that the new life that all people need needs to be breathed into them in a way analogous to God's creation of Adam. Just as at the beginning God breathed into Adam so that he became a living physical being, so also in our day if a person is to be saved God must breathe into him or her by his Holy Spirit once again from above, just like the first time so that the person might become spiritually alive. We may be physically alive without the new birth, but if we are to become spiritually alive God must breathe his Spirit into us.

The image of wind in Jesus' discussion with Nicodemus was not an extraneous idea, as it seems to us, but a vivid way of talking about the Spirit's work, which even Nicodemus must have recognized.

Here is one more text: Isaiah 2:22. "Stop trusting in man, who has but a breath in his nostrils. Of what account is he?" On the surface it sounds sort of foolish to say, "Stop trusting in man, who has but a breath in his nostrils." Why talk about breath or nostrils? It even seems a bit grotesque. It is not when you think along these lines: Isaiah is saying that man is only a one-breath person. He breathes in. He breathes out. If he stops breathing even for a few minutes, he dies. So, says Isaiah, Why pay so much attention to him? He says to stop trusting in man and to trust God. Why are we to trust in God? Because, to use this same imagery, God's breath is not in his nostrils. He is not a one-breath being. God does not live by breathing in and breathing out. God is one great and eternal breath. He is the source of all breath, the source of life. So what Isaiah is saying is that it is wise to trust God to give you the breath you need to live spiritually and carry on to the very end.

The Blowing of a Violent Wind

When we put this together we begin to get a sense of why the image of wind is so important in Acts 2. The text says, "Suddenly a sound like the blowing of a violent wind came from heaven and filled the whole house where they were sitting." That sounds very much like the story of the Spirit of God hovering over the waters of the earth at creation. So the suggestion is that here, in Acts, we have a new creation—as important (more important in many ways) as the original creation of the heavens and the earth. That heaven and earth are destined to pass away, but what is done by the Spirit at Pentecost is eternal.

Again, the account in Acts sounds like Genesis 2, where God breathes life into man. Pentecost is a life-breathing experience.

The account is also like John 3, where Jesus told Nicodemus, "You must be born again."

Obviously the coming of the Holy Spirit as a violent wind was meant to symbolize the coming of the creative power of God to inaugurate a new era in which men and women should be brought to spiritual life.

Filled with the Spirit

We need to look at another term in this account, the word "filled." It occurs twice. First, the house in which the disciples were was filled. And then, they themselves were filled by the Holy Spirit. I call attention to this because if we are to understand what is said about the Holy Spirit in the New Testament, we must see that there is a distinction between being *baptized* with the Holy Spirit, which we hear a great deal about today, and being *filled* with the Holy Spirit, which we hear about much less.

People talk about the baptism of the Holy Spirit as if that is what Pentecost was about. Usually they mean that Pentecost "baptism" is a special experience that involves the gift of being able to speak in tongues. They would say that the ability to speak in tongues is the only sure evidence that a person has been baptized with the Spirit—or even, perhaps, is a Christian.

The Bible does talk about a baptism of the Holy Spirit, of course, but not in those terms. The baptism of the Holy Spirit has to do with regeneration or being born again. It results in the regenerated person being identified with Jesus Christ, spiritually in the sight of God and publicly before other men and women. Significantly, that is what the sacrament of water baptism also signifies. It does not have anything to do with imparting some kind of special blessing. It is an identification of the baptized individual with Christ. It is done once, because a person is only saved once. To be baptized by the Holy Spirit is to be a Christian. John R.W. Stott wrote correctly, "Water-baptism is the initiatory Christian rite, because Spirit-baptism is the initiatory Christian experience."[3]

To be filled with the Holy Spirit is different, and it is this that is being talked about here. The early believers did not become Christians at Pentecost. They already were believers. They believed in Jesus. They were meeting together. They were praying. They were studying the Bible. But now the Holy Spirit came upon them in a special way to empower them for their task. The word used to describe the experience is "filled."

As I wrote in a previous chapter, the word "fullness" or the phrase "filled with the Holy Spirit" occurs fourteen times in the New Testament, but four of them concern the period before Pentecost and are therefore more in line with Old Testament than with New Testament experiences. There is one isolated reference in Ephesians. The other nine references are in Acts.[4] The interesting thing is that the circumstance common to every case is that whenever Christians were filled with the Holy Spirit they immediately began to testify forcefully and effectively to Jesus Christ.

It is not that they spoke in tongues, though this did occur at Pentecost and possibly elsewhere. It is not that they did miracles, though occasionally miracles were performed. No, when the Holy Spirit came upon his people in a special way, filling them, they immediately began to testify verbally about Jesus.

Someone might say, "Yes, but at Pentecost they did it in tongues." True enough. But that is not the emphasis, nor is it part of the other examples of "filling." In Acts 2 the emphasis is upon the fact that everyone *heard* about Jesus.

So if you ask whether a person is "Spirit-filled," the only way to answer the question is by determining whether or not he or she speaks often and effectively about Jesus. It is not by whether he or she speaks in an unintelligible language or does miracles. The question is, Does he or she testify to Jesus Christ, and does God bless that testimony in the conversion of men and women?

The Second Symbol: Fire

That is why, when the second symbol for the Holy Spirit is introduced, as it is in verse 3, it is as *tongues* of fire, and not fire alone. This is not just a way of saying that these were little flames. Tongues are that by which we speak. And when we speak, what do we do? We breathe out. That is how we make our larynxes work. It is how we produce sounds. So the main point is reinforced again: When the Holy Spirit, the breath of God, enters a person to enable him or her to give out some of what God has first given, that individual talks about Jesus Christ.

I wonder if you have experienced this phenomenon. Most preachers who are at all faithful in trying to explain the Scriptures know of it. When they are studying a passage of Scripture to try to communicate it to other people, sometimes the Holy Spirit seems to take over and bless the work in such a way that people observe afterward, "When I heard you speak yesterday (or today), I felt that I wasn't just hearing you. I was hearing God speak." This is what we should be seeking.

The second image for the Holy Spirit in the account of Pentecost is fire. I have indicated how this symbol links up with the first in that it is introduced as "tongues of fire." "Wind" and "fire" both involve speech. Yet there is more to this image than that.

What does fire chiefly symbolize? Well, we go back to the Old Testament again, and when we do that we see that quite often fire is a symbol of God's presence. The earliest instance I can think of is in the fifteenth chapter of Genesis, where God made his covenant with Abraham. Abraham had a vision. The vision was of God, suggested by symbols. Abraham had performed an ancient rite of covenant making. He had cut animals apart and put them in two rows on the ground. It was customary in his day for the two parties to the covenant to walk between the separated parts of the animals and take their vows there. (The vow was understood to be particularly sacred because of the shed blood of the divided animals.) However, in this particular vision, Abraham slept—he did not participate—and while he slept, he saw "a smoking firepot with a blazing torch," which symbolized God's presence, pass back and forth between the slain animals (Gen. 15:17).

The symbolism taught that this was a unilateral covenant. It meant that God was establishing it on his own authority entirely apart from Abraham's participation. Sometimes there are bilateral covenants. Human beings enter into those. God does something and they do something. But this time God did not ask Abraham's participation. Abraham did not have to do anything.

A bit later in the Old Testament we come to where God appeared on Mount Sinai. There the presence of God was symbolized by fire and thunder. It was a holy presence. No one was allowed to climb up the mountain to see what God was like except for Moses, who was invited. If another person did, he or she would die. This is what the author of Hebrews was thinking of when he wrote at the end of chapter 12, "For our God is a consuming fire" (v. 29).

What does fire do? It does two important things.

Fire Brings Light

We tend to forget that fire is a source of light because we live in an age of electricity. When we think of light, we think of flipping a wall switch and having a bulb light up. In the ancient world, there was no electricity. So light came either by the sun or by fire. When the Holy Spirit came upon the disciples at Pentecost, the first experience they had was what we would call "spiritual illumination." That is why Peter could preach such a persuasive sermon. He understood the Old Testament as he had not understood it before. He was given ability to preach it to enlighten those who heard him.

Wherever the gospel of Jesus Christ has gone into the world it has always brought enlightenment.

We live in a fairly bright age and forget how dark the world was before Jesus' coming. We glorify the days of the Roman Empire, for instance, probably because of movies starring actors like James Mason. How could the Romans possibly be depraved if they were like James Mason! Or we think of the Greek philosophers and reflect on how enlightened the Greeks must have been. They were not enlightened. Oh, there were sparks of brilliance. Plato was brilliant. But he said that philosophers are like men in a dark cave. They look toward the opening and see certain shapes illuminated from behind, silhouettes. They cannot really tell what they are. The forms only suggest the reality that lies behind. Plato's description of philosophy shows that he knew he was very dark in understanding. His knowledge of that is an indication of how wise he really was.

Apart from God's self-revelation men and women have no more than a faint idea of who God is. But when the gospel comes there is light. People can see as they could not see before. They can see who God is and what the gospel is. Perhaps as significant as anything, they can see what they are apart from Jesus Christ and what they can be in him.

Fire Brings Warmth

The second important use of fire in the ancient world was for warmth. If you were a bedouin camped out by a tent at night, you had a fire and drew near it to keep warm. In the same way, when the Holy Spirit is at work, one thing people notice is what we can call the warming of one's heart. It is what John Wesley experienced when the Lord reached him in that little chapel at Aldersgate in London. He said as a result of hearing the gospel explained on that occasion: "My heart was strangely warmed."

The problem is not just that the world we know is in darkness. The world is certainly in darkness—as black as any night when the sun goes down. But the world is also "out in the cold"—unwarmed, unloved, uncomforted—until

God, after whom our hearts long and in whose image we are made, draws near to warm us.

Christianity is meant to be a spreading flame. The Lord Jesus Christ said on one occasion, "I have come to bring fire on the earth" (Luke 12:49). Some of our translations say, "I came to cast fire on the earth." When I read that I think back to John the Baptist's testimony: "I baptize you with water. . . . But after me will come one who is more powerful than I. . . . He will baptize you with the Holy Spirit *and with fire*" (Matt. 3:11, italics mine).

When Jesus said that he had come to pour fire on the earth, he meant a fire that was destined to sweep over all the earth. How do we know? We know because of the way he spoke in giving the Great Commission. He said, "You will receive power when the Holy Spirit comes on you; and you will be my witnesses in Jerusalem, and in all Judea and Samaria, and to the ends of the earth" (Acts 1:8). This prophesied expansion of the Christian gospel began at Pentecost. That is why the second paragraph of Acts 2 talks about the many different people who were present in Jerusalem and who heard the gospel in their own language on that day: "Parthians, Medes and Elamites; residents of Mesopotamia, Judea and Cappadocia, Pontus and Asia, Phrygia and Pamphylia, Egypt and the parts of Libya near Cyrene; visitors from Rome (both Jews and converts to Judaism); Cretans and Arabs" (vv. 9–11)—people from all over the world, all the way to Rome and even beyond it. These individuals, reached for the first time at Pentecost, spread out in all directions like ripples on a pond.

When the Holy Spirit comes in power, what we are to have is not some particularly intense experience. We don't have to speak in tongues so that in a miraculous way everybody will hear our words in his or her language. Rather, we need to have a widespread speaking about Jesus. Everyone will hear as the gospel spreads through the testimony of those who are obeying the Great Commission. That is what you and I are called upon to do. That is the task to which the Lord Jesus Christ sends us.

In his book *The Incendiary Fellowship*,[5] Elton Trueblood describes the character and company of those who are filled by the Holy Spirit. "Incendiary" means "set ablaze." It refers to Christians themselves. But "incendiary" also means the act of setting other people ablaze. It refers to those in whom the fire of the Holy Spirit is so intense and so meaningful that they just cannot keep the message of the Spirit to themselves. So they speak of Jesus, and, as a result, here and there little fires spring up. And pretty soon there is a great raging fire of revival that spreads across the world. I do not think we have a raging fire in our time, though there are some places in the world where it may be beginning. But there is a fire. The Holy Spirit is working. We need to be part of that working and see the flames spread.

5

The Sermon that Won Three Thousand Souls

Acts 2:14–41

Then Peter stood up with the Eleven, raised his voice and addressed the crowd: "Fellow Jews and all of you who live in Jerusalem, let me explain this to you; listen carefully to what I say. These men are not drunk, as you suppose. It's only nine in the morning! No, this is what was spoken by the prophet Joel."

Acts 2:14–16

From time to time I read accounts of revivals in which the Spirit of God worked in such strong ways that many hundreds of people responded to the gospel. Yet in all those accounts I have not read of any in which a sermon was so blessed by the Holy Spirit that three thousand people who before it were lost in sin and blinded in their ignorance, far from God and far from faith in Jesus Christ, turned from sin, responded to the gospel call, and entered the company of God's people within the church. Yet that is what happened at Pentecost as God blessed the first great sermon of the church age.

Sometimes we look at what happened and get very excited about the miracle of speaking in tongues—each one heard the preaching in his or her own language—and we want to duplicate that today. We want another miracle. Well, speaking in tongues at Pentecost certainly was a great miracle, and an exciting one, one Peter used in a powerful way as an introduction to the sermon he preached about Jesus. But it was not the essence of Pentecost. It was an important miracle. But the most important thing is that those who were filled by the Holy Spirit began to be Christ's witnesses, as he had told them they would be (see chapter 2 of this study).

Peter's Pentecost sermon is a model sermon. We would expect it to be since it was the first sermon of the Christian era, preached by the most prominent of the apostles, and resulted in great blessing. It is a sermon every preacher should study. Yet, more than that, it is a sermon all Christians should study because although in a formal sense most Christians do not preach sermons, all nevertheless have many opportunities—they must have them—to speak about Jesus Christ. So the principles that govern the formation of a great sermon must govern the informal witness of the people of God in other circumstances. This sermon was centered on the Bible, it centered on Christ, and it was fearless and reasonable.

Centered on the Bible

First, this is a great biblical sermon, which means that it is centered on the Bible. Peter did not have the New Testament before him when he preached at Pentecost, but he had the Old Testament. And not only did he have it, he knew it. I suggested, when we were studying the end of chapter 1, that Peter had spent the days immediately before Pentecost studying the important Old Testament texts bearing on Jesus' ministry. And probably the other Christians who were gathered together on Pentecost had done so too.

The Lord had started them on this track. He had explained the nature of his work by referring to these texts, saying that the disciples were foolish and slow of heart to believe because they did not see that what had happened to him had been the fulfillment of prophecies. We know that when Jesus met with the Emmaus disciples, he began with "Moses and all the Prophets" and explained to them in "all the Scriptures"—that is, in all three sections of the Old Testament—the things that concerned himself. Now suddenly, Pentecost came, and Peter, never a person to be shy or idle, seized the opportunity.

In our day a preacher will usually take one text and develop three (or at most four) points from it. So you have "three-point" or "four-point" sermons. This is because people's attention span is rather short today. In Spurgeon's day, one hundred or more years ago, four-point sermons were the norm. People used to talk about a great "four-pointer." If we go back to the time of the Puritans, we are astounded to find that they could go on to eight, nine, ten, twelve, or sometimes more points. And they were not just little items either. They were developed at length and over a long period of time. People knew how to listen then. They could think. So there was a time when there were sermons with many, many points.

When we turn to Peter's sermon we find that it is not as much a case of his having many points as of his having many texts. He does not just take *one* text and expound it, as most of today's preachers have been taught to do. He has three texts, and he expounds each of them.

Joel 2:28–32

Joel was written on the occasion of a disaster that had come upon Israel. There had been a locust invasion, and the plague had destroyed every green thing in the land. In a rural, agricultural economy this destruction was an extremely serious thing. It was a matter of life and death for most people. So Joel talks about it. But instead of saying, as some of us might say under those circumstances, "Well, every cloud has a silver lining. Things will get better. Don't worry about it," Joel actually says, "As a matter of fact, things are going to get worse; judgment by locusts is only a foretaste of a greater, final judgment to come."

In the middle of this very gloomy book Joel talks about a blessing that is to come in the latter days. He says that God is going to restore the years that the locusts have eaten. There is going to be a time when God blesses the people so that they will be satisfied. It is at this turn in the prophecy, as Joel begins to speak comforting words, that the verses that became Peter's first text on Pentecost occur. He quotes God as saying:

> And afterward,
>   I will pour out my Spirit on all people.
> Your sons and daughters will prophesy,
>   your old men will dream dreams,
>   your young men will see visions.
> Even on my servants, both men and women,
>   I will pour out my Spirit in those days.
>
> Joel 2:28–29 (see Acts 2:17–18)

Peter referred to this text first because it was the clearest and most obvious Old Testament prophecy of the outpouring of the Holy Spirit. Then, with marvelous clarity and urgency, he linked it to what everyone in Jerusalem was noting: namely, the clear, powerful proclamation of the gospel of Jesus Christ to everyone in his or her own tongue. "This is what was spoken by the prophet Joel," was Peter's contention. What was happening was what Joel prophesied.

Psalm 16:8–11

Peter then repeated his procedure, reviewing what everyone knew of the ministry of Jesus and explaining it on the basis of a second great text. Psalm 16:8–11 was important to the early Christian preachers; the apostle Paul also referred to this passage on at least one occasion (Acts 13:35). Although it was written by David and contains statements that apply quite literally to him, toward the end of the Psalm are words that could not apply to that great king of Israel: "You will not abandon me to the grave, nor will you let your Holy One see decay" (Ps. 16:10; see Acts 2:27).

This is about the decay of a body in a tomb, a decay that will not happen. But how could David say that about himself? David's body did see decay, and, as Peter points out, "His tomb is here to this day" (v. 29). Any person who doubted it could walk over to the tomb and dig up his bones. What was David talking about then when he said, "You will not . . . let your Holy One see decay"? Peter pointed out—as did the other early preachers—that David must have been speaking as a prophet, looking ahead to the Messiah, who, because he would be God and not a mere man like David, would not see decay. He would die, but his body would be preserved and would be raised incorruptible.

Psalm 110:1

Psalm 110:1 also was a popular text with the early gospel preachers. It is the verse of the Old Testament most quoted in the New Testament. It is quoted or referred to indirectly about twenty-five or thirty times. The Book of Hebrews alone refers to it at least three times directly and several other times indirectly.

> The Lord says to my LORD:
> "Sit at my right hand
> until I make your enemies
> a footstool for your feet."
> Psalm 110:1
> (see Acts 2:34–35)

It is easy to see why this verse was so important. In Hebrew the first word for "Lord" is "Jehovah." It refers to the one great God of Israel. The second word for "Lord" is "Adonai." It refers to an individual greater than the speaker. So here is a case of David citing a word of God in which God tells another person, who is greater than David, being David's Lord, to sit at his right hand until he makes his enemies a footstool for his feet. This other person could be no one other than a divine Messiah.

Jesus referred to this verse in Matthew 22, asking how David could refer to a mere human descendant of his as his Lord. If the Messiah were to be a mere human descendant of David, a mere human being, that form of address is improper. But the Messiah was to be no mere man. He was to be more than that. He was to be the God/man, the one the Father would exalt above every being in heaven and on earth, giving him a name that is above every name and allowing him to sit at his right hand until he should make all his enemies subservient. This text, as Peter rightly saw, refers to Jesus and to him only.

What is this sermon's emphasis? One way we can answer that question is to count the number of verses given to quotations of the Old Testament and put them against the number of verses that are exposition. If we do that, we have thirteen verses citing passages of the Old Testament, eleven verses of exposition, and two verses of application that come at the very end. So we have thirteen verses versus thirteen verses. In other words, the verses of citation and the verses of exposition are about evenly balanced, and perhaps the emphasis even falls on the citations.

I have been to seminary and have taken my share of homiletics courses. I have had people teach me how to preach. They have taught me many useful things. But nobody ever taught me, and as far as I know nobody has ever taught anybody else, that half of what a preacher says should be biblical quotations. There are perfectly good reasons for that lack of teaching. Quotation itself usually fails to draw listeners along. Besides, there is no sense quoting verses if those listening fail to understand them, which is especially likely in our biblically illiterate age. People today would not even know why one is quoting the verses. But the point made by the way Peter's sermon is passed on to us is that the very words of the Bible and the use of the Bible by God's Spirit are far more important in spiritual work than anything the preacher can say—even if he is an apostle. It is what God says, and what God does with his Word when it is proclaimed or expounded, that is important.

A Christ-Centered Sermon

Second, the sermon is Christ-centered. If the sermon is biblical and if the Bible is about Jesus Christ, then a biblical sermon is inevitably a Christ-centered sermon.

This was Pentecost, the Holy Spirit had come upon the disciples, and Peter had begun his sermon with a great Old Testament quotation dealing with the Holy Spirit. But at the very point at which we might have expected Peter to go on to teach what we would call "a doctrine of the Third Person of the Trinity," showing who the Holy Spirit is and how he operates, Peter actually shifts ground and instead speaks about the life and work of Jesus.

This is no accident. When the Lord Jesus Christ had been talking to his disciples in what we call "the final discourses," he told them that when the Holy Spirit came he would testify to him. In John 15:26 Jesus said, "When the Counselor [that is, the Holy Spirit] comes, whom I will send to you from the Father, the Spirit of truth who goes out from the Father, he will testify about me." Similarly, in John 16:14 Jesus declared, "He [the Holy Spirit] will bring glory to me by taking from what is mine and making it known to you." The Holy Spirit came upon the disciples; Peter began to preach; and because the Holy Spirit was guiding, Peter inevitably preached about Jesus.

Sometimes people who are into "signs and wonders" say, "When you see signs and wonders—when there are healings or speaking in tongues—there the Holy Spirit is operating."

There is a tradition in the Reformed churches that says miracles ceased with the death of the apostles. According to this view, the miracles were given to authenticate the apostles as messengers from God. God did authenticate them. Their message is preserved in Scripture. Therefore, today we no longer need miracles and, in fact, cannot have them. As I say, I do not take that position. God can do anything he chooses. If he chooses to do something miraculous, well, so be it. I believe he does so from time to time. I rejoice in it.

But that is far different than using miracles as evidence that the Holy Spirit is active and present. Satan can counterfeit miracles. And whatever the case with miracles may be, the Bible teaches that we can know the Holy Spirit is present chiefly because those who profess Christ testify powerfully to him. I made that point in previous chapters.

Whenever you find men and women being pointed to Jesus Christ as Lord and Savior, however or wherever that may happen, there the Holy Spirit is at work. Do you seek miracles? That is the greatest of all miracles. It is a miracle of spiritual regeneration.

Peter preaches about Jesus beginning at verse 22, after he has cited the text about Pentecost, and continues to nearly the end. What is missing in these words, that we might have expected Peter as one who had accompanied Jesus through three years of active earthly ministry to have included, is Christ's teachings. We might have expected Peter to have said, "The Lord Jesus Christ taught this or that or this other thing." But Peter does not include the teachings.

The teachings of Jesus Christ are certainly important. That is why we have the Gospels; the teachings of Jesus are recorded for our benefit. But here Peter is preaching to men and women who were not believers in Jesus Christ—to men and women who apart from the work of the Holy Spirit were dead in their sins—and he knew that no one can preach successfully to spiritually dead people by saying, "Do what Jesus tells you." Some of these people likely had crucified Jesus because they did not like what he was teaching. So Peter does not tell them what Jesus said but instead declares what Jesus did for them. He preaches the cross and resurrection.

We need more of this preaching in our churches. Many churches are filled with well-meaning people who share what Jesus says and somehow expect those who are not born again to follow it. They cannot. Instead, we need to preach first that God sent Jesus to die for our sins and to call men and women to faith in him. We need to declare that those who trust him will find salvation from their sins and new life by the Holy Spirit.

Peter manages to squeeze in, in just these few verses, much doctrine concerning Christ's work:

1. *His ministry.* This is described not as a ministry of teaching but as a ministry of miracles or signs, the point being that God accredited Jesus by them.

2. *The crucifixion.* Peter emphasized that the crucifixion was by the express plan and foreknowledge of God; that is, it was no accident. He also said that those who were responsible for it were guilty of the sin.

3. *The burial.* Peter contrasts Jesus' burial with David's burial, which was permanent. Jesus' burial was real but temporary.

4. *The resurrection.* Peter deals with the resurrection at greatest length, quoting Psalm 16:8–11 and then expounding it in verses 29–32.

5. *His ascension.* The ascension links the work of Christ to Pentecost, to what was the present. It is from his present position with the Father that Jesus "has poured out what you now see and hear" (v. 33).

6. *Christ's present ministry.* Pentecost is proof that Jesus Christ is still working.

These points are the heart of all the apostolic preaching. A number of years ago a scholar in England by the name of C. H. Dodd wrote a book called *The Apostolic Preaching and Its Developments* in which he pointed out that there is a certain core of "proclamation" facts that were almost always used by the early preachers. Dodd and others called this the *kerygma,* using the Greek term for "proclamation."[1]

We find this *kerygma* throughout the New Testament. Here is one example. Paul, when he was writing to the church at Corinth, said:

> What I received I passed on to you as of first importance: that Christ died for our sins according to the Scriptures, that he was buried, that he was raised on the third day according to the Scriptures, and that he appeared to Peter, and then to the Twelve. After that, he appeared to more than five hundred of the brothers at the same time, most of whom are still living, though some have fallen asleep.
>
> 1 Corinthians 15:3–6

Do you see what Paul is doing? He is doing here, many years after Pentecost, precisely what Peter did when he preached so powerfully on that earlier occasion. He is listing the basic gospel facts.

When I think about this, I cannot help but reflect on the sad state of so much Christian preaching and witnessing in our time. The problem with our preaching today is that it is so man-centered. Sometimes this is centered on the preacher. The minister will tell cute stories, often about himself or his children. Sometimes the preaching is centered on the hearers. It speaks to "felt needs." There is a certain sense in which that may be quite proper, of course. It is possible to reach people by speaking to their felt needs. But much preaching never gets beyond that. It is psychological or sociological in emphasis. It looks to the polls and asks, "What produces the maximum results? What best builds a big congregation?" That may succeed as the world measures success. You can build a big congregation by the same technique you use to build a big corporation or market hamburgers. But that is quite different from doing the work of God.

Fearless Preaching

Third, Peter's preaching was fearless. I say "fearless" because, after all, the sermon was being preached in Jerusalem, and it was in Jerusalem that the Lord Jesus Christ had been crucified. Peter was preaching to the very people who had called out, not many weeks before, "Crucify him! Crucify him!" Moreover, Peter was preaching in the shadow of the temple, no doubt overlooked by the same religious leaders who had plotted to kill his Master at that time—and had succeeded, humanly speaking. Peter and the others had cause to be afraid. Yet they were not afraid. And the reason they were not afraid is that the risen Lord Jesus Christ was with them. The Jesus they served was not merely a man who had been crucified. He was also the Son of God who had been raised from the dead, had ascended into heaven, and was now seated at the right hand of the Father, directing the outpouring of the Holy Spirit and the preaching of the gospel.

These men expected results. They said, This is what the work of the Lord Jesus Christ has led up to. He has died for sin. Now it is our task to preach this gospel. They expected the Holy Spirit to bless their preaching, and the Holy Spirit did.

An Eminently Reasonable Address

Let me say, finally, that Peter's sermon was also sound, by which I mean that it was eminently reasonable. Sometimes preaching can be eloquent and moving so that an entire congregation can be swayed by the rhetoric. Yet it can also be unsound in its reasoning. This was not the case here. I am sure that Peter was an eloquent man. I am sure that on this occasion, as on other occasions, he preached with great fervor and that the people noted this fervor. I am sure also that the Holy Spirit blessed his fervor and eloquence and everything else. But when we read this sermon, we are impressed not so much with his eloquence as by the fact that he was calling the people to think reasonably. He was saying: You know about Jesus. You know what he did. You know the miracles that took place through his ministry and by his hands. That was God's way of authenticating him. How could he have done miracles if God had not been with him? You know how the leaders—your leaders—arranged his crucifixion. You saw how he was killed. God raised him from the dead. We are witnesses of it. The resurrection is proof that God has accepted Christ and repudiated your repudiation. It is this Christ who has poured out the Holy Spirit, whose power you can see and witness now.

Then Peter went on to his conclusion, and that was reasonable as well: If this Jesus is the Christ, then you have killed your Messiah. What you should do now is repent of this great sin, believe on Jesus, and be baptized, and thus identify yourself with him.

That call was powerful because we are told as we come to the end of the sermon that Peter's hearers were cut to their heart and said to the apostles, "Brothers, what shall we do?" Three thousand believed and were baptized.

I long for a day when we will hear that cry in the church of Jesus Christ. I long for the day when preaching will be so biblical, so Christ-centered, so fearless, and so sound that men and women will cry out, "Oh, brothers, sisters, what must we do?" and when the answer is given, "Repent and be baptized, every one of you, in the name of Jesus Christ so that your sins may be forgiven," there will be great repentance.

6

A Model Church

Acts 2:42–47

*They devoted themselves to the apostles' teaching and to the fellowship, to the breaking
of bread and to prayer. Everyone was filled with awe, and many wonders and miraculous
signs were done by the apostles. All the believers were together and had everything in common. Selling their possessions and goods, they gave to anyone as he had need. Every day
they continued to meet together in the temple courts. They broke bread in their homes and
ate together with glad and sincere hearts, praising God and enjoying the favor of all the
people. And the Lord added to their number daily those who were being saved.*

Acts 2:42–47

Acts 2:42–47 describes the early
church. It is presented as a model church, but this does not mean that it was
perfect. A few chapters further on, we are going to find that it was far from
perfect. It had hypocrites in it, as our churches also have. It had doctrinal
errors. It certainly had sinful human beings of all types, as our churches do.
Yet it was a model in many important respects, and it is as such that it is
described in Acts 2. These verses tell what developed in the church and how
it functioned in those remarkable days after Pentecost. Obviously this description is intended as an example for us and our assemblies.

This was an inner-city church. It was a large church, and it had a multiple staff ministry. It needed the latter because of the 3,000 people who were added to the church at Pentecost, making the total number of believers 3,120 (the 120 of chapter 1 plus the additional 3,000). It began with the twelve apostles. But when the Twelve found that there still were not quite enough people to do the work, they asked the church to elect seven deacons. So they had nineteen officers at that time. And the success of the church, as we soon discover, was that all of the believers (and not just these nineteen) were doing the work of the ministry (see Eph. 4:11–13).

In this chapter we need to look at some of the things that are said about this model church. It was a Bible-studying church that practiced fellowship. It also worshiped and evangelized. The key verse is verse 42: "They devoted themselves to the apostles' teaching and to the fellowship, to the breaking of bread and to prayer."

A Learning, Studying Church

The first phrase says that they devoted themselves to "the apostles' teaching." In other words, this was a learning, studying church. There were a lot of other things Luke could have said about it. As we go on, we find that it was a joyful church, also an expanding, vibrant church. These are important items. Nevertheless, the first thing Luke talks about is the teaching. He stresses that in these early days, in spite of an experience as great as that of Pentecost, which might have caused them to focus on their experiences, the disciples devoted themselves first to teaching.

It could have been a temptation for the early believers to look back to Pentecost and focus on the past. They might have remembered the way the Holy Spirit came and how he used them to speak so that those in Jerusalem each heard them in his or her own language. They might have longed to experience something like that again. They might have been praying, "Please, Lord, do something miraculous again." This is not what we find. They are not revelling in their past experiences. Instead, we find them revelling in the Word of God.

I suggest that this is always the first mark of a Spirit-filled church.

A Spirit-filled church always studies the apostolic teaching. It is a learning church that grounds its experiences in and tests those experiences by the Word of God.

It is also interesting that the object of their study was the *apostolic* teaching. The apostles were people specifically chosen by Jesus Christ to remember, teach about, and authentically record the events and meaning of his ministry. The importance of this office is seen in the way the apostles went about choosing a replacement for Judas, who had betrayed Christ and then committed suicide. Peter led the way. He said that the replacement had to be, first, a person who was present with the Lord from the earliest days, who knew about his ministry and was a witness of the resurrection. Second, he also had to be one whom the Lord specifically appointed to the apostolic office. Many people had witnessed the events of Christ's ministry, but the Lord did not choose all of them. He chose a certain number. And he chose those to remember and record an official, Spirit-inspired compendium of his teaching. Jesus said in the last discourses, recorded in John's Gospel, that after he was gone he would send the Spirit to bring to their remembrance all that he had taught.

If somebody says, "But how do we know that these particular men were the true apostles of Christ and spoke with his authority?" the answer is by the "wonders and miraculous signs" mentioned in verse 43: "Everyone was filled with awe, and many wonders and miraculous signs were done by the apostles." I do not think we need to conclude that the wonders and signs were done by the apostles alone and by no one else. Others may have been the agents of miraculous occurrences too. But what the text does say is that miracles were done by the apostles, and the reason they were done by the apostles (this is said explicitly) is that it authenticated them as Christ's messengers and as bearers of the true Spirit-given teaching.

We find exactly the same case in 2 Corinthians 12:12. Paul is speaking: "The things that mark an apostle—signs, wonders and miracles—were done among you with great perseverance." In other words, these were given so that those who looked on could say, "These men are God's appointees. His blessing rests on them, and what they do, they do in God's name." When Peter and John and the other apostles spoke, saying that Jesus Christ did so-and-so and taught so-and-so, the early Christians could receive their words as an authentic record and interpretation of Jesus' life and rightly devote themselves to studying it. They studied this teaching and tested it against the Old Testament.

We live in a different age, of course. We live thousands of years after this teaching. Peter is not with us. James was martyred. John has died. So have all the others. Even Paul, who came along later, has gone. How is it possible for us to focus on the apostolic teaching? These men gave us the New Testament. This is the deposit of their teaching. When it came time to collect the books that were to become our New Testament, the criterion by which that was done was whether they came from the apostles or bore the apostolic blessing. Moreover, the fact that we have our New Testament is a fulfillment of what Jesus Christ said he would do through these apostles. In order for us to copy the New Testament church at this point, as we should, we are to study the book these men have left us. It is in the New Testament that the authentic teaching of the Lord Jesus Christ is to be found.

Let's put that in terms easy to understand: A Spirit-filled church is always going to be a Bible-studying church. Those two things go together. There have been periods in history when the Bible has fallen on hard times and been neglected by God's people. These have been dry ages for the church. There have also been periods when the Bible was not always readily available, sometimes because of political pressures. Sometimes even church officials kept the Bible from God's people. Nevertheless, wherever the church has been greatly blessed, where the Spirit of God has come upon God's people and the gospel has gone forth in great power and people have responded to it, these have always been ages in which the Bible has been studied carefully. Why? It is because the closer men and women come to God the closer they want to get to where he speaks to their hearts, and that is in the Bible.

What is true of the church is true for individuals also. If you are Spirit-filled, then you will be drawn to this Book. If you are not drawn to this Book, if you do not really want to study it, if you say, "Well, you know, I look at the Bible from time to time, but it seems rather boring to me: it never really does much for me," you ought to question whether you are really born again. Or if you are born again, you at least ought to question whether you are filled by the Holy Spirit. Because the Holy Spirit, whose chief task is to bear witness to Jesus Christ, inevitably draws the people of God to Jesus through the Scriptures.

This means, among other things, that evangelical, Spirit-filled, Bible-oriented churches should offer many ways for people to get to know the Bible. It must be done through the preaching. In fact, that is the preacher's chief task: to expound the Word of God. He is to study it and then teach it to others. It may be done through Bible classes and home Bible studies. We are going to see that the early Christians worshiped in their homes. So I am sure they studied the Bible in their homes. If we had been there, we would have said, "They're having home Bible studies."

Christian Fellowship

Not only did it devote itself to the apostles' teaching, but the early church also devoted itself to fellowship at many levels. Stott says that "the word 'fellowship' was born on the Day of Pentecost."[1] This is because Christian fellowship means "common participation in God," which is what had drawn the early Christians together. The apostle John wrote, "We proclaim to you what we have seen and heard, so that you also may have fellowship with us. And our fellowship is with the Father and with his Son, Jesus Christ" (1 John 1:3).

The Greek word for "fellowship" is *koinonia*, which has to do with holding something in common. The form of the Greek language spoken in the time of the apostles was not classical Greek but a kind of Greek called *Koine*. This is from the same root as the word for "fellowship," and it means "common." The Greek of the apostles' time was "common Greek" because it was the universal language of the day. It is that language in which the New Testament is written. The fellowship of the church was a common fellowship because of the great spiritual realities the believers shared in together.

If you have a fellowship that you think is so special (perhaps with only two or three of you) that you do not want anybody else to be part of it, then you had better question whether it is really the fellowship of the people of God. These early Christians had all participated in God the Father and in Jesus Christ. They were one in God. So because they were one in Jesus Christ and in God the Father, they quite naturally participated in a common life and shared everything with one another.

Fellowship with God and true fellowship with others go together. That is why John said, in the verse I cited a moment ago: (1) we want you to have "fellowship with us" and (2) "our fellowship is with the Father." Some people have said, "The stronger your vertical fellowship is, the stronger your horizontal fellowship will be." If you find yourself out of fellowship with God, you will begin to find yourself out of fellowship with other Christians. You will say, "I don't really like to be with other Christians very much. They all seem to be hypocrites." You will begin to drift off. But if you come close to God, you will inevitably find yourself being drawn close to other Christians. And it works the other way, too. If you spend time with other Christians, if you share a great deal with them, that fellowship will help to draw you closer to the Father.

When we talk about our participation in God, we are talking about a "sharing in." But this "sharing in" also results in a "sharing out." In other words, these Christians, who enjoyed their close fellowship, inevitably shared what they had with one another.

A few paragraphs earlier I gave a brief study of the word *koinonia,* pointing out that it is based on the idea of having things in "common," "participating in something together," or "sharing." *Koinonia* has a variant closely related to it, *koinonikos,* which means "generous." Those who share in God inevitably share in God's nature, which includes generosity, and they are generous with those around them. Verses 44–45 read, "All the believers were together and had everything in *common.* Selling their possessions and goods, they gave to everyone as he had need" (italics mine).

Because their generosity extended to the sharing of their goods, some have regarded this as a biblical endorsement of communism. It is not communism. In fact, it is the opposite of communism. Communism is a sharing of goods, but it is an enforced sharing on the basis that no one has the right to own anything. Communism is compulsory; therefore it has nothing whatever to do with generosity. Peter himself endorses the right to private property (see Acts 5:3–4 and pages 97–98 of this study).

The sharing of possessions that went on in the early church was not socialism either. Socialism acknowledges the right of private property, but it compels individuals to give a percentage of, or everything above a certain figure, to others. Socialism does not deny a person a right to own things, but it denies him the right to have too many of these things as measured by somebody else's standard. Most people would be astounded to hear that American life is socialistic, but it is very socialistic. Whenever there is a system that taxes those who have more at a higher rate than those who have less in order that the state can take these resources and redistribute them to those who have less, that is socialism, because it is being done not willingly but by force.

I am not saying we have full-blown socialism in America, only that we have a great deal of it. But the point I am making is not that socialism is bad or good or even whether or not we have it in America. My point is merely that this is not what was going on in the early church. The early Christians shared their possessions, not because they were communists or socialists—not because they were forced to share their things—but for a far better reason. They shared their goods because they were generous, and they were generous because they had learned generosity from God. God had been generous with them. So because God had been generous with them, they were determined to be generous with one another.

Sometimes we reason that because the early Christians were not forced to share their goods we are therefore justified in keeping what we have for ourselves. But we can't get off the hook quite that easily. It is true that we are not forced to be generous. But if we are followers of Jesus Christ, if we have learned from him, then we know that "a man's life does not consist in the abundance of his possessions" (Luke 12:15), and that "it is more blessed to give than to receive" (Acts 20:35). The standard set before us is the standard not of being served, but of serving. So our obligation is to use what we have for others, which is what the early church did. It is one measure of a Christian's sanctification and maturity.

A Worshiping Church

The third characteristic of the early Christian church was worship. There was "the breaking of bread" and "prayer." "Breaking of bread" stands for the communion service, and prayer, although it is something we can do individually and at different times, is in this passage actually the formal exercise of prayer in the assembly. In the Greek text the definite article occurs before the word "prayer." The text actually says, "to the prayers." They devoted themselves "to *the* breaking of bread and to *the* prayers." Obviously, that is a reference to something formal—to worship in which the people got together and praised God.

There is also a reference to formal worship in verse 46: "Every day they continued to meet together in the temple courts." "Temple courts" probably refers to the courtyard of the Gentiles, which was a very large place. On feast days, when everyone packed into it, it could accommodate perhaps two hundred thousand people. It was the only place in Jerusalem where you could get such a large crowd together. Indeed, it may have been here that the large meeting on the day of Pentecost took place, and if it was, then it would have been natural that on set occasions the early Christians returned to the place so they could all enjoy the worship of God as they broke bread in the communion service and offered up prayers.

Then, not only did the Christians worship in a formal setting, perhaps in the large courtyard of the Gentiles, but *they worshiped informally as well,* as the very next phrase says: "They broke bread in their homes" (v. 46). That is a deliberate repetition. Verse 42 says, "They devoted themselves . . . to the breaking of bread." Then verse 46 says, "They broke bread in their homes." It means that they did both. They had formal worship and they had informal worship. And the informal worship included, and perhaps was largely centered on, the communion service.

How about their music? What did they sing when they got together in the temple courts? They must have sung the psalms, participating in the regular liturgical patterns of Jewish worship. Our equivalent might be the many hymns of the Christian past. What did they sing when they met together in their homes? In that setting their music was probably far less formal, perhaps the equivalent of our so-called praise music or choruses. The psalms were the best worship music. They were based on an inspired text, after all. But that did not exclude the use of other music in its place.

Should Christian worship be formal? Or should it be informal? The answer is certainly that Christian worship should be both. Why should we have to choose between the two? There are different kinds of people, different settings, and different occasions on which we worship. Why should there not be worship appropriate to each occasion?

A Witnessing, Evangelizing Church

There is one other characteristic of the church mentioned in this text. It was a witnessing or evangelizing church. That is why we find as we get to the end of these verses that the Lord added "to their number daily those who were being saved" (v. 47). This verse does not say specifically that they were out witnessing. But we know that the way God reaches people is through the spoken word and that when the Holy Spirit came at Pentecost, those who received the Spirit immediately began to speak about Jesus. If we find, as we do at the end of this second chapter, that the Lord was adding to their number daily those who were being saved, it must have been because they were out witnessing.

How could they do otherwise? They had experienced something wonderful, the ministry of God's Son. They had been present in Jerusalem when Jesus had been arrested, tried, and killed. Some had been present when he died on the cross. They had in their number many who were witnesses of the resurrection. These were wonderful facts and theirs was a life-transforming message. They had to share it with other people. How could they not?

Yet, as they shared it, they did not make the mistake of saying, as some do, "We are the ones bringing in the kingdom. We are adding to the church. This is being accomplished by our skill, our eloquence, and our power." They knew perfectly well that they were only channels for what God was doing, only means to the end that God himself had determined. So they did not say, "We are building the church" but rather, "The Lord added to [our] number daily those who were being saved."

There is a sense in which both God and we do the work. God works through us, which means that we must work. If we do not work at witnessing, nothing happens. If we do not pray, little happens. But when we do and when it does, it is because God himself is working. To many people that sounds like a contradiction, but it is not a contradiction. It is good biblical theology. It is the way God operates. The apostle Paul wrote to the Philippians in a similar vein, saying to them, "Continue to work out your salvation with fear and trembling, for *it is God who works in you* to will and to act according to his good purpose" (Phil. 2:12–13, italics mine).

Not only was God saving people, but he was also adding them to the church. These two things go together too. Sometimes we say, "Well, let's get out and save people." We do. But then we let them go off and do their own thing, forgetting about them. That is not the way God wants it. When a person is brought to the Lord Jesus Christ, he or she is not brought to him individualistically. People are saved individually. That is, people become Christians by believing in the Lord Jesus Christ themselves. They come one at a time. But when they come, they come into the company of God's people. God saved many in these days following Pentecost, but when he did, he added them to the fellowship of the church—and the church grew.

Not only did God do the work of saving people and not only did he add them to the church, but he also did it daily. The text says, "The Lord added to their number *daily* those who were being saved" (italics mine). That seems to have been a normal pattern then, and I assume it should be a normal pattern for us too. Wouldn't it be wonderful if every day we had reports of those who have come to the Lord Jesus Christ as their Savior?

John Stott makes an interesting point in his recent commentary on Acts:

> Looking back over these marks of the first Spirit-filled community, it is evident that they all concerned the church's relationships. First, they were related to the apostles (in submission). They were eager to receive the apostles' instruction. A Spirit-filled church is an apostolic church, a New Testament church, anxious to believe and obey what Jesus and his apostles taught. Second, they were related to each other (in love). They persevered in the fellowship, supporting each other and relieving the needs of the poor. A Spirit-filled church is a loving, caring, sharing church. Third, they were related to God (in worship). They worshiped him in the temple and in the home, in the Lord's Supper and in the prayers, with joy and with reverence. A Spirit-filled church is a worshiping church. Fourthly, they were related to the world (in outreach). They were engaged in continuous evangelism. No self-centered, self-contained church (absorbed in its own parochial affairs) can claim to be filled with the Spirit. The Holy Spirit is a missionary Spirit. So a Spirit-filled church is a missionary church.[2]

The world does not really know what it needs. It does not even know what it wants. But what it needs and wants (or needs to want) are those relationships.

7

The First Miracle

Acts 3:1–26

One day Peter and John were going up to the temple at the time of prayer—at three in the afternoon. Now a man crippled from birth was being carried to the temple gate called Beautiful, where he was put every day to beg from those going into the temple courts. When he saw Peter and John about to enter, he asked them for money. Peter looked straight at him, as did John. Then Peter said, "Look at us!" So the man gave them his attention, expecting to get something from them.

Then Peter said, "Silver or gold I do not have, but what I have I give you. In the name of Jesus Christ of Nazareth, walk."

Acts 3:1–6

In chapter 3 of this study I pointed out that Acts is a transitional book. Acts comes between the Gospels and the Epistles. When we begin to read it, the Lord Jesus Christ is still here. The characters we come across are people who knew Jesus, those who in many cases had traveled with him during the days of his ministry. Most of them were witnesses of his resurrection. But then as we go on through the book, we come to people who did not have those experiences. Paul himself did not live with Christ during the days of his earthly ministry. And there are people like Timothy and Titus, Aquila, Priscilla, and Apollos, who had not even seen him. The flow of the book is from those early days in Jerusalem, when Jesus is still present, to Rome, which is where Acts ends. Acts is a transition in

63

another way too. It is a transition from an age in which miracles were common to a time more closely resembling our own.

Better Than Gold

Luke described the early fellowship of believers by saying, "Everyone was filled with awe, and many wonders and miraculous signs were done by the apostles" (Acts 2:43). In Acts 2 Luke does not give us any indication as to what those miraculous signs may have been. But now, when we come to Acts 3, we have the account of at least one of them.

Why did Luke choose to chronicle this particular miracle? The answer is two-fold: (1) because it was the occasion for a second sermon of Peter's, which Luke wants us to hear; and (2) because the miracle and sermon were the cause of the first persecution of the church.

Verse 1 tells us that Peter and John were going up to the temple at the time of prayer. We were told in chapter 2 that one of the things the early church did was gather in the temple courts to pray. In time God would cause a break with formal Judaism. But the break had not come yet. The apostles and other early believers were still Jews as well as being Christians, and they were continuing to take part in the worship that their people had enjoyed for centuries.

As Peter and John were doing this, they met a man who had been placed at the temple gate to beg from those who were entering. He was unable to walk. But he had friends, and they had put him in what was obviously a good position. They must have reasoned that it would be difficult for people to enter the temple, offer heartfelt worship to God, and then, as they left, utterly ignore a poor man who clearly needed help. Peter and John saw him and stopped. We are told that Peter fixed his attention on him and demanded that the man look at them.

That is what the man wanted. I can imagine that if his experience was that of most beggars, most people would simply have walked by. If you see somebody who is needy and you do not want to help, you try not to notice him. That is what most people would have been doing. So when Peter and John stopped, looked at him, and said, "Look at us," the man must have looked up very hopefully, thinking that they were going to give him something. I do not know what they begged with in those days. But if he had owned a tin cup, I imagine he would have held the cup out to them, no doubt thinking, This is going to be a good day. These people are going to give me money.

Then Peter uttered the words that most of us know very well: "Silver or gold I do not have. . . ."

Can you visualize what must have happened at that moment? The man was expecting silver or gold. So when Peter said, "Silver or gold I do not have . . ." his eyes must have dropped, and he must have put his cup down. But Peter went on, adding, "But what I have I give you. In the name of Jesus Christ of Nazareth, walk" (v. 6).

Notice, first, that it was to Peter's credit that he could utter both parts of that sentence. There is a story from the Renaissance period that I have come across in several different versions. It may or may not be true. In any case, the version I like best goes like this: St. Thomas Aquinas was in Rome. He was walking along the street with a cardinal. The cardinal noticed a beggar. Reaching in his pocket, he pulled out a silver coin and gave it to him. Then he turned to Aquinas, the great doctor of the church, and said, "Well, Thomas, fortunately we can no longer say, as Peter did, 'Silver and gold have I none.'"

St. Thomas replied, "Yes, that is true. But neither can we say, 'In the name of Jesus Christ of Nazareth, walk.'"[1]

It has always been sadly true that people have used religion as a means of acquiring wealth. We see much of this today, particularly in the way some "ministries" are promoted on television. The heads of these ministries make a great deal of money. Peter was not one of these people. I suppose that in the early church there were people who kept the church's money. Later on we find that there was a treasury. Perhaps Peter had learned something from Judas, who dipped into the common purse when he needed something. Peter apparently did not. So when he went up to the temple to pray, he said quite honestly, I do not have any money. His penniless state may even have been a factor in his being close enough to God that he could also say, "But I am going to give you what I have."

When Peter reached down, he took that man by the hand. Luke, who perhaps was interested in this miracle from the point of view of a physician, records with particularly vivid language how strength flowed into the man so that his feet and ankles could now bear his weight. He was completely restored to health. And he was so exuberant in his new-found health that he leaped—"walking and jumping, and praising God." The language itself literally leaps, just as he leaped. This was a great, great day. And the people who knew the man because they had gone in and out of that gate many times and had seen him often were filled with amazement and undoubtedly praised God also.

In the case of the man who had been born blind, whose story is told in John 9, the man's appearance was so altered that the people questioned whether or not this was the same man. In the case of the man healed by Peter there was no doubt at all. Everyone understood at once what had happened. A miracle had taken place by the same power that had been displayed in the resurrection of Jesus of Nazareth and at Pentecost.

Peter's Second Sermon

At this point Peter began to preach his second sermon. When we compare Peter's first sermon with this one, we find some differences. Yet there are similarities too, because regardless of the circumstances, Peter was trying to do the same thing here as on the earlier occasion: He was trying to point his listeners to Jesus as the Savior of the world. He also confronted them with their sin, appealed for their repentance, and gave reasons to repent and believe.

Christ-Centered

Just as in the sermon at Pentecost, this new sermon focuses on Jesus. I suppose it would have been possible for Peter to have focused on something else. He could have focused on the miracle itself. He could have said, "This is an important thing that has happened, and I want to make sure that you understand that this really is a miracle. Look at this man. Let's all gather around and examine him."

Peter's sermon could have led into a testimony service. He could have said, "Now, brother, you have been healed. Here's your chance to give a testimony. Stand up and tell everybody what Jesus has done for you." A testimony like that might have focused on the man. The man could have said, "Let me tell you about my experience. Let me tell you how I first came to be part of what is going on here today. . . ." The man could have gotten quite a bit of personal attention out of that.

Instead, Peter said, "Men of Israel, why does this surprise you? Why do you stare at us as if by our own power or godliness we had made this man walk? The God of Abraham, Isaac and Jacob, the God of our fathers, has glorified his servant Jesus" (vv. 12–13). Jesus! This is where the emphasis of the entire sermon lies.

In speaking about Jesus, Peter is inevitably biblical. I say inevitably because this sermon is not so obviously biblical as the previous one. When we were studying the sermon Peter gave at Pentecost, I pointed out that it focuses on three great texts (see chapter 5 of this study). The way Peter preached that sermon was to quote each text at length and then explain it. The fact that he is biblical is not so obvious in this second sermon—although at the end he does quote from Deuteronomy and Genesis. Nevertheless, Peter is biblical.

The biblical nature of the sermon is apparent in Peter's choice of words. When Peter refers to Jesus as God's "servant," as he does in verse 13, he uses the word for servant that occurs in the Septuagint (Greek) translation of Isaiah 52:13–53:12, where the coming servant of God (52:13) is described as the one who would be "pierced for our transgressions [and] crushed for our iniquities" (53:5). The concept of the "servant of the Lord" was well-known in Israel because of Isaiah 53 and other texts. So when Peter used "servant" and then went on to speak of "the Holy and Righteous One"—another title for the Christ that also appears in Isaiah—it is pretty clear that he was thinking of these chapters. He was teaching that Jesus is the Messiah promised in the Old Testament Scriptures.

When Peter talked about Jesus, he had a number of important facts to mention. One is that Jesus was a real man. Earlier when he spoke to the paralyzed man, he referred to Jesus as "Jesus Christ of Nazareth" (v. 6). It was not some imaginary, philosophical Jesus that Peter was proclaiming. It was a Jesus they all knew, a Jesus who had lived in Nazareth and who had traveled about the country teaching and doing good. But notice: That Jesus was also the same Jesus who had died for sin and then had been raised from death by the power of God. Peter was not retreating into philosophy, nor was he de-supernaturalizing the gospel, as some modern Bible critics have done. He was preaching a biblical Jesus who was both the Son of God and fully man.

When you think about Christianity, do you think primarily about Jesus Christ? And do you understand who Jesus is by the words and doctrines of the Bible? There is a lot more that Christians talk about, of course. But properly understood, those other things all relate to Jesus in some measure. Without Jesus you do not have Christianity, and the Jesus of Christianity is the Bible's Jesus. To be a Christian is to have a personal relationship with him. Therefore Peter was preaching about him in this sermon.

Grappling with Sin

Peter's sermon is also direct in speaking about sin. Even more than in his earlier sermon Peter emphasizes the sin of the people in disowning Jesus and handing him over to Pilate to be crucified.

He does it in a personal way. Where Peter begins to talk about the sin of the people he uses the word "you" (the second person plural pronoun) four times. In the previous sermon he only used it in that way once: *"You,* with the help of wicked men, put him to death by nailing him to the cross" (Acts 2:23, italics mine). That is pretty blunt. But I suppose that as Peter reflected on it (and even got a little better with practice), he figured that when he got around to preaching a second time he would give that point emphasis. So now he says, *"You* handed him over to be killed, and *you* disowned him before Pilate, though he had decided to let him go. *You* disowned the Holy and Righteous One and asked that a murderer be released to you. *You* killed the author of life, but God raised him from the dead" (vv. 13–15, italics mine).

Peter is saying this in the very city where the people had cried out against Jesus, saying, "Crucify him! Crucify him!" He is speaking to these same people, perhaps with the very same leaders who had urged them to cry out looking on, and he is saying, *You* did it; *you* crucified him. The verbs are powerful, too: "You *handed him over* to be killed. You *disowned* [him]. You *killed* the author of life" (italics mine).

From time to time when I am preaching I will say something about the death of Jesus and how the Jewish leaders handed him over to Pilate to be crucified. Whenever a study like that appears on the radio later, as many of my studies do, I get letters from people who object to my saying that Jews demanded the death of Jesus. That is understandable, of course, because it is a sensitive point in Judaism, and I usually answer by pointing out that the Gentiles in the person of Pilate were also guilty. We are all guilty of Jesus' death, and if we had been there at the time, we might all have joined in the cries of those who demanded Jesus' death. But I notice here that, sensitive as that point may be, it was certainly never any more sensitive than it was in this early day when Peter preached in Jerusalem. In spite of the sensitive nature of the issue, Peter did not allow people's feelings to stand in the way of preaching clearly. He did not say "Jews" to the exclusion of others. He included Pilate in his "you." He included the Romans. They had actually put him to death. But that was not what concerned Peter in this sermon. Peter's "you" meant everybody, including the Jews and perhaps even the Jews particularly. He was not pulling his punches.

We need to realize that we are all to blame for the death of Christ in one way or another. Even though we were not there at the time Jesus was arrested, tried, and crucified, it was our sins that took him there. And if Jesus were here today, we would spurn him today, just as the masses of Israel spurned him in Jerusalem long ago.

An Appeal for Repentance

Third, not only does Peter's sermon point to Jesus and highlight the listeners' sin—making it clear that the people of Jerusalem had something to repent of—but it also contains an appeal. This is because in the final analysis, Peter was not interested in merely condemning his hearers. On the contrary, he wanted them to repent of their sin and believe on Jesus.

He begins with the words "Now, brothers" (v. 17). He does not treat them as foreigners, aliens, or enemies. Indeed, how could he, since what he said earlier, "You disowned him . . . you disowned the Holy and Righteous One" (he repeated it), was the very thing Peter himself had done? Peter had denied Jesus on the night of his arrest. So he does not stand aloof now as he appeals to these people. He calls them brothers, saying, "I know that you acted in ignorance, as did your leaders." Their ignorance did not make them guiltless. Nevertheless, they were not fully aware of what they were doing, and Peter was in exactly that category himself.

Where our English text has Peter encouraging his listeners to "turn to God" (v. 19), the Greek text actually says "flee to God." That was probably intended to suggest a powerful image. In Israel there were cities set aside from other cities as "cities of refuge." If an Israelite accidentally killed someone else, he could flee to one of these cities and there be protected from an avenger of blood, a relative of the deceased who might try to kill him in retaliation. These cities were not to protect real murderers. If somebody intentionally killed someone, well, he was to be tried and punished, as he should be. But if the killing was accidental—if it was what we would call "manslaughter" rather than "murder in the first degree"—then the killer could flee to the city and be protected there. He was to stay there until the high priest died. Then he could go home.

There is something like that idea in Peter's sermon. Peter told the people that they were guilty of killing Jesus, but he taught that God would forgive their sin if they would repent of it and flee to the refuge that he has provided in Christ.

Peter tells them to "repent, then, and turn to God" (v. 19). These two things always go together. Sometimes we feel sorry for what we have done.

But it is not enough merely to feel sorry. Sorrow is not repentance. Repentance is feeling sorry enough to quit, and quitting means turning from sin to Jesus Christ. When Peter tells the people, "Repent... and turn to God," he makes the connection apparent and indicates exactly what we need to do.

Reasons to Repent and Believe

The fourth thing Peter does in this sermon is offer inducements to repent and believe on Jesus. The first is: "so that your sins may be wiped out" (v. 19), that is, so that you might be forgiven. Forgiveness is what people need, and the only place anyone will ever really find forgiveness is in Christ. A director of a large mental institution in England said to John Stott some years ago, "I could send half of my patients home tomorrow if only they could find forgiveness."

Most people carry heavy loads of guilt. This may be true of you. You may not have not told anybody what you have done. You are afraid that if you told someone else, that person would reject you. Nevertheless, you remember what you have done, and you carry the guilt of your actions around with you day by day, week by week, and year by year. Your burden keeps you from being what you might otherwise be. Moreover, you do not find forgiveness in the world. The world is not capable of that. The world can judge you for your sin or pretend to overlook it. But it is not capable of forgiving it. On one occasion the Lord Jesus Christ said to a man, "Your sins are forgiven," and the religious leaders who were standing by replied, "Who can forgive sins but God only?" They were absolutely right. They did not recognize that Jesus was God and therefore had the right to forgive sin. In that they were wrong. But their theology was right. Only God can forgive sin. That is why the world is so unsatisfactory in this respect. Peter is saying that God can forgive your sin; he can lift that great load of guilt. Clearly this is one great inducement to turn from sin and believe in Jesus Christ.

Peter has another inducement too. It is the "times of refreshing [that] come from the Lord" (v. 19). This may be understood in different ways. On the one hand, it probably concerns a future day of blessing when the Jewish people will turn to Christ in large numbers and a final age of national blessing will come. Paul talks about it in Romans 11. On the other hand, there are also "times of refreshing" for all God's people even now.

Many of us go through much of life feeling pretty stale in what we do. We feel like the horse that eats hay and oats on Monday, oats and hay on Tuesday, hay and oats on Wednesday, and so on throughout the week. Many people find, especially if they are in an unrewarding job, that life is often quite dreary. And sometimes even their Christianity becomes stale. They say, "I've been coming to church every week. But somehow it just isn't what it used to be. I feel so flat when I come." Well, that happens. We all go through dry spells. Times like that do not necessarily mean that we are far from God. They only mean that we *feel* far from God. Sometimes the cause is bad health. Sometimes the cause is the weather. A few days of gloomy rain and cold sometimes plunge me into a dark night of the soul. What we are told here is that in Christ there will be times of refreshing.

Haven't you known times when Jesus became so real and the gospel so vivid that your whole spirit, soul, and body were revived? If you want times of refreshing, times that make life really worth living so you can say, "Oh, it is good to be a Christian," turn from sin and follow close to Jesus.

There is another inducement here also, in verse 26. After Peter gets through saying that all that has happened in Christ is a fulfillment of prophecy and that they ought to know it because it is clear in their Bibles (he quotes from Deuteronomy 18:15,18,19 and Genesis 22:18), he says, "When God raised up his servant, he sent him first to you to bless you by turning each of you from your wicked ways." First to you! To whom? Well, to the Jews! But more than that, because it was not just to Jews generally that Peter was preaching on this occasion. Peter was preaching to Jews who had been instrumental in the death of Jesus. They handed him over to be killed, disowned him, asked that a murderer be released to them, and demanded that Jesus be crucified. It is to these people, the very ones who had been instrumental in the greatest crime in human history, that God now comes with the gospel of salvation. And he comes to them *first*. It is God's way of saying, "I know what you have done, but I do not hold it over you. I love you anyway. It is precisely for people like you that I caused Jesus to die."

You and I cannot say that God sent his servant to us first of all. Many have come to Christ before us in former ages of human history. But the principle is the same. Regardless of what you have done, the low self-image you may have, or the guilt you may carry, God proclaims his Son to you. And the reason the gospel is proclaimed to you is because God says it is for you that Jesus died.

8

No Other Name

Acts 4:1–12

Then Peter, filled with the Holy Spirit, said to them: "Rulers and elders of the people! If we are being called to account today for an act of kindness shown to a cripple and are asked how he was healed, then know this, you and all the people of Israel: It is by the name of Jesus Christ of Nazareth, whom you crucified but whom God raised from the dead, that this man stands before you completely healed. He is

> *"the stone you builders rejected,*
> *which has become the capstone.'*

Salvation is found in no one else, for there is no other name under heaven given to men by which we must be saved."

Acts 4:8–12

In the fourth chapter of Acts we have a record of the first persecution. I do not know if on this occasion Peter remembered what the Lord Jesus Christ had said about persecution. But it might be that when he was dragged before the Sanhedrin he recalled that Jesus had prophesied persecution for all who followed him:

> You will be handed over to the local councils and flogged in the synagogues. On account of me you will stand before governors and kings as witnesses to them. And the gospel must first be preached to all nations. Whenever you are arrested and brought to trial, do not worry beforehand about what to say. Just say whatever is given you at the time, for it is not you speaking, but the Holy Spirit.
>
> Mark 13:9–11

Peter may not have been thinking about these or similar words on the occasion of this first persecution, but he may have been. At any rate, everything Jesus foretold earlier was now fulfilled, and it was going to be fulfilled in similar situations even more as the church expanded.

The Force against Christians

I am sure that as Luke thought about this first persecution he was impressed with the great power arrayed against the disciples. The church was not strong. There were very few disciples, perhaps 3,100 or 3,200. These were the early days; the gospel had not expanded far. There were few leaders; none of them had much experience as leaders. They were a small band when measured against the total numbers of the Jewish people, and they were very weak—powerless actually—when measured against the rulers of the day.

I am struck by the way Luke lists those who were of the opposition. In verses 1–6 he lists no fewer than eleven different individuals or categories of individuals who were opposed to Christianity. Three of them are in verse 1: the priests, the captain of the temple guard, and the Sadducees.

Priests could include the Levites scattered throughout the entire land or the Levites actually in Jerusalem at that time to help with the temple worship. Levites served by rotation, and their turn to minister at the temple would come maybe once or twice in a lifetime. They would serve for about three weeks. However, I do not think Luke had in mind either the entire priestly tribe or the priests who were actually serving in Jerusalem, because in the New Testament "priest" usually refers to the high priest, priests, or their specific families. These men were not like the Levites who lived in the villages and who only came up to Jerusalem once in a while. They were the established priestly caste, and they were powerful. I suspect, because Luke is thinking of those who were specifically opposed to the Christians, that this is whom he had in mind.

Next he mentions the captain of the temple guard. He is probably referring to the captain of the temple guard along with the temple guard itself. These were not Roman troops. The captain was not a Roman officer. Still this was a force to be reckoned with. These were the soldiers who had arrested Jesus. The captain of the temple guard was the second most powerful person in Jerusalem, apart from the Roman governor and army. First, there were the Romans; second, there was the high priest; third, there was the captain of the guard. So Luke's mention of the captain of the guard is significant.

He also mentions the Sadducees. The Sadducees were not a terribly numerous party, but they were the upper class and a powerful, monied class at that. The Sadducees had recognized early on that if the Jews were going to survive the occupation, they would have to get along with the Romans. So they had established close ties with the authorities.

Here, then, we have the high priests and their families, the police force led by the captain of the guard, and the Sadducees, who because of their special relationship to the Romans were the most influential people in the land. It was a formidable opposition.

But it is not only these who were involved. In verse 5 Luke lists three more categories: the rulers, the elders, and the teachers of the law. Teachers of the law probably were those we call scribes, those whose task it was to know and copy the Scriptures. Elders were the distinguished older men who lived in Jerusalem and had great influence. Rulers probably were people in various positions of authority, the heads of government departments and committees.

This gives us six categories. But there are still more, because in verse 6, Luke also refers to individuals. There was Annas the high priest. He was the true high priest. The Romans had deposed him years before; they had installed Caiaphas, his son-in-law, in his place. But in Israel the high priest was a high priest for life. So in the minds of the Jewish people Annas would still have been the true high priest, regardless of what the Romans had done. Then there was Caiaphas, the acting high priest. These two men had conspired in the trial of Christ, Jesus having appeared before each of them. Finally, says Luke, there were John—not John the apostle, but a John in the priestly family—Alexander, and other men of the high priest's family. These were all present, and all of them were arrayed against the two apostles.

When I look at that list and realize how powerful these men were, I think of Thomas Kelly's hymn (1806) that goes:

> Zion stands by hills surrounded,
> Zion, kept by pow'r divine;
> All her foes shall be confounded,
> though the world in arms combine.

That last part, "Though the world in arms combine," is what was happening to Peter and John in these early days of church history. All the forces of the land were getting together against the early Christians. Yet, as the first part of the hymn says, clearly Peter and John were kept by God's power, as we are going to see.

Why Were the Rulers Upset?

What is it that disturbed these powerful rulers so much? We are told in verse 2. They were disturbed because the apostles were "teaching the people" and "proclaiming in Jesus the resurrection of the dead."

That they were teaching the people was itself naturally disturbing to the priests, Sadducees, rulers, elders, and teachers of the law, because these men were teachers, and teaching by others was a threat to their authority. This was one thing that had bothered them about Jesus Christ. He had not gone to their rabbinic academies. Nevertheless, he had an intrinsic authority. People marveled at it and flocked to him. Once they sent the temple guards to arrest Jesus, but his teaching was so powerful that it stopped the guards cold. They went back to their leaders and explained their failure, saying, "No one ever spoke the way this man does" (John 7:46).

These rulers had killed Jesus. But now they suddenly had this entirely new group of people to contend with, and they were like him. They had not been to the rabbinic schools either. They were just fishermen and tax collectors, simple, untaught people. But here they were teaching as Jesus had taught—with authority—and the people were listening to them.

A second matter disturbed them even more. These men were teaching about Jesus, and the central point of their teaching was that God had raised him from the dead. If the disciples had been teaching about the resurrection only, perhaps it wouldn't have been so bad, because, after all, the Pharisees also believed in the resurrection. The Sadducees did not, but the Pharisees did. On a later occasion Paul used that doctrine to divide the Sanhedrin (see Acts 23:6–9). But the disciples were not just teaching about the resurrection generally, that there is going to be a resurrection at the last day, they were teaching about the resurrection of Jesus. That changed everything. If it was true, it proved that Jesus was who he claimed to be, namely, the unique Son of God. It also proved the nature and value of what he came to do.

The Weapons of This World

The authorities used the world's methods in their offensive against the disciples. That is, they used their power, because naked power is the only weapon the world really has. Sometimes it is the power of wealth; people who have wealth will often use it to control, exclude, or oppress others. The government will use the courts, policemen, guns, and eventually the army, because in the last analysis this is the only power it has.

The first thing the Jerusalem authorities did was attempt to intimidate the disciples. In the Greek there is an emphasis that does not come across as strongly in English but indicates that when the priests, the captain of the guard, and the Sadducees came upon Peter and John, they came upon them suddenly. That is, they did not just meander up out of the back of the crowd and begin to talk to them. One moment Peter and John were there teaching earnestly. The next moment, there were the soldiers. They must have said, "Enough of this," grabbed them, and taken them away.

They were declaring: We have the power. If you are allowed to preach, as you have been preaching, it is because we have permitted you to do it. If we decide that you are no longer to be permitted to do that, well then, you can't do it anymore. Anytime we want, we can arrest you and carry you off to jail.

Throwing them in jail was also intimidation. The leaders did not have to arrest the disciples at this point. They could have picked them up the next morning. Peter and John were not hiding. The leaders must have said, "Let's just throw them in jail overnight. Let them cool their heels there. That will dampen their spirits. Then we'll see how they function in the morning." Peter and John had courage in spite of this intimidation, and that impressed the authorities (Acts 4:13). Intimidating the disciples didn't work, but that is what the authorities were trying to do all the same.

The world continues to operate this way, and that is one reason why the witness of Christian people often fails or is given in an ineffective way. If Christianity is true, it is the greatest message in the world. Yet we are afraid to proclaim it, and the major reason is the world's intimidation. We fail to speak because we are afraid someone might laugh at us or harm us.

The Jerusalem authorities also used threats. Verse 21 says so explicitly: "After further threats, they let them go." If there were further threats, there must have been earlier threats. And I suppose this is what is being suggested in verse 18, where it says, "They called them in again and commanded them not to speak or teach at all in the name of Jesus." They must have said, "If you speak about Jesus in public again, we are going to beat you and put you in jail. It will be decades before you see daylight again." Or they might have said (maybe as Peter and John were going out the door, perhaps in a whisper), "And don't forget what we did to Jesus."

I think Luke shows a sense of irony at this point, though the situation is hardly funny and perhaps it is only the irony of the situation itself that I notice. But here these men were, trying to intimidate the apostles, threatening them. Yet even before they give their witness, Luke records in verse 4 that "many who heard the message believed, and the number of men grew to about five thousand." The last figure we had concerning the size of the church was from the days immediately following Pentecost, when it was said there were about three thousand (Acts 2:41). At this point, not very long afterward, a couple of weeks or so at the most, there were five thousand. It was an increase of 60 percent.

The world thinks that it can stop a spiritual movement by threats, force, imprisonment, and death, but it cannot. A good idea, especially a true spiritual idea, will always spread.

I do not think you can stop any good idea, even a good secular idea, by threats. A good idea will always thrive and eventually permeate a culture. Perhaps you can slow it for a time. Maybe some good ideas have been stamped out temporarily by harsh rulers. But most have not been, and certainly you cannot stamp out Christianity. The rulers were trying to stamp it out. But what we discover in Acts, which we also find in later church history and see in our day too if we just look around, is that the more the church is oppressed, the more the gospel spreads. Justin Martyr said, "The blood of the martyrs is the seed of the church."

The Christian Offensive: Peter's Testimony

We have seen the forceful methods arrayed against these early preachers of the gospel. Now we are going to see the force of God and the methods the people of God use.

The force on the side of God's people is the Holy Spirit. It says that when Peter began to speak he was "filled with the Holy Spirit" (v. 8). When we were looking at the account of Pentecost I pointed out that in Acts, on every occasion, what follows specific mention of a person being filled with the Holy Spirit is strong verbal testimony to Jesus Christ. When people are filled with the Holy Spirit they always speak about Jesus. That is how you can know whether you are filled with the Holy Spirit.

Peter gave a formal reply. He had been arrested because of events growing out of the miracle of the healing of the lame man. So he began by speaking to that issue:

> Rulers and elders of the people! If we are being called to account today for an act of kindness shown to a cripple and are asked how he was healed, then know this, you and all the people in Israel: It is by the name of Jesus Christ of Nazareth, whom you crucified but whom God raised from the dead, that this man stands before you healed.
>
> Acts 4:8–10

This was a wise reply. Peter was basically saying, "The only thing you can possibly have arrested us for is this miracle—for doing good to that poor lame man. Doing good is no crime. But if you also want to know by what power or in what name we did it" (that is the question they had asked in verse 7), "then you need to know that it was in the name of Jesus Christ of Nazareth."

In your Bible you will find a comma at that point. It is a significant comma because so far as the accusation was concerned, Peter had by that point given a perfectly good answer. There could be a period. He did not need to go further. They had said, "By what power or what name did you do this?" and Peter had replied, "By the name of Jesus Christ of Nazareth." Question. Answer. End of the defense!

Yet Peter was not merely trying to defend himself. He did what Paul later did in Rome (see 2 Tim. 4:17). He used the opportunity to witness to Jesus Christ. This is why I think Peter may have had in mind the prophecy with which I began, the prophecy in which Jesus said, "On account of me you will stand before governors and kings as witnesses to them." Peter may have remembered those words and thought to himself, Here is a great opportunity to witness to governors about Jesus.

If he had been intimidated he would have been trying to save his skin. He would have said as little as possible, "taken the fifth," and refused to incriminate himself. But he wasn't intimidated. He was a servant of the living God, and he had the greatest message in the world. So he thought to himself, In all my life I have never had a chance like this; I may never have a chance like this again. Look at this audience: the priests, the captain of the temple guard, the Sadducees, rulers, elders, teachers of the law, Annas, Caiaphas, John, Alexander, and all the other members of the high priest's family. I will never do better than this again. Why, if we had put on a great advertising campaign, we could never have gotten all these important people to come. But here they are. So let's preach Jesus.

And that is what Peter did. There were four points to his sermon.

1. *They were guilty in crucifying Jesus.* The Jesus about whom Peter was speaking was the Jesus they had put to death. Verse 10 says, "the one whom you crucified." And it would not have done any good for them to have said, "Well, you know, we didn't actually do it. The Romans did it." It did not do Pilate any good to have washed his hands of the matter either. The washing did not excuse Pilate, and these words would not have excused the Jewish rulers. They were guilty, along with others. The first thing Peter did was remind them of that. What courage! No wonder verse 13 mentions the courage of Peter and John. They needed courage to remind this august body of leaders of the crime they had committed.

2. *Jesus rose from the dead.* In verse 10 Peter calls Jesus "Jesus of Nazareth . . . whom God raised from the dead." The message of Jesus' resurrection proves everything that is essential about Christianity. It proves that Jesus is God, that he is the Savior, that death is not the end for anyone, and that there is a resurrection. Furthermore, Peter says that God is the one who has done this, the very God they claimed to worship. They killed his Son, but God vindicated Jesus by raising him from the dead.

3. *The purpose of God was established in spite of opposition.* In verse 11 Peter says, "The stone you builders rejected . . . has become the capstone" (quoted from Psalm 118:22). When Luke quotes from the Old Testament, he almost invariably quotes from the Septuagint, the translation of the Old Testament used among Greek-speaking people, since he was writing to Greek-speaking people. But in quoting from the Septuagint at this point, Luke varied the quotation slightly, adding the word "you." The Septuagint says, "The stone the builders rejected has become the capstone." But Luke changes it to say, "The stone *you* builders rejected . . ." (italics mine). Why? Undoubtedly because that is the way Peter spoke it. Peter added the word "you" to reinforce what he had been teaching. He had spoken of the leaders' guilt. Then he took an impersonal Old Testament text and made it pointed.

There are lots of things about the gospel that the world does not like. It does not like to hear about human guilt. It does not like to hear about the resurrection. But of all the things the world does not like, probably the greatest is that God always accomplishes what he wants in spite of our opposition.

But God does accomplish it. He is going to accomplish it with you. You may fight him to the end. But in the end, it will be his will rather than yours that will be done. We do not like that, because the essence of sin is thinking and saying, "I can do without God. I can resist God. I do not have to do what God wants." Unfortunately for that point of view, we are not our own masters. We are God's creatures. Therefore, it is always God's purposes and not ours that will be established.

4. *Jesus is the one and only way of salvation.* "Salvation is found in no one else, for there is no other name under heaven given to men by which we must be saved" (v. 12). Oh, how the world hates such statements! If you want to be laughed at, scorned, hated, even persecuted, testify to the exclusive claims of Jesus Christ. Say that Jesus is the *only* Savior, that *only* by believing in him can one escape hell. The world will fight you to the death, because nothing is so offensive to the natural man as teaching that we cannot save ourselves, that we cannot choose our own way of salvation, and that if we are going to be saved it must be by God in the way he has appointed.

Why did Peter insist on this fact? He was an intelligent man. He knew he was saying these things at the risk of his life. Why would he take such a chance? He was saying it because he knew there is nobody else like Jesus Christ. There is no man who is God except Jesus, no one who could die for the sins of others. That is why Peter could proclaim him fearlessly.

You may say, "But that sounds so narrow." Yes, it is narrow.

"But it sounds so exclusive." Yes, it is exclusive.

"But it sounds intolerant." Yes, in a sense it is intolerant. But it is also true. And any man or woman who turns his back on what is true is simply foolish.

When the authorities began to interrogate Peter and John, they said, "By what power or what name did you do this?" Peter and John answered, "Jesus." That was correct. But when Peter got to the end and summed it all up, he threw their question right back at them and said, in effect, "It is not only the lame man who was healed by the name of Jesus. That name is the only name by which anyone can be healed. What needs to happen to you is what happened to the lame man. You too must be saved by Jesus."

Everett F. Harrison had it exactly right when he wrote:

> Salvation was the supreme concern of this prince of apostles (Acts 2:40; 5:31; 15:11; cf. 1 Peter 1:5, 9, 10). It is found exclusively in Christ and "no one else," and it is an imperative need for sinful men (they "must be saved"). What had happened to the physical condition of the cripple, in that he had been made whole (literally, saved), was a parable for the healing of the whole man by the power of Christ.[1]

In your sin you are as helpless in the sight of God as that lame man. You cannot save yourself. Only Jesus can heal you. You need to believe that and place all your faith in Jesus Christ, the only Savior.

9

Civil Disobedience

Acts 4:13–22

"What are we going to do with these men?" they asked. "Everybody living in Jerusalem knows they have done an outstanding miracle, and we cannot deny it. But to stop this thing from spreading any further among the people, we must warn these men to speak no longer to anyone in this name."

Then they called them in again and commanded them not to speak or teach at all in the name of Jesus. But Peter and John replied, "Judge for yourselves whether it is right in God's sight to obey you rather than God. For we cannot help speaking about what we have seen and heard."

Acts 4:16–20

God had used Peter and John to heal a lame beggar, and the leaders of Israel were unhappy with the miracle. So they arrested the disciples and brought them before the Sanhedrin. "By what power or what name did you do this?" they demanded. "Name" stands for authority. So they were actually asking, "By what authority did you accomplish this miracle?" The disciples answered, "It is by the name of Jesus Christ of Nazareth, whom you crucified." This sentence is the theme of chapter 4, and it carries us into this new section. There is a four-fold sequence.

1. The question: "By what power or what *name* did you do this?" (v. 7, italics mine).

2. The answer: "By the *name* of Jesus Christ of Nazareth" (v. 10, italics mine).

3. The application: "There is no other *name* under heaven given to men by which we must be saved" (v. 12, italics mine).

4. The response: "We must warn these men to speak no longer to anyone in this *name*" (v. 17, italics mine).

The leaders knew that they could not deny that the lame man had been healed. They would be a laughingstock in Jerusalem if they tried to do that. But they thought they could contain the damage to their position by a naked exercise of authority. So, turning to Peter and John, they said, "Whatever you do, don't preach or teach any longer in that name." The issue is authority. On the one hand, there is the authority of the rulers, who frequently set themselves against Jesus. On the other hand, there is the authority of Jesus Christ, who commanded the apostles to be his witnesses. Peter and John replied, "Judge for yourselves whether it is right in God's sight to obey you rather than God. For we cannot help speaking about what we have seen and heard."

The Problem Facing the Sanhedrin

Not long before this, Jesus had created a problem. And now here were more preachers and workers of miracles just like him. The text expresses the Sanhedrin's view of the problem when it says, "They saw the courage of Peter and John and realized that they were unschooled, ordinary men" (v. 13).

To call them unschooled did not mean that they were ignorant. There was a basic knowledge of the Old Testament Scriptures that was imparted to most men in the synagogues, and Peter and John certainly had that fundamental Jewish education. They both wrote letters to the churches, which we have in our New Testament, and they are letters of ability, exhibiting considerable knowledge. The Gospel of John especially is a great literary achievement, and Peter's letters radiate a warm, winsome vitality. Besides, the apostles had spent three years in the best seminary the world has ever seen. They had been traveling with the Master himself, and he had taught them, not only by precept as he unfolded the Scriptures to them, but also by example. He modeled the gospel for them. They were slow learners, just as we would have been. But they were on the way.

So when the text says that they were unschooled it means only that they had not been to the rabbinic schools. To have gone to the rabbinic schools was like having gone to an approved university. It was a ticket to success. If you wanted to be someone other people looked up to—a judge or a political figure—this was the way to do it.

Here was the remarkable thing. These two fishermen, these rather rough characters, stood before the Sanhedrin without fear and gave the testimony we read in the first section of the chapter (vv. 8–12). This was brilliantly done. So I am not at all surprised that the rulers were aghast when they saw both the rhetorical skill and boldness of the apostles. The authorities were ready to run over them like a steamroller, but these men were not the kind who were easy to run over.

There was something else that frustrated them. Acts 4:14 says, "But since they could see the man who had been healed *standing* there with them, there was nothing they could say" (italics mine). It is hard to miss seeing that Luke used this word "standing" intentionally, for emphasis, and perhaps for irony. He could have said merely, "They could see the man who had been healed with them." But this was a man who previously couldn't stand. And there is this too. The Greek word for "resurrection" is *anastasis*. The basic part of *anastasis, stasis,* is the word for "standing." To the Greek mind resurrected people were people who were standing up, as opposed to dead people, who were lying down. So there was a sense in which this "resurrected" man was a symbol of the very gospel Peter and the others were proclaiming.

I think the leaders were also a bit dismayed. The text does not use the word "dismayed." But I think dismay was part of their response, because the text says that they took note that Peter and John had been with Jesus. Maybe they did not know this at first. One would think they would know it, but as we read the chapter, it sounds as if this dawned upon them slowly, perhaps during the interrogation. Perhaps, as they looked at them intently, they began to say, "Haven't we seen these men before? Aren't these two of those who were hanging around with Jesus? What a troublemaker Jesus was! He was unschooled, too. He didn't know the law. He misinterpreted it all the time. He had to be done away with. Such people always have to be done away with. But now here are his disciples, acting like him. What are we going to do about it?" They had eliminated Jesus, but his influence was still with them—and spreading.

The Sanhedrin's Solution

The Sanhedrin did what the state always does. They resorted to naked authority. They simply insisted, "Don't do it anymore."

If you look at this response grammatically, you find something that you would not normally find in good writing. Verse 16 says, "Everybody living in Jerusalem knows they have done an outstanding miracle, and we cannot deny it." In that sentence "it" stands for the miracle. But then they go on to say, "But to stop this thing [the Greek text has "it" again] from spreading any further among the people. . . ." What does that "it" or "thing" refer to? Normally, you would take "it" to refer to the last main idea or noun, and that would be the miracle. They would be wanting to stop the miracle from spreading.

But that is not what they were thinking of. People were talking about the miracle. That news was spreading. But what these rulers were really concerned about was the gospel, the preaching of Jesus and the resurrection. At this point they hardly knew what it was they were trying to repress. So they just referred to it as "it": We don't want "it" getting around anymore. Let's contain "it." Let's squelch "it" right now. The words are almost humorous.

They brought the disciples back in. I suppose they lined up, put on their clerical vestments to look as solemnly official as possible. Then in very stern tones, they said, "Don't do it anymore."

The Sanhedrin did not have the power they had in earlier days because they were a subject nation at this point. The ultimate power was Rome's. But they had worked out an arrangement. They would support Rome if Rome would support them. When they made a pronouncement that concerned local affairs—the kind of thing Rome was not really concerned about—well, Rome would back them up. Therefore, when they told the disciples, in essence, "If you do this again, you are going to have to answer to us. We'll arrest you; we'll haul you in," that is exactly what they were able to do.

The Disciples' Response

The disciples responded by disobeying the state, and this raises the question of civil disobedience. The very thought disturbs many people. Some years ago, when Francis Schaeffer was still alive, this well-known Christian apologist published a book called *A Christian Manifesto.*[1] In it he said in clear language that in certain circumstances Christians are obliged to disobey the state. A lot of evangelicals got very upset at that. They said, "Oh, we mustn't disobey the state. God has established the state. We must submit to the state. Why, in Romans it says, 'The authorities that exist have been established by God. Consequently, he who rebels against the authority is rebelling against what God has instituted.'" They didn't like Francis Schaeffer's book.

This is an area in which we must be extremely careful, of course. We tend to rebel easily. We rebel when we should clearly submit. However, if you find yourself saying in categorical terms, "I must do whatever the state says I must do," then you are making the state your god. Unless the state is as wise and perfect as God, always expressing the perfect will of God, it is inevitable that in some situations the state is going to demand action that is contrary to God's laws. Then, if you are following God, you are going to have to disobey the authorities.

The Options

When we speak about the relationship between "God and Caesar," to use Jesus' words, there really are only four options: monastic, secular, cowardly, or biblical.

The Monastic Option

The first option is *God alone with the authority of Caesar denied.* This view emerged early in the history of the church, in monasticism. Monks said, "The world and its governments are so corrupt that we can have nothing to do with them. They are all of the devil. The only thing we can do as Christians is retreat from the world." So they did it. They moved into the desert. They became something of a curiosity, and people flocked to see them. There wasn't a lot to entertain a person in those days, of course, so a hermit in the desert became an attraction. When people went out into the desert to see them, these monastic figures moved farther into the desert and then still farther. Eventually some of them got the idea that the only way really to escape the world was to climb to the top of a stone pillar, where nobody could get to them. So they did.

One of these men, a very famous man, was Simon Stylites. He lived on the top of a seventy-foot-high pillar for about thirty years. It was from figures like these and other less extreme people that the monastic orders began.

We are not so extreme today. Americans are not very extreme about anything. We just take things as they come. We compromise right and left. Yet we have a form of this option that is withdrawal from what we would call "civic responsibility." People who fall into this category say, "I'm not interested in voting because, after all, politicians are all equally bad. None of them stand for anything. I am just going to stay home, go to church, raise my children, and ignore the world." That is our evangelical form of denying any legitimate place to civil government. Fortunately, we are seeing revival of civic responsibility among evangelicals in our day, and that is a healthy thing. Nevertheless, some still fall into this category.

When we talk about the state being a legitimate authority, we have the example of Jesus Christ to appeal to. When he was arrested and appeared before Pilate, not once in the entire trial did Jesus suggest that the authority of Pilate was illegitimate, even though Pilate was about to commit the great injustice of condemning an utterly innocent man. Jesus did not say, "We cannot tolerate injustice like this in our world. We must rise up against it. That is what I am going to tell my followers, 'This is a bad world. You must fight it. Raise an army. Get people like Pilate out of here.'"

In the course of the trial Pilate said to Jesus, "Don't you realize I have power either to free you or to crucify you?" The Greek word here for "power" is *exousia;* it really means "authority."

How did Jesus reply? He did not say, No, you don't. He said, Yes, you do. But notice how he said it: "You would have no power [authority] over me if it were not given to you from above. Therefore the one who handed me over to you is guilty of a greater sin" (John 19:11). Pilate had authority; Jesus recognized that. But when he brought the matter of sin into the equation he added the matter of responsibility, indicating that although Pilate had authority, it was a delegated authority. His authority was given to him by God. Therefore, he was responsible to God for how he used it.

Christians are not to deny the state's authority, still less assume civil authority themselves. But they are to remind the state that its authority comes to it from God. The state is responsible to God for what it does.

This accountability to God is what gives limits to the civil authorities. We see one of these limits in the story. When the state tells us that we cannot preach the gospel, that is an overextension of its authority, an illegitimate use of its legitimate authority, and we must resist it.

In our day we have an unfortunate interpretation of the doctrine of the separation of church and state. Originally that meant that the state was not to establish or hinder religion. But religion and the free practice of it anywhere were clearly protected by the constitution. Today this amendment has been interpreted in a purely secular way to say that there should be no religion in anything that involves the state—and the state seems to be everywhere. Thus the practice of religion has been excluded from the public schools, and it is increasingly under attack in other areas of our national life.

However, when we begin to wrestle with the problem and ask how we are going to deal with it, we need great wisdom. I believe Christians should argue for the right to pray in the public schools themselves, if they wish, and to present the Christian point of view on things, along with other points of view. Students should have the right to meet for Bible study, just as another group might meet for something else. Cases involving those matters have been before the Supreme Court.

But when the state tells us, "You can be religious, but you must do it privately," it is doing the very thing that was being done in Russia before the changes of 1989. The Soviet Union tolerated religion, but it had to be practiced privately. In the Soviet Union parents could not teach religion even to their own children. We are on the same path when our government says that we cannot have the practice of religion in the public schools.

When the state forbid the apostles from doing something God had told them to do, Peter and John disobeyed. They did not deny the state's authority. The state had the right to make whatever judgment it thought best. In fact, Peter and John acknowledged that authority. They said, "Judge for yourselves whether it is right in God's sight to obey you rather than God." That is, If you think in your wisdom that we should obey you rather than obey what God has told us, then you must exercise your punitive authority. But as far as we are concerned, God has told us to do something and we are going to do it, regardless of what you say.

The Secular Option

The second of the four possible options is *Caesar alone with the authority of God denied.* This option pushes God, rather than the state, out of the picture. It is the prevailing option of our day. It is the option of secularism. Today's secularism does not prohibit us from practicing religion privately, but we are not supposed to bring it out of the closet. We are to keep it on the reservation, because in the real world, Caesar is the only thing that matters.

This option is foolish. Why? Because we need God to appeal to when the state becomes evil or tyrannical. We need a check on Caesar. In America we have a government system of "checks and balances," that is, a system of limitations and controls among the various branches of government. For example, the President can propose programs, but the programs do not get underway unless Congress funds them. Congress can pass laws, but the laws do not go anywhere if the Supreme Court declares them unconstitutional. The President can appoint Supreme Court justices, but the Congress can impeach the President. Each branch of the government has a check or checks on other branches. We are greatly blessed having a document like the United States Constitution, because our founding fathers, recognizing the corruption of the human heart, said, "It is not wise to allow any one branch of government to have all the power."

It is the same in regard to God. If you push God out of the picture, you have trouble. Even if you have three branches of government that are supposed to have checks on one another, what happens if all three get together to establish a state that has no room for God or biblical morality? This is very close to what is happening in America today. When you have God in the picture, you can always call the state to account. It is the job of the church to do that. But if you push God out of the picture, you are at the mercy of your governors.

The Cowardly Option

The third option is *the authority of both God and Caesar but with Caesar in the dominant position.* This is the option of cowards. This is the position Pilate reflected in the trial of Jesus Christ. Pilate was no Jew; he did not know the Jewish God. He was certainly no Christian. Yet when he saw Christ and recognized that he was dealing with an extraordinary man, he may have had a pagan superstitious sense that he was dealing with one of the half-divine-half-human gods of Greek and Roman mythology. Pilate knew that it was bad to get one of these gods angry at you. What if he condemned Jesus and Jesus turned out to be one of those gods? What if he was just "a little bit" God? What if Jesus "zapped" him for it? He didn't want to take a chance. So he did everything he could to try to get Jesus excused. Pilate's problem was that he was far more afraid of Caesar than he was of any spiritual reality. So he did the wrong thing in the end.

The Biblical Option

The fourth option is *God and Caesar but with God in the dominant position.* This means that the state has a legitimate authority, as Paul writes in Romans 13. But this does not mean that the state is autonomous. Human beings are given certain spheres of authority. Church elders have authority; parents have authority over their minor children; employers have certain authorities over their employees; police have authority. There are many kinds of authority. But none is independent of God. All authority that has been given to someone or some group of people is from God. Hence, those who hold authority are responsible to God, who is the ultimate authority. That is why we have to obey God whenever the two come in conflict.[2]

That is what Peter and John did. And because they obeyed God they were used of God in launching a movement that has extended throughout the entire world, has transformed it, and is still with us today, centuries after the Jewish Sanhedrin passed away.

You and I are part of something eternal. We may look at the United States and say, as President Reagan once said on television, "I hope it lasts for two hundred more years." Well, so do I. But whether it is two hundred, three hundred, five hundred, or one thousand years, eventually even this great land of ours will be gone. Only the kingdom of God will never pass away. It is eternal. The important question is: What kingdom do you belong to? Where is your ultimate allegiance? To the state? Yes, we're called to give honor where honor is due, taxes where taxes are due, all of that. But most of all, we are called to be citizens of the kingdom of the Lord Jesus Christ and to live for him.

10

The Church at Worship and at Work

Acts 4:23–37

All the believers were one in heart and mind. No one claimed that any of his possessions was his own, but they shared everything they had. With great power the apostles continued to testify to the resurrection of the Lord Jesus, and much grace was upon them all. There were no needy persons among them. For from time to time those who owned lands or houses sold them, brought the money from the sales and put it at the apostles' feet, and it was distributed to anyone as he had need.

Acts 4:32–35

Do you enjoy getting missionary letters? In this age of voluminous and many times worthless communications I suppose there are Christians who get missionary letters and simply throw them away, the way they throw away the many worthless advertisements. But for my part, I enjoy missionary letters. I enjoy them because by reading them I feel that a window has been opened for me into Christian work in some other portion of the world. I am encouraged to learn what God is doing there.

Acts is something like a missionary letter, only the window it opens is not a window to a church that exists somewhere in the world today. It is a window to a church that existed almost two thousand years ago in the very first days after Pentecost. This early church had its problems. It had its sins, just as our churches today have sins. Still, when we look at the church in these early chapters of Acts, we find a portrait that is meant to be encouraging and a model for us and our churches.

We have studied one portrait like this already. It was found at the end of chapter 2 in verses 42–47. When we come to the end of chapter 4, we find another portrait of this church. The background for this portrait is the miracle performed by the apostles followed by their arrest and questioning (see chapters 7–9 of this study). This portrait shows the church at worship and at work. At *worship,* because in the first half of this section of Acts we find the apostles leading the people in a service of thanksgiving (vv. 23–31). John Stott says, "We have seen the apostles in the Council; now we see them in the church. Having been bold in witness, they were equally bold in prayer."[1] At *work,* because in the latter section of the chapter we see the church actually operating as a fellowship of renewed Christian people (vv. 32–37).

The Church at Worship

When the disciples left the council they rejoined the waiting Christians and had an impromptu worship service, thanking God for the outcome of their first significant encounter with the rulers of this dark world. Apparently they broke into prayer instinctively, for the text says, "When they heard this [that is, the report of Peter and John], they raised their voices together in prayer to God" (v. 24). Then the prayer was given. Much of it is a quotation from Psalm 2.

When God's people worship God, they always do two things: (1) they pray, and (2) they reflect on the Scriptures. Prayer is our talking to God; the Scriptures are God's talking to us, and the two always go together. You pray in a right way when you pray scripturally. You study the Scriptures in a right way when you study prayerfully. This is what the church was doing. They had been reflecting on the Scriptures. Now, as they began to pray, the Scriptures rose up in them, and they found themselves talking to God in God's own words.

That is amazing, because there was a time not very long before this—six, seven, eight weeks—when they did not even understand the Old Testament. Jesus had taught them that he had to fulfill the Scriptures by being arrested by the chief priests, delivered up to the Gentiles, tried, beaten, crucified, and resurrected. He was the greatest teacher that ever lived. He was expounding the Scriptures and the Scriptures were clear, but they did not get it because it did not fit their preconceptions.

On one occasion, Peter had the temerity to rebuke Jesus, saying, "Never, Lord! This shall never happen to you!" and Jesus had to say, "Get behind me, Satan! You are a stumbling block to me; you do not have in mind the things of God, but the things of men" (Matt. 16:23). He used the occasion to explain once again that he must die. But they still did not get it. Yet now, they understood the need for his death and resurrection and instinctively explained it by references to the Old Testament.

We saw in the first chapter of Acts that when they needed to choose a replacement for Judas they did so on the basis of two psalms. When Peter preached at Pentecost he based his sermon on three great texts from the Old Testament. In Acts 4, when Peter appeared before the Sanhedrin, he quoted Psalm 118:22.

Can you see what is happening? The minds of these early Christians were being scripturally transformed. Although as devout Jews they already knew the Scriptures in a certain sense, before this they had not understood them. It was only after Jesus died and rose again and the Holy Spirit came that their eyes were opened and they saw the Old Testament in its true light.

Think of how the Lord opened the minds of the disciples on the first Easter. The story is told in Luke 24. It speaks of three great openings.

1. *Jesus opened the Scriptures.* When Jesus met two disciples on their way home to Emmaus and found that they did not understand what had happened in Jerusalem over the weekend, he "opened the Scriptures" to them (v. 32). This opening is important in itself, because Jesus could have said, "Look, it's me, Jesus. Look at my wounded hands and side. Don't you understand?" But he did not point to his body. Instead he pointed these two disciples to the Scriptures and taught what the Bible said about the resurrection.

2. *Jesus opened their eyes.* While they were sitting with him and he broke bread in their home, "their eyes were opened and they recognized him" (v. 31). They had not recognized him earlier; their eyes had been blinded.

3. *Jesus opened their minds.* Finally, later on in the chapter, after the disciples had gone back to Jerusalem and were assembled with the others in the Upper Room, Jesus appeared in their midst, and "then he opened their minds so they could understand the Scriptures" (v. 45). For the first time in their lives they really understood the Old Testament. When they turned to Genesis, they found Jesus there. When they turned to Exodus, they found Jesus there. When they turned to the Psalms, Jesus was in the Psalms.

Because of this entirely new way of understanding the Bible, here in Acts 4 when the early Christians wanted to speak about Jesus in their prayer to God, the words of the Bible just naturally came tumbling out. Does that happen when you pray to God? Do you express your delight in him in the words of Scripture? It is natural to do it, if you know the Bible. If you don't, well, that is a great deficiency in your life and should be corrected.

The Christians' Use of Psalm 2

The verses that came to the minds of the Christians in this important worship service were from Psalm 2. Psalm 2 is a messianic psalm, but this is the first time its words have appeared in Acts. The psalm is a record of human rebellion against God and God's response to it, but it is the verses dealing with the rebellion itself that the believers cite.

> Why do the nations rage
>   and the peoples plot in vain?
> The kings of the earth take their stand
>   and the rulers gather together
> against the Lord
>   and against his Anointed One.
>
>   Acts 4:25–26
>   (see Psalm 2:1–2)

If you know this psalm well, you know what the leaders of the nations go on to say: "Let us break their chains . . . and throw off their fetters" (v. 3). Those leaders are saying, as Israel's leaders did in the days of Jesus, "We will not have this man to rule over us." They are shouting, as the later leaders did to Pilate, "We have no king but Caesar!" This is the very essence of sin (see chapter 8 of this study). Sin is telling God, "I will not have you to be my Lord or my God. You can be God for somebody else, but not for me. You can be Lord for somebody else, but not me. I want to be my own god and lord." In this Old Testament psalm we have a classic expression of this essential sin.

Why do Peter, John, and the others quote this psalm on this occasion? What the "kings of the earth" did in that psalm is precisely what the Sanhedrin had been doing. They had done it with Jesus. Now they were doing the same thing with the disciples.

Peter and John had been instrumental in the healing of a lame man and gave the glory to Jesus. The Sanhedrin should have been most sensitive to spiritual things. They should have searched out the cause of the miracle and given God the glory if it was of God. That was their duty as the spiritual leaders of the Jewish nation. But instead, they forbade the gospel's proclamation.

If you know Psalm 2, you also know what God's response is to such arrogance. The rulers of the world are taking up arms against the Almighty— gathering up their weapons, missiles, tanks, and guns to fight God and cast off his chains. But what does God do? Does God tremble at the united opposition of the world? He does nothing of the sort. God laughs at them. This is the only place in the Bible where we are told that God laughs. "The One enthroned in heaven laughs; the Lord scoffs at them" (Ps. 2:4). Perhaps the Lord says, "Ha, ha, ha! Do they really think they can break my bonds?" He points to the Lord Jesus Christ and says, "I have installed my King on Zion, my holy hill" (Ps. 2:6).

The Sanhedrin had killed Jesus. But God raised Jesus from the dead, brought him to heaven, and then seated him upon his holy hill of Zion. He made him King of Kings and Lord of all the earth. Now the rulers were starting down the same path with the disciples. They prohibited the disciples to preach in the name of Jesus. But the disciples replied that God would exalt Jesus; the leaders couldn't do anything about it; and as for them, they would praise him for what he would do.

Notice that the prayer begins with the words "Sovereign Lord" (v. 24). This is the first time in Acts that a prayer has begun in this way. Why? Because that is exactly what needed to be said in praise on this occasion. God is sovereign. Therefore, it does not make any difference whether men and women like his decisions. God does not ask their opinion. God is God. God is in charge, and it is his deepest determination to exalt Christ. These early Christians were saying, in effect, "How marvelous this is! How wonderful to know that by the grace and power of God those who believe on and follow Jesus Christ are on the winning side!"

Someone might say, "But they put the apostles in jail." True, they did put them in jail. Someone may say, "They put them in chains." Yes, they also put them in chains. "And they threatened to kill them." Yes, and not only that, they did kill some of them eventually.

But Jesus was and is upon the throne. He is the King. He is ruler in Zion. Servants you can bind, but the Word of God is not bound. And that unleashed, unbound, powerful Word of the gospel reached out from Jerusalem, that remote city of the Roman Empire, to permeate and eventually to transform the entire world.

The Church at Work

We come then to the second half of this last section of Acts 4, and here we see a vignette reflecting the life and work of the church in those days. It was a bit like living in Eden. True, the church was composed of sinful people. But still it was a glorious time. We are told three things about these people.

1. They "were one in heart and mind" (v. 32). The church was doing a great work, and oneness was the foundation of it. They were building a community that was one in heart and mind. The Greek literally says, "one in heart and soul." I do not know why the translators changed that to "heart and mind," perhaps because they remembered the old song "Heart and Soul, I Fell in Love with You" and felt an echo of those words would be inappropriate. Still, the new translation, though not literal, is accurate enough.

It suggests not only that the Christians were one in heart—that is, one in their emotional bonds with each other, being committed to the same thing—but also that they were thinking along the same lines, that they had the same theology. That is a very proper foundation for any Christian work. We should be one in everything.

The disciples were experiencing the unity for which the Lord Jesus Christ prayed:

I pray also for those who will believe in me through their message, that all of them may be one, Father, just as you are in me and I am in you. May they also be in us so that the world may believe that you have sent me. I have given them the glory that you gave me, that they may be one as we are one: I in them and

you in me. May they be brought to complete unity to let the world know that
you sent me and have loved them even as you have loved me.

                                                                    John 17:20–23

This unity is not conformity, where everybody is exactly alike. It is not orga-
nizational, where everyone must be forced into the same denomination. The
worst times in the history of the church have been when everyone has been
part of one large organization. It is not that kind of a unity. The unity for
which Jesus prayed is a unity patterned on the unity of the Father and the
Son. That is, it is a unity of mind, will, love, and purpose. That unity is what
the church should experience and what the church seemed to have achieved
in these early days.

There are things that divide us—different points of view on secondary
issues, for instance. We will always have those. We have different ministries,
and there are different talents and different gifts. We work differently. There
is nothing wrong with many of these differences. Indeed, they are given to
us by God. But underlying these, as a foundation for effective Christian work,
there must be basic unity.

2. *They "shared everything they had" (v.* 32). Not only were they one in their
work, but they also were generous in it. Most people are not very generous
apart from a saving relationship to Christ. Everyone is usually out for himself
or herself. People are polite about it. Enlightened people realize that if you
want to get something done, you usually have to get it done through other
people. So you have to treat them well. That is just good management.
Besides, it is wise to keep other people happy. But the basis of this is not generosity; it is selfishness. It is only in Christianity that something new and truly
generous comes into the world.

This is because Christians are people who have come to know God, and
God is gracious. Christians know that God did not have to do anything for
us. He could have turned his back on us and simply let us go to hell. He would
have been just in doing so. But God sent Jesus Christ, his greatest gift, to die
for us so that we might be saved. Nobody who has come to know that God
has been so gracious can ever be exactly like he or she was before. If somebody
says he believes the gospel but then lives exactly as before, that person is not
really born again. He or she is not saved.

When you realize what God has done for you, your nature is changed.
These early Christians realized God had been generous with them, and so
they shared what they had.

3. *They testified "to the resurrection of the Lord Jesus"* (v. 33). Not only did they
have a solid foundation for their work in their basic unity of heart and mind
and not only did they have a verification of it in their changed lives, being
made generous, but they also had the work itself. And that work, as we have
seen again and again, was to testify "to the resurrection of the Lord Jesus,"
which they did. This verse says that as they testified, "much grace was upon
them all."

When the believers were praying, one of the requests they had was that God would not abandon them but that he would stay with them and do great works. What we are told as we come to the end of this section is that God answered that prayer: "The place where they were meeting was shaken. And they were all filled with the Holy Spirit and spoke the word of God boldly" (v. 31). It is an echo of Pentecost. That is the work of God: to speak of Jesus Christ in the power of the Holy Spirit and find that God, by his Spirit, uses our witness to draw men and women to himself.

11

Two Whom God Struck Dead

Acts 5:1-11

Now a man named Ananias, together with his wife Sapphira, also sold a piece of property. With his wife's full knowledge he kept back part of the money for himself, but brought the rest and put it at the apostles' feet.

Then Peter said, "Ananias, how is it that Satan has so filled your heart that you have lied to the Holy Spirit and have kept for yourself some of the money you received for the land? Didn't it belong to you before it was sold? And after it was sold, wasn't the money at your disposal? What made you think of doing such a thing? You have not lied to men but to God."

When Ananias heard this, he fell down and died. And great fear seized all who heard what had happened. Then the young men came forward, wrapped up his body, and carried him out and buried him.

Acts 5:1–6

Whenever I come to the story of Ananias and Sapphira, who sinned against God by lying to him and were struck dead, I think of a sermon preached nearly thirty years ago by Donald Grey Barnhouse. It was entitled "Men Whom God Struck Dead." In those days, the word "man" included both men and women. Ananias and his wife Sapphira were both embraced by that title. But the sermon covered more than this one incident. It included the Old Testament story of Nadab and

Abihu, who offered improper fire upon God's altar and were struck dead, and the story of Uzzah, who reached out and touched God's ark when it was being transported to Jerusalem and was struck dead.

The sermon linked these three stories together and pointed out, quite rightly I believe, that so far as we can tell, each of these individuals was "a believer." That is, they were not in the same category as the heathen, who are ignorant of God, or kings or philosophers, who in the arrogance of their unbelief set themselves against God. These people were in the fellowship of God's family and were all engaged in what we would call either Christian worship or service. Moreover, they were struck dead for what, to us at least, seem to be—I hate even to use the word, but let's use it—*trivial* offenses.

When we put these stories together, we discover that in each instance, it was a time of important new beginnings for God's people. This may explain some of the severity of the punishment. Something new was being inaugurated; a new era was about to come in. It would seem that God established at the start of these ventures how seriously he considered the purity of the relationship of his people to himself.

An Illuminating Contrast

We cannot begin Acts 5 without looking back a few verses to the end of Acts 4. There is sharp contrast between chapter 5, which tells of a great sin, and the earlier chapter, which speaks of a time of particularly sweet harmony in the church.

Luke did not have to give us the picture of nearly ideal harmony in chapter 4, because in a way it is a repetition of what he already recorded at the end of chapter 2 about the unified life of the early church (see chapters 6 and 10 of this study). Why is that? Luke is too fine a historian merely to be repeating himself. He is painting this ideal picture of church harmony as a background for the disharmony that came as a result of Ananias and Sapphira's deception.

Not only does Luke describe what this time of sharing was about in general terms, but in 4:36–37 he also ties it to a particular individual. The man's name was Joseph, a Levite who came from Cyprus. We know him better as Barnabas. Luke says Barnabas "sold a field he owned and brought the money and put it at the apostles' feet."

This was an unusual time in the history of the church. What may throw light on this time of unprecedented sharing is to remember that Jesus had prophesied the destruction of Jerusalem. He had said that it was going to come soon and that when his disciples saw it, they were to leave the city immediately (Matt. 24:15–22). When the destruction finally did come in A.D. 70, some of the Christians remembered Jesus' words and left the city. In these early days the Christians were no doubt living with thoughts of the destruction of the city, and this may be why they were so willing to sell all they had. They might have thought, The Lord has told us that Jerusalem is going to be overthrown. Our possessions are not going to do us any good then. The thing to do is sell them and use them in the Lord's work now. I cannot prove that this was the case. But it would explain why such exceptional giving occurred early in church history and was not repeated later.

Yet there is an application for us: Someday we are going to die, and the good we can do with our possessions will end then. Doesn't it make sense to take care how we use our possessions and use them well now? We should make them count. I do not say sell all you have. Normally that would be an unwise thing to do. But make sure you use your possessions for the Lord.

In the case of Joseph (Barnabas) we have one man whose possessions probably were not even in Jerusalem but who nevertheless was willing to sell them and use the proceeds in God's service.[1] If that is the case, it might explain why this man was particularly remembered. He is mentioned several dozen times in Acts. Barnabas did not have to sell what he had. It did not even make sense, humanly speaking. But he did it, perhaps reasoning, "Even though my possessions are not in Jerusalem, I want them to be used for the needy and for the expansion of the gospel." He sold his field, took the money, and laid it at the feet of the apostles.

This man was given a new name by the early Christians. He was called Barnabas, the same Barnabas who later traveled with Paul. Barnabas means "Son of Encouragement." Maybe they called him "Son of Encouragement," which really means "The Encourager," because of the way he acted. "What an encouragement this man is!" they must have said.

Unfortunately, as it was soon to turn out, sitting over on the side of the church somewhere there were two people who noticed what was going on and who wanted to be acclaimed like Barnabas. Their names were Ananias and Sapphira. They thought, I wish people were praising us like that. Look at the attention Barnabas is getting. He sold his field and gave them money. They named him "Son of Encouragement." How marvelous it would be to be thought of like that by our friends. So they decided to sell their piece of property and do the same thing.

Sadly, as we read the story we find that they were not at all like Barnabas. Outwardly they seemed to be, but inwardly they were of quite a different character. Barnabas was giving his goods out of thanksgiving to God and concern for God's people. He was honest about it. Ananias and Sapphira wanted to be treated the way Barnabas was treated, but they were not honest. They sold the property, looked at the money, saw how nice it was, and then kept back some of it for themselves while giving the rest, pretending to give it all.

Maybe they had intended to give it all at first. But the more they looked at it, the more they loved it. And so, even if it had not been in their hearts before, the evil of their hypocrisy was hatched. They thought, Nobody knows how much we got for the sale of this property, and we certainly have enough expenses today. Why don't we just keep part of it? Nobody will know. Let's keep part and give the rest. Then people will say, "They are just like Barnabas."

No Perfect Church

There is no perfect church, not even the church of the apostles. I read Acts 4:32, "All the believers were one in heart and mind. No one claimed that any of his possessions was his own, but they shared everything they had," and I think, ah, there's the perfect church. But even this church had Ananias and Sapphira in it.

Someone once told Charles Spurgeon that they were leaving his church because they were going to find a perfect church. Spurgeon, who had a great deal of wit and sometimes was more forthright than people dare to be today, said, "When you find it, please don't join it, because you'll ruin it."

I worry when people come to Tenth Presbyterian Church in Philadelphia, where I serve, and express an exalted idea of what they find there. Nobody has ever told me that they are joining Tenth because it is perfect—I suppose because it would be perfectly evident that the church is not perfect, at least as long as I am around. But often people are quite enthusiastic when they come. They say things like, "I have finally found it. This is the church for me. It is what I have always wanted." I get worried because I think, Just let a week go by, a month, a year. Let them get to know us a little bit, and that enthusiasm will vanish. I would hope, because God does work in us, that they also find good things as well as disappointments. I know they can find fellowship, faithfulness to the Word of God, people who will be concerned for them and pray for them. Tenth is a good church. But there is no perfect church, and there was not even in Jerusalem.

We need to pray for our congregations. We need to pray that God will help us do better, protect us from Satan, and keep us faithful to himself.

Peter's Reply to Ananias

Beginning with verse 3 of chapter 5 we have Peter's reply to Ananias. It is very significant.

> Ananias, how is it that Satan has so filled your heart that you have lied to the Holy Spirit and have kept for yourself some of the money you received for the land? Didn't it belong to you before it was sold? And after it was sold, wasn't the money at your disposal? What made you think of doing such a thing? You have not lied to men but to God.

> Acts 5:3–4

Peter addresses three important concerns in this response: the right of ownership, the role of Satan, and sin's offense to God.

The Right of Ownership

First, he teaches the right of private property. This first item is not the first thing Peter mentions. I mention it first only because, to my mind, it is the least important. When Peter says to Ananias, "Didn't it belong to you before it was sold? And after it was sold, wasn't the money at your disposal?" he is repudiating communism, even a sanctified "Christian" kind of communism. Some people have looked at this period of sharing in the early church and have held it as a permanent ideal for all Christians. Peter's words make clear that this does not follow.

Peter was not inventing the right of private property. It is something that was already in the Old Testament. You have it in the Ten Commandments. The eighth commandment says, "You shall not steal" (Exod. 20:15). In order to steal, you have to take something that belongs to somebody else, something they own. Thus there is the right of private ownership. If a person does not have the right to something, then it is not stealing for someone else to take it. If he or she does own it, then taking it is wrong. This is what Peter recognized. "You have the right to it," said Peter, in effect. "You didn't have to sell it. And after you sold it, you didn't have to give it."

The problem was not that Ananias did not give everything he had, but that he pretended to be giving it when actually he was holding back some. The problem was his hypocrisy and lying, not the fact that he owned property. He was part of the church, and falsehood destroys its fellowship.

The Role of Satan

The second point Peter made was about the role of Satan: "How is it that Satan has so filled your heart that you have lied to the Holy Spirit?" (v. 3). When Peter spoke on this occasion, he was conscious of speaking under the direct impress of the Holy Spirit. There were times in Peter's life, especially before his conversion, when like many of us he simply blurted out whatever happened to be in his mind. Often it wasn't much! An occasion presented itself, and Peter said whatever nonsense he was thinking. That is just the way Peter was. Indeed, even after his conversion, though he was a much wiser and steadier man, there must have been occasions when Peter said things that were not true. He may have thought they were true, but they would not have been. Yet here Peter was a mouthpiece of God. He was speaking by inspiration of the Holy Spirit. So when he said, "How is it that Satan has so filled your heart that you have lied to the Holy Spirit?" it is certain that this is precisely what Satan had done.

We have a tendency to refer to Satan in glib terms. "The devil made me do it," we say. Or, "Maybe it was Satan." It is probably unlikely that Satan has ever tempted you personally, because he is only a creature and therefore can only be in one place at any one time. If you did wrong, you probably just did it on your own. Nevertheless, there is such a thing as spiritual warfare and it is quite possible to be tempted either by Satan or by one of those fallen angels who sinned with him.

In these early days Satan was outraged by what was happening in this Christian fellowship. Satan, the one who wants everything for himself—who makes people as selfish as he possibly can make them—must have hated the spirit of generosity and unity among the early Christians. So with devilish wisdom he must have said, "I'll turn this around. I'll use the spirit of sharing to break down the very generosity it is supposed to be expressing. I'll get them to lie and introduce chaos to the church."

Satan is a limited being. He is not omniscient, as God is. He does not know everything. He is not omnipotent, as God is. Only God is all-powerful. He is not omnipresent, as God is. He is not everywhere, though he certainly gets around, "roaming through the earth," as he said of himself in Job (Job 1:7; 2:2). No, Satan is not the equivalent of God. But he is powerful. He is a very formidable enemy.

Perhaps because of this incident or perhaps because of other things that happened to him later in his life, Peter said in his first letter, "Be self-controlled and alert. Your enemy the devil prowls around like a roaring lion looking for someone to devour. Resist him, standing firm in the faith" (1 Peter 5:8–9).

That is an important warning. If we go through periods of special blessing, as these early Christians had, personally or in our church, we can expect Satan or one of his demons to attack us. It is because Satan does not want the church of Jesus Christ to thrive. If you are only going through the motions of serving Jesus, Satan will not worry about you very much. If you are not attempting anything important for God, if you are not breaking new ground, not witnessing, not serving in any particularly effective way, Satan will probably leave you alone. On the other hand, if you really are trying to do something for God—if your church is effective, if you have a strong missions program, if you have people out witnessing, if you are trying to embody the gospel in social programs that minister to the needs of real people and demonstrate the real love of Jesus Christ—Satan will attack you. You will have to be on your guard against him.

How can you do it? Satan is stronger than we are. He was stronger than Ananias, a man who even sat under the apostolic preaching. James tells us: "Submit yourselves, then, to God. Resist the devil, and he will flee from you" (James 4:7). Some have tried to resist the devil without first submitting to God and have found that the devil does not flee then. The devil runs over us like a tank because he is more powerful than we are. We stand only when we first submit to God, because only then do we stand in God's strength. It is only because of God and his strength that the devil flees.

But how do we first submit to God? We do it through prayer and that devotional life of which prayer is a part. Our example here is Jesus, who resisted and overcame the devil in his temptation. Jesus had just spent forty days in close fellowship with God, so he was utterly submissive to God's will, as of course he always was anyway. Then, when Satan came, he responded by quotations from Scripture. It is in Scripture that God has expressed his will.

When Satan tempted Jesus to use his power selfishly to make bread from stones, Jesus replied, "It is written: 'Man does not live on bread alone, but on every word that comes from the mouth of God,'" a quotation from Deuteronomy 8:3 (Matt. 4:4).

When Satan urged Jesus to throw himself down from the temple parapets, trusting God to preserve him, Jesus said, "It is also written: 'Do not put the Lord your God to the test,'" a quotation from Deuteronomy 6:16 (Matt. 4:7).

When Satan made a bald plea for Christ's worship, Jesus replied, "It is written: 'Worship the Lord your God, and serve him only,'" a quotation from Deuteronomy 6:13 (Matt. 4:10). Jesus seems to have been meditating on Deuteronomy and was submissive to its teachings.

Sin Is Always against God

The third point Peter makes is the most important. Peter has affirmed the right of private property and pointed out that Christians are involved in spiritual warfare. Now, in the third place, he says, "You have not lied to men but to God" (v. 4). That is, Peter raised this situation to the highest possible level, affirming that the sin committed by Ananias was of great concern to God. I would place this in positive terms also, saying that no matter what you do, it matters to God. And it matters to other people also.

We live in a world where people do not want to take their bad actions seriously. They minimize them, saying, "It really doesn't matter" or "It doesn't matter much." Either positively or negatively, we seem to think what we do is unimportant.

It has always helped me when I find myself drifting into that kind of thinking to remember the way C. S. Lewis put it when he was talking about Christian morality. He wrote:

> Every time you make a choice you are turning the central part of you, the part of you that chooses, into something a little different from what it was before. And taking your life as a whole, with all your innumerable choices, all your life long you are slowly turning this central thing either into a heavenly creature or into a hellish creature: either into a creature that is in harmony with God, and with other creatures, and with itself, or else into one that is in a state of war with and hatred with God, and with its fellow creatures, and with itself. To be the one kind of creature is heaven: that is, it is joy and peace and knowledge and power. To be the other means madness, horror, idiocy, rage, impotence, and eternal loneliness.[2]

Men and women are eternal beings. If we are only creatures of this life—if we live now, die, and that is the end of it—then it does not really matter a whole lot what we do. You can be as evil as Dorian Gray, but at the end of life it is all over. All you have to deal with is the disposal of a disgusting portrait. But if we are eternal beings, then the choices we make matter eternally. They matter to God.

The Sin of Sapphira

The last part of the story concerns Sapphira, Ananias's wife. It is important not to forget her, because she bore a full measure of guilt and responsibility. Luke points out her guilt in two ways. In verse 2 he adds the phrase "with his wife's full knowledge." Then, after Ananias had been judged, he notes that she repeated her husband's lie.

When you and I do wrong things or when our culture does wrong things, we work hard at shunning responsibility, usually by some form of determinism. "Determinism" means that some outside factor has made us do what we did and therefore we are not responsible. One form of this is environmental: "I am what I am, because that is how my parents raised me." Or, "It is because I grew up in a particular neighborhood" or "because when I went to preschool at a young age, somebody didn't treat me properly."

There is also a determinism that is personal. We excuse ourselves on the basis of our genetic structure: "I'm just made like that. There is nothing I can do about it." In this way we excuse bad temper, lying, or whatever else it may be. The problem with these excuses is that we use them for ourselves but disallow them in the case of other people.

A little boy once said to his mother, "Mother, why is it that whenever I do something wrong, it's because I am a bad boy; but whenever you do something wrong, it's your nerves?" The mother was recognizing that her son was a creature made in the image of God and was responsible for what he did. But in her case, she excused her bad behavior by her genes.

When we blame somebody else for our conduct, in the final analysis the person we are actually blaming is God. If you try to excuse yourself on the basis of your environment, well, God is ultimately the one who is responsible for the environment, isn't he? If you appeal to internal factors, well, God created those. Whenever you try to excuse yourself for some wrong behavior, you are actually attempting to shift the blame for your sin to God.

But that will not do. Sin is still sin. God is not its cause. And in the end God will judge it.

Let me point out that when we talk about God's judgment on Ananias and Sapphira, who so far as we know were believing people, we are not saying that God consigned them to hell. True Christians do not lose their salvation by sinning. The punishment of Ananias and Sapphira, though extreme, was for this life only. Still it was serious, and what it teaches is that God is not indifferent to his people's sins. Peter wrote in his first letter, possibly remembering this incident, "It is time for judgment to begin with the family of God; and if it begins with us, what will the outcome be for those who do not obey the gospel?" (1 Peter 4:17). Peter knew that the church in his day was far from perfect and that God judges sin.

The first occurrence of the word "church" in the Book of Acts is at the close of this story, where we read, "Great fear seized the whole church and all who heard about these events" (v. 11). "Church" is the translation of the

Greek word *ekklesia,* and it refers to a gathered community or fellowship, which is what these early Christians were. This community is always under attack by Satan. But his attacks are not always from without. They are often from within, which was the case here. The lies of Ananias and Sapphira harmed the church's fellowship. Therefore, God moved through Peter to arrest the deception in an unforgettable and even frightening way.

12

Suffering Disgrace
for Christ's Name

Acts 5:12–42

His speech persuaded them. They called the apostles in and had them flogged. Then they ordered them not to speak in the name of Jesus, and let them go.

The apostles left the Sanhedrin, rejoicing because they had been counted worthy of suffering disgrace for the Name. Day after day, in the temple courts and from house to house, they never stopped teaching and proclaiming the good news that Jesus is the Christ.

Acts 5:40–42

We have advanced far enough in our study of Acts to see Luke's pattern in these chapters. His plan is simple. Luke alternates between a picture of the church by itself—a portrait of the believers alone in their fellowship, in which he talks about their life, witness, and joy—and a portrait of the church as it exists in its relationship to the world. This second portrait increasingly deals with persecution.

103

Here is how this pattern has unfolded:

- In the first chapter of Acts, we see the church alone. The believers are gathered together after the return of the Lord Jesus Christ to heaven, conducting their own business. They elect an apostle to replace Judas.
- In Acts 2, after the Holy Spirit has come at Pentecost, we see the church with the world. On this occasion Peter preached the first great Christian sermon, and many people believed and were added to the church.
- At the end of chapter 2 beginning with verse 42, Luke goes back to his portrait of the church by itself. Here occurs that classic description of the Christians.
- In Acts 3 and the first part of Acts 4 through verse 22, we see the church in relationship to the world again. Before this, the church has been with the world in a witnessing situation only. This time Luke brings in the matter of opposition or persecution.
- Beginning with chapter 4 verse 23, Luke shows the church alone again. He lets us see a bit into one of their early worship services and almost repeats the description of the church found at the end of chapter 2.
- The fifth chapter continues the portrait, but now there are divisions in the church, hypocrisy, and judgment. The judgment is important, because it is only out of this judgment that we have the renewed picture of blessing that occurs at the start of the section that is the subject of this chapter.

This alternating pattern alerts us to two important realities for the church. Sometimes you have a church that goes so much over to the side of its own fellowship and the joy and wonder of its gathering together that it loses sight of the fact that it is called to be a witness in the world. The world tends to be forgotten. On the other hand, the church sometimes goes the other way. The Christians are in the world all the time doing good works but without the necessary base that comes from the unity, worship, and prayers of the Christian community.

Luke is teaching that both are necessary. If we have service without inner strength, soon the service becomes superficial and essentially no different from the kind of social work the world does. On the other hand, if we focus on our fellowship and forget the task, the church becomes self-centered. The two have to go together.

Acts 5:12–42 contains two main sections: (1) a look at the church in the process of reestablishing itself after the fiasco with Ananias and Sapphira; and (2) a long section in which the apostles are once again arrested, testify to the Sanhedrin, and are physically assaulted.

Restoration and a New Blessing

The Christians had gone through a very difficult experience as a result of God's judgment upon Ananias and Sapphira. They had been shaken by that judgment. The text says, "Great fear seized the whole church" (Acts 5:11). The believers may have wondered if they had lost the blessing of God permanently or at least for a time. Harmony was broken. Trust was destroyed. Would they ever find those great moments of blessing again? Luke reports that they did. In fact, it would seem that at this period God did even more wonders among them than he had done previously. There had been miracles earlier, the miracle of the healing of the lame man that led to Peter's sermon in the temple area, for instance. But there do not seem to have been many miracles. Now Luke tells us that "the apostles performed *many* miraculous signs and wonders among the people" (v. 12, italics mine).

Furthermore, "More and more men and women believed in the Lord and were added to their number" (v. 14). So not only were miracles being done, but also the gospel was being preached with such force that people were actually responding to it in large numbers.

A new and extremely important thing we are told is that the gospel was beginning to spread beyond Jerusalem. Verse 16 records that "crowds gathered also from the towns around Jerusalem, bringing their sick and those tormented by evil spirits, and all of them were healed." This is the first time there has been any mention of any area beyond Jerusalem.

Jesus had said, "You will receive power when the Holy Spirit comes on you; and you will be my witnesses in Jerusalem, and in all Judea and Samaria, and to the ends of the earth" (Acts 1:8). Now this was happening. Up to this point the disciples had been witnessing in Jerusalem only. But now the gospel was spreading into Judea, that is, to the little towns around Jerusalem in the old tribal territory of Judah.

Opposition to the Gospel

The second and major section of Acts 5:12–42 shows that the blessing described in verses 12–16 was accompanied by a time of renewed persecution (vv. 17–42). It begins, as chapter 4 did, with the frustration of the Jewish leaders. Christianity was beginning to spread. Thousands were responding to the gospel. Those who were in charge of the religious and political life of the nation were justifiably distressed at what was going on in the city and were afraid it might disrupt the stable social order they were enjoying and their place in it. Three things bothered them.

1. *The name of Jesus.* The leaders were bothered that the preaching of the apostles and the miracles being performed were in "the name" of Jesus of Nazareth, whom they had crucified. The way they speak of "that name" again and again shows how disturbed they were by it.

From their point of view, Jesus was only an upstart rabbi. He had come from who knows where and had taken it upon himself to be a rabbi. It is true that he did it powerfully and winsomely, so that he gained a large following. But if he was not who he claimed to be, and they were not ready to bow to that claim, Jesus of Nazareth was a false prophet, a blasphemer. He cleverly made out that he was God. He did not state his claims too openly, because if he had, they could have summoned witnesses, convicted him of blasphemy, and gotten rid of him early on. In the end they did get rid of him, but here was the devilish thing: They had destroyed him, but "that name" was still being proclaimed before the people. I detect, as I read these chapters, that although they would have said, "We were right to do what we did," deep in their hearts they felt guilty for having destroyed what was quite obviously a very righteous man.

2. *The resurrection.* The leaders were also frustrated by the fact that the preaching of Jesus involved the resurrection. Luke notes at this point that "the high priest and all his associates . . . were members of the party of the Sadducees" (v. 17). The Sadducees did not believe in the resurrection. It would be bad enough to be a Pharisee, to have condemned Jesus, and then to have it preached in Jerusalem that God raised him from the dead. You would have been responsible for his execution, yet you would have at least believed in the resurrection. How much worse for the Sadducees! They did not believe in the resurrection. For them, the preaching of Christ was an attack on their knowledge of the Scriptures and their theological position.

Moreover, the resurrection, if it was true, was proof of Jesus' claim to be the Messiah. This was an extremely dangerous possibility for those in their position. In fact, for them it was an intolerable assertion.

3. *Jealousy.* Luke adds one other thing. He says that the leaders were jealous. I suppose that if you opposed Jesus on the basis of his being a false prophet, you could at least do so with a certain degree of nobility. You could stand on a platform of truth, as crusaders usually do: "Falsehood is falsehood. We must defend truth. Jesus must be opposed, as reluctant as we may be to do it." As far as the resurrection goes, you could attempt an argument from Scripture. You could say, "I am not convinced that the Bible teaches that there will be a resurrection. The doctrine of the resurrection is wrong."

Yet what Luke tells us here is that the leaders were not really dealing with the claims of the apostles on a noble level. There was something beneath their opposition, something that had been festering away. It was jealousy. Jealousy of whom? Were they jealous of Jesus? Jesus who was dead? Were they jealous of the apostles, these whom they had observed had no education? The answer is probably yes to both possibilities.

They were jealous of Jesus because it was his name, rather than theirs, that was being proclaimed. They were also jealous of the apostles because they were preaching powerfully and doing miracles and because people were following them. The religious leaders wanted both of these things: They wanted to be well known, to have a "name" among the people; and they wanted people to follow them.

Many of our contemporaries, even ministers, want to be well known and have a following. Much of the evil in the world happens as a result of jealousy. It is seldom given that name, of course. Still, when attacks are made on those who are being much used by God it is usually jealousy that lies behind it. People resent the fact that someone else is getting the attention.

A Rising Tide of Persecution

All this caused the leaders to move against the apostles again, only this time more forcefully than before. The first time they hauled the apostles in and made threats and told them not to preach anymore. The disciples continued to preach about Jesus. The next thing they did was arrest them again and unleash a proceeding that eventually ended in the apostles' being beaten. What else could they do? They had no options, only force. That is why such procedures almost always lead to an attempt to kill people who are not liked. If it were simply a matter of truth contending with falsehood, the result would be a free and open debate. That is not what was going on. This was hatred born of jealousy. Since they were unable to contend with the disciples on the level of truth, they resorted to naked authority and force. First, threats. Second, a beating. Ultimately, death.

If we are very angry about something, especially in religion, it is probably a sign that we are on the wrong track. There is such a thing as righteous anger, of course. The Lord had that kind of anger against those who were keeping others from the truth, who were setting up barriers for them and making merchandise of spiritual things. That is why I say that anger *probably* shows that we are on the wrong track. But when anger is not righteous, as it usually is not, we need to deal with it. The leaders' anger was an indication that something was wrong.

Verse 26 tells us that the leaders brought in the disciples carefully, because the apostles were popular and the leaders were afraid. Afraid of what? The verse says, "They did not use force, because they feared that the people would stone them." They wanted to do away with the apostles, probably by stoning, but here they were, afraid that the people would try to stone them instead.

When they were ready to proceed with the trial they sent the captain of the guard to bring the apostles out of jail and into court, but when he got to the jail there were no apostles. They were gone. Luke tells us what happened. God sent his angel during the night, and he opened the doors of the jail and brought the apostles out. The angel then apparently locked them again, because when the officers came to the jail they "found the jail securely locked, with the guards standing at the doors" (v. 23). They had to report to their superiors that the apostles just weren't there.

Here the situation becomes humorous, at least it seems so to me. The leaders were standing around in the council chamber, having sent for the apostles and having it reported that they were no longer there. They were probably saying, "What are we going to do now? How are we going to find them?" when suddenly, someone came in and said, more or less, "It's not going to be hard to find them. I can tell you exactly where they are. They are back in the temple courts preaching. They are in the same place they were the last time you tried to arrest them." So they went out and arrested them again. They brought them before the Sanhedrin once more, and again they began their accusations.

This time the accusations went a step further.

They accused them, first of all, of disobeying orders: "We gave you strict orders not to teach in this name" (v. 28). That was a simple assertion of authority. It did not make any difference whether the apostles were right or wrong.

They went on to say, "Yet you have filled Jerusalem with your teaching and are determined to make us guilty of this man's blood." At the trial of Jesus Christ this was the very thing they had willingly taken upon themselves. Pilate had said, "I am innocent of this man's blood. It is your responsibility!" (Matt. 27:24). They had replied, "Let his blood be on us and on our children!" (v. 25). Now it was, and they were appalled at the consequences.

The blood of Jesus is upon us because we, like these Jewish rulers, set our face against the Lord and his Anointed. Today Jesus is not here to be physically mistreated, but that is what we want to do and would do if we could. In the meantime, we at least turn our backs on him and repudiate his rule, if we are not Christians.

The rulers did not have to be made guilty. They already were guilty, and they knew it. We know they knew it by the way they were talking about "this name" and "this man." They were guilty of murder, and they did not like the consequences at all.

Peter's Response to the Sanhedrin

Peter had a chance to give a brief sermon in his defense before the Sanhedrin (though it may have been considerably longer than the account Luke has preserved for us). The sermon contains what in formal New Testament studies has come to be called the *kerygma,* the fixed structure to almost all New Testament presentations of the gospel message (see discussion of *kerygma* in chapter 5).

C. H. Dodd distinguished *kerygma* from *didachē,* which means "teaching." The latter word refers mostly to ethical instruction, the kind of thing we find in the Sermon on the Mount and large portions of the New Testament letters. *Kerygma,* by contrast, refers to the basic gospel facts. These facts include: Christ's death for sins, his burial, his resurrection, his ascension to heaven, and his appearance in his resurrected form to chosen witnesses. We find perhaps the clearest example of this proclamation pattern in 1 Corinthians 15. But it is also found elsewhere and is the basic structure for the four Gospels. It is precisely what we find in Peter's short sermon to the Sanhedrin:

- *The crucifixion:* "whom you had killed by hanging him on a tree" (v. 30)
- *The resurrection:* "God . . . raised Jesus from the dead" (v. 30)
- *The ascension:* "God exalted him to his own right hand as Prince and Savior" (v. 31)
- *The witnesses:* "We are witnesses of these things" (v. 32)

Where is the ethical teaching of the New Testament? It is not present. Most of what Jesus taught in the Gospels was ethical teaching—sometimes in the form of parables, sometimes in more formal discourses. But when we come to this early Christian preaching we find that the apostles did not do as he did. Why not? Did they consider Jesus' ethical teaching unimportant?

Obviously, the reason the disciples began with the *kerygma* is that they knew, as we should also know, that a person must first come to Jesus Christ as Savior before he or she can take on the burden of his teachings. It is true that we cannot have one without the other. But unless a person first believes on Jesus as his or her Savior and thus has the new life of Christ within, that person cannot even begin to live the life Christ commanded. As a matter of fact, unless you first confess your sin and find forgiveness, you only go on into increasing sin, which is what these leaders did.

The apostles did not tell the Sadducees to "do unto others as you would have others do unto you." Instead they told them to repent of their sin and come to Jesus Christ for cleansing from it. That is the message we have been given for a perishing world today.

Gamaliel's Unexpected Advice

At this point the disciples found an unexpected ally in Gamaliel. He is the teacher under whom the apostle Paul had studied and was possibly still studying.[1] Gamaliel was obviously a great and unusual man. He was great as a rabbi. He was also great, as we would say, as a human being.

Here he basically said: "Before you kill these men stop and consider what you will be doing. I have lived a long time and seen many things. I have observed that movements like this tend to pass away quickly if God is not in them. I think of Theudas. Do you remember him? He raised about four hundred soldiers and proclaimed himself as the Messiah, but was killed. He wasn't the Messiah. So his movement ended by being nothing. The same thing happened with Judas the Galilean. He also was killed and his followers scattered. I have learned that if something is of God, it will prosper. If not, it will collapse of itself. So my advice is to do nothing to these men. If they are being led by God and you oppose them, you will find that you are fighting against God."

That was very wise advice. Yet, although I praise Gamaliel as a wise, gracious, and understanding man, it was still only good worldly advice. It did not deal with the real issue. It did not go far enough.

Gamaliel should have said everything he did say, but he should have added, "And in the meantime, since we are so closely tied to this and are supposed to be the spiritual leaders of the nation, let's investigate this matter and see whether what these men are teaching is true. If there is nothing to it, then we will let it run its course. It will go away. But if there is something to it, if Jesus really did rise from the dead, then our doctrine is wrong: There is a resurrection; and what is more important, our views of Jesus are wrong. If he rose from the dead, he must be the Son of God. His death really was a substitutionary sacrifice for sin. If this is the case, we dare not be neutral. We must believe on him and become his witnesses, as these men are."

Gamaliel did not do that. What happened is that events did run their course, and this little religion, Christianity—although it did not even have a name in those days—did not fade away. Instead, it spread throughout the whole world. It grew in power. It has even come to America, a land that was not even known at the time Peter and John appeared before the Jewish Sanhedrin. It has prospered because it is not of man but from God.

13

The First Deacons

Acts 6:1–7

In those days when the number of disciples was increasing, the Grecian Jews among them complained against the Hebraic Jews because their widows were being overlooked in the daily distribution of food. So the Twelve gathered all the disciples together and said, "It would not be right for us to neglect the ministry of the word of God in order to wait on tables. Brothers, choose seven men from among you who are known to be full of the Spirit and wisdom. We will turn this responsibility over to them and will give our attention to prayer and the ministry of the word."

This proposal pleased the whole group. They chose Stephen, a man full of faith and of the Holy Spirit; also Philip, Procorus, Nicanor, Timon, Parmenas, and Nicolas from Antioch, a convert to Judaism.

Acts 6:1–5

The good days are over, at least those exceptionally good days that marked the start of the Christian era. The problem we find in this passage was quite different from the one involving Ananias and Sapphira. The first was about deception. Ananias and Sapphira did not have this song then, but if they did, they would have sung:

> I surrender all, I surrender all.
> All to Thee, my blessed Savior, I surrender all.

111

But they were keeping back part. Whenever you are tempted to say, "I have given up everything for Jesus," remember that it is probably the case that you have not. Ananias and Sapphira had not. What is more, they knew they had not, which is what made the situation so serious.

In Acts 6 no one was being particularly evil, lying to the Holy Spirit or anything of that nature. It was a question of administration, resulting from the church's growing pains. The people of Jerusalem spoke different languages. We know this because of Pentecost, where people "each heard [the apostles] speaking in his own language" (Acts 2:6). Among these many languages two were most prominent: Aramaic, a form of classical Hebrew spoken by those of Jewish descent, and Greek, spoken by those who had settled in Judah as a result of the conquests of Alexander the Great three hundred years earlier. Greek was the *lingua franca* of the day. These two languages understandably resulted in two main divisions of the church, and it was this that led to the problem.

A Problem of Administration

We have not been told anything about any distributions of food thus far. This is because in Luke's day everybody just naturally understood what was involved. One of the duties imposed on Jewish people by law was care of widows and orphans. There were times when this was neglected, of course. The minor prophets frequently chastise the people of their day for this failure. But generally one could not just pretend to be a pious Israelite while neglecting the care of these persons.

The early church apparently followed this pattern with its own widows. For those who were Jews, there were provisions for meeting the needs of the orphans and widows through the temple authorities. Money was regularly collected for that purpose. But relations were not all that good between the temple authorities and the early Christian community. So rather than depend on the temple authorities to take care of their widows, which they might have had a legal right to expect, these early communities were taking care of the widows by themselves.[1]

It seems that the widows of the Greek-speaking communities were neglected, or at least the Greek division of the church thought they were. We do not know why. It may be that the Jewish Christians were thinking of themselves more as Jews than as Christians, were depending on the Jewish state to take care of their needs, and were assuming that the Greek-speakers would have separate means of dealing with their own problems. Or perhaps there was just an unequal distribution, the widows of the Greek congregations just not getting enough. Whatever the case, misunderstandings developed and the objection was raised.

Alternative Solutions

How were the apostles to deal with this problem? I find it interesting that on this occasion there apparently was no divine revelation as there had been in the case of Ananias and Sapphira. We do not even find that the apostles held a prayer meeting, though I am sure they prayed about the situation. What we have is an administrative decision. The apostles considered the problem and, no doubt guided by God, said to those who were members of the church, "It would not be right for us to neglect the ministry of the word of God in order to wait on tables. Brothers, choose seven men from among you who are known to be full of the Spirit and wisdom. We will turn this responsibility over to them and will give our attention to prayer and the ministry of the word" (vv. 2–4). That is what the church did. The story tells who were elected and what the results of their service were.

It would be good to compare what the apostles did with what might have been done—and has been done in the church since. Some branches of today's church would throw the complainers out. But if there had been anything like a division before due to the two languages being used in the church, a division that had not yet become serious, it would certainly have become serious at this point. The church would have been divided formally, and there would have been a First Apostolic Church of Jerusalem on one corner of the city and across the street on the other corner there would have been a Second Apostolic Church of Jerusalem.

Another solution that is sometimes followed in churches is to shun the difficult people. They are not thrown out. That is "un-Christian." They are just not talked to; they are ignored. "Let them sit by themselves for a while and see how they like it. That will teach them not to make trouble," is the common attitude.

One of the things Presbyterians especially do is to outvote the dissenters. We call a meeting. We ask people to speak. We make a motion, being careful to follow *Robert's Rules of Order.* Then when we have our motion and our second, we vote to cut off debate, vote, and the majority prevails. Our will is done, and everything has been accomplished democratically. Who can complain? The losers have to keep quiet because the decision has been made. Unfortunately they do not always keep quiet, and ruptures still occur. I have heard people say, "The Holy Spirit speaks through the fifty-one percent vote." But that is usually not the case, to judge by the outcomes.

Sometimes people separate: a fourth attempt at a solution. "Those people are always causing trouble," the purists say. "We'll just leave them to themselves. We'll start our own church." That works well until somebody dissents in the "pure" church. Then you have to start another church, and then another one. The pure church always gets smaller and smaller until eventually it is gone. That can hardly impress us as the ideal solution.

The apostles might have formed a committee. That would be a fifth approach. Committees do not have to do anything positive. All they have to do is discuss the problem, knowing that if you can delay long enough, the problem may go away or be superseded by a still larger problem that will get all the attention. The committee may not have to do anything.

Once, before preaching on this passage, I was talking to Roger Nicole, who was then professor emeritus at Gordon-Conwell Divinity School, and I mentioned what I was going to be preaching on. He said, "I preached on that once. I made a list of all the solutions the apostles didn't use, and I had ten of them." Well, I have given five. If you like, you can think up five (or ten) more.

A Spirit-Led Decision

The apostles did not use any of these approaches. They went to the congregation itself and, I suspect, appealing chiefly to those who were complaining of the difficulty, basically said, "Look, just choose people who, in your judgment, are able to oversee the distribution fairly." The apostles were not trying to protect their own rights. They were not even protecting their own point of view. They simply wanted to solve the problem.

The church got together and chose the first deacons, seven of them. The significant thing about their choice is that every one of these men, to judge from their names, was a Greek-speaking Christian. Isn't that wonderful? The Greeks were the ones who were complaining that their widows were neglected. I would imagine there were more Aramaic-speaking Christians in the church than there were Greek-speaking Christians, but the church as a whole said, Let's elect Greek-speaking leaders.

They might have said, "There should be a few Greeks on this board to represent the Greek point of view. But we are the majority. At least four of the seven, maybe five of the seven, should speak Aramaic." But they did not operate that way. Either they deliberately picked the Greek-speaking leaders, or else they just picked out the seven best men. Here are their names.

1. *Stephen.* Luke says he was a man "full of faith and of the Holy Spirit." We will see him again in this and the next chapter.

2. *Philip.* We will see him again in Acts 8. Later in the book he is called an "evangelist" (Acts 21:8), the only person in Acts to be so named.

3. *Procorus.* We know nothing more about Procorus from the Bible, but tradition says he became a bishop of Nicomedia and was martyred at Antioch.

4. *Nicanor.* We know nothing about this man from the New Testament.

5. *Timon.* Nor of Timon.

6. *Parmenas.* Nor of Parmenas.

7. *Nicolas.* He was from Antioch and had been a convert to Judaism.

These men then became the first official body of officers in the church other than the apostles, who were appointed by Jesus Christ.

Sound Principles of Church Leadership

The selection of these men gives us important principles for sound church leadership. We also see these principles elsewhere in the New Testament.

A Division of Responsibility

Once I was talking to a young man who had been coming to Tenth Presbyterian Church to get away from the problems of his own congregation. I asked him how things were going, and he told me that although there were a number of difficulties the chief problem was that his minister thought he had to do everything—preach, make decisions, evangelize, and so on. Moreover, what he decided was always what was done. He was unable to listen to anybody else about anything. I do not know whether that was actually true of this minister, but it is true of many ministers and congregations. A situation like that denies the gifts of the Holy Spirit to the whole body of Christ. It unduly exalts the minister, demeans the other members of the church, and impoverishes the body.

Paul writes about spiritual gifts at various places in his letters, stressing always that the Holy Spirit gives gifts to each one. This means that every Christian has at least one gift. So if you have a situation in which people are not exercising their gifts, the result is always an impoverished church. No one person has all the gifts. So if the gifts he does not have but that others have are unused, the church is poorer by that amount.

People who study church growth factors say that in order to have a maximally healthy church at least 60 percent of the people should be engaged in some church work. I do not know where that precise statistic comes from, and I do not quarrel with it. The principle it articulates is a good one. If you have a church where 60 percent of the people are engaged in some work for Jesus Christ, that church is in ministry. It is working, and others who are on the fringes tend to get drawn in.

On the other hand, as valuable as that 60 percent figure may be as a goal to shoot for, it can never be the ideal. The ideal is 100 percent, and the apostles, with the wisdom given to them by God, recognized this principle when they suggested the election of these deacons.

A Plurality of Leadership

Not only was there to be a division of responsibility, but there was also to be a plurality of leadership even in a specifically designated area.

I have in my office a sign somebody gave me some years ago that says, "God so loved the world that he didn't send a committee." I can understand what it means. Committees are inefficient, indecisive, and slow. We think how much better it would be just to do away with them and get the job done quickly. Well, sometimes that may be necessary. But the problem is that the directions taken are often wrong or unbalanced, and this is what a plurality of leadership corrects. The gifts of Christ to the entire body are needed to correct such imbalances. It is significant that in the New Testament the Holy Spirit never seemed to have led anyone to appoint merely one elder or one bishop in a place. It is always elders (plural) or bishops (plural).

Spiritual Qualifications

The third principle for sound church leadership is suggested in the instruction given to the people before the election. The apostles said, "Brothers, choose seven men from among you who are known to be full of the Spirit and wisdom" (v. 3). These words point not to administrative skills or abilities but to spiritual qualifications.

When a congregation chooses a pastor, it usually knows that it is supposed to choose him on the basis of his spiritual qualities. At least that is what everybody says. The trouble is that when you talk to the people afterwards, you often find that the real reasons they chose him were quite different. Some liked the wave in his hair. Or they liked his smile or his jokes. Some liked the tone of his voice. Or they admired his educational background. Others found his family attractive. What a mistake this is! The church, above all institutions, should know how to choose leaders on the basis of Christian character and spiritual maturity.

This is a striking point in the choice of these first deacons. The job they were being chosen for was the distribution of food to the widows. If we were doing this today, many would say, "We might run short of supplies in this work. What we need are men who have private resources. Then, if the food runs short, they can supply the need out of their own pockets." Or, if we don't have people like that, "We need people who know the stock market and can invest the meager resources we have wisely. If we run short of food, we can live off the income from our investments."

I do not mean to suggest that we do not sometimes need people who can manage money well or that we do not need people who have had experience in business. One of the good things about working in a church is that you usually have people with a variety of such experiences, and that is usually an asset. But when this church was choosing leaders it was not concerned about how much money the men had or how much management experience they had acquired, but whether they were wise and Spirit-filled. The reason was that their main problem was not money or the lack of it, nor even food or the lack of it. The problem was essentially spiritual. Therefore, it needed persons who were Spirit-filled to deal with them.

And people with wisdom. When a person is young the person basically thinks that he or she knows just about everything. But as we get older that changes, or ought to change. Mark Twain said that when he was fifteen, he thought his father was a very ignorant man. By the time he was twenty-one, he was surprised to discover how much his father had learned in those six years. We start with self-confidence. But as we get older, we see that problems are not always susceptible to simple solutions and we begin to discern our own inability to handle them.

Deaconal Ministry

By electing deacons as the first administrative officers in the church other than the apostles, the church was electing people to do what above all else is most essential to true Christianity. This is because their service was patterned on the servant ministry of Jesus Christ. "Deacon" means "servant." And Jesus was the servant of everybody.

When we think about success we have to remember that the Bible's evaluation of success is completely different from the world's evaluation. If you ask people of the world, Who are the really important people? Where are those who are really great? the world answers that it is those at the top of the administrative pyramid. It is those who have a lot of people under them. If we are talking about a person's private circumstances, it is those who do not need to work. People work for them. They have servants. And of course, the more servants they have, the more important they are.

If we are talking about those who do work, which is most of us, the principle is the same. Most people are near the bottom of the pyramid, so many do not think they are very important at all. Supervisors are more important. Next is middle management. Then at the very top you have the chief executive officer, the president, or the chairman of the board. The person at the top of the administrative pyramid is the most important person.

That is not the way Jesus spoke of greatness. Jesus said:

> The kings of the Gentiles lord it over them; and those who exercise authority over them call themselves Benefactors. But you are not to be like that. Instead, the greatest among you should be like the youngest, and the one who rules like the one who serves. For who is greater, the one who is at the table or the one who serves? Is it not the one who is at the table? But I am among you as one who serves.
>
> Luke 22:25–27

Jesus also said, "If anyone wants to be first, he must be the very last, and the servant of all" (Mark 9:35).

If you want to be great in God's sight, try serving people. Be a true deacon. If you want to be even greater in God's sight, serve even more people. The more people you can serve, the greater you will be. And that includes doing things for them that the world would call menial.

Remember Jesus. When he was about to be crucified and wanted to give his disciples a graphic demonstration of what true greatness was, he removed his clothes, wrapped himself with a towel, knelt before them, and washed each of the disciples' feet. The Lord of the universe—the Lord of glory, the King of Kings—knelt before Galilean fishermen and performed a servant's task. Peter understood how incongruous this was, at least from his point of view. He told his Master, "You shall never wash my feet." But notice that he did not say, "No, Lord, let *me* wash their feet." He just didn't want the Lord to wash him. The Lord taught him how to be a servant.

When we are talking about these deacons, we are talking about what is absolutely essential because we do not have real Christianity without this vital function. That is why these men now became the leaders of the church. They did not replace the apostles, of course. The apostles had their own, special role. Theirs was a unique function. But apart from these specially chosen and commissioned apostles, the deacons (who were servants) became the first true leaders in the church.

Up to this point the apostles have been doing their thing: Peter at Pentecost, Peter and John before the Sanhedrin. They testified and were put in jail; sometimes they were beaten. In everything they counted it an honor to suffer for Christ. But from this point on we do not find those apostles appearing very much. What happens is that the deacons become the prominent and most effective witnesses.

It begins even in this passage, as Luke starts the story of Stephen, the first deacon: "Now Stephen, a man full of God's grace and power, did great wonders and miraculous signs among the people" (v. 8). We have his sermon and the story of his martyrdom in Acts 7. In Acts 8 we have the story of the second deacon, Philip. The gospel spread to Ethiopia through him. In each case, the gospel spread beyond Judaism not through the apostles but through the deacons. It was these men who really carried the ball.

So here is the challenge from this great story: Be a deacon, a servant, as these men were. How? Well, if you want to be a deacon, you will have to be like Jesus Christ. He is our model. He counted his equality with God not something to be grasped after or clung to. Rather he emptied himself and became a man, humbling himself even unto death that he might serve us (Phil. 2:5–8). You say, "I don't like that; I don't want to serve anybody." Well, no, of course you don't. We never want to serve others naturally. We want people to serve us. It is only in Christ that we become different.

The world will hate you if you take this path, just as it hated Jesus, Stephen, and the others. It will say, "Let's get rid of that person." And it may! But if it does, you will be able to say, even as Stephen said, echoing the words of his Master, "Lord, do not hold this sin against them." He was thinking of others and serving them even as he died.

Do you want to be like that? It is what Jesus wants for you, and if you are willing, he will teach you how.

14

Stephen: The First Martyr

Acts 6:8–7:60

When they heard this, they were furious and gnashed their teeth at him. But Stephen, full of the Holy Spirit, looked up to heaven and saw the glory of God, and Jesus standing at the right hand of God. "Look," he said, "I see heaven open and the Son of Man standing at the right hand of God."

At this they covered their ears and, yelling at the top of their voices, they all rushed at him, dragged him out of the city and began to stone him. Meanwhile, the witnesses laid their clothes at the feet of a young man named Saul.

While they were stoning him, Stephen prayed, "Lord Jesus, receive my spirit." Then he fell on his knees and cried out, "Lord, do not hold this sin against them." When he had said this, he fell asleep.

Acts 7:54–60

The second half of Acts 6 (vv. 8–15) tells of the arrest of Stephen, the most prominent of the early deacons, and leads into the record of his sermon before the Sanhedrin in Acts 7. Stephen's sermon is the longest address in this book. It is essentially a pointed survey of the history of Israel, and the points it makes are unfolded and reinforced throughout.

Stephen was the first Christian martyr. A martyr is a person who dies for his or her beliefs, and a Christian martyr is a person who is killed because of his or her witness to Jesus Christ. Martyr comes from the Greek word *martys*, which means "a witness" or "one who bears a testimony." Stephen was an out-standing witness for Jesus Christ, and it was because of his witness that he was put to death.

The Nature of Stephen's Sermon

Before we look at Stephen's speech in its particulars, it will be good to look at it in general, thinking about some of its characteristics.

First, it is not actually a defense. That is, Stephen is not dealing directly—at least not point by point—with the accusations that had been made against him. When Peter had been called before the Sanhedrin, Peter answered his accusers directly. They demanded to know "by what power or name" Peter had healed the lame man, and he had given a direct answer to the accusation (Acts 4:7–10). Stephen does not follow Peter's procedure. He answers the accusations against him indirectly as he goes along.

Second, this speech is not like the sermon of Peter at Pentecost. When Peter spoke at Pentecost he quoted a verse of Scripture, explained what it meant and how it had been fulfilled, then quoted another verse of Scripture and explained what that meant, and so on. Stephen's address is different. It is not that he is not biblical. In a sense, he is entirely biblical, since he is retelling the Old Testament. But he is not quoting Bible verses as he goes along, nor is he explaining them. Only toward the end does he begin to bring in some specific texts, quoting first from Amos 5:25–27 and then from Isaiah 66:1–2.

Something else is noticeable when Stephen's speech is contrasted with Peter's. Peter preached about Jesus throughout. He preached the resurrec-tion. In Stephen's speech Jesus is not mentioned at all until the very end, and even then he is not mentioned by name as Jesus or Jesus Christ. He is called "the Righteous One" (v. 52). Again, Stephen does not mention the resurrection, the doctrine that was so prominent earlier.

This sermon has a number of easily identifiable parts. Verses 2–8 deal with Abraham. Verses 9–16 deal with Joseph. A major section, verses 17–43, deals with Moses, followed by a section that contrasts the wilderness tabernacle with the temple in Jerusalem (vv. 44–50). Finally, there is a summation in which Stephen makes bold accusations against the Sanhedrin (vv. 51–53).

This is a fairly straightforward recital of Jewish history, as I said. But if we read it carefully, we discover that the section that deals with Moses actually answers the first of the charges that had been made against Stephen—that he had blasphemed against Moses; and his discussion of the tabernacle answers the second charge—that he had blasphemed against God.

Stephen was from the Greek-speaking portion of the early church. That is perhaps why he spoke so differently from Peter, who was a Jew. Stephen seems to have perceived, with a brilliance that surpasses that of the apostles and anticipates the keen insight that was later given to the apostle Paul, that the old order of things was passing away and a new order was coming. This becomes particularly clear when he talks about the temple. It was cherished by the Jews. But it was destined to pass away, and Stephen seems to have sensed that. His speech is a transition speech that paves the way for presenting the gospel to the Gentiles, which begins in the very next chapter of Acts.

The Calling of Abraham

The first section of Stephen's speech deals with Abraham. It is found in verses 2–8. There were many things that Stephen could have said about Abraham, since a very long section of Genesis is given to Abraham's story, but Stephen is selective. What he emphasizes is the clue to his thought.

1. *God appeared to Abraham in Mesopotamia.* Stephen says, "The God of glory appeared to our father Abraham while he was still in Mesopotamia, before he lived in Haran" (v. 2). This is different from the impression that we have reading the early chapters of Genesis. Genesis seems to suggest that God appeared to Abraham when he was in Haran, but Stephen is saying that God actually appeared to him even before he got to Haran—that is, when he was in Mesopotamia.

Why does that matter? How is that important?

It is important in the context of the address because what we are going to find, not only here but later on also in the case of Moses, is an emphasis upon the fact that God is God not of one limited geographical place only, such as the land of Israel, but of the whole world. So it is significant for Stephen to have begun by saying that God revealed his glory to Abraham first when Abraham was far away in Mesopotamia.

2. *God himself appeared to Abraham.* The fact that Stephen mentions the God of glory appearing to Abraham is also new. In Genesis we are told that God spoke to Abraham, but here Stephen adds that God appeared to him. So it is not as if Abraham was in Mesopotamia and God, perhaps from Mount Zion many hundreds of miles away, shouted to him, "Abraham, come over here. I want you to come to Palestine." Rather God appeared to him right there in Mesopotamia in all his glory, and that revelation caused Abraham to respond by setting out on his journey.

3. *Abraham remained a pilgrim even in Canaan.* When Stephen talks about Abraham's time in Canaan, he emphasizes that Abraham remained a pilgrim even there. Even though this was the land that God was giving him and his descendants, the land in which the people settled and the temple was built, for Abraham Canaan was only a land through which he was passing. He didn't own even a small bit of the land, says Stephen (v. 5).

This statement must have been meant as a rebuke to these settled leaders of the people. They were in the land God had given. It was a blessing. But they were too much at home in the land. They had forgotten that, wonderful as possession of the land of promise was, they were nevertheless only to be pilgrims in it as Abraham had been. Without this orientation, they lacked the spiritual depth that characterized their ancestor. Abraham, we are told in Hebrews, was not looking for an earthly city, but "to the city with foundations [the heavenly city], whose architect and builder is God" (Heb. 11:10). These rulers had ceased to look forward. They were looking back, and they had taken the things of the world and the blessings of the world to be permanent. They had allowed God's temporal blessings to eclipse their sense of God's presence.

The Abuse of Joseph

Next Stephen talked about Joseph (vv. 9–16), and his chief point here is that Joseph was mistreated by his brothers.

I noticed when I was studying Genesis some years ago that although Joseph is a remarkable illustration of the Lord Jesus Christ in the way he was mistreated, was sent into a foreign land, and there became the salvation of his people, nowhere in the Bible is Joseph ever made a direct type of Christ. The New Testament never says, as it does in Moses' case, for example, that Jesus is the second Joseph, or something like that. But if ever there is a place where that comparison is at least in the background, even though it may not be said openly, it is here. The point Stephen is making is that all through their history, the Jewish people persecuted and killed the prophets sent to them, just as Joseph's brothers persecuted Joseph. And, of course, that is what the leaders had done in the case of Jesus Christ. They had killed him.

The Case of Moses, the Lawgiver

When Stephen begins to talk about Moses, it is similar, only he deals with the story of Moses at greater length because Moses was the one the Sanhedrin was chiefly concerned about. Moses was the one through whom God had given the law, and these leaders had built their whole lives around keeping the law of Moses.

1. *Moses was rejected by the Jewish people.* One of the first things Stephen says about Moses is that Moses also was rejected by his people. There were other things that Stephen could have said, just as in the case of Abraham. But he emphasizes that when Moses perceived that his heart lay with his people and he wanted to be identified with them rather than with the Egyptians, they rejected him.

We know the story. Moses killed an Egyptian, thinking, no doubt, that this might be something like a rallying cry for revolution. He had received a wonderful education. He was uniquely qualified to lead the people. Now he was taking his stand for righteousness against an injustice. Perhaps Moses knew that the time prophesied for the coming of a deliverer had arrived (cf. Gen. 15:13–14). The four hundred years that had been foretold for the time of slavery in Egypt were up. Now is the time, he must have thought. I must be the deliverer. They will follow me.

But they did not follow him. The people rejected him, and when word of his action got around, he had to flee. He fled to Midian where he spent the next forty years of his life.

2. *God appeared to Moses when he was in Midian.* This is the same point Stephen made earlier in his recital of Abraham's story. God appeared to Abraham when he was in Mesopotamia—that is, when he was in Gentile territory. Now we are told that he also appeared to Moses when Moses was in Midian. It was there, "after forty years had passed, [that] an angel appeared to Moses in the flames of a burning bush . . . near Mount Sinai," and the Lord said to him, "Take off your sandals; the place where you are standing is holy ground" (Acts 7:30–31). This "holy place" was not Jerusalem. It was a mountain in Gentile territory. Yet God was there, and because God was there, the ground was holy.

By now we should be getting Stephen's drift, and we may suspect that the Sanhedrin was beginning to get his point as well. Stephen was saying: This neat little hold you think you have on God, this little thing that makes God Jewish and not the God of the Gentiles as well is a corrupt thing, and it is corrupting you. If you were faithful to your tradition, if you were guided by what your Scriptures tell you, you would know that God is the God of all people and that you, just because you have been given special privileges, have the enormous responsibility of being a witness to them.

This is true for us as well. We have a hymn by William Cowper (1769) that says:

> Jesus, where'er thy people meet,
> There they behold thy mercy seat;
> Where'er they seek thee, thou art found,
> And every place is hallowed ground.

Stephen was teaching that God is everywhere and that in every nation he has those who seek him.

3. *Moses was rejected again even after the Exodus.* Stephen continues Moses' story, showing that the rejection Moses experienced when he killed the Egyptian was followed by an even more substantial rejection after he had led the people out of Egypt. While he was on the mountain, receiving God's law—that very law on which the Sanhedrin prided itself and that they were accusing Stephen of breaking—the people were down in the valley breaking it. God had brought them out of Egypt. He had revealed himself to be the true God. The first of the Ten Commandments said, "You shall have no other gods before me" (Exod. 20:3). Yet that is exactly what the people were doing. At the very time the law was being given, the people were making idols for themselves, just like the idols of Egypt. They were committing adultery and no doubt breaking each of the other laws as well.

In rejecting God, they were also rejecting Moses.

At this point, Stephen brings in the first of his direct quotations. There are a few other places where he seems to refer indirectly to certain passages, picking up some specific Old Testament words and phrasing. But here for the first time, he gives a full quotation.

In the New International Version there is a footnote giving the reference as Amos 5:25–27. The note comes after the word "exile" and before the words "beyond Babylon." There is a very good reason for that. It is because Amos did not say "beyond Babylon," but rather "beyond Damascus." Amos wrote "beyond Damascus" because he was a prophet to the people of the northern kingdom, and he was prophesying their exile. They were taken beyond Damascus by the Syrians. But Stephen, who quotes the text, alters it, because he is not talking to the people of the northern kingdom but to the leaders of Israel in the south. It is their history he has in mind. When they were carried away into captivity, it was not by the Syrians, who took the people of the northernmost Jewish state into exile beyond Damascus in 721 B.C., but rather by the Babylonians, who took them "beyond Babylon" in 586 B.C. As we would say, that is "where the rubber really met the road" for the Sanhedrin.

Stephen was telling them that the rebellious attitude of Joseph's brothers and the people who came out of Egypt has been characteristic of Jewish people throughout history. The Sanhedrin were part of that history. They were descendants of those who returned to Canaan from Babylon, and the spirit that took their ancestors to Babylon was still in them.

They had told Stephen he was blaspheming against the law of Moses, and they were going to condemn him for that.

Stephen responded: You have been breaking the law of Moses all your lives, and because you have been rejecting Moses you have also been rejecting the truth about Jesus. You are going to be judged by him when he returns to judge the living and the dead.

Where Is God's House?

Another section of the speech is found in verses 44–50. So far Stephen has been talking about individuals: Abraham, Joseph, and Moses. Now he turns from individuals to deal with the "tabernacle of the Testimony." The tabernacle was the portable temple the Jews carried with them during their desert wanderings. It came with them into the Promised Land and was retained in part up to and including the time of King David. It was only during the reign of Solomon that a permanent temple was built. Stephen contrasts the wilderness tabernacle with the later, magnificent temple that was built by Solomon, rebuilt after the return from exile and then again in an even more marvelous fashion by King Herod.

The temple of Herod was the glory of Jerusalem at this time. Much of it was covered with gold. So as a person drew near Jerusalem, he saw it shining against the skyline. The temple had never been as glorious as it was in that day, and the priests, like priests who serve in cathedrals everywhere, loved the temple and could not see beyond it.

Stephen compares the wilderness tabernacle, which was not glorious, with this great temple of Herod. The tabernacle was not spectacular from a human point of view, but God could be found there. What about Herod's temple? Was God there? Commentators differ about this, wondering if Stephen could really be criticizing the existing temple or the temple service. Is he saying that the building of the temple was a mistake, that Christians, and perhaps the entire body of the Jewish people, should not be worshiping there? On the one hand, his quotation of Isaiah 66:1–2 may imply it.

> Heaven is my throne,
>   and the earth is my footstool.
> What kind of house will you build for me?
>   says the Lord.
> Or where will my resting place be?
> Has not my hand made all these things?
>   Acts 7:49–50 (see Isaiah 66:1–2)

On the other hand, as some commentators point out, God had appeared in the temple, Jesus honored the temple, and even in Stephen's day Christians were still worshiping in the temple. It is hard to think that Stephen could really be saying that the building of the temple was a mistake.

The place this speech occupies in Acts leads me to think Stephen is saying that the day of the temple was passing. It had been built by Solomon. It had been a blessing. That was all very good. But it was passing away now simply because the Lord Jesus Christ had come. He was the real temple. Besides, those who believe on him themselves become temples of the Holy Spirit as the living God comes to dwell in them. If this is what Stephen is saying, then there is a sense in which he is admitting that the accusation made against him in Acts 6:14 is actually true. His enemies said, "We have heard him say that this Jesus of Nazareth will destroy this place and change the customs Moses handed down to us." Stephen is admitting, Yes, that is what I have said, because God is not God of the Jews only but of the Gentiles too, and it is to the Gentiles that the gospel will now go.

This speech has prominence in Acts because it marks the closing of the Jewish mission and is an indication of the opening to the Gentile communities.

Summation and Application

At the end of his sermon (vv. 51–53) Stephen applied what he said in true prophetic fashion. In doing so he made three accusations against the religious leaders: (1) they were resisting the Holy Spirit, as they had always done; (2) they were persecuting and killing the prophets, as they had always done; and (3) they were breaking the law of Moses, as they had always done. At this last point, their anger against Stephen reached such a heat that they would not hear him anymore and rushed him outside and stoned him.

We are told that before he began his address Stephen's face glowed like that of an angel (Acts 6:15). Here at the end of his address, knowing what was going to happen, he looked up and saw not an angel, but the Lord Jesus Christ, whom they had crucified. I said earlier that Stephen did not mention the resurrection in his sermon. But Stephen *saw* the resurrected Jesus and called attention to him, saying, "Look, I see heaven open and the Son of Man standing at the right hand of God" (v. 56).

People have wondered why Jesus was standing in this vision, since in Hebrews 10:12 we are told, "But when this priest had offered for all time one sacrifice for sins, he *sat down* at the right hand of God" (italics mine). Hebrews makes a contrast between Jesus, who sat down, and the temple priests, who always stood for their work (there were no chairs in the Jewish temple), signifying that their work was never finished. They had to make sacrifice upon sacrifice because their sacrifices were only types of Christ's sacrifice. When Jesus had made his sacrifice, his work was done. That is why we say in the words of the Apostles' Creed that Jesus *"sitteth* on the right hand of God the Father Almighty" (italics mine). We do not look for an additional atonement.

But now Jesus is standing. Why?

There have been two suggestions, and I think both may be valid. One is that Jesus stood up to receive his martyr Stephen. Sometimes we hear stories like that of the death of Christians. They are lying on their beds, but as they die they lift their arms and rise upward, sometimes even saying something like, "Look, I see Jesus." Then they fall back and die. My own great grandfather died that way, reacting in astonishment to what he saw of the heavenly glory as he died. Perhaps that is the explanation of why Jesus stood when Stephen died.

But there is another explanation, and I think that it may be valid as well. Jesus said in Matthew 10:32: "Whoever acknowledges me before men, I will also acknowledge him before my Father in heaven." In view of this verse, it may be that we have a case of Jesus standing to plead Stephen's cause as his advocate. That is, Jesus takes the position of a defender and witness before the Father's throne.

If this is the case, then what Stephen caught a glimpse of was that second and much greater trial in which he was involved. Up to this moment he had only been able to see the earthly trial. He was condemned by the earthly court. But at the moment of his death he caught a glimpse of that greater, heavenly trial, in which he was acquitted. In this trial the Lord Jesus Christ took his side, pleaded his case, and prevailed. Perhaps he said something like this to the Father: "Stephen is my follower. He is confessing me. I am going to take him with me into heaven forever." I find that immensely encouraging.

In this life we go through many situations in which we are on trial, and although we try to do our best, we often fail and are even misunderstood.

We get discouraged. But we have to remember that the trials we go through in this life are not the final trial of history. They may be important. We want to do as well in them as we possibly can. That is why we have to be strong and bear a faithful testimony in all circumstances. But the trial that really matters, the verdict that counts, is the verdict that is given by the Lord Jesus Christ and by God the Father.

I do not know what the Lord Jesus Christ says when he looks down, sees us, and pleads our case before the Father, though I am sure it varies in every case. But I do know that if we are his, he owns us and pleads our case in heaven. He says in effect, "This one is mine. That one is mine. I died for these people. My death covered their sin. They are clothed in my righteousness." As long as that is true, we can carry on. We can fight the good fight of faith, stand firm to the end, and bear a victorious testimony.

PART TWO

The Witness
in Judea and Samaria

15

Samaria: The Widening Stream

Acts 8:1–25

On that day a great persecution broke out against the church at Jerusalem, and all except the apostles were scattered throughout Judea and Samaria. Godly men buried Stephen and mourned deeply for him. But Saul began to destroy the church. Going from house to house, he dragged off men and women and put them in prison.

Those who had been scattered preached the word wherever they went.

Acts 8:1–4

Before he was taken back to heaven the Lord Jesus Christ told his disciples that after he was gone his enemies would persecute and kill them, thinking they were doing God a service (Matt. 24:9). The early disciples remembered that teaching, no doubt. Still it must have been a shock when Stephen, their most outstanding layman and deacon, was killed. He was a distinguished Christian leader, one who had proved himself pious, strong, and useful to the church. He was also the first believer to be martyred.

As we move from Acts 7 to Acts 8 we find that Stephen's killing was the signal for a widespread outbreak of persecution against many. It was led by Saul, who was present at Stephen's stoning (Acts 7:58) and gave approval to

131

his death (Acts 8:1). There had been persecution already. The apostles had been beaten because they had refused to remain silent about the person and work of their Master. But that earlier persecution was against the apostles only, and here for the first time we find persecution not only of the leaders but also of the membership of the church at large.

Good in Spite of Opposition

To make the picture of these days even worse, for the first time we find the leaders of Judaism united in their opposition. They had not been united before. When the apostles were brought before the Sanhedrin Peter referred to the resurrection, and because the resurrection was something in which the Pharisees believed and the Sadducees did not, the apostles' assertion immediately divided the ruling body. Acts 23:6 recounts a similar case involving Paul.

Between Peter's arrest and the persecution recounted in Acts 8 the gospel had spread among the Hellenists—those Greek-speaking persons who were Jews in the sense that they were sympathetic with Judaism and worshiped the God of the Jews in a Jewish way, but who were Gentiles by birth and were now becoming Christians.

The leaders of the early church (apart from the apostles) were from this number, and their leader had been Stephen. The apostles were worshiping at the temple, going through the religious rites of Judaism. They did not seem to see any problem with that. Stephen understood that the surviving Jewish accretions to Christianity needed to pass away and indeed were destined to pass away. In fact, he knew that even the temple would be gone soon, since Jesus had said this would happen. It was on this ground that Stephen was brought before the Sanhedrin, and on that point not just the Sadducees but the Pharisees too were up in arms.

So things were getting bad for the Christians. Saul, whom Luke introduces as an agent of the persecution (Acts 8:1), became the first truly great and deadly enemy of the church. Not much is said about him here. He is simply mentioned as being present, "giving approval to his death." But Luke knew that Saul went on to intensify the persecution of the church so that not only were the disciples scattered, as the text says they were, but they also were actually pursued in their scattering as Saul hounded them to death.

Verse 3 says, "Saul began to destroy the church." Other versions say he "ravaged" it. The tense of that verb, whether "ravage" or "destroy," is imperfect, which means that he ravaged it and kept on ravaging it. The translation of the New International Version, good as it is, seems to suggest that Saul just started in to make trouble. But the real idea is that he continued to make trouble. He was making trouble, and he was going to keep on making trouble—until God stopped him.

The trouble Saul and the others were making was ineffective in the end. Saul was setting out to destroy the church. But the more he tried, the more the gospel spread. This was because those who were persecuted and thus scattered throughout Judea and Samaria planted the seeds of the gospel everywhere.

There are different words for "scattered" in Greek. One means dispersed so that the item is gone from that point on, like scattering a person's ashes on the ocean's waves. That is not the word used here in verses 1 and 4. The word used here means scattered in order to be planted. It is exactly like the Hebrew word *jezreel*, meaning "scattered" but also "planted." It is what God did with Israel, scattering the Jews throughout the world because of their sin; but he also brought them back and planted them in their land. The disciples were scattered as a result of the persecution. But all the leaders did by scattering the disciples was to plant them in the places to which they had been scattered, for there they "preached the word" (v. 4).

Is that true of you? Wherever you find yourself—whether scattered by work or family or education or some other means—have you considered yourself planted in that place? Have you put down roots and born fruit for Jesus Christ? That is what these early Christians did. It is because of this activity that even the bad things that had happened to them served to advance the cause of Christ. Later Paul would write, "We know that in all things God works for the good of those who love him" (Rom. 8:28). The persecution of the early church, even the stoning of Stephen, illustrates that principle.

Philip the Evangelist

Now the mantle of leadership passes from Stephen to Philip, who actually begins the church's Gentile mission. Philip began his ministry in Samaria. That place name should ring a bell in our minds because it was mentioned in Acts 1, where Jesus outlined his plan for the expansion of the missionary enterprise (v. 8). When we were looking at that verse at the beginning of this book, I pointed out that Judea and Samaria are probably to be taken together as embracing one region. The verse should be read as describing three regions: (1) Jerusalem, (2) Judea and Samaria, and (3) the regions beyond.

Through the end of Acts 7, Luke has described the preaching of the gospel in Jerusalem. It had been effective. Thousands had believed. In fact, others had flocked into the city to be with the apostles and experience the healings that were taking place. Now, beginning with chapter 8, the gospel expands to Samaria, and Philip becomes the instrument of the first great missionary outreach.[1]

It was bold of him to do it, because there was a long-standing and very deep-seated hostility between the Jews and the Samaritans, going back to ancient times. When the Assyrian army had overthrown Samaria and carried the Jews of the northern kingdom away to Assyria, some Jews were inevitably left behind. These soon intermarried with the foreigners who had been settled in Samaria in their place, which made the Samaritans both ethnic and religious half-breeds, and they soon compounded the problem by setting up a rival temple on Mount Gerizim. This was prohibited in the Old Testament, but the Samaritans solved the problem by rejecting the Old Testament except for the first five books. The Jews looked down on the Samaritans and had no dealings with them (John 4:9). So it was a very novel thing for Philip to lead in the evangelization of this area. He was a Gentile too, a part of the Hellenistic branch of Judaism and now also Christianity.

When Philip began his ministry in this new area, we find him doing exactly what the apostles and other evangelists had been doing before him. Verse 4 says, "Those who had been scattered preached the word wherever they went." Now verse 5 gives a specific example of one who did this: "Philip went down to a city in Samaria and proclaimed the Christ there." In other words, he preached the gospel. The gospel was centered in Jesus Christ, and they had been preaching Jesus all along.

Why did they not adopt some new methods? Why did they not hold rap sessions or set up therapy groups or hold discussions about important books? Paul explains the reason for their choice in Romans 1:16: "I am not ashamed of the gospel, because it is the power of God for the salvation of everyone who believes: first for the Jew, then for the Gentile." It is through the preaching of the Word (in formal settings) and testifying to the Word (in informal conversations) that the power of God is known. That is how God has chosen to reach people. Transformations take place through the preaching of the Word. Philip preached the gospel, and God blessed his teaching.

Philip is the first person—indeed, the only person—in the New Testament to be called an evangelist (Acts 21:8). It is interesting that he was a layman. It has always seemed to me that those people who have been particularly effective in telling others about Christ have been laymen. We usually think that ministers are to be evangelists, and certainly there are ministers who are evangelists. But my experience has been that those who are most effective as evangelists are laypeople.

Although some ministers are evangelists, the chief task of the ministry is not evangelism. It is, as Paul says to the Ephesians, "to prepare God's people for works of service, so that the body of Christ may be built up" (Eph. 4:12). Works of service include evangelism. So a minister's job is to teach the Bible so that those in the church who are taught, particularly those who have the gift of evangelism, can exercise their gift (or whatever other gift they may have) in reaching others.

We do not know where Philip received his teaching. He may have been a disciple of the Lord, though I do not think so. Probably he learned what he knew from the apostles. However and wherever he learned it, he took the message to distant places boldly. And God blessed him, even with the ability to do miracles! The text says that "evil spirits came out of many, and many paralytics and cripples were healed" (v. 7).

The Strange Case of Simon

Miracles are particularly significant in view of the story that follows. One of the reasons and perhaps the chief reason God allowed Philip to do the miracles he did was for the impact they had on a man whose name was Simon. Simon was a miracle worker. He had impressed the people of Samaria by his tricks for some time, giving out that he was some great person. The text says that he called himself "the Great Power" (v. 10). The Latin word for "great" is *magus*. So Simon was usually referred to as Simon Magus. This is like "Blackstone the Great" or "Simon the Magnificent"! He had been making a magnificent impact on the city before Philip came.

Now for the first time in his life Simon saw a power that really did what it seemed to do. He had been doing tricks. He had been fooling people and knew that he had only been fooling them. Suddenly Philip was doing the real thing, not operating at all the way Simon was operating, not trying to draw attention to himself but rather pointing to Jesus Christ, and it was through the power of this Christ that real miracles were being done. It was in a sort of a professional capacity that Simon thought to himself, If I am going to advance in my profession or even just recapture the following that I have had until now, I had better get the power that the Christian has.

This is a puzzling story, however, and what makes it so puzzling is verse 13, which says, "Simon himself believed and was baptized." Was Simon actually a believer? Was his baptism a true baptism? Or was he just carried along by his enthusiasm for Philip, professing something that had not really happened in his heart? The easiest answer is that Simon was not a true believer. But it is possible to make a case for the other side, as some commentators do, though they do not necessarily endorse the position.[2] They suggest that nothing is said in the story that necessarily excludes the fact that Simon may have been a true Christian.

I suppose that is true. Later Peter, who had come to Samaria by this time, says, "May your money perish with you, because you thought you could buy the gift of God with money! You have no part or share in this ministry, because your heart is not right before God" (vv. 20–21). That is strong language. But when Peter says, "You have no part or share in this ministry," it is interesting that he employs the same words Jesus used for him when Peter had objected to Jesus' washing his feet in the Upper Room. Jesus said, "Unless I wash you, you have no part with me" (John 13:8). Strong words. Still Peter was not an unbeliever; he was just out of the will of God.

So I say that it is possible, just possible, that Simon was a believer. Nevertheless, this seems rather to be a case of one who had been exposed to strong preaching, was impressed by the miracles, and wanted to tap into the evident blessings of the gospel, but who did not have that genuine change of heart that would have meant that he was born again. We can apply the story either way.

If Simon Was Born Again

If Simon was saved, we are warned against what in the history of the church has come to be known as "simony." In the narrowest sense simony is "the crime of buying or selling ecclesiastic preferment." Because it is based on the notion that God's blessings can be bought, it can refer more broadly to any theological system in which we suppose we can pay God for what we want from him. We may think of this as old-fashioned, perhaps merely a medieval idea that thrived when people were trying to buy papal favors or buy their way to heaven by the purchase of indulgences to release their souls from purgatory. But we have the same thing today in the thought, all too common in some Christian organizations, that we can obtain the blessing of God on our work if only we can raise enough money.

When God really blesses his church, when revival sweeps over God's people, it is generally in unexpected ways and never linked to how much money they have. God just chooses to do it. His Spirit moves. His people are revived. Then, from beyond the walls of the church, people hear what is happening and the Holy Spirit draws them in. That is what we are lacking today. We are rich in things but poor in soul.

If Simon Was Not Born Again

If Simon was not a believer, though he thought he was, then his case is a warning to anybody who thinks that just because he or she has made a profession of faith or has gone through certain motions expected of Christians that he or she is right with God for that reason. That is not the case.

About thirty years ago, when I was working for the evangelical magazine *Christianity Today,* editor Carl F. H. Henry, who was effective at bringing different branches of the church together, did a series of parallel articles accompanied by an editorial in which he pointed out a strange anomaly regarding different churches' practice of baptism. He noted that those that practiced infant baptism were tending to delay it later and later because so many disagreed with the practice, while on the other hand, those who believed in adult baptism (as opposed to infant baptism) were tending to baptize children earlier and earlier for the sake of gaining new members and enlarging their rolls. The ages of those being baptized were moving closer and closer together. I know nothing about that tendency personally. But it occurs to me that something like that happens frequently in churches.

We are often so interested in getting members into our churches that we make the demands for membership almost meaningless. As long as a person will say a few right things, we consider the person to be regenerate and proceed to the baptism. Then we add such persons to our rolls, saying, "We increased our congregation by 13 percent last year, and the year before that we only increased it 10 percent. Things are really going well."

None of this is necessarily the work of God. I suspect that when we add members to the church that easily, what we are actually doing is inoculating them against the real article, against the gospel.

Compare how churches function today in terms of membership with how they functioned in what was probably the strongest period of all for American churches, the age of the Puritans. In those days membership in the churches did not represent a large percentage of the population, perhaps only 6 or 7 percent of the population as contrasted with 45 or 46 percent now. Yet the churches were tremendously effective. One reason is that today, if a church has a membership of two thousand people, it probably knows where about one thousand of those members are, and about five hundred come to church. But in the days of the Puritans, if a church had five hundred members, one thousand were in church and the congregation was having an impact on at least two thousand. The Puritan practice suggests that it is not wise to make membership in a church too easy.

Yet when Simon came to the apostles saying he believed in Jesus Christ and wanted to be baptized, the apostles accepted his profession. That was necessary because as human beings we cannot see into another person's heart. All we can do is judge on the basis of what we call "credible profession." That is what Philip did. When Simon confessed Christ, Simon was baptized, though I believe he probably was not a true believer.

A Divine Person or a Power

When Simon the sorcerer offered Simon Peter money to get the gift of the Spirit, his conception of the Holy Spirit was not different from that of many Christians today. They think of the Holy Spirit as a power, and they reflect that if you want to have power in your life, the thing to do is to get more of the Holy Spirit. They are not thinking of buying the Holy Spirit, of course. But they are thinking of ways to get more of this power. If we have *it,* then we can use *it* to integrate our lives, overcome our problems, live victoriously, or whatever.

The Holy Spirit is not an "it." The Holy Spirit is a Person. He is God. When we get that clearly in mind, then we can see that the object of our relationship to the Holy Spirit is not that we might have more of him so that we can use him, but rather that he might have more of us and use us. Simon did not understand this, and neither do many believers today.

The proper contrast with this story in Acts 8 is what we find at the beginning of Acts 13, at the start of Paul's missionary enterprise. In that chapter the Holy Spirit spoke to the church, saying, "Set apart for me Barnabas and Saul for the work to which I have called them" (v. 2). Think about that. When you contemplate the Third Person of the Trinity, do you think of him as a power that somehow you should get a hold of and use? Or do you think of him as God, the One who should have and use you, as he used Saul and Barnabas?

This section ends with Peter's words to Simon. Peter tells Simon, "Repent of this wickedness and pray to the Lord. Perhaps he will forgive you for having such a thought in your heart. For I see that you are full of bitterness and captive to sin" (vv. 22–23).

Simon replied, "Pray to the Lord for me."

Does that sound pious to your ears? "Pray to the Lord for me." That is the sort of thing ministers hear all the time. We talk to somebody about spiritual things, and he or she says, "Well, pray for me. Pray for me."

I do not want to be misunderstood: It is good to pray for people. If somebody says, "Pray for me," I try to do it. But Peter had told Simon to pray. He was to repent of his wickedness and pray to God. So when Simon replied by saying, "Pray for me," he was not being pious at all but rather disobedient. His words were what we would call in colloquial English "a cop out." He was refusing to do what he had been told he should do and was passing the buck to Peter.

Do you do that? Do you pass the buck for your spiritual growth to other people? Do you pass it to your minister? Lots of people try to pass the buck to me. They think that somehow I can solve their problems. I cannot. I cannot even solve my own problems, let alone their problems. If you are sinning, *you* are the one who must repent of the sin. If prayer is needed, *you* are the one who must pray.

The Bible says that it is our "iniquities" that have separated us from God. It is because of our "sins" that "he will not hear" us (Isa. 59:2). If you have sinned, you must confess it and repent of the sin; then you can pray. You must come to God like the prodigal, saying, "Father, I have sinned against heaven and against you" (Luke 15:21) or like the tax collector at the temple, "God, have mercy on me, a sinner" (Luke 18:13). It is hard to pray in that fashion. But if you do it, you will find, as Peter suggested to Simon, that God will forgive your sin, cleanse and restore you, and save your soul.

16

Philip and the Ethiopian

Acts 8:26–40

Now an angel of the Lord said to Philip, "Go south to the road—the desert road—that goes down from Jerusalem to Gaza." So he started out, and on his way he met an Ethiopian eunuch, an important official in charge of all the treasury of Candace, queen of the Ethiopians. This man had gone to Jerusalem to worship, and on his way home was sitting in his chariot reading the book of Isaiah the prophet. The Spirit told Philip, "Go to that chariot and stay near it."

Then Philip ran up to the chariot and heard the man reading Isaiah the prophet. "Do you understand what you are reading?" Philip asked.

"How can I," he said, "unless someone explains it to me?"

Acts 8:26–31

The movement of the gospel to Samaria was centered on the ministry of Philip, as we have already seen. Philip was one of seven deacons who had been elected to carry out important works of service in the church at Jerusalem, but it was not long before he became an effective evangelist too.

Although the deacons were elected to do what we would call works of mercy or service ministries—which is what even today we think of the deacons primarily as doing—these men did not consider themselves to be limited to such functions. At least two of them were great preachers. They were steeped in the Scriptures, and they were men of great courage. Stephen, the first, was able to stand before the highest tribunal of his day, give an articulate, well-reasoned analysis of Israel's history, and advance the gospel.

Now Philip is on the scene, and he is another outstanding man. He earned the title of evangelist, because when the church was scattered, he made his way north to Samaria, where he preached Jesus. Acts 8 contains two stories about him: the impact of his preaching on Simon the magician, which we looked at in the last chapter; and his witness to the Ethiopian eunuch, which we will look at carefully in this chapter.

The Calling of Philip

The setting in which the call came to Philip to share the gospel with the Ethiopian is noteworthy.

A Time of Revival

This was a time of unusual blessing on the church. To judge from the story, it would even seem that the revival in Samaria was still growing. Philip was an important part of this, being the chief evangelist. Peter and John had been sent to inspect the work, but they had then gone back to Jerusalem to report. Philip was the front-line man. He seemed to be utterly indispensable. Yet it was at precisely this moment when God called him to leave the area.

A Desert Area

The other striking fact about this call was the area to which the angel sent Philip. He was in a good area, doing a good work, reaching many people. But the angel of the Lord said he wanted Philip to go down to the desert road that stretches south to Gaza on the way to Egypt (Acts 8:26).

Isn't it interesting that God should call Philip at such a time and to such a place? We are not told that Philip objected, and I do not think he did. What God called him to do he did joyfully. But if we were in his place, we might very well have raised objections. I can think of the kinds of objections I might have raised. I might have said, "All right, Lord, but not now. We can get to that region, and no doubt we will—in the proper time. We are in the midst of great blessing here in Samaria, and it would be a great mistake to turn our backs on it. I am the one you sent to do it, through whom, humanly speaking, all this blessing has come."

Or I might have said, "Not me." I might even have said it humbly. I might have said, "Lord, I'm not the only Christian around. I am involved in work here. Why, look at all those apostles sitting around in Jerusalem. They received the Great Commission too. In fact, they received it from Jesus directly. Why don't they go? They're not doing anything except checking up on my work to see if I am doing it right."

Or I could have said, "All right, Lord, but not there. Not to that desert area. Nobody even lives down there. The place to be is where the people are, like right here in Samaria."

But, as I say, I do not think Philip had any of those thoughts at all, because Philip knew something we need to know and that will be very helpful in our lives: God's ways are not our ways; his thoughts are not our thoughts. How do we know this? We know it because God tells us (Isa. 55:8). This means that although Christianity is not an irrational thing and although none of us are called to be irrational, nevertheless when we are engaged in spiritual work there are always going to be areas we will not fully understand. We will find ourselves asking, "Why does God do that?" Or "Why does he do that rather than something else?" That is just the way it is going to be.

Haven't you ever asked questions like that? I know I have. Take the case of someone who is extremely effective in some particular branch of Christian work. He is the one who gets sick or dies. Do you find yourself asking, "Why that one, Lord? There are all sorts of Christians you could dispense with. Why take the one that is so valuable?"

Or we look at a good Christian work. It is spiritual. It is a pioneer effort in some difficult area. But that is the work that does not seem to get the necessary funds to keep going. It struggles and struggles, while other projects that seem weak, superficial, and unnecessary thrive. Don't you find yourself asking, "Why, Lord? Why are those who work in difficult places struggling?"

I can think of some answers to these questions, of course. It is good to struggle. Struggle builds character, just like tribulation builds patience—that sort of thing. But those answers are not always satisfactory.

The real answer from our side of things is that really there is often no answer, at least none that we can comprehend. God's ways are just not our ways. We just do not know what God is doing. Someday we will know, I think, though it might take us an eternity to find out. We might have to ask God questions one after the other for perhaps one thousand or two thousand years until we get it sorted out. But now we cannot understand it.

When Philip was given this call, he did not know what God was going to do with him. I am sure it did not make sense to him to leave what he was doing and go to the desert near Gaza. But that is what God had told him to do; so he did it. Whenever it comes to a choice between our way of thinking and what God says, you know as well as I do that there is no real choice. We must do what God says. If you read the Bible and what you read does not seem to make sense to you but you understand what it is telling you to do, well, you had better do it. That is the only way you or anybody else will find blessing.

A Chapter in a Very Ancient Story

On the road to Gaza Philip came upon an Ethiopian eunuch. He was part of a history that might have gone back one thousand years. Ethiopia is a name that in ancient times was given to a large area of Africa south of Egypt. Today that land is more limited; it is a smaller country to the southeast of Egypt. But in that day it referred to the whole region of the upper Nile, approximately from Aswan to Khartoum.

It is the area from which the Queen of Sheba came in the days of King Solomon. In other words, there had already been a link between that area of the world and Judaism. The Queen of Sheba had been greatly impressed by King Solomon, and Solomon had certainly shared the Scriptures of the Jews with her. Who is to say what may have happened? Over those hundreds of years, who knows what remnant of the true religion may have survived in far-off Ethiopia? We do not have that kind of a history of Ethiopia. But here, in the time of the early church, there was an Ethiopian who for some reason had gotten the idea that in Jerusalem, hundreds of miles away, there was a religion that he should investigate if he was serious about finding God. Perhaps it was something he heard, some tradition that had been passed down to him.

So he made the long, long trip to Jerusalem. Another man would not have been able to do it. It was hard to travel in those days, and this was a very long and costly journey. If he had been even a minor official in the court of Candace, he would not have been free to make the journey. But he was an important man, the keeper of the treasury of what was acknowledged by all to be a very rich country. He was free to go because of his position.

There is nothing in the story to indicate that he heard anything about Jesus, though it is hard to think that he could be in Jerusalem in those days and get no wind of what was going on. But he was not Hebrew-speaking. He did not know Aramaic. Probably he knew Greek, and it was probably from the Greek Old Testament (the Septuagint) that he was reading. Those who study textual matters closely say the way Isaiah 53 is quoted is a clue that this was a Greek Old Testament and not Hebrew.

Because the Ethiopian probably did not know Hebrew or Aramaic and because he had been in Jerusalem for what was perhaps a relatively short time, it is possible that he really had not heard about Jesus. But he had certainly entered into the religious life of the Jews. If he was a religious man, as he obviously was, he would have fallen into the category of those the Jews called "God-fearers." These were people who had not become Jews by circumcision. They could not participate in the formal rites of Judaism. But they could attend the synagogues and discuss religion with the rabbis. This man was a God-fearer; he had reverence for the traditions of Israel. So there was a special place for him. He would have been welcome.

Yet I wonder what he found in the religious life of Judaism in those days. We know what Jesus found and what the early apostles were finding. The religious leaders of the nation had great traditions; they had the Old Testament; but they had become hopelessly legalistic. They were more concerned with the jots and tittles of the law than with its spirit. So I suspect that this man from Ethiopia must have been badly disappointed as he confronted Judaism.

I suspect too that he found the religion of Israel to be political and disappointing for that reason. If the Pharisees were the party chiefly responsible for the keeping of the law, the Sadducees were the chief political figures. The high priests and his family were Sadducees. They were the ones who had access to the Romans.

It is not much different today. People go to churches hungering and thirsting after God, but instead of finding God they find people who are concerned about rules, or politically-minded people.

This man had not found God but he had found something. He had found the Scriptures, the religious books of Judaism. Now he was reading them. He was reading from Isaiah, which he had purchased in the city. And now, although he had not found much in the actual religion of the people, he was reading the Word of God.

Did he know how valuable the Word of God was? I do not know. Probably that was the very question he was asking, pondering whether this particular religious book, Isaiah, had been worth his long journey.

I imagine that he started at the beginning. He had probably read about Isaiah's call to the ministry: "In the year that King Uzziah died, I saw the Lord seated on a throne, high and exalted, and the train of his robe filled the temple" (Isa. 6:1). He would have read about the seraphim singing, "Holy, holy, holy is the LORD Almighty" (Isa. 6:3). I think if he had come to this chapter, he would have said to himself, Ah, that is what I long for. I want to know God, the holy God. I want a vision of the One for whom my soul is thirsting.

As he went on, did he read about the sins of the people and of the fact that sin bars the sinful one from God?

Did he read about God's holiness and his just judgments of human sin?

Did he read this great invitation?

> Come, all you who are thirsty,
> come to the waters . . .
> Come, buy wine and milk
> without money and without cost.
>
> Isaiah 55:1

If he had read all that, he must have understood something about himself and the people among whom he lived. He must have learned that although God invites us to come to him, we are nevertheless unable to approach him, being sinners.

Whatever the case, at this point of his journey he had come to Isaiah 53, and he was reading the words:

> He was led like a sheep to the slaughter,
> and as a lamb before the shearer is silent,
> so he did not open his mouth.
> In his humiliation he was deprived of justice.
> Who can speak of his descendants?
> For his life was taken from the earth.
>
> Acts 8:32–33 (see Isaiah 53:7–8)

He was puzzled. What is this speaking about? he wondered. Of whom is the prophet writing? Is he writing about himself?

This was the moment Philip saw the chariot and approached it. There are no accidents in the life of God's people. Philip came at precisely the right moment, the moment the Ethiopian had reached what most people regard as the very heart of this prophecy, which also means the heart of the Old Testament.

We are not given the whole conversation between the Ethiopian and Philip. But I imagine that Philip gave a friendly greeting and the man in the chariot gave a greeting back. In those days people generally read everything out loud, so Philip had already heard him reading from Isaiah. Philip asked, "Do you understand what you are reading?" (v. 30). It was a good question—inoffensive, yet a subtle but gracious offer to explain the passage if the Ethiopian official was interested in receiving one.

"How can I unless someone explains it to me?" the Ethiopian replied. He then invited Philip to sit beside him, and Philip began to expound the passage.

Some years ago there was a director for the work of Campus Crusade for Christ at the University of Pennsylvania who used to worship at Tenth Presbyterian Church. His name was Ron Blankley. I had been preaching on the genealogies of Jesus in Matthew and Luke, showing how they fit together, and I was showing how they proved that Jesus is not only the promised Messiah but also the only possible Messiah. Blankley had been in the service, and the following week as he was going through one of the student lounges, he noticed a young man reading a Bible. He remembered the Ethiopian reading his Bible. So he went to the student and asked Philip's question: "Do you understand what you are reading?"

The student said, "I'm reading the genealogies of Jesus. I'm trying to make them fit together. They seem to be different."

Blankley then sat down and explained them, using the points I had made the previous week. The young man became a Christian.

That is precisely what happened with the Ethiopian eunuch. He was reading the chapter that portrays Jesus as the suffering servant who came to be our Savior. These verses contain the principle of vicarious atonement. In fact, they are the strongest statement of this principle in the Old Testament. They show how Jesus "took up our infirmities and carried our sorrows" (Isa. 53:4). They show how he was "pierced for our transgressions" and "crushed for our iniquities" (v. 5). They showed how "we all, like sheep, have gone astray" but that "the LORD has laid on him the iniquity of us all" (v. 6). As he explained the meaning of these words to the Ethiopian, Philip told him about Jesus, who had fulfilled this prophecy precisely just a short while before.[1]

I like to think that it was as Philip got to the end and said that just before Jesus was taken into heaven, he told his disciples to go and make disciples of all nations, baptizing them in the name of the Father and of the Son and of the Holy Spirit that the Ethiopian must have exclaimed, "Look, here is water. Why shouldn't I be baptized?" (v. 36). So he was.

That Very Scripture

Just before the baptism there is a tremendous verse that says, "Then Philip began with that very passage of Scripture and told him the good news about Jesus." I wonder if you are able to do that—to start with a given passage and preach Jesus. Isaiah 53 is an easy one, of course. But how about the genealogies? How about Revelation? Or Genesis? Can you begin with those passages and preach the good news about Jesus?

It can be done, you know. It is because the Bible from beginning to end is about Jesus. You cannot explain Genesis 1:1 ("In the beginning God created the heavens and the earth") without explaining something about Jesus, because Jesus is God. He was active in this work of creation, and it is through him that the God of creation is made known to us. You cannot explain the end of Revelation either apart from Jesus. Revelation 22:20 says, "Yes, I am coming soon." Who is coming soon? The answer is Jesus. Philip knew his Bible. So he was ready when the Ethiopian asked for an explanation.

I am glad Philip didn't get hung up on some church procedure about baptism. There are places where a request like that would be referred back through channels, lest something inappropriate or contrary to the "Book of Order" should be done. Philip could have said, "It's important to be baptized, but you have to do it in the right way, and this is an unusual case. I think I had better get back to the apostles in Jerusalem to find out what I should do." Instead he said, "Well, of course, of course." So there in the desert in the presence of the treasurer's entourage, which of course did not have any idea what was going on, this high-ranking official of the Court of Candace, the queen of the Ethiopians, was baptized. He came to God not as the treasurer of the Ethiopians, as an important man, but as a sinner availing himself of the blood of Jesus Christ, who had died in his place.

The text says he "went on his way rejoicing."

Philip went on his way rejoicing, too, and he had a great career after this. He went up the coast to the north. He preached in many cities, Azotus for one. Eventually he arrived in Caesarea, where he settled down and had a family. Acts 21:8 says that Luke and Paul stayed with Philip when they arrived in Caesarea from Macedonia, on the way to Jerusalem, and by this time Philip had four unmarried daughters who were prophetesses (v. 9).

John Stott calls attention to the differences between the two samples we know of Philip's evangelism. In the first case, he spoke to people of mixed race, part Jewish, part Gentile. In the second case, he evangelized a pure-blooded Ethiopian who was wealthy and of great influence. Two very different cases. But the message was one and the same message, because there is only one gospel of Jesus Christ.[2]

What happened to the Ethiopian? Can we fail to believe that God blessed him and his witness in his homeland? He did not have even a single Gospel—no Matthew, Mark, Luke, or John. He did not have Romans. These books were not yet written. But he had Jesus. He understood that Jesus had died in his place, and he was one of Christ's disciples. I am sure he spoke about Jesus to others and that a sound church grew up in his land.

17

The Conversion of Saul

Acts 9:1–19

Meanwhile, Saul was still breathing out murderous threats against the Lord's disciples. He went to the high priest and asked him for letters to the synagogues in Damascus, so that if he found any there who belonged to the Way, whether men or women, he might take them as prisoners to Jerusalem. As he neared Damascus on his journey, suddenly a light from heaven flashed around him. He fell to the ground and heard a voice say to him, "Saul, Saul, why do you persecute me?"

"Who are you, Lord?" Saul asked.

"I am Jesus, whom you are persecuting," he replied.

Acts 9:1–5

The ninth chapter of Acts contains Luke's account of the conversion of his friend Saul. But the story is told twice more, once in chapter 22 and again in chapter 26. These later accounts are not mere summaries of Saul's conversion. They are full accounts, each with its own particular emphasis. It is significant in so short a book attempting to cover the expansion of Christianity from its small beginnings in Jerusalem to a religion that filled the whole empire that the tale of one man's conversion should be so greatly emphasized.

It is striking, but not surprising. For more than any other individual in these early years, Saul of Tarsus picked up the banner of the cross of Jesus

147

Christ and carried it throughout the Roman Empire. Obviously and rightly, Luke considered Saul's conversion to be a watershed event.

Lord Lyttleton and Gilbert West

In the eighteenth century there were two young men in England whose names were Lord Lyttleton and Gilbert West. They were unbelievers. In fact, they were strong in their unbelief. They were also both lawyers, with keen minds, and they thought they had good reasons for rejecting Christianity. One day in a conversation one of them said, "Christianity stands upon a very unstable foundation. There are only two things that actually support it: the alleged resurrection of Jesus Christ and the alleged conversion of Saul of Tarsus. If we can disprove those stories, which should be rather easy to do, Christianity will collapse like a house of cards."

Gilbert West said, "All right, then. I'll write a book on the alleged resurrection of Jesus Christ and disprove it."

Lord Lyttleton said, "If you write a book on the resurrection, I'll write on the alleged appearance of Jesus to the apostle Paul. You show why Jesus could not possibly have been raised from the dead, and I'll show that the apostle Paul could not have been converted as the Bible says he was—by a voice from heaven on the road to Damascus."

So they went off to write their books. Sometime later they met again, and one of them said to the other, "I'm afraid I have a confession to make. I have been looking into the evidence for this story, and I have begun to think that maybe there is something to it after all." The other said, "The same thing has happened to me. But let's keep on investigating these stories and see where we come out."

In the end, after they had done their investigations and had written their books, each had come out on exactly the opposite side he had been on when he began his investigation. Gilbert West had written *The Resurrection of Jesus Christ,* arguing that it is a fact of history. And Lord Lyttleton had written *The Conversion of St. Paul.*[1]

By treating the resurrection of Jesus Christ and the conversion of the apostle Paul as two great pillars of Christianity, these men were saying that if the apostle Paul was not converted as the ninth chapter of Acts says he was and as he himself declares in his own recorded testimonies both before the Jews and the Gentiles, then Christianity loses one of its two most important bulwarks. Moreover, it loses its most able theologian and is considerably weakened.

Was Paul converted as the Bible says he was? One important factor in the answer is the account we are to study now.

Saul's Past in Judaism

We have already met Saul at the beginning of Acts 8. What can we say about this man? One thing is that he had received a remarkable education.

Sometimes when I am talking to young people who are thinking about Christian work and are wondering whether taking time to get an education is worthwhile, I ask them, "Who was the man who was most used of God in the Old Testament?" The answer to that question is obviously Moses. So I say, "Did he have an education or not?" The answer is that he did.

"What kind of an education did he have?" He had the best education that it was possible to get in his day, and it was a secular education. True, he had been trained along spiritual lines in his home; he knew the Lord. When the time came in his life when he was confronted with a choice between the pleasures, wisdom, prestige, and power of Egypt and God's people, he chose to identify with the people of God, even though that was obviously going to involve great self-denial and suffering (Heb. 11:24–28). He was a spiritual man, but his formal education was nevertheless secular. Stephen, as recorded in the last chapter, said that he was "educated in all of the wisdom of the Egyptians" (Acts 7:22).

Then I ask, "Who was the man most used of God in the New Testament, apart from Jesus Christ?" The answer undoubtedly is the apostle Paul. "How was he educated?" The answer is that he had the best possible education a person in his time could have. "What kind of an education was it?" It also was a secular education—overtly secular in his home town of Tarsus, but also secular in Jerusalem. In Jerusalem Saul received what in that day would have been called a religious education. He had studied under Gamaliel. This was like going to Harvard University and registering in the religion department. It was a thorough study of religion, and Paul did learn the traditions of Israel. But it was not a truly spiritual education. Paul's heart was not yet touched by God.

What would Paul have thought of Christianity before he met Jesus? He would have thought that it was wrong, of course. That is clear enough. He was a monotheistic Jew. Christians were claiming that Jesus was God. He would have regarded that as polytheism. If Jesus is God and if Jehovah is God, there must be two gods at least. Christianity would have been incompatible with Judaism.

But there would have been more to his rejection of Christianity than this. Not only would Paul have considered Christianity wrong, he would have considered it deceptive. This is because it made such great claims. It claimed not only that Jesus was the Son of God, but that he also had proved this by his resurrection from the dead. If Christianity was wrong, as Paul believed it was, then Jesus had not risen from the dead and was not God. Those who were going about saying that he had been raised from the dead and therefore was God were obviously and consciously trying to deceive the Jewish community.

Frank Morison, who wrote the classic book, *Who Moved the Stone?* emphasizes that the early Christians were preaching the resurrection in the very city in which the tomb was located.[2] It had been discovered by the priests, as well as by the early Christians, to have been empty. If the enemies of the gospel had been able to produce the body of Jesus Christ in those days, they would have done it, because nothing would have destroyed Christianity as quickly or as thoroughly as that. That they could not produce the body was a great embarrassment to them. Nevertheless, they tried to explain it. The traditional explanation is the one reflected at the end of Matthew's Gospel, namely, that the disciples came and stole the body (Matt. 28:11–15).

That is what Saul must have thought. So it was not just a matter of Christianity being wrong. Rather, Christianity was a damnable deceit. It was leading people away from the truth.

If Saul needed justification for his fierce actions, he could have found it easily in the Old Testament. There is the story of Phineas, for example. Phineas killed an immoral man and woman with a spear, and God honored the action by halting a plague. Phineas is praised by God. Saul was trying to stop a plague of "false" religion.

Therefore, having helped in the persecution of Christians in Jerusalem and hearing that the sect of the Nazarenes, which in this story is now called "the Way," had begun to spread and was taking roots in Damascus, he turned his persecution in that direction. It was on his way that God converted him.

God's Preparation of Saul

In the version of the story found in Acts 26, the Lord is quoted as having said to Saul, "It is hard for you to kick against the goads" (v. 14). This means that Saul was bothered in his conscience. Why, if he was convinced he was doing what was right? What was his state of mind? The explanation must come from his exposure to Stephen at the time of Stephen's death.

In the trial and martyrdom of Stephen, perhaps for the first time in his life, Saul must actually have come face to face with a true and articulate Christian. What an impression it must have made on him! Saul was educated; so was Stephen. Stephen may not have had the equal of Saul's superb education—at least technically—but when Stephen gave his testimony before the Sanhedrin, he demonstrated a knowledge of the Scriptures that was at least equal to that of his chief persecutor. Moreover, he displayed it effortlessly. It was a natural part of him. Stephen also made his points clearly. Could Saul have given an address that powerful?

I think, too, that he must have been impressed with Stephen's final words. As Stephen died, he looked to heaven and said, "I see heaven open and the Son of Man [Jesus] standing at the right hand of God" (Acts 7:56).

Could Stephen have been lying? In those circumstances? At that moment, the moment of his death, when he was to appear before the great Judge of all? Is it possible to think that a man in circumstances like those would cling to such an evil deception? If this was a deception, it was a deception of a most remarkable order. And Saul, having the mind he had, must have been impressed with it.

There was also the way in which Stephen died. As he died, he repeated the words of his Master: "Lord Jesus, receive my spirit" and "Lord, do not hold this sin against them" (Acts 7:59–60). I suspect that Saul asked himself whether he could have died like that. Was his faith as strong as Stephen's? Could he die with peace of mind and heart? Did he have a moral character that could ask forgiveness for his murderers at the moment when he was being killed?

Prejudices die hard, however. Although Saul may have been kicking against the goads, he was nevertheless still kicking against them. It was while he was in that frame of mind that Jesus met him.

The Spread of Christianity

Saul was concerned that the religion called the Way was spreading. It had started in Jerusalem; he was doing everything he could to stamp it out there. But he heard rumors that the faith was taking root in Damascus, a Gentile city in Syria. We have been reading how the gospel spread to Samaria. Now it had gone even beyond that. It had spread the whole way to Damascus, 120 miles to the north—this in spite of Saul's persecution.

But there is an irony. In the chapter immediately before this we have been told about Philip and the Ethiopian and how the gospel was spreading to the south. Saul was concerned that the gospel was spreading north. But while he was on his way north, God picked up Philip from Samaria and leap-frogged him over Saul, sending him down the Gaza road in the direction of Ethiopia. Saul was trying to stamp out Christianity in one direction, while God was advancing it rapidly in the other.

On the way to Damascus, the Lord stopped Saul in his tracks. There was a bright light from heaven, and a voice.

"Who are you, Lord?" Saul said.

"I am Jesus, whom you are persecuting," came the reply. "Now get up and go into the city, and you will be told what you must do" (Acts 9:5–6).

What a thunderbolt in Saul's intellectual sky! Saul was so sure of himself. True, he had been resisting the goadings of God concerning Stephen. Nevertheless, he believed that the Christians were wrong. Suddenly, in this remote place—as barren as the area in which the Ethiopian was traveling, without a Christian anywhere around—there was a light from heaven, God spoke, and God was Jesus.

What an utterly revolutionary event!

Unless Saul was hallucinating, the appearance of Jesus proved that Jesus was alive and that Jesus was God. This was a theophany. This was not like merely meeting a man walking along the road. This was a voice from heaven. Moreover, this Jesus who was God was identifying himself with the very people Saul was persecuting.

Saul was blinded as a result of the bright light. So they led him into the city, and while he was in the city, praying, God sent a Christian leader named Ananias to him. God told Ananias, "Go to the house of Judas on Straight Street and ask for a man from Tarsus named Saul, for he is praying. In a vision he has seen a man named Ananias come and place his hands on him to restore his sight" (Acts 9:11–12).

Ananias knew who Saul was. He answered, "I have heard many reports about this man and all the harm he has done to your saints in Jerusalem. And he has come here with authority from the chief priests to arrest all who call on your name" (vv. 13–14).

The Lord told him, "This man is my chosen instrument to carry my name before the Gentiles and their kings and before the people of Israel. I will show him how much he must suffer for my name" (vv. 15–16).

Verse 17 says simply, "Ananias went to the house and entered it." When God spoke to him, Ananias was strong enough to believe God and do what he said, trusting God for the consequences. He might have said, "Oh no, Lord, you're mistaken. I know you have been able to convert many people, but you have not converted Saul. If ever there was an inconvertible enemy, it is Saul." But Ananias did not say that. If God said Saul was converted, Ananias was willing to believe it. So he went.

I wonder if your faith is as strong as the faith of this great man of Damascus. Many of us pray for people. Sometimes it is for a son or a daughter, sometimes a parent, sometimes a friend, sometimes a wife or husband. We ask God to change his or her life and save the person. But often we really do not think God can do it. We pray, but we mutter beneath the surface of our prayers, "I know you saved others, but I really don't believe that you can save my wife or husband or son or daughter."

We should be greatly encouraged by the fact that God saved Saul. God turned this great persecutor of the early Christians into the first great missionary. He took the man who had been doing most to harm the church and turned him into the man who did most to build it up. If God could do that with Saul, God can do the same thing today. If you have a son or daughter whom you are worried about, a child who is off somewhere not serving the Lord, or a husband or wife who is unconverted, keep praying for him or her. God can (and frequently does) do something remarkable.

What Are the Options?

Let me return to Lord Lyttleton. As he wrestled with the account of Saul's conversion, Lyttleton concluded that there are only certain ways a person can honestly think about this story. If it did not happen the way it is described in Acts, then Paul must have been: (1) an imposter, (2) an enthusiast (that is, one who got carried away with himself, one who was virtually out of his mind), or (3) deceived by others. In his very systematic legal way and with relentless logic, Lyttleton examined each of these options.

Was Paul an Imposter?

Luke was Paul's friend; he undoubtedly got the story from Paul directly. That should count for something. But maybe it was just a big put on. Perhaps

Paul was pretending something happened, but it never really happened. Paul knew the truth, but he fooled his friend Luke as well as many others.

If that is the case, we have to ask what could have possibly been Paul's motivation. If Paul had gone to such lengths as to invent this story and then try to persuade others of its truthfulness, why would he do it? Some might do something like this to try to get ahead in life. It might be a way of impressing people and making a mark for oneself. People sometimes do that in religious circles today. They pretend a faith they do not have because they think it is a good thing to be a member of a church and be highly thought of. Others want to be popular as an evangelist or some other type of religious leader. So they invent impressive stories of how God spoke to them or called them to some ministry.

But, said Lyttleton, that was hardly the case with Paul. Paul had a bright future, and that bright future was not with the persecuted Christians. He had been doing very well in Judaism. He was a Pharisee of the Pharisees. If anybody was going to make a name for himself in Judaism, it was Paul. Paul could not have invented the story to get ahead. In fact, the opposite happened. Humanly speaking, he got behind rather than ahead. He gave up everything and suffered many things as a consequence of having thrown in his lot with the Christians.

Lyttleton also pointed out that people will sometimes claim a special revelation from God to excuse some sinful behavior, some sin they want to commit. They'll say, "God told me to do it. I had a vision, and God said, 'Do it.' So what I want to do is all right." Did Saul do that? Did he live a sinful life? Did he use the story of Jesus' appearance to him merely to indulge himself in some wickedness? The answer is quite the contrary. He lived an upright, selfless, morally exemplary life. A desire for sin does not explain Saul's motivation.

Was Paul an Enthusiast?

In the nineteenth century "enthusiast" meant one who was virtually out of his mind, an "off the wall" fanatic. Does that explain Paul? Was that the kind of mind Paul had? Did he have a mind or personality naturally given to fantasies? We have to remember that Saul was not a Sadducee, who did not believe in the resurrection, but a Pharisee, who did. Moreover, he was one who had heard stories of Jesus' resurrection but did not regard them as valid. This is not a picture of an enthusiast. It is the picture of a man who says, "I know that the Bible teaches that there will be a resurrection at the end of time, and I believe the Bible. But I have lived a long time, and although there may be a resurrection someday, it is for the future. Right now dead people do not rise. If the Christians are saying that Jesus rose from the dead, they must be trying to deceive people." This is exactly the opposite of a person who is religiously unbalanced, which is what this explanation demands.

Was Paul Deceived by Others?

This is the third possibility. But we then have to ask, Who would have deceived him? It would have had to have been the Christians. Could they even have thought of the possibility of inventing something to deceive their great enemy? Hardly! They were trying to stay as far away from him as they could. They weren't capable of such a deception. Even if they were, how could they have carried it off? A bright light from heaven? A voice that Saul believed to be the voice of God?

What is the conclusion? Obviously, if each of these other explanations has to be discarded, the only remaining possibility is that the story is true: that there was a genuine appearance of Jesus to Saul followed by an authentic conversion.

Here is how Lyttleton puts it:

> I shall then take it for granted that he was not deceived by the fraud of others, and that what he said of himself cannot be imputed to the power of that deceit, no more than to wilful imposture or to enthusiasm. . . . It follows that what he related to have been the cause of his conversion and to have happened in consequence of it, did all really happen, and therefore the Christian religion is a divine revelation. . . . It must be . . . accounted for by the power of God. That God should work miracles for the establishment of a most holy religion, which, from the insuperable difficulties that stood in the way of it, could not have established itself without such an assistance, is no way repugnant to human reason. But that without any miracle such things should have happened as no adequate natural causes can be assigned for, is what human reason cannot believe.[3]

Lyttleton's arguments are still valid. He was converted by the truth, and so are people today. There are non-genuine, spurious conversions. They pass away. But all true conversion is a result of the work of this same Jesus Christ who knows his sheep, "calls [them] by name and leads them out" (John 10:3). Christianity does not rest on a foundation of sand. It rests on the work of God, as is demonstrated in the conversion of Saul.

18

Saul's First Preaching

Acts 9:19–31

Saul spent several days with the disciples in Damascus. At once he began to preach in the synagogues that Jesus is the Son of God. All those who heard him were astonished and asked, "Isn't he the man who raised havoc in Jerusalem among those who call on this name? And hasn't he come here to take them as prisoners to the chief priests?" Yet Saul grew more and more powerful and baffled the Jews living in Damascus by proving that Jesus is the Christ.

Acts 9:19–22

It is sometimes helpful to compare parallel accounts of Bible stories. Parallel accounts are generally not quite identical, and the variations usually throw light on one another or on the meaning of the passage in which each occurs. That is the case with the stories of Paul's conversion. Luke makes different points in each one.

There is also different information in each. When we read Acts 9, we find Paul asking Jesus, "Who are you, Lord?" (v. 5). In response Jesus told him, "I am Jesus, whom you are persecuting. Now get up and go into the city, and you will be told what you must do" (vv. 5–6). However, when we read Acts 22, we find that Paul also asked a second question: "What shall I do, Lord?"

155

(Acts 22:10). This is an important addition to the story and a significant combination of ideas, because together the two questions form a sound basis for a strong Christian life.

Many people approach Christianity on the basis of the second question only. They want to know what to do. So they become great activists and rush about doing many good things. This is not necessarily true Christianity. On the other hand, others ask, "Who are you, Lord?" They are the speculative ones, the theologians. They love doctrine, but they are not very interested in practical matters. They do not want to know what to do; they want to know what to think. This is not necessarily a true form of Christianity either. We need both.

Christianity begins with the question, Who are you, Lord? That is because the deity of Jesus Christ is the foundation for everything that follows. Without that foundation we rush around doing things that appeal to us, things that seem good, but are not necessarily the Lord's plan for us. But having established that base, we also need to ask the second question: What shall I do? This is because God has appointed certain good works to be done by every Christian (Eph. 2:10).

Paul got it right from the very beginning. He began with the question, "Who are you, Lord?" But then he submitted himself to this one who was the Lord and asked quite properly, "What will you have me do?"

The Early Preaching

We get the impression from the verses that describe Paul's early ministry in Acts 9 that the events recorded happened very quickly. Luke uses phrases like "several days" (v. 19) and "after many days had gone by" (v. 23). That sounds like maybe a week or two. But we learn when we read what Paul says in Galatians that it was actually a three-year period. Sometime during this period, Paul went into Arabia and returned to Damascus. Then after he had returned to Damascus, three years now having passed either in Damascus or in Arabia, he went to Jerusalem. These time details teach that even the apostle Paul needed significant time for preparation.

This need for preparation does not mean that Paul was not ready to speak for Jesus, however. We are told in this section that as soon as he was converted and had received his sight again, "At once he began to preach in the synagogues that Jesus is the Son of God" (v. 20).

Sometimes when people are talking about their conversion, they say things like, "Well, I'm converted, but I want to be inconspicuous about it. I want to be a silent Christian." I doubt if that is possible, though I suppose there are people who are naturally shy and afraid to speak up for that reason or another. Other people no doubt have a difficult time speaking for Christ because of circumstances—pressure from their parents or friends, a hostile government, or whatever. But although it is often hard, at some point early in the life of a person who has come to believe on Jesus Christ there must be a verbalized expression of that faith. If there is not, it is doubtful whether the new life of Jesus Christ is really there.

The new birth is a lot like physical birth, and physical birth is used in the Bible as an illustration of what the new birth is like. What happens in physical birth? First of all, new life is created within the womb of the mother. There is a combination of the sperm and the egg. Until that happens there is no life, but once that union takes place, life begins to grow. It grows for nine months. Then the moment of birth comes, the baby cries, and everyone is pleased with the cry because it is a sign of a healthy baby.

It is the same spiritually. The sperm is compared in Scripture to the Word of God (1 Peter 1:23). It meets with the ovum of saving faith in the heart of the one God is saving, and a new life comes into being. It is a very small thing at the beginning; often we do not even know it is there. But it begins to grow, and the time finally comes when the spiritual birth takes place. Someone is holding a meeting. A person gives an altar call and says to the people, "If you'll receive Jesus Christ as your Savior, I want you to put up your hand and come forward." This individual does, and someone says, "Oh, he or she has been born again." But actually, the new birth had already taken place. The Word had been sown. It had been received by faith. The new life had begun to grow. The putting up of the hand is only the proof that the person has been made spiritually alive.

If a baby is born and the baby doesn't cry, something is wrong. So also in spiritual terms. When a person is born again, there has to come somewhere at the beginning that moment when he or she verbalizes what has happened. When the person does, those who are looking on and have understanding in such things say, "Well, that's wonderful. That proves that the Holy Spirit has really brought the person into new life."

This is what happened to Paul. Paul was a very bright man, and he had a great deal of understanding. True, he was still young in the faith; he needed time to learn. That is one reason why he went into Arabia and spent three years there. That was his seminary training. Nevertheless, although he had a great deal to learn and although the chief work of his life was still many years ahead, he verbalized his faith and began his first preaching by declaring rightly that "Jesus is the Son of God" (Acts 9:20) and "Jesus is the Christ" (v. 22). Thus, from the very beginning, Paul became a preacher.

The Essential Message

If you had said to Paul at this stage, "Paul, we want you to write down a theological statement of what you understand about the Christian faith," this is what Paul would have written down: (1) Jesus is the Son of God, and (2) Jesus is the Christ.

I do not know how much he understood about this basic creed at that time, but I think he probably understood a great deal since it says in verse 21, "All those who heard him were astonished," and in verse 22, "Saul . . . baffled the

Jews living in Damascus by proving that Jesus is the Christ." They would not have been astonished or baffled just by his saying, "Jesus is the Son of God" or "Jesus is the Christ." It was because he could explain what he meant and why he believed it. Later on, we find that the Grecian Jews were impressed with him because he argued theology with them—undoubtedly on the basis of the Old Testament.

Jesus Is the Son of God

We have had a form of liberal theology in recent history in which the term "Son of God" has been changed to mean merely that everyone is made in God's image, that is, that we are all sons of God and daughters of God. With this definition there have been liberal theologians who are quite willing to admit that Jesus is the Son of God. "Of course, he is the Son of God," they say. "Everybody is a son or daughter of God." But that is not what this term meant on the lips of Jesus Christ. Nor is that what it meant to Paul. The proof is that Paul was persecuted for his profession. Why would he be persecuted for saying this if all he meant by the words "Son of God" is that Jesus was another human being?

Knowledge of spiritual things is based upon the identity of Jesus Christ as God. Why? Because if Jesus is the Son of God, then Jesus is God. God does not err; if Jesus is God, Jesus does not err. Everything Jesus tells us can be trusted. If he tells us God is a certain kind of God, we can believe it because he is God himself and speaks truthfully. If he tells us, as he does, that the Bible can be trusted, that it comes from God, that heaven and earth will pass away but the Word of God being divine in nature will never pass away, then we can trust the Bible. In a sense, nearly everything we know of spiritual things is based on the confession: "Jesus is the Son of God."

Our salvation is also based upon it, because the value of Jesus' death is linked to his being God. If Jesus were a mere man, even if he were a sinless man, his death could only have availed for himself. It could not have been of infinite worth. Besides, if he were nothing but a man, he would be sinful, as other human beings are, and his death would be no different from the death of any other human being. But Jesus is not merely man. He is a man; he had to be a man to die. He had to take on human flesh. At the same time, being God as well as man, he died as God and thus accomplished what God alone could accomplish.

Jesus Is the Christ

Paul also preached that Jesus is the Christ (v. 22). The word "Christ" is the same as the word "Messiah" (Christ is the Greek word; Messiah is the Hebrew word), and both mean "anointed." When they refer to a specific individual they mean "the Anointed One," that is, the one promised in the Old Testament as the ultimate fulfillment of God's promises. Therefore, when Paul began to prove from the Scriptures that Jesus is the Christ, he must have gone back to these Old Testament promises to show that Jesus was the one God had promised. He was the one who was going to redeem (and who had now redeemed) his people.

At one time, Paul's idea of the Messiah would have been the same as that of the majority of the Jewish people of his day. They thought the Messiah was going to be a political figure who would rally the nation and drive out the Romans. They thought he would reestablish an earthly throne of David.

Jesus had not done that, of course. So Paul must have gone back to the Old Testament and asked himself, "If the Messiah was not one whose primary function was to drive out the Romans, what was he to do?" I think at that point—though I admit that I am speculating somewhat here—Paul probably reflected on the word "anointed" and asked, "Who in the Old Testament was anointed for a specific function?" The answer was prophets, priests, and kings. The people had been thinking in terms of a political king, but Paul must have realized that Jesus came to fulfill a prophetic and priestly function too.

Jesus must be a prophet, the last and greatest of the prophets. We do not know whether Paul wrote Hebrews, because the authorship of that book is uncertain; he was certainly capable of having written it. Hebrews says, "In the past God spoke to our forefathers through the prophets at many times and in various ways, but in these last days he has spoken to us by his Son" (Heb. 1:1–2). As he reflected on the Old Testament, Paul would have been able to say that since Jesus is the Christ, he is a final word from God to us. He is the one from whom we are to learn what God is like.

Then Paul must have reflected on the fact that the priests were anointed as well, and he must have concluded, If Jesus is the anointed one, then he must also be God's great priest. He must be the one who was to offer himself as the only truly adequate sacrifice for human sin. He offered himself once as the perfect sacrifice forever (Heb. 5–10).

Jesus was also a king. David was the greatest of the kings, but he grew old and died, and his throne was taken by another. Jesus rose from the dead to live and reign forever. When Paul got around to thinking about that, he must have reflected on his encounter with Jesus on the road and on how Jesus said to him, "Now get up and go into the city, and you will be told what you must do." It meant that Paul was now no longer his own master but the rightful servant of the true King of Israel and the Lord of Lords. This King, Paul's Master, was sending him to the Gentiles.

The Inevitable Persecution

In these verses we also find the beginning of something else Jesus spoke of: Paul's sufferings for Jesus' sake. He had his first taste of this from the Jews of Damascus. It is a dramatic story. When Paul had returned from his time in Arabia, "the Jews conspired to kill him" (v. 23). He needed to leave the city, but his enemies were keeping a twenty-four-hour watch on the gates and a normal exit was impossible. Fortunately, the disciples in Damascus were resourceful. They knew of a place where there was an opening in the wall. They put Paul in a basket and lowered him down. In this way he escaped by night and so foiled this first plot against his life.

It was the beginning of many escapes for Paul, and sometimes he didn't quite escape. Sometimes they caught him, imprisoned him, beat him. He did indeed have to suffer many things for Jesus' sake (v. 16).

This chapter of Acts also gives us a glimpse into another kind of suffering, not the outright persecution Paul frequently suffered from overt enemies of Christ, from those who would have killed him if they could, but suffering that came from the suspicions of the early Christians.

I imagine that this hurt Paul more than anything. He came to Jerusalem, where he had started out some years before and, as it says in verse 26, "tried to join the disciples, but they were all afraid of him, not believing that he really was a disciple."

We can hardly blame them, though perhaps we should. God is the God of the unexpected. He saves the most unlikely people. If he did not, why would we be Christians? Still, we find it hard to think like this, especially when some great enemy is involved. Saul had been an enemy. So the Christians found themselves saying, Well, it is true that God saved us—and no doubt we were all difficult cases—but how could he possibly save a person like Saul? Saul is an outright enemy. God might kill somebody like Saul, strike him down (it would serve him right), but not save him. It must be a trick.

One of the most delightful things about the Christian life is getting to know the kind of people God saves, because they are generally not the kind you would expect. It is impossible to figure out what God is going to do, because God does not have to do what we expect and usually doesn't.

Here are some examples.

When I was in seminary, one of the people who was talked about a lot was the late Episcopal Bishop James Pike. He had made a name for himself by his denials of basic Christian doctrines. He denied the virgin birth and the resurrection. He was even brought up on what almost amounted to a heresy trial, and to be charged with heresy in the Episcopal Church in those days required some doing. Pike had a terribly messed up theology. He had a messed up life also. He got into the occult. One of his sons had committed suicide, so he tried to contact him through a Philadelphia medium named Arthur Ford. This event was widely publicized. Then he went to Israel to research a book on the historical Jesus, which he said was going to be the most shocking thing that he had done yet. While he was there investigating the countryside for the background for this book, he got lost in the desert and died.

A person might look at that as I did in those days and say, "Can anything good come out of such a life?" It is hard to see anything good in it. Pike seemed to have left only rubble behind him. But Pike had another son whose name was Christopher. In 1967, when Christopher was about sixteen years old, he got into the drug culture and drifted out to California. He was at the University of California at Berkeley, where many wild things were going on in those days. He seemed to be on the same path his brother had been on. But while he was there, he heard a converted hippie testifying about Jesus Christ on the steps of Sproul Hall. He found himself wondering whether Christianity could perhaps actually be true. He went into seclusion and began to read the New Testament. He had never actually read it before. As he began to read it, he found the very truths that his father had rejected and denied. He found the real Jesus. He was converted and became active in Christian work. Unusual? Yes, but not for God.[1]

In more recent times we have Madalyn Murray O'Hair, the well-known atheist, who got prayer and Bible reading out of the public schools through a court case. Not long ago, her son, who was raised on her particularly angry form of atheism, found Jesus Christ as his Savior and wrote a book about it, confessing the errors of his early days.

I think of Chuck Colson, a shrewd but ruthless politician. He was part of Richard Nixon's White House staff and was so committed to Nixon that he said he would walk over the body of his grandmother if it would mean getting his boss reelected. Colson spent time in prison as a consequence of his part in Watergate. Yet God reached and transformed him, and he is now working in the prisons of the world to help those who, like himself, have been prisoners. His testimony is that when he was successful, his success accomplished nothing. It was in his great humiliation, when he was actually sent to jail for his Watergate offenses, that God used him.[2]

That was what God was doing with Saul, the great persecutor. But the Christians in Jerusalem didn't understand it and were afraid of him.

There was one person who was not. His name was Barnabas, the "Son of Encouragement." Barnabas has already been introduced to us as a Levite from Cyprus who sold his property and gave the proceeds to the early church (Acts 4:36–37). Later we will see him traveling with Paul on his first missionary journey (Acts 13–14). In this chapter we see him seeking out Paul when everybody else was afraid of him, listening to him, recognizing that his testimony was genuine, and then bringing him to the apostles. Perhaps he said to them, "You are wrong about Paul. He was on a journey to Damascus, and Jesus revealed himself to him on the way. The man is changed." Barnabas brought Paul to the apostles, and Paul spent the next few days in Jerusalem with others who knew the Lord.

It was not a long time. Paul tells about it in Galatians, stressing how little contact he had with the Christian leaders. He wrote, "After three years, I went up to Jerusalem to get acquainted with Peter and stayed with him fifteen days. I saw none of the other apostles—only James, the Lord's brother" (Gal. 1:18–19).

I imagine Paul cherished this time, even though it was short. Later in his ministry, when he was on his own in hostile areas of the world, he must have thought of those days and rejoiced that God had made him one in spirit with those other apostles who were back in Jerusalem. What do you suppose he and Peter talked about during that momentous fortnight? Undoubtedly they talked about Jesus, about his teachings and miracles, above all about his death and resurrection. Peter would have instructed Paul in these things.

Eventually his enemies got after him in Jerusalem, too. He had tried to debate with the Hellenists, taking up the mantle left by Stephen. Probably Paul was trying to make up for his role in Stephen's death. But the religious leaders hated Paul even more than they had hated Stephen, and they tried to kill him. When the Christians learned of this, they took Paul to Caesarea and sent him to Tarsus.

John Stott notes the strange irony of this situation. "The story of Saul's conversion in Acts 9 begins with him leaving Jerusalem with an official mandate from the high priest to arrest fugitive Christians, and ends with him leaving Jerusalem as a fugitive Christian himself."[3]

Paul the Unknown

What happened then? We might suppose since Paul was now back in Gentile territory that he began his missionary activity at once. But as a matter of fact, he did not. Something like ten years passed before Paul finally emerged again at Antioch and was chosen by the Holy Spirit. At that point Barnabas and Paul became the first official missionaries of the Christian church, and Paul in particular became a model pioneer missionary.

Paul was not at all prominent up till then. In fact, Paul says in Galatians that he was "personally unknown to the churches of Judea" during those years (Gal. 1:22). I suppose they must have had some memory of him. They must have said, "Oh, yes, years ago there was a man who was very active in persecuting us. The rumor is that Jesus met him somewhere on the way to Damascus and that he was converted. We haven't heard anything about him for a long time. I wonder if he is still alive."

Paul the unknown!

That is what he was. What a title for the most influential man in the New Testament period, if not of all Western history. Yet during these "unknown" years, God was working in his life, teaching him and training him for future service. Paul was searching out the Scriptures to learn about the faith more thoroughly. The bottom line is that God's ways are not our ways. His timing is not ours. We need to learn to wait on him patiently.

We pray for people. Nothing seems to be happening. But that does not mean that nothing is happening; it only means that we cannot see it. God is working. In fact, one of the joys of getting older in the Christian life is that you begin to see some of the things God is doing. Problems we prayed about earlier are being resolved. People whom we might have given up on early in life we now see changed. So do not give up. Keep your eyes on the Lord.

19

In the Steps
and Power of the Lord

Acts 9:32–43

In Joppa there was a disciple named Tabitha (which, when translated, is Dorcas), who was always doing good and helping the poor. About that time she became sick and died, and her body was washed and placed in an upstairs room. Lydda was near Joppa; so when the disciples heard that Peter was in Lydda, they sent two men to him and urged him, "Please come at once!"

Peter went with them, and when he arrived he was taken upstairs to the room. All the widows stood around him, crying and showing him the robes and other clothing that Dorcas had made while she was still with them.

Peter sent them all out of the room; then he got down on his knees and prayed. Turning toward the dead woman, he said, "Tabitha, get up." She opened her eyes, and seeing Peter she sat up. He took her by the hand and helped her to her feet. Then he called the believers and the widows and presented her to them alive. This became known all over Joppa, and many people believed in the Lord.

Acts 9:36–43

The last section of Acts 9 contains two new stories about Peter, but it is a bit surprising to find stories about Peter here. We have just had the story of Paul's conversion, and we might have expected the continuation of Paul's story. Instead, we do not have it until

163

Acts 13. What is going on in this portion of the book? When we analyze Acts, we find that the first twelve chapters are mostly about Peter. Beginning with chapter 13, Paul becomes the central figure. What we have in chapters 9–12 is a blending. As Peter recedes, Paul comes forward.

Yet, this is not just an overlapping. As Luke puts this material together, he shows that Peter, the great apostle to the Jews, and Paul, the great apostle to the Gentiles, were not teaching or doing two different things but were actually one in their doctrine and work.

One Lord, One Task

If you know the history of liberal scholarship in the last century, you will know that most German theologians made a distinction between what they called the primitive teaching of the Jewish community, centered in Peter, and the later, quite different teaching of the Gentile communities, centered in Paul. It was a form of the "historical dialectic" theory developed by the great philosopher Georg Wilhelm Friedrich Hegel. Hegel had taught that history flows from a dominant idea, which he called the thesis, to a contrary idea, which he called an antithesis, to a synthesis, which in turn becomes the new thesis. From there the process repeats itself indefinitely.

There is a certain thoroughness about the German mind, according to which any winning theory is at once applied to nearly everything, and this is what happened to Hegel's idea.

Another German professor, Ferdinand Christian Bauer, took Hegel's theory and used it to explain the early history of the church. The thesis was the primitive Jewish theology centered in Peter. This produced the antithesis of Paulinism, which became the dominant Gentile theology. Then there was a struggle—Bauer went to the chapters of Acts we are studying and to Galatians, which actually does record a disagreement between Peter and Paul—and the result was the synthesis of the early Catholic Church.

Unfortunately for Bauer, chapters 9–12 of Acts do not support this idea. Luke does not suggest even for a moment that Peter and Paul were going in different directions. On the contrary, he is showing that the two great apostles were actually of one mind and heart in their work.

One thing we notice is that although (in chapter 9) Jesus had called Paul to be the apostle to the Gentiles, in chapter 10 God also called Peter to this same ministry. That is, although Peter remains the chief apostle to the Jews, it is actually Peter, and not Paul, who opens the door of the gospel to the Gentiles. Together chapters 9 and 10 provide us with parallel accounts, two great breakthroughs, that launch the next great step in the church's worldwide expansion. The church had expanded from Jerusalem into the neighboring areas of Judea and Samaria. Now it is expanding to the Gentiles.

True, Philip had carried the gospel up and down the Mediterranean coast. But that was still a basically Jewish area. Here for the first time there is to be a breakthrough to the Gentile community.

There are other parallels, too. Each of these chapters involve two sets of individuals. In chapter 9 it is Paul and Ananias. Ananias is hesitant about going to talk to Paul. In chapter 10 it is Peter and Cornelius, and Peter is hesitant about going to talk to Cornelius.

Peter in Lydda and Joppa

Peter was doing what he should have been doing in these days, and it is to his credit. Many (probably most) of the apostles had remained in Jerusalem, I think wrongly. Jesus had sent them into all the world with the gospel, but they had gotten entrenched in Jerusalem. However, even if the others were wrong in this, Peter at least was not making that mistake. He was the chief apostle to the Jews. So he was going around visiting the various Jewish communities into which the gospel had spread. He had already been to Samaria examining the situation there. Now he was making his way to the coast, which is where Philip had been. This was fairly early in church history, but already there were churches there. We see this in the story, because it is not just an isolated individual here and there whom Peter visits but actual groups of believers. These knew one another, prayed for one another, were concerned about one another, and were working together. In his capacity as the apostle to the Jews, Peter was checking up on these communities.

The Healing of Aeneas

The first place Peter visited was Lydda, the Lod of the Old Testament (1 Chron. 8:12). Here there was a paralyzed man named Aeneas. He had been confined to bed for eight years. But Peter addressed him in the name of Jesus, crying, "Jesus Christ heals you. Get up and take care of your mat." The healing was an echo, perhaps consciously on Peter's part, of Jesus' healing of the paralytic man early in his ministry. Jesus had said, "I tell you, get up, take your mat and go home" (Mark 2:11).

The Raising of Dorcas

The second of these stories is told at greater length. It concerns bringing a woman named Dorcas back to life after she had died, and it takes place in the ancient city of Joppa, today's Jaffa.

Joppa was a Jewish community. That is why Peter had gone there. But when this woman died, we notice that they did not bury her right away. Why not? When Ananias and Sapphira died they were buried that very day. Why were Ananias and Sapphira buried at once but Dorcas was not? It is because there was a law in Jerusalem that a body was not allowed to remain around for a second day. It had to be buried at once. Beyond Jerusalem the normal period between death and burial was three days. This was Joppa's custom. So it was during these three days that those who knew and loved Dorcas sent for Peter, undoubtedly expecting him to do a miracle.

When Peter went to the room where they were weeping and crying, the women showed him the robes and other clothing that Dorcas had made while she was still alive. It was the women, those who did similar things, who were appreciative of Dorcas's good deeds.

Like the earlier story about Aeneas, there are also parallels in this story to things Jesus had done, in this case to two of the resurrections he had performed during his ministry. The obvious one is to John 11, which tells of the raising of Lazarus. Jesus, like Peter with Dorcas, was not present when his friend Lazarus died. His sisters had to send for him, and the resurrection took place after a considerable passage of time. This was Peter's situation too. As Peter was making his way to Joppa, where Dorcas had lived, he was probably wondering what God might accomplish on this occasion and probably also thinking of the time Jesus raised Lazarus.

When he got to Dorcas's house there were circumstances that probably reminded Peter of the other resurrection in which Jesus was involved. It is told in Mark 5 and concerns the raising of the daughter of Jairus. It too was in an upper room. The people there were also distressed and wailing. On that occasion, Jesus put them out so there would be quiet. Then he called to the girl—a young girl who was only twelve years old—"Little girl, I say to you, get up!" (v. 41).

When Peter saw the mourners and saw Dorcas lying in the upper room that story must have come immediately to his mind. So he followed in Jesus' steps. He asked the women to leave. Then he knelt and prayed. He must have prayed fervently. He was an apostle, of course. God had been doing miracles through him. Still it must have required a great deal of faith for Peter to get up from his knees, turn to the dead woman and say, "Tabitha, get up."

God's Unlikely Agent

What an unlikely person to be used in such a great way by Jesus Christ. Think of the major moments in Peter's life thus far.

Peter's Calling

Peter was a fisherman, and he had been fishing when Jesus first called him. Jesus saw him mending his nets and said to him, "Come, follow me." I suppose that it was in response to a rather quizzical look on Peter's face that Jesus then explained himself, saying, ". . . and I will make you fishers of men" (Matt. 4:19).

In Luke's Gospel there is a fuller account of that calling. In Matthew and Mark (Mark 1:17) we are told how he called Peter, saying, "Follow me." But in Luke there is an expanded account that tells how Jesus did a miracle in causing Peter to catch a great number of fish. Peter was astonished by the miracle. He realized that it was not the proper time of day for catching fish and that the number was unusually large. This was a revelation of the power and the glory of Jesus. So Peter, overcome by this great revelation, responded by saying, "Go away from me, Lord; I am a sinful man" (Luke 5:8). He meant, "Why are you calling me? You are the Holy One. I am just a fisherman, and a sinful one at that. I don't deserve to be your disciple." Peter spoke truly. But, of course, that is just what God uses—sinful men and women. If God did not use sinful men and sinful women, he could not use anybody. All of us are sinful.

It is not what we are or where we come from that is important. It is what God makes of us. So it was not Peter's background that mattered. It was what Jesus chose to do through Peter. Later, when Paul came to write about God's use of this procedure, he said:

> Brothers, think of what you were when you were called. Not many of you were wise by human standards; not many were influential; not many were of noble birth. But God chose the foolish things of the world to shame the wise; God chose the weak things of the world to shame the strong . . . and the things that are not—to nullify the things that are, so that no one may boast before him.
>
> 1 Corinthians 1:26–29

Peter's Great Confession

If we run through the major events of Peter's life, the next we come to is when Peter gave his confession of faith concerning Jesus Christ. Jesus had been teaching the disciples and had stopped to ask them who the people thought he was.

"Some say John the Baptist; others say Elijah; and still others, Jeremiah or one of the prophets," they said (Matt. 16:14).

"But what about you?" Jesus asked. "Who do you say that I am?" (v. 15).

This made the question very personal. The text does not say that there was a moment of silence at this point, but I suppose there must have been. Until Peter, who was always the first to speak—usually foolishly—said, "You are the Christ, the Son of the living God" (v. 16). It was so unusual for Peter to get something right that Jesus had to stop to point out that Peter was actually right this time and that the reason he was right was that God had given him a special revelation.

Unfortunately, Peter, who had just had this marvelous insight, instead of being humbled by it must have been saying to himself, Why, that's tremendous. And I want you to take notice of that, guys. The Holy Spirit spoke to me. I know who Jesus is. That is why when Jesus went on in the next breath to explain that he would have to go to Jerusalem to suffer and die and then rise again, Peter rebuked him, saying, "Never, Lord! This shall never happen to you" (v. 22).

This time Jesus had to rebuke him. He recognized that the one speaking through Peter now was not the Holy Spirit but Satan, trying to keep him from the cross.

What a day that was in Peter's life: One moment he was the vehicle of God's revelation, the next a vehicle for Satan. Yet that was Peter! And that is what we are like too. Or, to use another example, we are like Elijah. One moment we are up on the mountain, calling down fire from heaven. The next we are down in the valley, saying, "Lord, let me die." There are none stable but the Lord.

Peter's Denial

Later in his life Peter denied the Lord. Again Peter was feeling high on himself. It was the final week of Christ's earthly life. His enemies were gathered. Storm clouds were settling over Jerusalem. Everyone knew that it was dangerous for Jesus to be anywhere near Jerusalem. Yet Jesus proceeded as if everything was under control, which it was. Peter stepped forward, saying in effect, "I don't know if these other disciples can be counted on. You've said that everybody is going to abandon you, and they probably will. But there is one thing I want you to know, Jesus. I am going to stick with you to the end, even to death, if that's what's coming."

He really thought he was! When they came to arrest Jesus in the garden, it was Peter who pulled out a sword. He was ready to fight. They could have killed Peter at that moment because he was serious about not abandoning Jesus. In fact, when they arrested Jesus, Peter still tried to do the best thing he knew to do. He followed a long way off.

But it was while he was separated from Jesus, waiting in the courtyard of the high priest, that Peter denied his Lord. He was frightened when the servant girl recognized him as a follower of Jesus. The servants in the courtyard kept at him, and finally Peter denied his Lord three times, even with "curses" (Mark 14:66–72). That was Peter.

Peter wept when he realized what he had done, but he did not fall away. And the reason he did not fall away is that Jesus had prayed for him. Jesus told Peter, "Satan has asked to sift you as wheat. But I have prayed for you, Simon, that your faith may not fail" (Luke 22:31–32).

A farmer would put wheat on a threshing floor, run over it with something heavy to separate the wheat from the chaff, then throw it up in the air where the wind would blow the chaff away and allow the grain to settle down so it could then be gathered up. Jesus was telling Peter that Satan wanted to blow him away, believing that he was nothing but chaff. "If you give me a chance to blow on him, Peter will be gone," Satan might have said. Peter was chaff, of course, except for the grain Jesus had put in him. But because Jesus prayed for him, Peter was actually strengthened by his failure.

Peter's Race to the Empty Tomb

At the time of the resurrection, when most of the disciples were not even in Jerusalem, having scattered back over the Mount of Olives to Bethany where they had spent most of their time that week, Peter and John were in the city. So on Easter morning, when word came from the women that the tomb was empty, it was Peter and John who rushed to the tomb—John getting there first, but Peter rushing in and being the first to see fully that the tomb was empty.

Peter's Recommissioning

Then there was the moment when Jesus appeared to the disciples in Galilee. They had been told to go there, and they had. But Peter was restless. He had taken the others out fishing, and it was while he was fishing that Jesus appeared to them, calling from the shore. Peter had denied the Lord three times. Now Jesus used the occasion to recommission him three times. "Simon son of John, do you truly love me more than these?" he asked.

Peter answered, "Yes, Lord, you know that I love you."

Peter may have said many foolish things in his day and boasted of a strength he didn't have. But the one thing that was sublimely true of Peter is that he had come to love Jesus. If he loved him before, which he did, he certainly loved him even more now after the Lord's death and resurrection. Certainly the Lord knew that Peter loved him.

Still Jesus repeated his question: "Simon son of John, do you truly love me?" Peter said, "Yes, Lord, you know that I love you."

The Lord repeated it a third time: "Simon son of John, do you love me?" The text says Peter was "hurt" because Jesus had asked him the question not once but three times. He answered again, "Lord, you know all things; you know that I love you." Jesus said, as he had after each of Peter's three answers, "Feed my sheep," and later, "You must follow me" (John 21:15–22).

This is what Peter was doing in the chapter we are studying: He was following Jesus. He was doing exactly what Jesus had been doing, serving in the same way, preaching the same message, demonstrating the same character. The same Spirit was working in Peter as had worked in Jesus Christ.

Reflections on the Story

It was not very long into what we call "the Christian era," but already Christianity had spread south to Ethiopia, north to Samaria and Damascus, and now west to the coast of the Mediterranean. Moreover, Paul had gone back to Turkey and had undoubtedly begun to preach there.

Why was this happening? It was because the gospel spreads. It is like perfume. If you take the stopper out of a perfume bottle, the odor of the perfume soon spreads throughout the room. You can't stop it. The gospel is the sweet smell of true doctrine, a gospel centered in a gracious, loving God, who sent his Son to die for our salvation. A message like that just can't be bottled up. If that message is bottled up in you or your church, it is because you do not really understand it. You have not actually entered into it. These people had, and it was spreading. Here in Lydda and Joppa, there were Christians who were already worshiping and serving Jesus Christ.

The second point is how practical the Christian gospel is. Dorcas had been doing so many good deeds that many people were weeping and crying because they had lost her. She was valuable as a Christian and as a human being.

One thing preachers hear again and again is that they are always up in the clouds or that they have no contact with practical things. I would imagine that anybody who has ever been in the ministry has heard that dozens of times. But exactly the opposite is the case. A person can escape being practical in different areas or callings of life, but not in Christianity. Christianity has a gospel of salvation from sin, and flowing from that is a practical calling to help and serve other people. Yes, Christianity calls people to turn from sin and respond to Jesus Christ in saving faith. But if they have done that, it then calls them to serve others also.

Before the coming of Jesus Christ there were no hospitals in the world. If somebody got sick at home, there would have been family members to take care of them. There were doctors, but there were no hospitals. Nobody established institutions to take care of those who were ill, certainly not those who were poor and unable to pay for their treatment. But where Christianity came, the light of medicine followed and hospitals were founded everywhere.

Before Jesus Christ came there were no orphanages in the world. People did not care for children who had no parents. The world was too full of people already. Orphans did not even deserve to live. Letting them die was considered the best thing. Even worse, good Greek and Roman families would expose their own children to perish from the elements if they thought they had enough children. When a Roman baby was born, it was brought to the father. If he picked it up in his arms, that meant he was going to acknowledge it as his child and keep it. If he did not, they discarded it. That is the way the people of those days treated children. If by some means some rejected child should manage to grow up to a reasonable age, even then nobody would take the child in. He or she would just roam the streets. Generally, such children fell into male or female prostitution.

There were no leprosariums in the world before the coming of Jesus Christ. Everyone feared leprosy and fled at a leper's approach. There was no compassion or humanitarian care for those who were suffering as a result of this disease.

There were no disaster relief organizations in the world before the coming of Jesus Christ. You never in all of ancient literature read, for example, of the community in Rome getting together to take up an offering to send to the starving poor in Egypt. People thought about themselves. Yet at even this very early stage, when the Christians were for the most part quite poor themselves, you find the apostle Paul going around the Greek communities collecting money to send to the poor in Jerusalem because there had been a famine there. Christians felt a tie to one another and to other men and women because of a common humanity.

There were not even any great schools in the ancient world. There was education, of course. Plato and Aristotle had their academies. But there was nothing like common education. There was no concern for those who did not have means or were not from wealthy families. Christians brought that concern. It is Christians who have gone into the cities of the world and have hunted out the poor, the young, the sick, the uneducated, and have brought them into schools to train them and give them skills that enabled them to be something other than destiny would seem to have chosen for them.

This is just biblical religion. And here was Peter, a poor fisherman, doing exactly that.

Although Peter had followed in the steps and power of his Lord for many days, his journey was not over yet. In fact, in the very next chapter Peter is going to be sent to Cornelius, the Gentile, and by this means God is going to use him to open the door of the gospel to those who were not Jews. God was working in his life, but God had not finished working.

God is not finished with you either. It does not make any difference where you have come from or what you have learned or how far you have come or have not come in your Christian life and walk. If you are alive and know Jesus Christ as your Savior, God has not finished with you. You are to keep on learning, doing, serving, loving.

20

No Favorites with God

Acts 10:1-35

About noon the following day as they were on their journey and approaching the city, Peter went up on the roof to pray. He became hungry and wanted something to eat, and while the meal was being prepared, he fell into a trance. He saw heaven opened and something like a large sheet being let down to earth by its four corners. It contained all kinds of four-footed animals, as well as reptiles of the earth and birds of the air. Then a voice told him, "Get up, Peter. Kill and eat."

"Surely not, Lord!" Peter replied. "I have never eaten anything impure or unclean."

The voice spoke to him a second time, "Do not call anything impure that God has made clean."

Acts 10:9–15

Ｏne of the things Jesus told Peter when he made his great confession of faith in Jesus as the Christ was that he was going to give Peter the keys of the kingdom. Did this mean that Peter somehow had a right as the first of the apostles or, as he was later called by some sectors of the church, as the first pope, to say whether a man or a woman should be allowed into heaven? Or did it refer rather to a right given to all ministers to say on the basis of the Word of God that sin has been forgiven when it has been confessed to Christ and that it has not been forgiven when

172

it has not been confessed? The first of these interpretations is the Roman Catholic interpretation. The second, generally speaking, has been Protestant.

I would like to suggest another interpretation. It is that when Jesus gave the keys to Peter he appointed him to open the door of the gospel to two distinct bodies of people: Jews and Gentiles.

I suggest that Peter was given two keys. He used the first key to open the door of the gospel to the Jewish people at Pentecost, when he preached the first of all Christian sermons. He used the second key to open the door of the gospel to the Gentiles, when he preached before the Roman centurion Cornelius on the occasion recorded in Acts 10. Peter was the apostle to the Jews, so he preached to the Jews first. But although he was the apostle to the Jews, Peter was also the first to bring the gospel to a strictly Gentile audience.[1]

An Important Forward Movement

However we interpret the keys, it is evident that this event of bringing the gospel to Cornelius was very important.

A number of the incidents in this book are recorded more than once—that is, they are told once as a historical happening, and then they are repeated again and sometimes even a third time as those who were involved in the incidents tell others. It is a way Luke has of emphasizing something. This was true of the conversion of Paul, as we have already seen (see chapter 17).

The same thing is true of the story in Acts 10, only here the repetition is in the story itself. In one way or another it is told twice and perhaps even three times. First, the Lord gives Peter a vision meant to show him that the gospel is not to be restricted to Jews but is for Gentiles too—Gentiles who may come to Christ not as Jews first, but as Gentiles. Second, Peter repeats the lesson he had received to Cornelius, perhaps even telling the vision of the sheet, though Luke does not include that specifically. Finally, in chapter 11, when Peter arrived back in Jerusalem, he explained what had happened to that audience (vv. 4–17). Obviously, Luke is saying that this event is pivotal.

It is also pivotal in the structure of the book. With this incident, Peter begins to fade out in terms of the narrative, and Paul, who carries on the mission to the Gentiles now inaugurated by Peter, becomes dominant. So what is happening here is significant from the perspective of Luke's theology and also from the perspective of the place of this event in the narrative.

The story of Peter's preaching to Cornelius and his household is a long story, occurring in six sections: the introduction of Cornelius (vv. 1–8), the preparation of Peter (vv. 9–16), Peter's meeting with the messengers (vv. 17–23), Peter's journey to and arrival in Caesarea (vv. 24–33), Peter's sermon (vv. 34–43), and the results of this encounter (vv. 44–48). We will look at the first four of these points in this chapter and the last two in the next.

The Introduction of Cornelius

Cornelius is a Gentile first of all. He is also a centurion. A centurion was a Roman military officer who had command of one hundred men. Cornelius's group was called the Italian Regiment.

This is not the only place in the New Testament where we are introduced to a centurion; we find these men several times in the Gospels and in Acts, and in every instance they are highly commended. One of them, who came into contact with Jesus, was praised by him with the words: "I tell you the truth, I have not found anyone in Israel with such great faith" (Matt. 8:10). Cornelius followed in this path.

We are told a number of additional things about Cornelius in verse 2 of chapter 10, all of which are indications of his genuine faith: He was devout; he was God-fearing; he was active in his piety, giving to all who were in need; and he prayed to God regularly.

That Cornelius was a "God-fearer" meant that although he worshiped Jehovah he had nevertheless not become a Jew by circumcision. God-fearers were Gentiles who expressed interest in Judaism and attended worship in the synagogue but who, because they had not yet fully converted to Judaism by circumcision, had to sit in the back as observers rather than as full participants in the community. In the eyes of Jewish people it was a good thing to be a God-fearer. It meant that they were on the right religious track. Nevertheless, because they were not yet Jews, it was improper for Jews to associate with them socially.

Peter would have had no trouble associating with Cornelius if Cornelius had previously come into the fold of Judaism by circumcision. His being a Roman would have been no problem. If he was a Jewish proselyte, Peter could have gone to him easily. But Cornelius had not converted. Though he had been exposed to the God of Israel, he was nevertheless still a Gentile.

This raises an interesting question in my mind: Was Cornelius regenerate? Was he born again? This question is not as easy to answer as one might think. It would be hard to put him in the category of the pagans described in Romans 1, or even those described in Romans 2. Granted, he had nothing in his background that could commend him to God. Granted, he was ignorant of Jesus Christ. That is what Peter was sent to Caesarea to tell him about. But Cornelius was seeking the true God. He was attending synagogue services. He was listening to the Jewish Scriptures. He was praying. Is it possible to seek God—really seek God—unless God is first at work to draw a person to him? Is it possible to pray so that God hears the prayer and responds without first being born again? Is it possible to do good deeds that God notes and recognizes without being regenerate?

As I say, I am not sure of the answer we should give to that question. Part of it depends upon how we define what theologians call "prevenient grace," that is, the work of the Holy Spirit in preparing one to receive the gospel.

But whether this man was already regenerate and now just needed to be taught more fully, or whether (if I had to choose, I would say that this is probably the case) the Holy Spirit was merely at work in his life in what we would call an "external way," making him dissatisfied with his paganism and bringing him into contact with a better way so he could begin to learn about the God of Israel, it is certainly the case that Cornelius had been prepared for what Peter was being sent to Caesarea to tell him.

Everyone needs to have his or her heart prepared by God if that person is going to receive the gospel. Yet the person also needs to hear the way of salvation.

The Preparation of Peter

We are told of the preparation of Peter for his task (vv. 9–16). Did Cornelius need preparation? Yes, and God prepared him. Did Peter need preparation? Yes, Peter needed preparation too.

The problem was that although Peter had become a Christian, he still thought as a Jew, and according to the Jewish way of thinking, God did not save Gentiles as Gentiles. They had to become Jews first. God had already been preparing Peter to think differently. It had begun in Samaria. The gospel had spread there earlier, and Peter had been sent to Samaria to investigate. Samaria was not entirely Gentile; the people were part Jewish and part Gentile. But it was this very mixture that was so important in moving Peter away from his strictly Jewish prejudices. Peter checked Samaria out, and because he had the germ of the truth in him in spite of his prejudices, he concluded, God really is at work here. He was quite rightly pleased.

Then we are told, at the very end of chapter 9, that when Peter went to Joppa he stayed in the home of a tanner named Simon. Tanners work with leather. In order to work with leather they have to handle dead animals. Dead bodies were unclean, according to Jewish thinking. Anyone who touched them became unclean. So a normal Jew would have nothing to do with such people. Yet Peter stayed with Simon. Simon was a Christian brother, and this was the right thing to do. This was another experience in which God was beginning to break down Peter's defenses.

Still, Simon was a Jew. And Peter was now going to be told to go to the household of the Gentile Cornelius. Let me emphasize again that the problem was not that God did not save Gentiles. He did. The Old Testament has a number of examples. But when these Gentiles were saved, they were saved not as Gentiles but through their becoming Jews.

There was Rahab, for example. She was a harlot in Jericho. She was not a member of God's people, but she had heard rumors of what the God of the Jews had done and she had come to believe in this God. When the Jewish spies came into Jericho she protected them, recognizing them as God's servants. She saved the spies and so was saved herself when Jericho was taken. But what happened after that? As we read the sequel, we find that she was then incorporated into Israel. She married into the tribe of Judah and became an ancestor of the Lord Jesus Christ (Matt. 1:5).

There is also the example of the Moabitess Ruth. She got to know the true God through her mother-in-law Naomi. Later, when Naomi's sons died and Naomi decided to return to her own land, Ruth determined to return to Israel with her. She said to Naomi, "Don't urge me to leave you or to turn back from you. Where you go I will go, and where you stay I will stay. Your people will be my people and your God my God" (Ruth 1:16). The order of that last sentence is particularly important. Ruth wanted the God of Naomi to be her God; she would be a worshiper of Jehovah. But before she could say "your God will be my God" she had to say "your people will be my people." Ruth became a member of Naomi's tribe. She married Boaz. Their son was Obed, the father of Jesse, who was the father of King David (Ruth 4:21–22; Matt. 1:5).

Could Peter preach salvation, offering it freely on the basis of the finished work of Christ, to one who had not come to God by way of Israel, in this case by the rite of circumcision? We know how God answered. The vision of the sheet was intended to show that God was not calling the Gentiles unclean, regardless of what the Jews might be doing, and that Gentiles could come to Christ as Gentiles without first having passed through the very narrow door of Judaism.

The story tells us that Peter was on the roof of the house of Simon the tanner in the middle of the day, waiting for his noon meal. The houses had flat roofs, and there was usually a staircase to the roof from the outside. So the roof was a nice place to go to escape the bustle within. Probably there was a bit of an awning there, and stretching out under it, Peter fell asleep. (This awning may have been supported by four posts, and maybe this is how the vision of the great sheet supported at the four corners came about.) As Peter was dozing, he had a vision. A great sheet was let down from heaven, and in the sheet were all kinds of animals—some that the Jews would call clean and others that the Jews would call unclean.[2] While Peter was wondering what this vision meant, a voice from heaven told him, "Get up, Peter. Kill and eat" (v. 13).

Peter responded instinctively: "Surely not, Lord! I have never eaten anything impure or unclean" (v. 14).

Some have pointed out that this seems to have been a very incongruous statement on Peter's part. The Lord was giving Peter a command. And Peter, while acknowledging Jesus as his Lord, nevertheless contradicted him, saying, "Surely not!" That would be an incongruous reply, of course—if Peter's words are to be understood that way. But I do not think that Peter's words were a flat contradiction. I think he understood this to be something of a test and therefore approached it biblically on the basis of his knowledge of the law, as he was right to do. When the voice from heaven said, "Kill and eat," Peter would not have taken the words as a command but as a test to see whether he, a Jew, would disobey God's written law. He answered rightly on the basis of the understanding he had: "Lord, I can't do that, as you well know. You know what you wrote in Leviticus. I can't have anything to do with food that is unclean."

At this point the voice said, "Do not call anything impure that God has made clean" (v. 15).

Peter must have scratched his head at that. He had never heard anything so strange. What in the world was that about? he must have been thinking. Is God contradicting himself? While he was thinking about it the same thing happened again, then a third time. I suppose, although we are not told this explicitly, that Peter's response would have been the same each time: "No, Lord, I can't do that." By the time the drama had been acted out the third time, Peter must have begun to get the idea that God was trying to tell him something, even though he did not know exactly what it was.

Peter's Meeting with the Messengers

While he was puzzling over the vision (v. 17), the men Cornelius had sent arrived in Joppa. Joppa was to the south. Caesarea was to the north. It was a three days' journey between them, and the men had arrived in the south hunting for the house of Simon the tanner and for Simon Peter, who was staying there. God told Peter to go down and welcome the three men.

Perhaps Peter saw significance in the number of men and the number of times the dream had been repeated. But whatever the case, God had told him: "Simon, three men are looking for you. So get up and go downstairs. Do not hesitate to go with them, for I have sent them" (vv. 19–20). So Peter went down and asked why they had come. They said that they had been sent by Cornelius the centurion. "He is a righteous and God-fearing man, who is respected by all the Jewish people. A holy angel told him to have you come to his house so that he could hear what you have to say" (v. 22).

Now notice this: Verse 23 says, "Then Peter invited the men into the house to be his guests." Peter was learning already. A Jew would not normally have done that. Normally a Jew would have said, "Well, it is nice to meet you, but we need to stay out here in the street. You can't come inside." Or he might have said, "If you go down this street a little way, I think you'll find an inn where you can stay." Or, "You can camp out on the beach. I think you'll manage all right there." No orthodox Jew would have invited Gentiles into his house. He would not have sat down at the same table with them. He would not have had fellowship with them. It was forbidden. Peter had gotten the point of the vision thus far. God had called these men clean. And since God had called them clean, he was not to call them unclean. So they came in.

Peter's Arrival in Caesarea

The next day Peter started out with them to Caesarea, taking some of the brothers from Joppa—that is, some of the other Jews—with him. It was a smart move on Peter's part. I suppose he anticipated what was to happen and the misunderstanding and opposition that would result, and he judged that what-ever God was leading him into it would be good to have some of the other Jews along to verify the outcome.

At Caesarea they met Cornelius and those whom he had assembled to hear Peter's message. What a wonderful thing! It would be wonderful if every evan-gelist or preacher, when he stood up to preach, should find the reception Peter found when he got to Caesarea. Cornelius had been prepared by God, and Peter had been prepared by God. But these were not the only ones who had been prepared. Cornelius had prepared his whole household, and now they were all waiting to hear Peter. I suppose Cornelius had figured out how long the trip to and the return from Joppa would take. He knew that those he had sent would not delay. He knew exactly when they would arrive. So there he was. He had everybody assembled. God had prepared Cornelius, the preacher, and the audience.

Today, in communication theory, people talk about what happens in the communication process. Communication is not simply a question of saying something and automatically having it communicated to the people who hear it. First there is the idea that is to be communicated; then the "encoding" of this message, usually in human speech or language, though it can also be by visual symbols such as facial expressions or gestures; then the transmission of the encoded message to the one who is to receive it; then the "decoding" by the receiver; and finally the passing of the idea into the mind of the one who receives it. That is a complicated process. And the point students of com-munication make is that communication does not happen until what the speaker thinks actually gets into the mind of the person listening.

Here God was communicating, and true communication did take place.

In communication theory there is also a necessary intellectual preparation for understanding what is to be said. There must be an intellectual framework with which to receive the new material. Here it was not merely a case of mental preparation. This was a spiritual message, and it required spiritual perception. So the preparation God made was also in the hearts and souls of these Gentile hearers. To use the idea present in one of the Lord's parables, God had already made them receptive ground.

That is when things really happen after all: when God prepares both the messenger *and the hearts* of those who are to hear the message. I speak to a lot of different audiences, and I find that although one can never be abso-lutely sure of this, it is sometimes possible to tell when one is getting through as one speaks. Sometimes you think you are not getting through and find out later that you did. Or sometimes you think you are and find out later you did not. But it is not always that way, and sometimes as you look out on a congregation, audience, or class, you can tell very well what is happening. Generally those audiences to which one readily communicates are those that have come prepared to respond to the message.

When you go to church, do you want to receive a good message? If so, the best way is to come with a prepared heart. I know that the preacher must be prepared too. But when God prepares the messenger as well as those who are to hear him, then tremendous things happen, as they did in Caesarea in the household of Cornelius.

Notice what Peter said when he arrived: "I now realize how true it is that God does not show favoritism but accepts men from every nation who fear him and do what is right" (vv. 34–35). I wonder if we really believe that. We would all probably say, "Oh, yes, yes, that is true. After all, we are Gentiles, and God has accepted us. And, yes, there are also Jews, and God accepts them." But I wonder if we really believe that God does not show favoritism.

I am glad Peter used that word, because it is just a bit closer to what our problem really is than *prejudice,* which is the word I used earlier. We know prejudice is wrong. So although we may have prejudices, we try to reject them. But favoritism—well, that is not quite the same. God showed favor to us, we reason. Aren't we the kind of people to whom God might show favor? When our minds begin to work like that it is only a very short step from favor to favoritism. What we must never forget is that God has shown favor to us precisely because he does not show favoritism. That is the only way you and I ever became Christians. If God had shown favoritism, we would not have been saved. Therefore, we must never show favoritism in our presentation of the message. The gospel is for all who will come to Jesus.

Harry Ironside tells a personal story at this point. It concerns the death of his father. As his father was dying, he kept muttering something, and the family couldn't quite understand what it was. But finally they got it. Mr. Ironside was thinking about this vision, thinking about the sheet full of animals. He was saying, "A great sheet and wild beasts and, and, and . . ." He couldn't quite finish it. A friend bent over and whispered, "John, it says, 'creeping things'" (KJV).

"Oh, yes," he said. "That is how I got in. Just a poor good-for-nothing creeping thing, but I got in—saved by grace."[3]

Whenever you see yourself, not as the clean animal but the unclean animal, not as the attractive beast but as the creeping thing, as one who by the grace of God got into that sheet and is pronounced clean by the sheer grace of God in Jesus Christ, then you are ready to open your heart and arms to other people. And it does not make any difference who they are. God does not show favorites. If you got in, the gospel must be for everybody.

21

Even Gentiles

Acts 10:34–48

While Peter was still speaking these words, the Holy Spirit came on all who heard the message. The circumcised believers who had come with Peter were astonished that the gift of the Holy Spirit had been poured out even on the Gentiles. For they heard them speaking in tongues and praising God.

Then Peter said, "Can anyone keep these people from being baptized with water? They have received the Holy Spirit just as we have." So he ordered that they be baptized in the name of Jesus Christ.

Acts 10:44–48

The tenth chapter of Acts is one of the most important chapters in Acts, perhaps also one of the most important chapters in the Bible. It is so important because it tells how a gospel that was originally thought of in exclusively Jewish terms came by the intervention and revelation of God to be practically as well as theoretically a gospel for the whole world. Gentiles should be especially thankful for this chapter, since it is because of this revelation that they are able to come to God as Gentiles (see chapter 20).

Today the gospel is preached to Gentiles as Gentiles, and it is not demanded of us that we become Jews in order to become followers of Jesus

Christ. Jesus, as Peter says in this sermon, "is Lord of all" (Acts 10:36); that is, he is the Savior and Lord of Jews as Jews and of Gentiles as Gentiles. So Gentiles do not have to come to church wearing coverings for their heads. They do not have to eat kosher food. They do not have to make yearly pilgrimages to Jerusalem for the required feasts. This was not always so, and the reason it is not so now is because of what is recorded in this chapter. Acts 10 is of crucial importance for the way in which Christianity has become not a Jewish religion but a world religion.

In our last chapter we looked at the first four parts of Acts 10. Now we consider Peter's sermon and its results.

A Three-Part Sermon

Peter's sermon has three parts. It has an opening section in which Peter describes how he got where he is and how he perceived what God was doing. Second, there is the message proper, beginning with verse 36. Finally, at the end of the sermon, there is what we would call an invitation. It is not phrased as an invitation explicitly, but it is a call for faith in Christ as a result of which, Peter says, God will forgive the sins of those listening.

The important thing about this sermon is that it is simply the basic gospel. Christians are always tempted to reinterpret, rework, or re-create the gospel because they think if they do that, somehow they will make it more appealing to the people to whom they speak. There is a proper concern here, and there is a proper way of doing this. Obviously we have to use the language of the people to whom we speak. And this is not just a matter of learning a particular language—English, French, Greek, or whatever it might be. It is also a matter of speaking in a people's cultural idiom. For these reasons there is a sense in which the preacher does properly adapt his expression of the gospel to a given audience. But the point I am making is that we must not change the gospel itself. The important thing is the faithful declaration of the message that was given to the apostles at the very beginning and that has formed the substance or heart of Christian preaching throughout all the long centuries of the history of the Christian church.

In the last chapter I described the metamorphosis of Peter's thinking. God had been teaching Peter that the gospel was for Gentiles as well as Jews. So when Peter got into Cornelius's house and actually had a Gentile congregation in front of him, he began by acknowledging that truth: "I now realize how true it is that God does not show favoritism but accepts men from every nation who fear him and do what is right" (vv. 34–35).

We ought to realize it too. But, of course, we often do not—since we have prejudices of our own. We have denominational prejudices, believing that God is more willing to work with our denomination than with others. We have racial prejudices, thinking that God prefers one race or prefers working with one race to working with others. We have national prejudices, supposing that our nation is somehow intrinsically superior to all others. We must learn that

God does not show favoritism. The gospel is for all who will come to him through faith in Jesus Christ.

The Apostolic Gospel

In verse 36 Peter gets to the sermon proper, introducing it by the words: "You know the message God sent to the people of Israel, telling the good news of *peace* through Jesus Christ." Do you remember C. H. Dodd's *kerygma*? This is the fixed structure of the basic gospel message the apostles preached (see pages 52, 108, 109). This basic gospel is what we find Peter's sermon in Acts 10 to be. So when we go through it we are studying not just any sermon but rather what Peter and the other apostles thought was essential for all people everywhere to learn.

Understand that this is not just a historical study. I am not merely saying, "Well, back in the early days of the church, this is what Peter thought." Peter was an apostle, and what he thought and the way he expressed the gospel are both normative and binding. Because of his and the others' apostolic authority, this gospel is also for today. If we teach something else, we do so to our harm and the weakening of the church.

Here is what Peter thought the gospel to be.

The Good News of Peace

The gospel is "the good news of peace through Jesus Christ, who is Lord of all." This is a summary statement or introduction to the gospel. The reason the gospel is good news of *peace* is that apart from the work of Jesus Christ, we are not at peace with God. We are at war with God. Paul puts it in other terms in Romans, saying that we are actually under God's wrath. The world says, "I'm okay; you're okay." But God says that everything is not okay. God says the world is in rebellion against him. Humanity wants to fight him to the death. When almighty God actually did take a form in which mere human beings could fight him to the death, that is precisely what they did. So, as I say, we are at war with God. And the first announcement of the gospel is that peace with God has been made for those who will have it. Peace has been made by Jesus Christ.

When Peter says, quite appropriately in this context, that Jesus is "Lord of all," he is saying not only that Jesus is the Savior of the Gentiles as well as of the Jews, but also that he is God. The "Lord" is God. Only God is able to establish peace by removing the offenses we have erected.

E. M. Blaiklock notes how remarkable this emphasis is.

Peter was the first to declare that Jesus was the Messiah, and in his exposition of the gospel to his Gentile audience he covers the same theme fully and faithfully. . . . "This startling claim made by St. Peter with reference to Jesus of Nazareth, with whom he had lived on terms of closest human intimacy, and in whose death he might well have seen the destruction of all his hopes is a further evidence of the change which could only be accounted for by the belief that this same Jesus was risen, and declared to be the Son of God with power."[1]

The Baptism of Jesus

The second thing Peter mentions is the baptism of Jesus by John the Baptist. This is a much more important part of the early preaching than we would imagine, as is proved by the fact that each of the four Gospels begins at this point.

Why is Jesus' baptism so important? When we talk about the baptism of Jesus, generally we talk about it in terms of Jesus' identification with us. He stressed that point himself when he was baptized. When John protested about baptizing him, Jesus said, "Let it be so now; it is proper for us to do this to fulfill all righteousness" (Matt. 3:15). He was saying in effect, "I want to identify with people; I want to go through all that is proper for me to do." That is important in its own place. But that is not the primary reason why the baptism of Jesus by John has such an important place in the *kerygma*.

The reason it is involved in all these basic proclamations of the gospel is that when Jesus Christ was baptized God the Father spoke from heaven, authenticating him as his Son, and on that occasion Jesus was anointed visibly with the Holy Spirit for the task he had to do. John saw the Spirit of God descending like a dove upon him, and the voice from heaven said, "This is my Son, whom I love; with him I am well pleased" (Matt. 3:17).

It is significant in this respect that the four Gospels do not begin by giving us information about the Lord's early life, the time between his birth and the start of his public ministry about thirty years later. Some but not all tell of the birth. Luke mentions his growth "in wisdom and stature, and in favor with God and man" (Luke 2:52). That is something but not much. Rather, each of the Gospels passes quickly to the baptism of John. And Mark does not even mention the birth! Mark just starts with John's baptism. This is because at his baptism God set his seal of approval on Jesus. He identified him as his Son and messenger, the one to whom we should pay heed.

The Public Ministry of Jesus

The third part of Peter's summation of the gospel is the public ministry of Jesus: "how God anointed Jesus of Nazareth with the Holy Spirit and power, and how he went around doing good and healing all who were under the power of the devil, because God was with him" (Acts 10:38). This ministry involves two things: good deeds and special acts that demonstrated Christ's power over Satan.

The significant thing about this summation of the public ministry of Jesus is that, as in his previous sermons, Peter does not mention Christ's teaching. In the Gospels we find whole chapters filled with Christ's sayings, parables, and discourses. In Matthew the Sermon on the Mount takes three chapters and the Olivet Discourse takes two. Chapters 14–16 of John contain what we call the final discourses. The reason for this omission is that until people come to understand what Jesus Christ accomplished by his death, turn from sin, and follow him, they are incapable of responding to his teaching. In the Sermon on the Mount Jesus said that his disciples are to be poor in spirit, meek, pure in heart, and peace-makers, to live by the teaching of the Scriptures, and to follow a standard higher even than that found in the Old Testament. These teachings are important and necessary for those who are Christ's. But if they are taught to those who are not yet converted, to those who are incapable in their unconverted state of doing them, these teachings are misleading and harmful.

If we speak about the teachings of Jesus without first speaking of the need for repentance and faith in Jesus as our Savior from sin, people quite naturally begin to think that Christianity is merely about doing good. It is learning what Jesus taught and trying to put it into practice. This only encourages self-righteousness, a trust in human righteousness, which is harmful. Whenever Christianity has fallen into that pattern of teaching it has made a great mistake.

Well, someone says, didn't the disciples share what Jesus taught? Of course they did. The proof is our New Testament, which contains that teaching. But this came afterward—after people had turned from sin and had come to God through faith in Jesus (see chapter 12).

The Crucifixion of Jesus

The central item in this list of essentials is the crucifixion of Jesus, though Peter mentions it only briefly, perhaps because it was so well known: "They killed him by hanging him on a tree" (v. 39). We may rightly suppose, however, that as questions were asked, this is the chief thing Peter would have spoken about.

What was the point of Jesus' dying? Jesus was God's messenger. He is the one to whom we should listen. Why should he have died and not have remained alive to teach us? And why is his death such an important part of the gospel proclamation? The answer is that he died for us, in our place. This is how he made peace between ourselves and God the Father, the truth with which Peter started (v. 36). Jesus made peace, as Peter's fellow apostle Paul says in another place, by taking the law that we have broken and that condemns us and "nailing it to the cross" (Col. 2:14).

Our sin is like a great wall between God and us. We cannot bridge it in order to make peace with God. We are on the far side of this wall, fighting God all the time. How can that wall be removed? The cross is God's answer. At the cross God took our sin, placed it upon Jesus Christ, and punished it there. Jesus did not die for himself; he had not sinned. He did not die merely because he was a man. He died for us.

This is the symbolism of the sacrifices. One who had sinned could take an innocent animal, bring it to the priest, have it killed, and then go away knowing that an innocent had died in the guilty one's place. Of course, a mere animal does not take away sin. But the animal pointed to Christ, who could take away sin. Because Jesus is God and infinite, his death had inexhaustible value. When we trust him, coming to God on the basis of his death, our sin is removed. And what was before a relationship of hostility becomes a bond of peace.

The Resurrection of Jesus

The next item in Peter's list of gospel truths is the resurrection: "But God raised him from the dead on the third day and caused him to be seen. He was not seen by all the people, but by witnesses whom God had already chosen—by us who ate and drank with him after he rose from the dead" (vv. 40–41).

Peter stresses eating and drinking with Christ because that is a way of saying that Christ's was a real resurrection. In the resurrection of Jesus we are not dealing with some mystical appearance of a disembodied Christ, not the kind of resurrection you sometimes see in Hollywood movies. It was not a resurrection in the sense that "Jesus died, but what he stood for lives on." The disciples were not suffering from a hallucination as if they loved him so much that they just couldn't bear the thought of having him dead and so imagined that they saw him in various places. Nor was it that his Spirit was just somehow present with them, inspiring them. No, it was a real resurrection. The resurrected Jesus had a real body. They sat down at a real table with this real Christ, and together with him they ate and drank real food.

This took place in the Upper Room, as Jesus asked for food to show them he was real. When they first saw him they thought he was a ghost. But when he ate with them they knew that he was really risen from the tomb.

Jesus as Judge

Peter's final point is that God appointed Jesus "as judge of the living and the dead" (v. 42), adding that Jesus also commanded that this truth be preached to the people. This is part of the gospel, but it is the first specific mention of Christ's role as judge in Acts.

Repent and Believe

When Peter got to the end of this sermon he gave what I would call an application or invitation, though he does so cautiously and even indirectly. Peter said, "All the prophets testify about him that everyone who believes in him receives forgiveness of sins through his name" (v. 43).

Sometimes you hear people talking about different kinds of gospels. In the last century there was something called "the gospel of inevitable progress." It was a secular philosophy, having to do with Darwinism and the Industrial Revolution. But it also had a religious version that maintained that Jesus came to establish an earthly kingdom and that this kingdom would advance in the world inevitably. Sin was going to be wiped out, and everything was going to be perfect. That was not the real gospel.

Jesus Christ does have a kingdom, of course. That kingdom will be established. I believe it will even be established upon earth. But the preaching of an inevitable kingdom to be brought in by the church is not the gospel. The gospel is what we find in Acts 10.

Sometimes people talk about a "social gospel." There was an emphasis upon that in the earlier decades of this century by men like Walter Rauschenbusch, Washington Gladden, and others. They saw that the social aspects of Christianity had been neglected and began to stress these things. For them and their followers Christianity became feeding the poor, helping the downtrodden, and so on.

Good as these things may be, we must nevertheless remember that the gospel is what we find here: peace with God through the work of Jesus Christ. And this is no imaginary Jesus. He is the one God sent—who was anointed with the Holy Spirit at his baptism, who went about doing good, demonstrating power over Satan and the forces of evil, who was crucified by wicked men, who was raised the third day, and who will return one day as the judge of all people. This is the gospel God blesses. Whenever we preach something else, we may indeed produce certain visible results. People may be pleased by it and say, "Isn't that wonderful!" But it is not the gospel, and it will not be blessed by God in the rescue of sinners and the changing of human lives. What God uses to turn men and women from a life of sin to righteousness and empower them to live righteously through the Spirit of the living Christ is the good news of Christ crucified, risen, and coming again.

And that is the way the chapter ends: "While Peter was still speaking these words, the Holy Spirit came on all who heard the message" (v. 44). What message was that? The message of the social gospel? The message of liberation theology? The gospel of inevitable progress? No. It was the message of Christ crucified. It was while they were hearing *that* message that the Holy Spirit came upon them and saved them.

This was a puzzle to those Jews who had come up from Joppa with Peter, because they could not understand how the Holy Spirit could be poured out "even on the Gentiles" (v. 45). They had been thinking that the Gentiles would have to become Jews first. The Gentiles had not become Jews, and yet the Holy Spirit came to them exactly as he had come to the apostles prior to Peter's first preaching at Pentecost. The Gentiles are brought into an exactly parallel position, not merely with normal Jews (or even Samaritans) who had believed on Jesus, but with the apostles themselves. When Peter preached at Pentecost, people repented, were baptized, and after that the Holy Spirit came upon them. When Peter and John went to Samaria, the people had already believed, but they did not receive the Holy Spirit until the apostles laid their hands on them. Here, the Gentiles in the house of Cornelius—this entirely and unabashedly Gentile congregation—received the Holy Spirit just as the Jewish apostles had received the Holy Spirit in the Upper Room.[2]

And they were not compelled to be circumcised! Peter looked at them and said, "Can anyone keep these people from being baptized with water?" He meant, If you can give a reason, here's the time to do it. Speak up or forever hold your peace. "They have received the Holy Spirit just as we have" (v. 47). Nobody had anything to say. So they baptized them. Thus, without being circumcised, without becoming Jews, they were received rightly, properly, and victoriously into this one great, growing, international, and multiracial church of Jesus Christ.

22

No Further Objections

Acts 11:1-18

The apostles and the brothers throughout Judea heard that the Gentiles also had received the word of God. So when Peter went up to Jerusalem, the circumcised believers criticized him and said, "You went into the house of uncircumcised men and ate with them."
Peter began and explained everything to them precisely as it had happened. . . .
When they heard this, they had no further objections and praised God, saying, "So then, God has granted even the Gentiles repentance unto life."

Acts 11:1–18

The story of Peter's preaching to the Gentiles was of great importance to Luke. He tells it three times, twice in chapter 10 (once briefly) and again in chapter 11, the chapter we are to study now. Luke was composing under the direct influence and guidance of the Holy Spirit. Thus we know that this story was not only important to him but to God also. If God tells us something once, we should listen. If he tells us something twice, we should pay extremely strict attention. How then if he tells us something three times over, as is the case here? In that case, we must give God's words the most intent, comprehensive, sympathetic, and obedient notice possible.

188

A Major Readjustment

If the Gentiles had not been received into the church as they were, as believing Gentiles, without their first having to become Jews, the church of Jesus Christ would never have become the universal missionary force it has proved itself to be throughout the long centuries of church history. It would have remained a limited ethnic community, as Judaism itself was at the time of Christ and for the most part continues to be today.

From this time on, people were to become members of God's family by faith in Jesus Christ alone and it would not be necessary for them to go through the door of Judaism first. Moreover, Jews who were Christians were to have fellowship with their Gentile brothers and sisters who had not become Jews but had nevertheless believed in Jesus. There was to be one church—not two churches, which is what would have happened otherwise.

E. M. Blaiklock writes:

> It required . . . a major readjustment of all thinking for a people, fiercely conscious of racial privilege and stirred anew by the thought that the Messiah of promise had appeared and spoken, readily to abandon the thought that a unique national destiny approached fulfillment. To accept a re-interpretation of ancient prophecies, to admit a spiritual rendering of old promises accepted and cherished as literal and material, to see Israel melt into the church, and the minority of the chosen lose identity, and privilege, and special place in a global organization, called for insight, faith, self-abnegation, magnanimity, and a transcendent view of God rarely found in any but the most enlightened souls.[1]

That is not an overstatement. The terms by which Gentiles were to become Christians required an adjustment and needed to be addressed forcefully and directly—which is what the Holy Spirit was doing through Peter in this story.

When Peter got back to Jerusalem, his Jewish brethren, who had already heard about what had happened in Caesarea, approached him and expressed their objections. They did not say, "It is not right for you to allow the Gentiles to become Christians." They knew better than that. But what they did object to is what we find in verse 3. They said to Peter, "You went into the house of uncircumcised men and ate with them." They meant, "You broke kosher." That was the thing that really bothered them, because if it was right for Peter to have done that, then Gentiles obviously had the right to come into their homes and the church as Gentiles and as the Jews' equals. And that is where the prejudice lay.

We do not have this exact problem today, but we do have something like it. We are glad to have other people join us as long as they become like us.

We may not want charismatics—unless, of course, they will give up their charismatic behavior.

If we are white Christians, we may be glad to have a few blacks join our fellowship—as long as they do not act too ethnic and as long as there are not too many of them. And maybe blacks—although I think that they as a minority have more understanding and are more adaptable than whites at this point—are not too glad to welcome whites.

The point is that God takes people as they are. They do not have to become something else before they can come to Jesus.

A Wise Response

Peter could have said, "I am an apostle; God speaks to me and through me. God told me that going to the house of these Gentiles was all right. So if you don't like it, you can just leave my church." Some Christian leaders handle controversy in that way. Peter did not. Peter did not flaunt his apostolic authority. Instead he began with a humble recitation of what happened. The Greek makes this particularly clear. It indicates that Peter began at the beginning and explained everything *precisely*—a very strong word—as it happened.

If anybody questioned his particular presentation of the facts, well, there were the six brothers who had gone to Caesarea with him. They could say, as undoubtedly they did, "It is exactly as Peter has reported."

Lessons in Divine Guidance

People often ask ministers: How does a person come to know the will of God? How does God lead people? How am I to know whether or not I should do this or do that? Some people think that God never gives guidance except through application of a specific Bible text. Others speak of open or closed doors. Some, like the eighteenth-century evangelist George Whitefield, speak of "intimations." Still others declare, "The Lord told me to do such and such." Here Peter tells how he was led.

He Was Praying

Prayer is an important starting point, isn't it? It was a good preface to what Peter was going to say next too, since this was not a case of Peter's simply having the notion pop into his head that now might be a good time to take the gospel to the Gentiles or of his being caught off guard when the Gentiles arrived in Joppa from Caesarea. No, Peter said, I was praying. I was seeking the will of God. And it was while I was in that frame of mind, seeking God's will, that God led me in this matter (v. 5).

More than thirty years ago I listened to a tape by Donald Grey Barnhouse on "How to Know the Will of God." He made the point that God leads in three ways and that when you get all three of these in line you can be sure that it is God who is leading you.

First, "You need to be willing to do the will of God even before you know what it is." God does not give options, allowing us to choose one or another or even choose whether we want to follow a specific course of action. He waits until we are ready to obey him. Then he tells us what we should do.

Second, "God speaks through Scripture." God never leads contrary to Scripture. So if we are to be led by God, we must be men and women of the Book. We must know it and understand its principles.

Third, "You need to look to God on a regular basis—daily and, at times, even hourly." Barnhouse referred to Psalm 32:8, which in the King James Version says, "I will guide thee with mine eye." Barnhouse said that if God is to guide us with his eye, he must catch our eye. So we need to look to him regularly through periods of personal Bible reading and devotion.

It is the third of these points that Peter mentions first. He was praying—trying to catch the eye of God to see the way in which God might lead him. It was while he was in that frame of mind that God provided the new direction.

He Received a Revelation

Revelation does not happen to everybody. Peter was an apostle. We are not. In this important case, Peter was given a vision of the sheet let down from heaven with clean and unclean animals in it and told to eat (vv. 5–10). That was a revelation about food, if nothing else, and Peter would have picked that up. He would have remembered that on one occasion, when Jesus was asked about defilement from eating unclean food, the Master had said, "What goes into a man's mouth does not make him 'unclean,' but what comes out of his mouth, that is what makes him 'unclean'" (Matt. 15:11). By such teaching Peter would have been prepared to learn that kosher restrictions were to be a thing of the past. God was now purifying peoples' hearts rather than their dishes.

But more important than that, God was saying that Peter was not to call those whom God was calling to faith in Jesus Christ unclean. The frame of mind by which Peter approached eating was to be changed, and that in turn would change how he approached other people. The only way anybody, Jew or Gentile, was ever really to become clean was by the work of Christ, and that was now being offered to everybody.

We are not to expect special revelations like Peter's today. I have friends who deny even the possibility of that kind of a revelation for this age. They do it on the grounds that God gave special revelations at a time when the Scriptures were not yet given and that now that the Scriptures are given all special revelations have stopped. As I said before, I am not willing to say categorically that God cannot give such revelations in our times, for who can tell God what he can or cannot do? God can do anything he pleases. I do not know anybody who has had such a vision. I would be very skeptical if I met somebody who claimed that he or she had. But I will not say it can't happen.

If it does happen that God gives some persons special revelations or visions, it happens very rarely. And the chief and only sure way God guides his people today is by the Bible. So what we have in these first two means of guidance that Peter talks about—prayer and a divine revelation—is paralleled by what we have in our times of prayer and Bible study. When we open our hearts to

God, asking for his leading, and then study his Word, God takes that Word and applies it directly to our situation.

If Peter were speaking before the Jerusalem council today, he might say, "I prayed about it, and we searched the Scriptures. I believe this is what the Bible teaches and that it applies in this way."

He Appealed to Circumstances

Peter said that while he was praying and immediately after he had received the vision, suddenly men from the household of Cornelius came to him (vv. 11–12). Timing like that could not have been accidental. God rules this world so that nothing is accidental. We may not always see his hand in circumstances, but God does have a purpose when things happen.

Think what would have happened if the men had come only an hour earlier. Simon the tanner, who was a Jew, would have said, "I am sorry but you cannot come in here. This is a Jewish home." Or if he had not said that, Peter would have. Suppose they had come a day later. By that time the meaning and impact of Peter's vision might have begun to fade, and Peter might have found himself thinking, Maybe it was just something bad I ate for breakfast. Get those Gentiles out of here. I don't want to get in trouble with my brothers in Jerusalem.

It did not happen that way. The Gentile visitors came exactly at the time Peter had received the vision. The vision had been repeated three times, and here were three men. Perhaps that also helped Peter to recognize that God's hand was in the circumstances.

First, Peter had been praying.

Second, he had the equivalent of what we would call a Bible study.

Third, circumstances began to fall into place.

The order is important, because many Christians like circumstantial leading and want to depend on circumstances without first praying and studying the Scripture. And they are often terribly misled. This is because circumstances can be read in different ways. Sometimes when things come into our lives, we say, "This is God's circumstantial leading," when actually we are only interpreting the events to make them what we want them to be. It is only safe to trust circumstances after we have first been praying and studying the Bible. Circumstances are only good direction if they confirm what God is teaching.

He Confirmed His Decision by Witnesses

The Old Testament required two or three witnesses for the establishment of any fact (Deut. 19:15). Peter probably figured, "To be safe, I need at least three." But this was a very serious matter. So he may have said, "And to be doubly safe, I had better have six." So he brought along six friends (v. 12). Confirmation by others is a valuable thing when we are talking about the will of God.

There is an illustration in the way we talk about an individual's call to the ministry of the Word in a Presbyterian church, and probably some other communions too. It is customary for those who are examining a candidate to look for three things.

First, the individual should have a sense of God's calling. No one can tell somebody else what the will of God is in such a matter. The person must know that God has called him or her. This is a subjective matter, and we speak of it as the internal call.

Second, the call should be confirmed by the presence of the necessary abilities or gifts. If a man says, "I am called to be a preacher" but is so shy or stammering that he cannot speak or is so mentally deficient that he cannot read or understand the Bible, most people would rightly conclude that his sense of call should be re-examined at least.

Third, there should be a confirmation of the call by the church from which the individual comes and by the presbytery. That is what ordination is about and why a minister goes through various tests before he is approved for ordination. There has to be the sense that this is not just a matter of an individual call, though that is important and necessary, but somehow also that it is confirmed by other Christians. These others should be concerned about it and should be praying through it with the individual.

If Peter had been the only one who saw the leading of the Lord in this way, he probably would have rightly thought, I had better think this through again. None of the others agree with me. But Peter's friends experienced the same things and saw what had happened in the same way. So he was not being a Lone Ranger in this important matter. Their agreement was a significant confirmation of God's leading of him personally.

Peter Found the Ground Prepared

Finding the ground prepared was also a circumstantial matter, but I mention it separately because it seems to have meant something special to Peter. He was rightly impressed with how the Gentiles were ready, willing, and waiting to hear the gospel message (vv. 13–14).

This does not mean that if Peter had not received a good hearing he would not have been led to that point of his life by God. Lack of immediate success is not proof that one has taken a wrong step in trying to follow after God. Sometimes God leads us into difficult situations. Missionaries in difficult areas of the world sometimes spend many long years before they see even an initial convert to the faith. But if you arrive in a place and find that the ground is prepared and people respond to the gospel, that is obviously a great confirmation.

Peter had difficulty preaching in Jerusalem. He had been arrested and beaten for it. He was not out of the will of God then, just because he had difficulties. But here the household of Cornelius was waiting and eager, and that was an important encouragement.

God Blessed Peter's Preaching

When Peter began to preach to them, the Gentiles heard the message and believed it, and God showed their acceptance with him by sending the Holy Spirit, just as he had sent the Holy Spirit upon the apostles on the day of Pentecost (v. 15).

I suppose, although the text does not say this explicitly, that there was the sound of the rushing, mighty wind and perhaps even the tongues of flame that had been seen on that earlier occasion. Yet whether or not this was the case, the Gentiles did experience speaking in tongues (Acts 10:46). In the face of such divine favor, not one of the Jews present had the audacity to say, "But they are not circumcised. Let's attend to that first, and then they can be baptized."

Peter Ended with Scripture

Peter said, "Then I remembered what the Lord had said: 'John baptized with water, but you will be baptized with the Holy Spirit'" (v. 16). In other words, Peter had been led by Scripture initially, and now his experience and decision had been confirmed by additional reflection on the Word of God (v. 17). Peter did not have our New Testament. The New Testament was yet to be written. But he had heard Jesus' teaching and remembered what he had heard, and now these words were beginning to direct his thinking.[2]

A Fortunate Outcome

The results of Peter's explanation and defense were all good. Verse 18 says, "When they heard this, they had no further objections and praised God, saying, 'So then, God has granted even the Gentiles repentance unto life.'"

I notice two things about this response. First, the Jews of Jerusalem were convinced that this had been of God. Peter had explained the situation, and they were intellectually convinced. Second, because they were convinced, they praised God. What God had done was perhaps not what they would have preferred. It certainly was not what they expected. Nevertheless, there was evidence that this was truly God's work. And if God was working, then God was to be praised.

However, although the Jews were convinced by Peter's presentation, it was only for a time. They praised God, but not for long. Not very long after this a party began to grow up in the Jerusalem church that rejected this position. These people said in effect, "We must not allow the Gentiles to ignore the law of Moses. If we let down the barriers in this way, pretty soon everyone will start acting like Gentiles. And we all know how the Gentiles act. We have to preserve the law of Moses (and our traditions). We have to insist that Gentiles be circumcised, come under the law of Moses, and then keep the regulations that we have been keeping for centuries." So these questions had to be battled out again and again. Acts 15 tells about one such struggle, and the matter appears again in Paul's writings, particularly in his letter to the churches in Galatia.

Prejudice dies hard. But we need to learn from these early lessons regarding the scope of God's grace in the gospel. Often we find it difficult to believe that God can accept other people without these others first becoming like us. Yet God does accept them. And it is good he does, because if he did not, you and I would never have become Christians. We would have been excluded. The only reason we are believers is that God does not show favoritism. That is why we are "in." Therefore, we must not show favoritism ourselves. We must reach out to everyone, and we must not count it a threat when God brings into our fellowship somebody who from our perspective just doesn't seem to fit.

What matters is not whether other people fit in with us. What matters is that they have been accepted by God.

23

Christians First at Antioch

Acts 11:19-30

Now those who had been scattered by the persecution in connection with Stephen traveled as far as Phoenicia, Cyprus and Antioch, telling the message only to Jews. Some of them, however, men from Cyprus and Cyrene, went to Antioch and began to speak to Greeks also, telling them the good news about the Lord Jesus. The Lord's hand was with them, and a great number of people believed and turned to the Lord. . . .

Then Barnabas went to Tarsus to look for Saul, and when he found him, he brought him to Antioch. So for a whole year Barnabas and Saul met with the church and taught great numbers of people. The disciples were called Christians first at Antioch.

Acts 11:19–26

Acts 11 continues the story of the expansion of Christianity to the Gentiles, which began in chapter 8. Acts 8:4 said, "Those who had been scattered preached the word wherever they went." Now Acts 11:19 says almost the same thing: "Now those who had been scattered by the persecution in connection with Stephen traveled as far as Phoenicia, Cyprus and Antioch, telling the message."

When the gospel was preached in Caesarea, Cornelius was at least what is described in the story as "a God-fearer" (see chapter 20). Now, however, in the city of Antioch, we find Christians preaching not to Jews, not to those who were part Jewish and part Gentile, nor even to Gentiles who were God-fearers, but to those whom we would call utter pagans, since Antioch was an utterly pagan city.

The progression reminds us that Acts is not a haphazard telling of the story of Christianity but rather a step-by-step unfolding of what happened, which was the expansion of the Christian gospel and the Christian church throughout the known world.

When we understand this movement we also begin to understand why it was necessary to have the previous chapters. We might think that the material in Acts 11 should have followed immediately after Acts 8. After all, the gospel was moving along the Mediterranean coast from south to north. Why didn't Luke just go on to show that it took root next in Antioch? The answer is because of the preparation found in chapter 10. God was showing that it was possible for the Gentiles to hear the gospel, believe on Christ, and then be received into the church of Jesus Christ without first becoming Jews.

Moreover, the gospel did not have to be preached only to those Gentiles who had already shown some interest. It was to be taken everywhere, allowing the Holy Spirit to use it to bring forth fruit in many places.

Another way of saying this is that by the time we get to chapter 11, we are getting close to the kind of evangelism we know today. In today's churches we speak largely to those who have some acquaintance with the gospel, even if they are not converted. But the chief field for our evangelistic witness is those who are without. We are to go into the whole world with the gospel, even to those who do not want to hear it.

In Acts 13 we find that it is from Antioch that the great missionary movement starts. Since the church was made up of people converted out of paganism, they naturally had the needs of pagans on their hearts.

The City on the Orontes

After the death of Alexander the Great, the kingdom he had established divided into four parts. One of these was ruled by a man named Seleucus, who founded Antioch. Antioch was on the Orontes River, which made it possible for it to maintain trade with the big Mediterranean cities. Yet it was far enough inland to be a strategically-centered command post for the rule of Syria. For the Arabs, whose world was the desert, the natural capital of Syria was Damascus. But for the Greeks, who came from the west and whose world was the world of the Mediterranean, Antioch was the natural capital.

1. *A political center.* Over the years Antioch grew in importance. When Ptolemy, another of Alexander's generals, later conquered Seleucus and thus incorporated Syria into his more southern kingdom, he made Antioch the official capital of this new area.

As we read about the various cities of the Roman world in Acts, we find that each is quite properly given its own character.[1] Jerusalem is a Jewish city, filled with volatile temperaments and seething with the Jews' great hatred of the Gentiles. Rome is quite different. It was the capital of the empire and was very power conscious. Athens was the intellectual center of the world. Antioch was distinguished by being cosmopolitan. There was a tremendous mix of people in this city, as its geographical location might indicate. It was not far north of the Jewish states, so many Jews were found there. Josephus tells us there were 25,000 in his day. But Antioch was actually located in Syria, which meant that there were many Arab peoples too. And there were also Greeks, who were descendants of the Seleucids and Ptolemy, and Romans, since they were the occupying power. By Luke's time Antioch had grown to be the third most important city in the empire. Rome was first, Alexandria in Egypt second, then Antioch of Syria because of its extensive Mediterranean trade.

2. *A commercial center.* Antioch was chiefly a business city. The wealth of the east flowed through Antioch on its way to Rome. The armies of Greece and Rome marched through Antioch. Antioch was sophisticated and tolerant. Yes, tolerant—because all these different peoples, each with its own background, had to live and function side by side. Antioch was somewhat like the "melting pot" of the American ideal.

3. *A morally corrupt center.* Even the ancients thought Antioch was corrupt. Outside the city there was a park or grove of trees called "the Grove of Apollo." It was notorious as a location for licentious sexual indulgence. It was like an outdoor brothel, and people went there specifically to indulge their sensual appetites. Antioch was so well known for its debauchery that not long after this when a Roman senator was trying to describe how Rome, which had been morally upright in the days of the republic, had become corrupted by the moral degeneracy of the east, he said in picturesque language, "The Orontes has flowed into the Tiber."

Yet it was here in this cosmopolitan, commercial, and most corrupt city that a great church was established. This church that had a mixture of races was grounded in the Word of God, and, because it was grounded in the Word and was anxious to obey Jesus Christ, it became the first great missionary church of the New Testament.

The Gospel Comes to Antioch

Luke begins his account of the church at Antioch by telling how the gospel became established there. Believers who had been scattered as a result of the persecution in connection with the killing of Stephen "traveled as far as Phoenicia [to the south], Cyprus [off the coast] and Antioch, telling the message only to Jews" (v. 19). There were some of them, however, no doubt of Jewish background though perhaps with good contacts with their Gentile neighbors, "men from Cyprus and Cyrene" [in north Africa] who "went to Antioch and began to speak to Greeks also, telling them the good news about the Lord Jesus" (v. 20). We are told that "the Lord's hand was with them, and a great number of people believed and turned to the Lord" (v. 21).

This news got back to Jerusalem.

News was always getting back to Jerusalem, and I suppose it is always that way. Whenever anything is done, there is always somebody who will run to those who are supposed to be important and say, "Do you know what's going on?" They get their own sense of importance by being busybodies. Somebody went to Jerusalem and perhaps said, "They are preaching to the Greeks in Antioch. Did you know that? It is bad enough that Peter spoke to Cornelius, but at least Cornelius was a God-fearer. In Antioch they are just going out into streets and talking to everybody. You had better do something about it." The church sent Barnabas to investigate.

"Son of Encouragement"

Barnabas was a godly man. We know something about him already, because he has already been introduced to us, no doubt in anticipation of his role in Antioch and later. At the end of Acts 4, after the wonderful paragraph describing how the Christians were so united in spirit that they shared all they had, we read that "Joseph, a Levite from Cyprus, whom the apostles called Barnabas (which means Son of Encouragement), sold a field he owned and brought the money and put it at the apostles' feet" (Acts 4:36–37). Those two verses tell us a great deal about Barnabas.

> *His given name was Joseph, and he was a Jew.* In fact, he was a Levite, which means that he was a member of the priestly tribe. That was a very important thing for a Jew to have been.
>
> *He came from Cyprus.* Cyprus was a Gentile area. So although Barnabas was a Jew, even a prominent Jew, he must have known many Gentiles and have been familiar with the racially mixed environment he was to find at Antioch.
>
> *He was generous.* He sold a field he owned and gave the money to the apostles. In this action he stands in striking contrast to Ananias and Sapphira, whose story follows immediately after this first introduction of Barnabas, in Acts 5.
>
> *He was an encourager.* The apostles gave him the special name Barnabas to acknowledge this quality.

Barnabas was the man the Jerusalem Jews decided to send to Antioch. Why not Peter? It might be that Peter was busy or away somewhere else. Or it might be that they wanted someone who would be able to look at the situation with fresh eyes, not "tainted," as they might suppose Peter was by his experience at Joppa and Caesarea. Whatever the case, Barnabas was a good man. Perhaps they said, "If anybody has good judgment and can handle a delicate situation well and report back on what is happening—whether God is in this or not—surely Barnabas is the one to do it." So Barnabas went to Antioch.

We are told first that when Barnabas arrived and saw the evidence of the grace of God "he was glad" (Acts 11:23). I suppose it is possible to pass over something like that and say lightly, "Well, of course, he was glad; he ought to have been glad. God was working. Gentiles were getting converted."

Yes, but we must remember that this was a new situation, and it was not a foregone conclusion that a Jew, particularly a Levite, would rejoice in it. He might have opposed preaching to Gentiles entirely. Or he might have said begrudgingly, "Well, I guess the Gentiles have a right to hear too, if they must. If God is determined to include them, I won't stand in his way." But Barnabas did not react like that. On the contrary, when he saw that the gospel was bearing fruit in the Gentile communities, he was delighted to see it. These were not his people. Antioch was not his home city. But God was working, and he was pleased.

We need to learn from Barnabas in this respect—to be happy when God works somewhere else. All of us are happy (or at least most of the time are happy) when God works among us, blessing our denomination, church, people, or family. When he blesses somewhere else, well, we are not always so happy. We are restrained in our enthusiasm.

Then again, not only did Barnabas rejoice at what was going on, he also encouraged the believers. The text says, "He . . . encouraged them all to remain true to the Lord with all their hearts" (v. 23). I suppose he was thinking, If God is working here, well, I want to be at work here also. So he exercised his gift of encouragement and strengthened others.

When a person is really glad about something God is doing, he normally works with the others among whom God is doing it. And when the person works with other people, he or she is almost inevitably glad about the work. The reason some of us are so sour, I suppose, is that we stand back, saying, "Let God work," or, which may be even worse, "Let others work. Let them do the job." We don't like other people or what God is doing among them, so we don't pitch in. If we would, some of the blessing would rub off.

If you are not involved in witnessing to someone else, you ought to be, because there is joy in seeing how God blesses any faithful witness.

If you are not involved in a Bible study where God is bringing people to Christ and people are growing, you ought to be, because there is joy in the fruit of such studies.

If you are not participating in the life and worship of an active, working, worshiping, witnessing church, you ought to be, because there is joy in seeing how believers grow together into a fellowship where others are helped and in which the Lord Jesus Christ can be seen.

A Man Full of the Holy Spirit

We have seen what Barnabas did. Let's ask why he responded in this positive and encouraging way and not in some of the other ways we have suggested. The answer is in verse 24. It was because "he was a good man, full of the Holy Spirit and faith."

It is hard to read "he was a good man" without thinking of the way the Lord Jesus Christ handled a similar statement when the rich young man came to him and said, "Good teacher, what must I do to inherit eternal life?" (Luke 18:18). Jesus answered, "Why do you call me good? No one is good—except God alone" (v. 19). Jesus' point was that if the young man wanted to learn from him, he needed to start with a higher view of Jesus than his merely being a good man. He was calling him "good teacher," which was the equivalent of calling him "good man." Jesus wanted him to see that either he was the "good God" or he was a "bad man." Yet here, when Luke speaks of Barnabas, he says without any apparent difficulty or embarrassment, "He was a good man."

How can this be? The answer is in what comes immediately after, for the next phrase explains that Barnabas was good because he was "full of the Holy Spirit and faith." That is, he had the Spirit of Jesus Christ within him, and he had faith, which is a fruit of the Spirit. He was strong in these graces. It was because of the presence of Jesus Christ within him that when he got to Antioch he was able to rejoice at what was happening. The Spirit within him was bearing witness with the Spirit that was in the Gentile converts, and he found himself saying, "It is marvelous what God is doing among us."

The True Spirit of Christ

We learn another thing about Barnabas, and for this he is perhaps most to be praised. Barnabas was self-effacing.

Barnabas was the official delegate from Jerusalem. He was probably one of the most prominent figures in the church. As such, he could have been quite authoritarian. He could have said, "I am the official representative from Jerusalem. I am going to tell you what to do and how to run your church. You must do it like the Jerusalem church does, and you must report to me." Barnabas did not seem to have had any of that spirit. Instead, he rejoiced at what was happening and encouraged the work. Then he went out of his way to get a man he had known years before in Jerusalem and whom he recognized as being just the one to help the church.

This was a mixed church with very little knowledge of the Word of God. What did a church like this need if it was not to go off in one crazy direction after the other? Obviously, it needed sound teaching. In order to have that, it needed someone to teach the new converts. Who could do it? Who was capable of that kind of systematic teaching for Gentiles? Barnabas thought, That isn't my gift. I am an encourager. I am not the one to teach them, but there must be somebody who can. He thought of Saul.

Where was he? Saul had been in Jerusalem, which is where Barnabas had first met him. But he had gone back to his home in Tarsus, in what is now Turkey. Tarsus was about one hundred miles from Antioch, but Barnabas was not deterred by this distance. He set the time aside and made the journey.

Harry Ironside, in his commentary on Acts, has a bit of speculative dialogue based on his sense that perhaps Saul was feeling just a bit discouraged. God had called him to be a missionary to the Gentiles, telling him that he would stand before kings to testify. But Saul hadn't stood before any kings, and we do not even hear of wonderful things happening in Tarsus. Ironside imagines Saul thinking, The Lord cannot use me. People are not willing to receive my message. Suddenly there is a knock on the door, and there is Barnabas.

"Saul, I have come to take you to Antioch, to help the church there."

"Why, what do you need me for?" Saul asks.

"There is a great opportunity. You are just the man for the job."

Saul replies, "Oh, no; I am not worthy. I persecuted the Christians."

Barnabas persists, "You are the very man for the place. Come with me." So he brought him to Antioch.[2]

When they got there, Barnabas introduced Saul and then probably stepped back to let him preach. In this way, Saul began his ministry. The text says, "So for a whole year Barnabas and Saul met with the church and taught great numbers of people" (v. 26). That phrase "great numbers of people" is the very phrase used in verse 21 saying that a great number of people were brought to the Lord. Verse 26 is saying that all who were brought to the Lord were now taught. God saved many; now Barnabas and Saul taught many. They did this jointly, which is how it should be.

One of the weaknesses of much church planting in our day is that we send a single individual to do it. The person does the best he can. God blesses many of these efforts. But this is not the best way to proceed. When the Lord sent out his disciples, he sent them two by two. Here we have two also, Saul and Barnabas working together with mutually supporting gifts—Saul, the expositor or teacher, and Barnabas, the encourager.

Congregations need to understand the value of this biblical arrangement. Usually they look to one pastor or another and expect that one person to have all the gifts. That is a great mistake. God gives one gift to one person and another gift to another, and every gift is needed. Churches need to recognize this fact and support all people in the exercise of the gifts they have been given.

The First "Christians"

The church at Antioch was a church of many races with the dual ministry of Paul and Barnabas to lead it. It was a church that is closer to today's churches than any that we have seen so far in Acts. It is here for the first time that the disciples of Jesus Christ were called "Christians." The text says, "The disciples were called Christians first at Antioch" (v. 26).

They had been called a lot of other things before this. The first word that had been used to describe them was "disciples." They were disciples of their Master. That name prevailed through the lifetime of Jesus Christ.

Afterward, they were called "saints." Jesus had given them that word, calling them "holy ones." A saint is one who is committed to or devoted to God, which we all are if we are followers of Jesus Christ.

They were called "believers." This does not refer only to their intellectual beliefs, but also to the fact that they had responded with joyous commitment when the gospel was preached to them.

They were called "brothers." A new sense of brotherhood and sisterhood enveloped these members of the early church. They knew they were part of a new order of humanity.

They were called "witnesses." Jesus said, "You will be my witnesses" (Acts 1:8), and so they were. They witnessed to the truth about Jesus Christ throughout the whole world.

Here, for the very first time, these disciples—saints, believers, brothers, and witnesses—were called Christians. What is that? A Christian is a "Christ-one." Where did the believers in Antioch get that name? They did not get it from the Jews, because Christ means "Messiah" and the Jews would never have used that word of Jesus. They did not get it from one another either, because they already had all these other names. They must have gotten the name Christian from the pagans around them, for the Gentiles would have looked at these followers of "the Way" and said, They are Christ-ones. They are trying to be like Jesus. I do not think they said this in a derogatory way, though in some cases it could have been derogatory. I think instead that it was a genuine acknowledgment of what seemed to motivate these people.

Ironside says that when he was traveling in China years ago he was frequently introduced as "Yasu-yan." At first he did not know what the word meant, but he asked about it and learned that *Yasu* was the Cantonese word for Jesus, and *yan* was "man." So he was being introduced as a "Jesus man," which is fine, because that is what a Christian really is.[3]

It is appropriate in view of their being called "Jesus men" that the last paragraph of the chapter shows how the Christians in Antioch functioned. A prophet named Agabus, who will show up again later in connection with the apostle Paul, predicted that a famine was coming that would spread across the Roman world. We are not told that Agabus told the church what they should do about it; he merely prophesied. But they, being filled with the Spirit of Christ, immediately asked what Christ would do in such a situation. The result was, "The disciples, each according to his ability, decided to provide help for the brothers living in Judea" (v. 29). So they collected money and sent the gift to Jerusalem by Saul and Barnabas.

As far as I know, this is the first charitable act of this nature in all recorded history—one race of people collecting money to help another people. No wonder they were called Christians first at Antioch.

When the text says that "the disciples were called Christians first at Antioch" it means that Antioch was the first place they were given that name. But, taking that sentence another way, we might also observe rightly that they were

Christians *first of all,* before anything else. They could have been Gentiles first and only Christians second, in which case they would have said, "We are Gentiles. Why should we send money to the Jews?" They could have been pagans first and Christians second, in which case they would have said, "Why should we worry about anyone but ourselves?" Actually, they were neither of these. They were Christians first. And because they were Christians first, they felt a bond with all other believers and were determined to help them when the need arose.

Are you a Christian *first?* Is that the most important thing about you? Are you happy most of all to be a follower of Jesus Christ? If you are, then the gospel will go forward. God will bless it, and many other people will be brought to the Lord Jesus Christ through your witness.

24

Victory in Spite of Unbelief

Acts 12:1-19

It was about this time that King Herod arrested some who belonged to the church, intending to persecute them. He had James, the brother of John, put to death with the sword. When he saw that this pleased the Jews, he proceeded to seize Peter also. This happened during the Feast of Unleavened Bread. After arresting him, he put him in prison, handing him over to be guarded by four squads of four soldiers each. Herod intended to bring him out for public trial after the Passover.

So Peter was kept in prison, but the church was earnestly praying to God for him.

Acts 12:1–5

The church had suffered relatively little persecution since the persecution that followed the death of Stephen, but in chapter 12 we read about another. As a result of the last persecution the Christians were scattered throughout Judea and Samaria and carried the gospel to those areas. Now there was a new persecution and the church began to expand again, this time by the missionary journeys of Paul, which we are told about beginning with chapter 13. However intently the church is persecuted, the result is always the extension of the faith into new areas.

Persecution: The New Wave

The new wave of persecution unleashed against the church was probably connected with the expansion of the gospel to the Gentiles. What bothered Jews was the thought that Gentiles could be saved without becoming Jews first plus the corresponding thought that traditional Judaism would be superseded by a largely Gentile Christianity. Stephen had suggested this in his speech to the Sanhedrin and was martyred for it. Now the gospel was expanding to Gentiles in exactly the manner he suggested and renewed persecution broke out. It began when Herod arrested James and had him executed. James was one of the three most prominent leaders of the Jerusalem church. These "firsts among equals" were Peter, James, and John.

It would seem from the story that Herod arrested James as a test. This was Herod Agrippa I, and one thing we know about him is that he was very anxious to please the Jewish people. He seems to have thought, If the Jews are against this new movement, I'll strike out against the Christians and see how things go. So he arrested James and executed him. I suppose Herod waited a bit then, stepping back to see what the reaction would be. But when he was informed that the execution pleased the Jewish leaders, he thought, Well, I'll just move on to the next one. So he arrested Peter and was undoubtedly planning to have him killed also. It was Passover time, however, and since Herod did not want to break any of the rules surrounding these special days in the Jewish calendar, he put Peter in prison, intending to bring him out afterward and kill him.

Peter was guarded by "four squads of four soldiers each" (v. 4). It is hard to imagine Peter being as dangerous as all this, but that is the way Herod and the others seemed to be thinking about him. Peter was chained to a soldier on the right and another on the left, with two remaining outside the door of the prison to keep watch. It sounds as if Peter was being regarded as Public Enemy Number One. And in a certain sense he was. He was no real enemy to the public, but he was a threat to the public order that his enemies knew.

We remember that at the time of Christ's arrest, Pilate presented the people with a choice: Barabbas or Jesus. Barabbas was a zealot and a murderer besides. We would think that a person like that would be a major enemy, to be kept in jail at all costs. Jesus had gone about doing good. Jesus should be released. But that is not what happened. Barabbas was released and Jesus was executed. The people preferred a murderer to Jesus because Jesus was turning the world upside down by his preaching, and truth was more dangerous to them than Barabbas.

In the same way the Jews considered Peter, who had done nothing but preach the truth about Jesus, to be their chief enemy now. He was upsetting their world by his teaching. So here he was in prison, chained to soldiers.

What was Peter's reaction to all this? A little later in his life, when he came to write his first letter, he advised the believers to whom he was writing to "cast all your anxiety on him [that is, God] because he cares for you"

(1 Peter 5:7). Apparently, the man who wrote those words practiced them, because in prison on what was to be his last night, Peter was found sleeping. Sleeping! Obviously Peter knew what it meant to have cast all one's care upon God.

When Chains Fall Off

While Peter was sleeping, the Lord suddenly sent his angel to bring Peter out of the prison. There are some humorous elements in this story, and one of them is that Peter was sleeping so soundly that the angel had to poke him in the side to wake him up. I suppose Peter was one of those people who sleeps deeply. So the angel had to poke him quite hard, probably saying, "Peter? Come on, Peter. Peter, it's time to get up. Peter, we're getting out of here. Peter, come on, wake up." Peter did, of course, but even then he was so groggy that he thought he was having a dream. Peter did not really come to himself until he was outside the prison.

Sometimes we hear stories like this from missionaries. I am inclined to believe them. The Indian evangelist Sundar Singh had been witnessing in Nepal and had been forbidden to preach in a particular city. However, he went on preaching and was arrested. They put him in a dry well with a lid on top. He was there to die, because they didn't intend to feed him. In fact, Singh was sitting on the bones of people who had died before him. While he was there praying he heard a noise, looked up, and noticed that somebody was releasing the lid. Soon a rope was lowered. The rope had a loop in the end, so he put his foot in it and hung on. He was drawn out. But when he was up on the top and looked around to see who had pulled him out, there was nobody there.

His deliverance sounds perfectly natural so far because we can imagine how a sympathetic person might rescue him and then quickly run away so he would not be detected. But when Singh looked around, he saw that the cover was back on the cistern and that it was locked again. How had that been accomplished? Singh was merely thinking that whoever rescued him had certainly done his job efficiently.

However, the freed evangelist went back to the city and started preaching again. He was arrested again the next day and was brought before the priest, the chief man in the city. The people thought some sympathetic person had freed him, just as we would. But when they searched to see who had the key to the cistern's lid and how Singh might have gotten it, they found that the key was on the belt of the priest, where it had been all the time. At this point Singh believed that God had sent his angel to deliver him. He may have.

Lessons in Deliverance

There are a number of lessons from this first phase of the story that teach us to trust God and yet not presume on him.

1. *Peter's deliverance came at the last possible moment.* Peter had been arrested some time before and had been kept in prison during the week-long Feast of Unleavened Bread. He could have been delivered on any one of those previous nights, but he was not. It was only on the last night before he was to be brought to trial and executed that the angel came.

Many of us get into situations from which we also need deliverance, but we are not willing to wait for it. I find that it is usually at the very last minute that God intervenes to do something for us. Take knowing the will of God, for example. We would like God to reveal his will in advance, because we think we could do a better job of serving him if we could plan carefully. But God usually doesn't bow to our wishes. He does not reveal his plan to us until what we would call almost the last minute. He lets us wait—often, I am sure, with the very good purpose of leading us to trust him and accept his will in advance, whatever it may be.

2. *The experience of Peter must be balanced with that of James.* These were both chief apostles. Yet Peter was delivered and James was executed. Why? The story does not give us the answer to that question. You say, "Well, there must have been more for Peter to do. That is why he was spared." No doubt! But notice that we are not told what Peter did after this. There are no more stories about him so we could point to them and say, "Well, God obviously spared Peter to do such-and-such." God is sovereign in our lives and does what he will do. He chooses one to glorify him by his or her life. He chooses another to glorify him by his or her death. It is not for us to make that determination.

3. *The story illustrates the nature of spiritual deliverance through the gospel.* Peter's case was hopeless, humanly speaking. He was in prison, surrounded by guards. He was asleep. He was condemned to die. His case pictures us in our sin. We are chained by sin and are unable to escape. We are even asleep in sin, insensitive to it until God sends his Holy Spirit to break our shackles and free us.

I think it was this picture of the imprisoned Peter that was in Charles Wesley's mind when he wrote the fourth verse of his hymn "And Can It Be":

> Long my imprisoned spirit lay
> Fast bound in sin and nature's night;
> Thine eye diffused a quickening ray;
> I woke, the dungeon flamed with light;
> My chains fell off, my heart was free;
> I rose, went forth, and followed thee.

That is a good picture of what God does with us in salvation. He sends his light to illuminate the spiritual darkness of our lives and strikes off the shackles of sin so that we might be set free to follow Jesus.

Just a Prayer Meeting

Peter was now out on the streets of Jerusalem in the middle of the night. He had been delivered from prison, but he knew that he would have to leave the city since those who had arrested him would certainly arrest him again. What should he do? Should he leave at once? Peter was unwilling to leave without relating his deliverance to those he knew would be concerned for him.

His best bet was to go to the house where everybody usually met, the house of Mary, the mother of John Mark. Mary must have had a large home, and it was probably in this home that the disciples had gathered on the day of Pentecost when the Holy Spirit had come on them. Peter did not know the believers would be there now praying, though we do, because earlier in the story we were told they were so we might understand that Peter's deliverance was given by God in response to these prayers. Verse 5 says, "So Peter was kept in prison, but the church was earnestly praying to God for him."

This is a lesson about the importance of prayer. Sometimes people who have not lived with the Lord a long time (or perhaps have not studied the Bible's teaching about prayer carefully) say, "Why should Christians pray? If God is sovereign, as we believe he is, won't God do what he wants to do anyway? If God wants to save John Smith, won't God save John Smith? How can it matter if I pray for John Smith to be saved or don't pray for John Smith to be saved if he is going to be saved anyway?"

Other people say, "God is omniscient. He knows what we need. Why should we have to pray at all?"

These are valid questions, but they have a good answer. The answer is that although God is sovereign and does things in his own sovereign way, he nevertheless does what he does through means, one of which is prayer.

Witnessing is another means. It is true that God can save anybody he chooses even without us. But he has chosen to do it through the vehicle of human testimony. Because of this it is proper to say, "If God is going to save John Smith, God will save John Smith." But it is not proper to say that God will save John Smith anyway, apart from your witness to John Smith, if God has determined that it is by your witness that he will save him.

When we apply this to prayer we can say, as James does, "You do not have, because you do not ask God" (James 4:2). We do not get something because we do not ask for it. By contrast, we do get something else because we do ask for it. Why is that? It is because God has ordained the means as well as the ends. So when he ordains an answer to prayer he also ordains that the answer be obtained through the channel of prayer, which is the case here.

Somebody says, "Well, God would have saved Peter anyway."

It is not quite right to put it that way. God had determined to save Peter and certainly would save him. But the problem with the statement "God would have saved Peter anyway" is in the word "anyway." God had determined to save Peter, but the way in which God had determined to save Peter was in response to the prayers of the Christians who were praying. Without their prayers Peter would not have been saved. But he was saved through their prayers because that was the way God had determined to save him.

The story is a lesson about prayer's importance. But it is also a lesson about the nature of prayer. Verse 5 gives us four points.

The Christians Were Praying to God

It was to God that the Christians were praying. Someone may object, "That is hardly worth mentioning because, after all, aren't all prayers offered to God?" Well, no, not all prayers are addressed to God. Our questioner might reply, "Well, yes, I can understand that the heathen somewhere out in the jungle or on a remote island might be praying to trees or mountains or idols, that sort of thing. I mean the prayers of educated people." But that is not what I am talking about.

Someone else might say, "You must be thinking of those branches of the church that pray to saints." That is not what I am talking about either. I am talking about many normal prayers uttered by supposed Christian people in Christian assemblies, and I am suggesting that many of them are not really offered to God. Perhaps that is true of many of your prayers as well.

Some years ago I heard of a minister in Boston who was known for his eloquent prayers. In those days what went on in prominent churches on Sunday was still reported in the newspapers, and it was reported in the Boston papers the day following one of this man's services that his was "the most eloquent prayer ever offered to a Boston audience." The paper was not trying to be humorous, though they were directly on the mark. The prayer probably was offered to the audience rather than to God, and there are probably very many other prayers like it—only perhaps not so eloquent. Ministers pray in a way they hope will please the people, and sometimes laypeople do the same.

One of the best books I have ever read about prayer is *The Power of Prayer* by Reuben Torrey. At one point he relates how a discovery that prayer is actually meeting with God transformed prayer for him.

> The day came when I realized what real prayer meant, realized that prayer was having an audience with God, actually coming into the presence of God and asking and getting things from him. . . . The realization of that fact transformed my prayer life. Before that prayer had been a mere duty, and sometimes a very irksome duty, but from that time on prayer has been not merely a duty but a privilege, one of the most highly esteemed privileges of life. Before that the thought that I had was, "How much time must I spend in prayer?" The thought that now possesses me is, "How much time may I spend in prayer without neglecting the other privileges and duties of life?"[1]

The Christians Were Praying Together

What is involved in this particular example of prayer is not individual prayer, important as that may be, but what we would call "united prayer":

Christian people meeting together to pray in harmony. There is great value in that! The value is in the unity of mind and spirit that corporate prayer brings.

Most often we think of the value of united prayer in quantitative terms, probably because Americans usually think of quantity before quality. We suppose that if one prayer is good, well, two prayers must be better. If ten prayers don't get what we want, we should get twenty people praying. If we have a big project or want something very important from God, we start a prayer chain. For us the value of an all-night prayer vigil is not in the seriousness and fervency of the prayer but in the fact that we are able to get more prayers offered in that way and get them offered around the clock, at all hours, in case God is not paying attention in the day time. That is not a Christian concept, of course. It is pagan. It has more in common with the worship of Baal than of Jehovah. The value of united prayer is that the minds and hearts of God's people are being brought together on that matter.

The Christians Were Praying Earnestly

We discover how earnest the Christians' prayers were when we get into the story and find that although Peter was released in the middle of the night, when almost everyone in Jerusalem was sleeping, the Christians were nevertheless gathered together praying. They must have been praying all night, since in those days it was not safe to wander around the streets in the dark. They must have collected after work when it was still light. Now it was much later and they were still praying. If Peter had not come, they would have gone on praying until morning. That is a good biblical example of earnest prayer—something we know very little about today, at least in the United States.

Those who have studied revivals tell us that there has never been a great revival that has not been preceded by strong, fervent, united prayer by Christian people. Usually it starts small, perhaps with two or three getting together saying, "Let's pray that God will visit us and send a revival in our time." But these groups grow until there are many whose hearts are united to pray for it. It is out of such prayer that great revivals come.

The Christians Were Praying Specifically

Not only did the Christians pray to God, pray together, and pray fervently, they also were specific. The text says they were praying to God "for him [that is, for Peter]" (v. 5). It never hurts to be specific in our prayers. We know that sometimes we pray wrongly, of course. We ask amiss, as James says, especially when we pray for ourselves or something we very much want. In such cases we get our selfish desires mixed up with our proper desires. We have a much better chance of praying rightly and therefore getting what we pray for when we pray for someone else or when we pray for spiritual rather than material or physical things.

Two Qualifications

We may be saying to ourselves, "What a perfect example of prayer! How wonderful!" Yet the irony of the story is that although this is a great example of what true prayer should be, it was nevertheless also prayer that was somehow largely unbelieving. Unbelieving? Can prayer that is truly prayer to God, involves the whole church, is earnest and specific also be unbelieving? Apparently, because when Peter was delivered and came and knocked at the house door, nobody in the prayer meeting believed it was Peter.

We can understand what happened, because we have all been in prayer meetings in which everybody is trying to concentrate and something disruptive occurs. The telephone rings, for example. Whoever is praying keeps praying; everybody else tries to concentrate. But everybody is also aware that the phone is ringing, and they are all wondering who is going to get up and answer it. That is what happened here. I imagine the following scenario. The Christians were praying, "Oh, Lord, please deliver Peter. We need Peter. We don't want Peter to be executed the way James was executed."

Knock. Knock. Knock.

"Please save Peter. Please save Peter."

Knock. Knock. Knock.

People began to glance around. Wasn't somebody going to do something about that knock? Mary owned the house, so I suppose she looked up and saw Rhoda. Rhoda was a servant. Mary probably indicated to her, perhaps by a sign, that she should go to the door. Rhoda did. When she got there Rhoda recognized Peter by his voice, but she was so overjoyed and shocked that she went back to the group without even opening the door. She interrupted the prayer meeting, saying, "Peter is at the door!"

Did you ever hear anything so crazy in your life? Peter? How could it be Peter? Peter is in prison. Why would we be praying for God to save Peter if Peter is at the door?

So the others said to her, not very charitably: "You're out of your mind! I don't know who you saw out there, but you are out of your mind. And besides that, you are interrupting our prayer meeting. Sit down over there and let us pray."

But Rhoda kept insisting that it was so.

Obviously Rhoda had seen something that looked like Peter. So they said, "Well, Peter must already be executed then. He's dead, and it's his ghost (or angel) come to bid us good-bye." They did not really believe that God was going to deliver Peter.

But Peter kept on knocking. I know that in seances there is supposed to be something called "spirit rapping." But this was no spirit rapping. This was Peter knocking. And Peter didn't knock like a ghost, especially after he had been kept waiting outside, being the impatient man he was. I imagine that by this time he was banging on the door pretty firmly. Eventually, of course, they opened the door, and Peter came in and told his story.

Many people pray like that. I heard a story that illustrates what I mean. A couple had a nice house, but the view from their living room was blocked by a large hill. They read in the Bible that if two on earth agree about anything, they can pray and it will be done. They can say to a mountain, "Be removed and be cast into the sea," and it will be removed. So this couple said, "Let's pray that this mountain will be removed." They spent much of the night praying that God would remove their mountain. When they got up the next morning and went to the window and looked out, the hill was still there. And the husband said, "I knew it wouldn't be removed." Obviously, the man was not praying in faith, because he did not expect God to answer his request.

I have pointed out that these early Christians were not strong in believing that God would answer their prayer, even though they were praying rightly. But in spite of their unbelief, God did answer them. If their prayer was effective, though unbelieving, why should our prayers not be effective also? They were the same kind of people we are. The Bible says of Elijah, "Elijah was a man just like us." But he prayed that it would not rain, and it did not for three and a half years (James 5:17).

The questions for us are: Do we really pray? Do we pray to God? Do we pray with other Christians? Do we pray fervently? And do we have specific requests in mind?

25

The Death of Herod

Acts 12:19–25

On the appointed day Herod, wearing his royal robes, sat on his throne and delivered a public address to the people. They shouted, "This is the voice of a god, not of a man." Immediately, because Herod did not give praise to God, an angel of the Lord struck him down, and he was eaten by worms and died.

But the word of God continued to increase and spread.

When Barnabas and Saul had finished their mission, they returned from Jerusalem, taking with them John, also called Mark.

Acts 12:21–25

The twelfth chapter of Acts brings us to the end of the second major section of this book, but in a strange way. It tells of the death of King Herod, and our reaction is likely to be, "So what?" The death of a king is not remarkable. In fact, most deaths are not. A couplet from Shakespeare's play *Cymbeline* says:

> Golden lads and girls all must,
> As chimney sweepers, come to dust.

Quite true. Everyone must die, golden lads and girls included.

214

Or we might think of Shelley's poem "Ozymandias." Ozymandias was a mythical ancient king, and the poem by that title was written on the occasion of the author's reflection on an imaginary statue of the king now found to be lying prone in vast sandy wastes of a forbidding desert. The statue bore the inscription: "Look on my works, ye mighty, and despair."

Herod was only a man, though a king also. What is remarkable about his demise?

We might raise this question because of where we are in Acts. This bit of narrative material might have been inserted at any inconspicuous space in the story. But it does not come just anywhere. It comes at the end of chapter 12, where Luke is wrapping up the second section of the book. We recall that in the first chapter, in Acts' version of the Great Commission, Jesus told his disciples that they were going to be his witnesses: (1) in Jerusalem, (2) in Judea and Samaria, and then (3) throughout the whole world. The story of Herod ends part two and prepares the way for part three. Is this a proper way to end the second section? I think it is.

First, we need to know who Herod was. There are five Herods in the New Testament, and they are related. That is, they were part of one dynasty.

1. *Herod the Great (reigned from 34 to 4 B.C.).* The first and most prominent king in this dynasty was Herod the Great, the ruler who controlled Palestine at the time of the birth of Jesus Christ. He was a ruthless man. He exterminated all potential rivals to his throne, including at least one wife and several sons. We know him best as the king who ordered the murder of the babies of Bethlehem, thinking that if he killed all who were under two years of age, he would inevitably kill the pretender, that "king of the Jews" who had been sought by the wise men (Matt. 2:2).

2. *Herod Archelaus (reigned from 4 B.C. to A.D. 6).* Herod the Great was succeeded by his son Archelaus, the worst of his descendants. Archelaus was so bad that the Jews complained to the emperor about him, and he was removed from office in A.D. 6. He is mentioned only once in the New Testament (Matt. 2:22).

3. *Herod Antipas (reigned in Galilee from A.D. 6 to 39).* After the removal of Archelaus, Judea was governed for a time by Roman procurators. But the line of Herod the Great continued through another of his sons who reigned in Galilee until his banishment to Gaul in A.D. 39. His name was Herod Antipas, and he is the Herod who killed John the Baptist. He emerged in a cameo role at the trial of Jesus Christ.

4. *Herod Agrippa I (reigned as tetrarch of Trachonitis from A.D. 39 and then as king of Judea from A.D. 41–44).* He was the son of Aristobulus, Herod the Great's son by his second wife, Mariamne. This is our Herod, the one who appears in Acts 12.

5. *Herod Agrippa II (reigned over various territories from A.D. 50 to 100).* This Herod was a son of Herod Agrippa I, but he was only seventeen at the time of his father's death, and the emperor Claudius was persuaded not to give him his father's kingdom owing to his youth. In time, however, Agrippa II

was given other territories. This was the Herod before whom the apostle Paul appeared and made a defense some years later, a story recounted in Acts 25 and 26.

Herod Agrippa I

Herod Agrippa I, the Herod of Acts 12, was raised in Rome, and while he was there became a friend of Gaius Caligula. That was not a great honor. Caligula turned out to be shockingly corrupt even in a shockingly corrupt age. But Herod got to know him, and when Caligula came to the throne, he appointed Herod to a prominent position in the empire. In A.D. 39 Herod contributed to the fall of Herod Antipas and received his tetrarchy as a result. After the ascension of Claudius in A.D. 41, Herod also received Judea and Samaria and therefore ruled at last over all the territory of his grandfather.[1]

We do not know a great deal about some of the Herods, but we do know a lot about Herod Agrippa I, primarily because Josephus has written much about him. One thing Josephus tells us is that Herod tried hard to get on the Jews' good side. If we are cynical, we might say that he did this for political reasons. He knew Judea was a trouble spot. He wanted to keep both peace and his position. But perhaps Herod also had a genuine respect for Judaism. He was half Jewish himself, and we are told that he even took part in some of the temple ceremonies, such as reading the law publicly on certain occasions.

Acts 12:19–25 is a place where something we are told about in Acts is also found in secular literature. Josephus tells about Herod's death. The account is much like what we find here, although Josephus adds a few embellishments to the story. If it were the other way around—if the account in Josephus were the more straightforward and that in Acts elaborated—liberal scholars would dismiss the biblical account as untrue. As it is, they are inclined to accept these additions. Conservatives believe the Bible over Josephus and would accept it even if there were a contradiction. But there are no real contradictions, and there is no reason to question Josephus any more than the Bible in this case. Here is what Josephus tells us.

> After the completion of the third year of his reign over the whole of Judea, Agrippa came to the city of Caesarea. . . . Here he celebrated spectacles in honor of Caesar. . . . On the second day of the spectacles, clad in a garment woven completely of silver so that its texture was indeed wondrous, he entered the theater at daybreak. There the silver, illumined by the touch of the first rays of the sun, was wondrously radiant and by its glitter inspired fear and awe in those who gazed intently upon it. Straightway his flatterers raised their voices from various directions—though hardly for his good—addressing him as a god. "May you be propitious to us," they added, "and if we have hitherto feared you as a man, yet henceforth we agree that you are more than mortal in your being." The king did not rebuke them nor did he reject their flattery as impious. But shortly thereafter he looked up and saw an owl perched on a rope over his head. At once, recognizing this as a harbinger of woes . . . , he felt a stab of pain in

his heart. He was also gripped in his stomach by an ache that he felt everywhere at once and that was intense from the start.[2]

Josephus says that Herod endured this pain for five days before departing life in his fifty-fourth year. The lesson of Herod's death was not lost on those who were present, certainly not on Josephus. No mere mortal dare take the glory due to God alone. Herod did that, and God struck him down.

The Fall of an Even Greater Ruler

When I read this story I think of a similar one in the Old Testament, the story of Nebuchadnezzar. The fourth chapter of Daniel tells of the time Nebuchadnezzar stood on the roof of his great palace in Babylon, looked out over the famous hanging gardens that were one of the so-called wonders of the ancient world and on the city beyond with its great walls and said, "Is not this the great Babylon I have built as the royal residence, by my mighty power and for the glory of my majesty?" (Dan. 4:30). It was a classical statement of what we call secular humanism, the persuasion that everything in life is of man, by man, and for man's glory.

While Nebuchadnezzar was still speaking a voice came from heaven saying that because he had not given glory to God but had taken God's glory to himself, he would become insane, be driven from the company of human beings, and become like an animal, living in the fields for seven years until he should acknowledge that the Most High God was the true God and sovereign over human kingdoms. That is what happened. Nebuchadnezzar became insane, was driven from the palace, and lived like an animal for seven years. At the end of that time, as he himself said, his "sanity was restored" (v. 34), and he praised God. This was not just a matter of intellectual sanity, but also of spiritual sanity. It means that Nebuchadnezzar came to his senses spiritually, acknowledging that Jehovah really was the true God.

It is easy to see the parallel between this and the story of the death of King Herod. But there is also a great contrast. Nebuchadnezzar was judged in a way that allowed him by the grace of God eventually to regain his right spiritual mind and acknowledge that God is the true God. Herod had no opportunity to do that.

Most of us will never be in a position to take such glory to ourselves, and I trust that no such judgment is ever going to come upon us. Nevertheless, we do have a tendency to take praise to ourselves when it should go to God. People will say, "Aren't *you* wonderful!" When that happens there is always a tendency to smile in a half-prideful, half-humble way, thinking, Well, yes I am; thank you for noticing it.

We are on dangerous ground when we do this. What we must learn to do is to give glory to God. We have no talent that God has not given. We have achieved no success that God has not made possible. We can do no good of which God is not the source. We need to acknowledge that source, as the Bible teaches we should.

God's Word Is Not Bound

The reason Luke includes the story of Herod's death, in my judgment, is not primarily to show that it is wrong to take the glory of God to ourselves, though that is obviously true and is part of the story. Rather, it is to provide a contrast with the two verses ending this second section of Acts.

Verse 24 says, "But the word of God continued to increase and spread." Herod dies, but the gospel lives. Verse 25 adds, "When Barnabas and Saul had finished their mission, they returned from Jerusalem, taking with them John, also called Mark." These verses lay the ground for the missionary expansion of the church introduced in the very next verse.

Herod had been the individual who was most effective in opposing the progress of the gospel. At the beginning of the story the persecutions of the church were not really very intense. The Sanhedrin did not like it when the apostles went around saying that Jesus had been raised from the dead. They liked it even less when the apostles accused them of Jesus' murder. But there was still a certain tolerance among these religious leaders, and they were not terribly hostile so long as the traditions of their fathers were respected and upheld. Mostly they just told the disciples to go home and be quiet.

It was quite different with King Herod. Herod executed James and arrested Peter and was going to execute him too. Herod was opposed to the expansion of the gospel. But now, as this section of the story ends, it is he who is struck down by the Lord's angel, and the gospel prospers.

John Stott writes:

> At the beginning of the chapter Herod is on the rampage—arresting and persecuting church leaders; at the end he is himself struck down and dies. The chapter opens with James dead, Peter in prison, and Herod triumphing; it closes with Herod dead, Peter free and the Word of God triumphing.[3]

It is always that way. The enemies of the cross have always opposed the gospel. But in spite of them, the good news spreads. Why is it that the gospel continues to spread when so many other messages flounder and become relics of the past? Let me suggest a few reasons.

The Word of God Is Effective

Second Timothy 3:16–17 says, "All Scripture is God-breathed and is useful for teaching, rebuking, correcting and training in righteousness, so that the man of God may be thoroughly equipped for every good work." The key word is "useful," because it teaches that one reason the Word of God continues to spread is that it accomplishes what needs to be accomplished. It is a practical thing.

Many messages we hear and to which we give a great deal of attention are not useful. They are actually useless, if the truth be told. Most of what we hear on television is useless. The stories are useless; they accomplish nothing except perhaps to fill up an idle hour that would be better spent reading a good book, getting some exercise, helping a neighbor, playing with one's children, or something else. The commercials are especially useless. So is most of what we read in the newspapers; we prove it by forgetting what we have read even before we put the paper down. It is like this with most of this world's messages, however urgently they are thrust upon us.

The Word of God is not useless. It is effective. We need to be taught, and it teaches us—about God, ourselves, and the way of salvation. We need to be rebuked, and it rebukes us—about our sin and unrighteousness. We need to be corrected, and it corrects us—showing us the way we should go, the way of blessing. We need to be trained in righteousness, and it trains us—through daily application of its teaching. I suppose someone could say of Herod that he did many useful things. He was a great builder, for example. But compared with the gospel, which brings spiritual life out of spiritual death, what Herod did was of little value.

The Word of God Is Penetrating

Hebrews 4:12 says, "The word of God is living and active. Sharper than any double-edged sword, it penetrates even to dividing soul and spirit, joints and marrow; it judges the thoughts and attitudes of the heart." This means that the Word of God gets through to us as no merely human words do. We set up barriers against God and cover ourselves with suits of secular armor to protect us against the truth of what we are, who God is, and what the future holds apart from Jesus Christ. But the Word of God strikes through that armor to show that we are sinners in need of salvation. When the Word of God penetrates our defenses, it does so not to destroy or kill us, as a sword would do, but as a surgeon's scalpel to heal us and restore us to life.

The Word of God Is Life-Giving

Isaiah 55:10–11 says:

> As the rain and the snow
>   come down from heaven,
> and do not return to it
>   without watering the earth
> and making it bud and flourish,
>   so that it yields seed for the sower and bread for the eater,
> so is my word that goes out from my mouth:
>   It will not return to me empty,
> but will accomplish what I desire
>   and achieve the purpose for which I sent it.

The rain and snow that come down from the sky water the earth so it can begin to produce fruit conducive to life, and that is the way the Word of God operates. It not only saves people from sin, but it also makes them fruitful so from that time on they can contribute to the world and be a fount of spiritual blessing in it.

The Word of God Is Eternal

Matthew 24:35 says, "Heaven and earth will pass away, but my words will never pass away." We look about us and conclude that all things are temporary. People are born and die. Even the dreaded Herod died. Even the earth on which we stand will be destroyed. Nothing lasts. But there is one thing that will not pass away, namely, the Word of God. Nothing can stop it.

A person who has understood that truth knows that although there is some value to the visible, material things we work for and achieve in this life, these things, important as they seem, will still pass away. The only things that last are those that are invisible. And these come about only as God works through his Word to transform the hearts of men and women. That is why Christians are so anxious to teach the Word of God and why they are anxious to have men and women believe it. It is only then, when they do believe it and are born again, that something of lasting value occurs in their lives.

People say, "Nothing can be more precious than life." But that is not true. Physical life is precious. We go to great lengths to preserve and enhance it. But it is not the most precious thing of all. Spiritual life is more valuable.

Therefore, Christians have been willing to give up their physical lives for the sake of what they know lies beyond. They want to link their lives to the gospel because they know that whoever builds on the foundation of Christ's teaching will never be destroyed. They know that when the floods of life come they will be found secure upon that rock. Is it any wonder that a faith like that endures, increases, and spreads throughout the world?

Opposition to the Gospel

I think of those who have tried to oppose the gospel over the centuries. There were times when Christ's enemies tried to oppose the expansion of the Word of God by the sword, just as Herod did when he executed James. The powerful said, "If you continue to preach this gospel, we will take away your lives." And they did. There have been countless martyrs in the history of the church. Yet the Word of God has not been bound. The more the enemies of Christ have killed his followers, the more the gospel has spread outward like ripples on a pond.

Others have tried to suppress the Word of God by ridicule. They have concluded that physical persecution does not work. Killing people does indeed often turn them into martyrs, and Christ's enemies do not want to give the church heroes, so they have ridiculed Christianity and attempted to tear the heroes down. They laugh at us, saying, "Who in his right mind would ever believe a foolish thing like that? No enlightened, no modern person can believe such foolishness." The French agnostic philosopher Voltaire tried to destroy the church by ridicule, predicting that within fifty years people would have forgotten even who Jesus Christ was. But the very year he said that the British museum purchased a Bible manuscript from Russia for $500,000 while a copy of one of Voltaire's books sold for eight cents in the book stalls in Paris. Fifty years after his ignorant prediction, the Geneva Bible society was running off thousands of Bibles on presses that had been set up in Voltaire's former home in Geneva.

Others have tried to bind the Word of God by neglect, by pretending it no longer matters, just getting on with their utterly secular lives. Yet the gospel spreads.

People have tried to bind the gospel by creating substitutes for it, counterfeits. They say, "Well, all right, we'll have religion, but we'll have it without Christ. We don't need this business of the cross and an atonement. We'll just take the beautiful things like Jesus' ethics." That kind of religion, a Christ without the cross, has no power and appeals to no one except those seeking a substitute for the true thing. Thus do people fight, oppose, and ridicule the gospel we hold dear. Yet that true gospel of God goes on from strength to strength while the other secular gospels and their advocates fade along the way.

Although the Word of God is always advancing, as the text says, it does not do so without human channels, which is why I think Luke closes this section by a reference to Barnabas, Saul, and John Mark. The gospel is going to expand. God has decreed that it will. But he has also decreed that it is to advance by human messengers like Barnabas, Saul, and the others. It spreads by all those whom Jesus in Acts 1:8 appointed "witnesses" (all Christians).

I am glad Luke mentioned John Mark. If he had only mentioned Barnabas and Saul, we might have said to ourselves, "Well, naturally. Paul and Barnabas were apostles. They were the ones to carry out Christ's mission. There are people like them today—great leaders, evangelists. The task is for people like that, not for me." But Luke mentions Mark.

John Mark was the author of the Gospel of Mark. He was a friend of Peter and Barnabas. He was also a cousin to Barnabas, and he traveled with him much of the time. At the beginning of the Christian mission Mark was young. Later there was a period when he seems to have abandoned the missionary call—at least in Paul's judgment—though Paul later judged him to be useful again. He was an ordinary person. I suppose he was typical of the next generation of Christian missionaries after the apostles and is mentioned here for that very reason.

Do you look to others who have been in the faith a long time and think they are the ones to carry the gospel on? They are, or course. They are doing it to the best of their ability. But you, like Mark, are also called by Jesus to the same assignment. Will you do it? You must, because God has determined that the Word of God shall "increase and spread" through you, as it has through other normal people in earlier generations of the church.

PART THREE

The Witness to the World

26

The Start of the Missionary Era

Acts 13:1-12

In the church at Antioch there were prophets and teachers: Barnabas, Simeon called Niger, Lucius of Cyrene, Manaen (who had been brought up with Herod the tetrarch) and Saul. While they were worshiping the Lord and fasting, the Holy Spirit said, "Set apart for me Barnabas and Saul for the work to which I have called them." So after they had fasted and prayed, they placed their hands on them and sent them off.

Acts 13:1–3

No matter how a person chooses to outline Acts, it is evident that chapter 13 begins a new section. It describes a third stage in the expansion of the gospel.

I have outlined Acts by the pattern Jesus set in Acts' version of the Great Commission. Jesus told the disciples to remain in Jerusalem until they should receive power from the Holy Spirit but that after the Holy Spirit had come upon them they were to be his witnesses "in Jerusalem, and in all Judea and Samaria, and to the ends of the earth" (Acts 1:8). Chapters 1–7 of Acts concern the preaching of the gospel in Jerusalem, where foundations were laid for a theologically healthy church. Chapters 8–12 tell of the work in Judea and Samaria, the area just beyond Jerusalem. Finally, beginning with chapter 13, we have the expansion of the gospel to the entire Roman world. Chapter 13 therefore marks the beginning of what is rightly called "the missionary era."

The word "missionary" has to do with sending. The Latin word *mitto, mittere,* means "to send"; "mission" and "missionary" come from the forms *missi* and *missum.* The mission of the church is the sending of people by the church at the leading of the Holy Spirit into areas of the world where the name of Christ is not known and God is not worshiped.

As we study this chapter, we need to examine the church base from which this missionary outreach was conducted. Second, we need to think of the work of the Holy Spirit in calling, equipping, sending, and blessing the missionaries. Third, we need to see the nature of the task as it is illustrated in the work that took place on Cyprus, the first missionary target of the church in the Roman Empire.

The Church at Antioch

God does what he does through tools, and in the case of missionary work the tool God uses is his church. At Antioch we have an example of a mighty missionary tool, a church that was established, well-taught, integrated, active, and seeking God's direction.

An Established Church

Acts 11 describes how the church started. Later the pillar saints in Jerusalem wondered if anything sound could take place in purely a Gentile community and sent people from Jerusalem to Antioch to investigate. When they came back the delegation reported the church was doing well.

A church that is floundering is inadequate even for its own needs, and it certainly is not alert to the needs of others. A church that does not know where it is coming from, why it is here, or where it is going is not likely to be of use in the missionary enterprise. This was a church that in a very short time had become very sound indeed.

A Well-Taught Church

Notice how Acts 13 begins: "In the church of Antioch there were prophets and teachers." The words are plural in each case—more than one prophet and more than one teacher. Then there is a colon, and the text lists "Barnabas, Simeon called Niger, Lucius of Cyrene, Manaen (who had been brought up with Herod the tetrarch) and Saul." There are five names in this list, and we do not even know that it is exhaustive.

Where did this great body of teachers come from? Well, when we were in Acts 11 we saw that Barnabas, when he came to Antioch, recognized the church's need for sound teaching. He thought of Saul and then went all the way to Turkey to fetch him from Tarsus. Perhaps Barnabas had recruited the other teachers also. We do not know. But whatever the case, Barnabas's sense of this need certainly established teaching as a priority in the thinking of this church.

An Integrated Church

I am sure that the Christians in Antioch did not use the word "integrated," but that is what they were, though in a far richer sense than we normally use the word today. When we talk about integration we usually think of an integration of black and white persons. There were blacks and whites at Antioch, but the integration was more than that. There was also an integration of those who were from high levels of society with those who were from lower levels of society, the disadvantaged or slaves. And there was a mingling of Greeks and Jews too. The church had within it all the various groupings of people in the Roman Empire.

In the empire these groups usually had very little to do with one another. Greeks did not like Romans very much. Romans did not like Greeks. Jews did not like anybody. The rich despised the poor, and the poor hated the rich. The educated people looked down on those who were uneducated, and so on. But not in the church at Antioch! The five names of teachers tell an enormous amount about this church.

There was *Barnabas*, first of all. We know who he was. He was a Levite; that is, a Jewish priest. He did not come from Jerusalem, however. He came from Cyprus, so he was a Jew of the diaspora, those Jews who were scattered beyond Judah in Gentile lands. This means that he was a Jew who was in touch with Greek culture, perhaps even sympathetic to it.

Simeon was called Niger. "Niger" means "black." So people have surmised—I think on sound grounds—that this was a man of black skin. He too was a distinguished leader.

There was *Lucius* of Cyrene. It was men from Cyprus and Cyrene who first went to Antioch and began to teach the Greeks (Acts 11:20). Since Lucius was from Cyrene and appears here only a few years later, we can assume that he was one of the men who went to Antioch to found the church. In other words, he was a missionary. Lucius is a Latin name, by the way. So he was probably brought up in a Roman culture.

Manaen is next. Manaen is a Greek form of a Hebrew name, so this man was probably a Hellenistic Jew. The significant thing mentioned about him is that he had been raised with Herod the Tetrarch. This Herod was Herod Antipas, the third of the five Herods I introduced when we were studying the death of Herod Agrippa I in the last chapter. If Manaen had been brought up with this Herod, he would have been what we might call a prince—a man of high station who knew the ruling dynasty intimately. He was an "important person," but here he was associating with the other "normal" Christians in the church.

It is interesting that Herod and Manaen went such different ways. They were brought up together. But the first killed John the Baptist and later became involved (though indifferently) in the trial of Jesus Christ. He gave not the slightest indication of any spiritual sensitivity or made any response to the gospel. Manaen, though he was brought up with Herod in the very same surroundings, became a Christian. Moreover, he became a leader in the church and is numbered among its teachers.

The last teacher mentioned is *Saul*, a former Pharisee who was an enemy of the church but who turned from a career of persecution to build up the faith he had once tried to destroy.

The church's integration demonstrated in the diversity of its membership the full unity of all people within the body of Christ. Because this church was established, well-taught, and integrated, it was well-equipped to go into the pagan world with Christ's gospel. As representatives of this church went to the Greeks, Romans, barbarians, slaves, and free persons of the Roman world, they could say, "The gospel is for you." If those to whom they spoke replied, "But how do you know it's for me?" they could answer, "Because of the way it functions in our church at Antioch." A church like this was quite naturally a very powerful force in the missionary enterprise.

A Multiple Staff Ministry

The early churches all had multiple ministries, and this was no exception. When Paul went to a place, he always took someone with him. And when he and his coworker or coworkers left the new church behind, they appointed leaders for it.

We have fallen away from that principle in our time through a pattern of organization in which churches usually are in the hands of just one minister. The people think, Well, he's the minister. It's his job to do Christian work. Let him do it. Such churches are weaker as a result. Churches should have multiple ministries. At the very least, they should use the gifts of all the church members. God has given each a spiritual gift to be used. But even in the formal pastoral leadership—"the ordained leadership," as we would say today—there should be a plurality wherever possible. There should always be more than one worker when mission work or new church planting is being done.

A Worshiping, Praying Church

In verse 2 we are told that while they were worshiping the Lord and fasting, the Holy Spirit spoke to them about sending Barnabas and Saul to the Gentiles. Sometimes churches forget that power in ministry comes from God, and they lose contact with him. That was not the case with this church. It was an active church, even blazing new ground. But it knew that its life came from God and therefore did not abandon its worship.

A Seeking Church

Sometimes when I am reading commentaries on a passage I come across humorous things, and that has been my experience here in regard to the word *fasting*. One person who obviously fasted very little, if at all, explained that fasting means that when you are working on a sermon you sometimes get so involved with it that you forget to eat a meal. Well, I often miss a meal because of my work too, and if that is what fasting means, I fast often. But I do not think that is what this verse is talking about. In the Bible fasting means to forego food for a time in order that in a spiritual frame of mind and having one's time given over to spiritual things one might seek God's direction for a new phase of life. The church at Antioch was seeking such direction.

Perhaps the church was seeking the role it should play in world missions. These people knew the Great Commission. The early preachers of the gospel undoubtedly shared it with the church. Paul had been told that he was to be a missionary to the Gentiles. Years had gone by. Perhaps Paul had even been talking about this, saying, "I think it may be time for me to get on with this task." The church at Antioch may have shared his thinking: "Perhaps it is time for us to do something about it too. Maybe it is time for us to be useful."

The church did not want to make this decision on their own, however, taking it upon themselves to fulfill a specific missionary function. Rather they waited upon the Lord and sought his leading. It was in a prayer meeting in which they were doing this that the Holy Spirit said, "Set apart for me Barnabas and Saul."

A Power or a Person

The second thing we need to notice in these verses is the work of the Holy Spirit. If mission work is to be successful, it is going to have to be the Lord's work.

If we try to do it in our own strength, nothing will happen. Our efforts will be as fruitless as Peter's efforts at Pentecost would have been if the Holy Spirit had not come. Peter would have stood up before those who had been instrumental in crucifying his Master, would have condemned their sin and called them to repentance, and not one would have repented. As a matter of fact, they would very likely have done to Peter what they did to Jesus earlier. But when the Holy Spirit blessed Peter's speaking, what a day earlier would have been entirely fruitless became fruitful, and three thousand people believed. At Antioch the Christians sought the will of God, the Holy Spirit led, Paul and Barnabas were set apart, and God eventually blessed what these first missionaries did.

The Holy Spirit is not a power for us to use. He is a Person, the Third Person of the Trinity. So rather than thinking of the Holy Spirit being a power that we are somehow to seize and use, we are to think of him as a person whose job it is to use us. Acts gives us this contrast. In Acts 8 we have Simon wanting to get and use the Holy Spirit, but in Acts 13 we have the Holy Spirit getting hold of and using Barnabas and Paul.

The people the Holy Spirit chose were the two most gifted leaders in the church. Paul was the most effective person in the extension of the Christian message to the Gentiles, and Barnabas must have been right there with him. I know Christians who say they do not believe in missions. They believe in giving to local work, supporting things they can see, but giving to mission work or sending people abroad . . . well, that just seems unnecessary. That is not the way the Holy Spirit leads. Moreover, the Holy Spirit apparently does not say, "Since you have to send somebody, pick out someone you can spare and send him or her." He wants the best. If we listen to him, we'll send the very best people we have.

If a seminary graduate is of average gifts, we think he should pastor a church. If he has above average gifts, we think he should pastor a large church. But if he has exceptional gifts, we think he should teach in seminary. I say in schools of theology that this is not the way it should be. In my view, the worst should teach, the more gifted men should pastor churches, and the very best should be missionaries. That may be a slight exaggeration, but I think Acts 13 does gives us insight into the mind of God in this area.

We have seen that the Holy Spirit sent the missionaries out. But notice that he did not just call them or send them; he went with them too. We see this clearly later on, because when the missionaries were opposed by Elymas the sorcerer, Paul was "filled with the Holy Spirit" as he replied (v. 9).

If we did not know that the Holy Spirit would go with us, we would not dare to do Christian work. We would be paralyzed even from attempting it. By definition missionaries go where the gospel has not been heard, and where the gospel has not been heard life is dark and the opposition is strong. Frequently, antagonism to the God of the Bible is intense and expressed in violent hatred. How would anybody dare to tackle such work unless the Holy Spirit is with him and working in him to bless the message? If we know God is with us, we can be bold to go anywhere at all.

The Work on Cyprus

Cyprus is a large island off the south coast of Turkey west of Antioch. It is the place from which Barnabas came. I do not know if that fact entered into the missionaries' decision to go there, but it probably did. Barnabas may have said, "I know Cyprus, and I think it would be a good place for us to start. Many cities have never heard the gospel. Let's start out in that direction." Whatever the reasoning, the two missionaries took a ship sailing from Seleucia, the port near Antioch on the coast, to Cyprus and arrived at Salamis. From there they traveled across Cyprus westward until they came to Paphos on the opposite side of the island.

I suppose they talked about Jesus everywhere they went and that many believed. But instead of telling what happened in each and every village, Luke tells us about one incident in Paphos. We see several things in this incident that are characteristic of what happens in Acts from this point on.

Great Opportunity

In this case, the opportunity was an invitation from the proconsul Sergius Paulus to speak the Word of God. This was a good opportunity because of the importance of this man. The word "proconsul" probably does not mean much to most of us. In some minds it might suggest something like "mayor" or "councilman." But it was much more than that. A proconsul was a Roman official placed over an entire province.

Cyprus had been annexed by Rome in 57 B.C. After it was settled to Rome's liking it became part of the province of Seleucia on the southern coast of Turkey. This happened in 55 B.C. In 27 B.C. Cyprus was made a separate province. During this entire period it was ruled by the emperor through an imperial representative, known as an imperial legate. In 22 B.C. the administration of Cyprus passed from rule by the emperor to rule by the senate, and when that happened, the person in charge of the province was no longer called an imperial legate, which indicated his relationship to the emperor, but rather a proconsul, which indicated his subordination to the Roman senate. Thus, it is no accident but a mark of accuracy on Luke's part that he calls Sergius Paulus a proconsul. The ruler of Cyprus was a proconsul at the time of Paul's visit, but he had not been a proconsul prior to 22 B.C.[1]

Serious Opposition

Opposition came from a man whose name was Elymas, also called Bar-Jesus. He is described as a Jewish sorcerer and false prophet. There were many like him in the ancient world. They would get into positions of power because they pretended to have special insight into what was going to happen and could offer "wise" advice to those who made decisions. This man had gained the proconsul's confidence. When Barnabas and Saul came along, Elymas recognized that if Sergius Paulus paid attention to them, his own days as an influential person would be numbered. As a result he opposed the gospel and did everything he could to turn the proconsul from it.

Divine Empowerment

It is here that the presence of the Holy Spirit is mentioned in a special way. We are not to think that the Holy Spirit was not with Paul and Barnabas earlier, of course. Certainly he was. But with the emergence of Elymas's fierce opposition, the Holy Spirit filled Paul in a powerful way to pronounce judgment on this man. Paul called Elymas "a child of the devil and an enemy of everything that is right."

Elymas's second name was Bar-Jesus, which meant "son of Jesus." Jesus was a popular name; it did not refer to Jesus Christ necessarily, though it may have. The gospel was spreading by this time, and Elymas could have been taking a name of somebody who was beginning to be regarded as important. But whatever the case, Paul referred to the name for contrast, saying, in effect, "You call yourself Bar-Jesus ('son of Jesus') but you are actually Bar-devil ('a child of the devil') because you oppose the work of God."

Significant Success

Paul said that Elymas was going to be blind for a time (v. 11). Eventually, we must suppose, God gave him back his sight. But in the meantime, his blinding made a great impression on the proconsul, as well it might. The story says that after "mist and darkness" came over Elymas so that he groped about, seeking someone to lead him by the hand, "the proconsul . . . believed" and followed the missionaries' teaching.

Some commentators have questioned the quality of Sergius Paulus's belief. They have called it belief that is mere impression only, the kind the devils have and yet are not saved. They say, "We do not see any evidence of a change in this man's life." Well, of course we don't. We are not told much about him at all. But why should we not think that Sergius Paulus was saved? He had heard the gospel and responded to it. Why should we not think that along with whatever others believed this man also believed and became the nucleus of a church that has endured all down through the ages to the present time?

John Stott argues that "Luke surely intends us to view Sergius Paulus as the first totally Gentile convert, who had no religious background in Judaism."[2]

Barnabas and Saul, Paul and Barnabas

In the middle of this story Paul is called "Paul" for the first time (v. 9). Before this he has been called "Saul," which was his Hebrew name. Now he is called "Paul," which is a Roman name. This is probably because the chapter marks the beginning of the missionary outreach to the Gentiles. Prior to this the growth of the church had been under the oversight of the Jewish leaders in Jerusalem; hence Saul was called by his Hebrew name. Now he is going to the Gentiles; so his name assumes a Gentile form.

Yet there is a change that goes beyond that. If we look back to verse 2, we find the words "Barnabas and Saul." In verse 7, where Sergius Paulus sends for the two missionaries, it is the same: "Barnabas and Saul." Then, in verse 9, Saul becomes Paul. Verse 13 says, "Paul and his companions." Finally, in verse 42 we find the words "Paul and Barnabas." I think these changes signify that at the start Barnabas was the leader. He had been in the faith longer. He had been effective, recruiting Paul, for example. But the time came, as God worked sovereignly in these two lives, that Paul became the natural leader of this missionary team.

Paul had been in the background for a long time. He seems to have faded from sight, at least to the eyes of the people in Jerusalem. Most had forgotten about him. Paul had spent three obscure years in Arabia, had been perhaps seven years in Asia Minor at Tarsus, and now had spent two more years at Antioch. Twelve years! Paul was getting on into middle age at this point, and he had not been used much—certainly not in any great pioneer work among Gentiles, which God had told him he would do.

But now the call came, and from this point on Paul leads the enterprise to which God had earlier set him apart.

You may be in a time of preparation too, even though you are thirty, forty, fifty, or more years of age. If you are, don't cut your years for preparation short. If you have been given such years, cherish them and use them wisely. Christians emphasize missions, and missions are important. Don't give up on missions, but don't give up on preparation for other Christian work either. The important thing is to keep close accounts with God, study the Bible, learn about others, and serve everyone as widely and as well as you can. It may be that in the years to come, you will look back on this very time and say, "God was working," and others will note that God was indeed preparing you for even more useful service.

27

One Sabbath in Antioch

Acts 13:13–43

From Paphos, Paul and his companions sailed to Perga in Pamphylia, where John left them to return to Jerusalem. From Perga they went on to Pisidian Antioch. On the Sabbath they entered the synagogue and sat down. After the reading from the Law and the Prophets, the synagogue rulers sent word to them, saying, "Brothers, if you have a message of encouragement for the people, please speak."

Acts 13:13–15

There were three missionary journeys of the apostle Paul. On the first journey (Acts 13:4–14:28), Paul and Barnabas sailed from Seleucia near Antioch to Cyprus. They traversed that island and then went to Perga in Pamphylia on the southern coast of what we call Turkey. They traveled inland to Galatia, ministered in Pisidian Antioch, Iconium, Derbe, and Lystra and then retraced their steps to the coast and returned to Antioch. At the start of the second journey (Acts 16:1–18:22), the two missionaries parted in a dispute over John Mark, who had left them on the first journey and was thought by Paul to be unfit for future service (Acts 13:13; 15:36–41). Barnabas took Mark and returned to Cyprus, while Paul took another missionary named Silas and went overland into Turkey. From there he went on into Europe, worked in Philippi, Thessalonica, Berea, Athens, and finally Corinth. On his way home, he made a short stop at Ephesus but did not stay there until the third journey. The final missionary journey (Acts 18:23–20:38) also began by an overland trip through the previously evangelized regions of Turkey, but the bulk of the time was spent at Ephesus. At the end of this journey, Paul sailed back to Jerusalem, where he was arrested.

These three missionary journeys changed the history of Europe forever and as a result the history of the world.

Through Thorny Ways

In Acts 13 we are at the start of these journeys, and it is not long before we find that they were not at all smooth sailing. As far as we know, there were no serious difficulties on Cyprus. But now we begin to notice some. We anticipated one in the last chapter: a shift in leadership. Somewhere along the line Paul began to take first place as leader of the missionary party.

We need not suppose that Barnabas did anything but take this graciously. He seems to have been an extremely gracious man. Still it must have been a bit difficult for him. Somebody once said,

> It takes more grace than I can tell
> to play the second fiddle well.

Barnabas had that grace, although it may not have been acquired easily.

Second, there is the matter of John Mark's desertion. Luke mentions John's departure briefly in verse 13, at this point passing over the fact that Paul and Barnabas must have reacted quite differently to it.

Mark had not been called by the Holy Spirit or commissioned by the church as the others had been. Mark was related to Barnabas, and Barnabas probably just said, "Let's take him along with us," which is what they did. Mark was with them on Cyprus. But when they arrived in Pamphylia, for some reason Mark left the others to return to Jerusalem. We do not know why he left, though there has been a great deal of speculation about it. What we do know is that Paul did not like it. He regarded it as a desertion.

There is also a third problem. It is not mentioned here, except that Luke may be alluding to it in saying that although the missionaries went to Pamphylia and might have been expected to carry on a ministry there, they actually left the coast and passed inland to Antioch in Pisidia (not Antioch of Syria, from which they started out). Pisidian Antioch was in the mountains at an altitude of about 3,600 feet. Since Paul mentions in the letter to the Galatians that he had a bodily affliction at this time, some scholars have supposed that Paul caught a disease, perhaps malaria, while living in Pamphylia's lower coastal plains and that he and his party pressed on into the healthier mountain climate because of it.

I do not know if this was the case, but the idea was worked out at some length by the British scholar William Ramsay. In the last century Ramsay did extensive travels in these areas and wrote a book about his findings called *St. Paul the Traveler and the Roman Citizen.* He did much to show the historical accuracy of Luke's account of Paul's travels.[1]

If Ramsay is right and Paul did get malaria, this might be related to Paul's particularly strong reaction to Mark's desertion. Ramsay suggests that Mark wanted to evangelize Pamphylia and that when Paul left Pamphylia for Galatia Mark regarded *this* as abandoning the work. Paul, for his part, would have thought Mark unsympathetic and unsupportive of him in his illness, perhaps even unresponsive to God's leading.

Regardless of the specifics of these events, clearly even these extraordinary apostles had disagreements. They were in the middle of a monumental missionary journey, led by the Holy Spirit, on the verge of what turned out to be a time of great blessing not only in Antioch but in the churches of Galatia as well. But they still had problems.

If these men had trouble in their work, we should not be too shocked if we have trouble too. We sometimes talk as if everything in the Christian's life should go smoothly, that nothing bad should happen. We expect total and unmitigated blessings. But Jesus did not promise us smooth sailing as his disciples. He promised suffering.

A person might say, "Well, yes, but I do not see a reason for these things. What was the purpose of Paul getting sick, if he did get sick? Or of John Mark leaving?" I do not know the answer to those questions, but God does. And just because we do not know the answer to why things fail to go smoothly in our lives does not mean there is no answer or God is not blessing us in spite of discouragements. These men had trouble, but in spite of their trouble they preached the gospel, people believed, and churches were established.

The Sermon at Antioch

When Paul got to Antioch he went into the synagogue with Barnabas. The synagogues of the diaspora were an open door for these early gospel preachers, most of whom were Jews. They were places of regular worship and were open to strangers, God-fearing Gentiles as well as Jews. It was the custom on a normal Sabbath to have two readings of the Scriptures: one from the law, the other from the prophets. After that people could give extemporaneous expositions.

This opportunity had been given to Jesus in the synagogue of Nazareth. The leaders had been reading from Isaiah at the time. So Jesus stood up, found the proper reading, and then expounded it. He said, "Today this scripture is fulfilled in your hearing" (Luke 4:21). This order of service was followed nearly everywhere. So Paul and the other missionaries customarily went into the synagogues, waited, and then when they were asked to speak used the opportunity to preach about Jesus.

Paul did this in the synagogue of Antioch, and the sermon that resulted was a great one. It is the first synagogue sermon by Paul that Luke records. In some ways, it is like the sermon Stephen preached before the Sanhedrin prior to his martyrdom. Stephen gave a long recital of God's acts on behalf of the Jewish people, a review of Jewish history. Paul did the same. In other respects, however, Paul's sermon is like that of Peter at Pentecost. Peter quoted texts from the Old Testament and then explained how they had been fulfilled. Paul did the same. Still, this sermon is distinctly Pauline. In fact, when we read it, we find that its themes are those developed by Paul later in his letters. The sermon may indicate that this was a time when the distinct doctrines of the next section of the New Testament, the letters, were beginning to crystalize in Paul's mind.

The Introduction: Jews and Gentiles

All good sermons have an introduction, some long, some short. This sermon has a brief introduction. It might be the case that Paul actually gave a much longer speech with a longer introduction and that Luke is merely summarizing here. But we have the drift of it in any case.

Paul addresses two categories of people who were in the synagogue that day, and he calls for their attention: "Men of Israel and you Gentiles who worship God, listen to me" (v. 16). This indicates that there was a mixed worshiping community in this synagogue. There were Jews, of course. But there were also some devout Gentile God-fearers (see chapter 20 on Cornelius). By going to a synagogue like this Paul had an opportunity to preach to Jews, which he felt an obligation to do, but at the same time also to make contact with those Gentiles who had sensitivity to spiritual things. These would already have been instructed out of the Old Testament and would therefore be fertile ground for his evangelizing.

The Sermon Proper: Four Points

Once past the introduction, Paul organized his sermon into four parts: a review of the Old Testament *kerygma,* a statement of the New Testament *kerygma,* a selection of supportive biblical texts, and an announcement of the gospel. The conclusion that follows this presentation is a warning of judgment to come if the Good News is not heeded.

The Old Testament Kerygma

We looked at the word *kerygma* in chapters 5 and 12. It has been used by biblical scholars since the time of C. H. Dodd to refer to the way God's specific saving acts are recorded in both the Old and New Testaments. For example, G. Ernest Wright applied Dodd's work to the Old Testament, pointing out that we find specific proclamation outlines not only in New Testament sermons like this one by Paul or the earlier one by Stephen, which refer to the Old

Testament, but even in the Old Testament itself, in some of the psalms, for instance. In each of these places a certain standard listing of the saving acts of God for his people is brought forward for the people's remembrance.[2]

Paul lists these acts briefly here, though we probably have a sharp condensing of his sermon by Luke. Because Paul is brief, we have to look carefully to appreciate the events of Israel's history that he had in mind.

> Verse 17: "The God of the people of Israel chose our fathers." This refers to the patriarchal period, as Jews (and the instructed Gentiles present) would understand. They would know Paul was referring to God's choice of Abraham, Isaac, and Jacob—the fathers of the people.
>
> Verse 17: "He made the people prosper during their stay in Egypt." This is when Israel began to grow into a great nation. "With mighty power he led them out of that country." This refers to the Exodus.
>
> Verse 18: "He endured their conduct for about forty years in the desert." This concerns the years of the wilderness wandering, during which Moses led them to the Promised Land.
>
> Verse 19: "He overthrew seven nations in Canaan and gave their land to his people as their inheritance." Here is the conquest, as recorded in Joshua.
>
> Verse 20: "After this, God gave them judges until the time of Samuel the prophet." This sentence embraces Joshua and 1 and 2 Samuel.
>
> Verses 21–22: "Then the people asked for a king, and he gave them Saul son of Kish, of the tribe of Benjamin, who ruled forty years. After removing Saul, he made David their king. He testified concerning him: 'I have found David son of Jesse a man after my own heart; he will do everything I want him to.'" These verses describe the first eighty years of the monarchy.

Wright and others think the Old Testament *kerygma* ends at this point, coming to a climax in King David. After this the history of the people goes downhill.

The *kerygma* tells us that the Jewish view of history was really the Jewish view of God. People have asked whether the Old Testament is a book of theology or a book of history. The answer is that in a sense it is a book of theology, just as the New Testament is also a book of theology. But what is most important is that the Bible is a book about God's saving acts, which is where the Bible's theology is seen. We see this reflected in Paul's words, for one of the things we notice is that he used the words "God" or "he" (referring to God) repeatedly: God did this, and God did that. It is always a case of God calling, moving, saving, delivering. This is wonderful theology. Even more, it is a theological worldview.

The New Testament Kerygma

The second part of Paul's sermon is a continuation of the first. Just as he has spoken of the Old Testament *kerygma,* so now he also speaks of God's acts in the New Testament period.

I am sure Paul was acutely conscious of what he was doing. He had been reminding his mostly Jewish hearers (in a Jewish synagogue) of what God had done in the past for his people. Now, embracing his Gentile audience also, which he had addressed at the beginning, Paul reminds his hearers that God is not a God of the past only or of the Jews only. God is still acting and has acted in recent times, doing something new. God established an old covenant, but now God has established a new covenant through the work of Jesus Christ.

C. H. Dodd studied three blocks of New Testament material: (1) the early Christian preaching, which includes the sermons in Acts, (2) the handling of this message in the Gospels, and (3) the summaries of the gospel in the writings of the apostles Paul and John. Dodd points out that in each of these three blocks of material the same essential core is presented. In its simplest form, it has to do first with the ministry of John the Baptist, who announced the appearance of the Messiah. Second, it concerns the trial and crucifixion of Jesus, the heart of the gospel. Third, it deals with Jesus' burial. Finally, it announces the resurrection, paying special attention to those who were the witnesses of it.

Notice how it works. In verse 23 Paul says, "From this man's [David's] descendants God has brought to Israel the Savior Jesus, as he promised." That is a summary of the *kerygma.* Then Paul spells it out: (1) the ministry of John the Baptist: "John preached repentance and baptism to all the people of Israel" (v. 24); (2) the trial and crucifixion of Jesus: "The people of Jerusalem and their rulers did not recognize Jesus, yet in condemning him they fulfilled the words of the prophets that are read every Sabbath. Though they found no proper ground for a death sentence, they asked Pilate to have him executed" (vv. 27–28); (3) the burial: "When they had carried out all that was written about him, they took him down from the tree and laid him in a tomb" (v. 29); and finally (4) the resurrection attested by witnesses: "But God raised him from the dead, and for many days he was seen by those who had traveled with him from Galilee to Jerusalem. They are now his witnesses to our people" (vv. 30–31).

Christianity is not just a philosophy or a set of ethics, though it involves these things. Essentially Christianity is a proclamation of facts that concern what God has done. That is why Christianity is not malleable. Sometimes people try to remake Christianity, thinking a new version might be more acceptable to our contemporaries. But this does not work, and the reason it does not work is that whether we like it or not Christianity constantly brings us up against the facts. Rather than trying to change them, we have to learn first to conform our thinking and conduct to these facts and second to proclaim not our own ideas but these very facts to other people.

A Selection of Supportive Biblical Texts

I said earlier that Paul's sermon is not only like Stephen's before the Sanhedrin in its review of Old Testament history, it is also like Peter's at

Pentecost in its citation of Old Testament texts. This is what Paul does in the third part of the sermon, beginning in verse 32. There are four texts here, and all of them are Old Testament support for or further explanation of what God accomplished in the incarnation and work of Jesus Christ.

The first text is Psalm 2:7: "You are my son; today I have become your Father." Here God the Father is speaking to God the Son, and Paul rightly sees this as having been written of Jesus.

The second text is Isaiah 55:3: "I will give you the holy and sure blessings promised to David." This text fits Paul's sermon well, for he has been trying to show that the promises made to David are fulfilled in Jesus.

The third text is Psalm 16:10: "You will not let your Holy One see decay." Peter used this same text in Acts 2:25–28, pointing out as Paul does that it was written of the Messiah, who though he died and was buried did not decay. Rather, his body was preserved, and he was raised again on the third day.

The fourth text occurs in the final part of the sermon, beginning with verse 38. It is Habakkuk 1:5: "Look, you scoffers, wonder and perish, for I am going to do something in your days that you would never believe, even if someone told you."

An Announcement of the Gospel

Everything that has been said up to this point leads to an announcement of the gospel and a plea for personal response: "Therefore, my brothers, I want you to know that through Jesus the forgiveness of sins is proclaimed to you. Through him everyone who believes is justified from everything you could not be justified from by the law of Moses" (vv. 38–39).

Someone has pointed out that "justification" means "just as if I'd never sinned." That is exactly right. It is not that you and I *have* never sinned, because we have. It is rather that because of the work of Jesus Christ, who bore the punishment of our sin in our place, we can now stand before God *as if* we had never sinned. It is as if we were Adam or Eve before the fall. Paul says the law could never do that. He mentions the law because he was speaking in a synagogue to those who loved the law and based their hopes of salvation upon keeping it. He knows whereof he speaks. He tried to live like that himself at one time. In those days he thought he was keeping God's law perfectly (Phil. 3:6). But when he met Jesus on the road to Damascus he learned that the law actually condemned him, since he was not keeping it, and that if he was to be saved it would have to be by Jesus doing for him what the law could not do. In Christ God atoned for sins committed and provided a basis on which he could justify sinners.

That is the good news Paul came to Galatia to proclaim. It is precisely what swept through Europe and transformed the world.

A Serious Conclusion

Paul does not end with good news but with a warning. It is where the quotation from Habakkuk comes in. "Take heed that you do not neglect this gospel," Paul in effect is saying. Why? Because although ours is an age of great grace, God is nevertheless also a God of great judgment, and sin must be judged if it is not atoned for by the work of Christ. The text from Habakkuk concerns the fall of Jerusalem, which was an expression of God's judgment upon Israel. On that occasion God judged his Old Testament people. Will he not also judge those living in the New Testament period who reject his offer of forgiveness through the work of Christ?

Remember that the Old Testament God and the New Testament God are one and the same. Therefore, if you will not have forgiveness of your sins through Jesus Christ, the wrath of God will come upon you.

When Paul finished his sermon, there was interest on the part of the people. They invited the apostles to return the next Sabbath and speak about Jesus further.

Some of these people undoubtedly believed in Jesus Christ eventually and presumably became active in promoting the gospel throughout this region of Asia. But at this point it seems they had a ways to go before they truly became Christians. They had to repent of their sin and trust Jesus for their salvation. Yet they were interested. They wanted to hear more, and many followed after Paul and Barnabas, asking questions.

28

Another Sabbath in Antioch

Acts 13:44–52

On the next Sabbath almost the whole city gathered to hear the word of the Lord. When the Jews saw the crowds, they were filled with jealousy and talked abusively against what Paul was saying. . . .

The word of the Lord spread through the whole region. But the Jews incited the God-fearing women of high standing and the leading men of the city. They stirred up persecution against Paul and Barnabas, and expelled them from their region. So they shook the dust from their feet in protest against them and went to Iconium. And the disciples were filled with joy and with the Holy Spirit.

Acts 13:44–52

Things from the past will sometimes pop into one's mind at the strangest times. This happened to me as I was thinking about these verses while preparing this chapter. I remembered a talk given at a Friday night InterVarsity meeting during my college years. I do not remember the details of the talk, but I remember it was about witnessing. The point was made that in order to witness effectively you need to make friends with those with whom you are trying to share the gospel. What I remember particularly is the speaker asking, "How long does it take to make a friend?"

242

I recall how we went about answering. We were college students, and we believed we thought deeply about things—not "superficially," the way some other people might. So we replied that it takes a long time. Somebody said, "I suppose it takes several years to make a good friend."

The person giving the talk was not satisfied. "Does it really take that long?" he asked.

Another student said, "Well, maybe not. I suppose a sensitive person might be able to make a good friend in six months."

Another said a week or two.

The speaker kept pressing, we kept reducing the time, and eventually he said, "I don't think it takes a great deal of time at all. I think you can make a good friend in five minutes."

Establishing a Church

As I was looking at the latter half of Acts 13 and thinking about the church that Paul and Barnabas established in Antioch on their first missionary journey, I remembered that InterVarsity meeting and found myself asking a parallel question: How long does it take to found a good church?

How long *does* it take to found a church? Presbyterians know the answer to that. We are not "superficial" people either. We *know* that nothing that is done well is done quickly. We believe that everything should be done decently and in order—and in as long a time as possible. We are careful about where we plant a church. We do demographic studies to determine whether the area is a good area with a rising population or a bad area with a declining population. We want to know what kind of people live there and whether there is a nucleus for a church. We screen our founding pastors carefully. There are tests they must take. We want to know whether they have the abilities and gifts to make the work successful. We raise money. Only when we have done all that do we have our first meeting and move forward. And even then our churches do not always move forward.

As I read Acts 13 and discovered what Paul and Barnabas did on this occasion I noticed that in this one case at least the establishing of a church took no more than a week. The apostles moved into the area. They preached on one Sabbath. There was interest in their preaching. They were invited back. Then, on the second Sabbath, when people literally thronged the site and many believed, the church was founded. Moreover, it was a good church, for it lasted not only through the members' lifetimes but also for hundreds of years. We read that "the word of the Lord spread through the whole region" by their witness (v. 49).

That last sentence probably embraces an indefinite period of time. What we are told about is two Sabbaths—a Sabbath of initial preaching, followed by a period of informal talking, conversing, witnessing, maybe canvassing, and then a second Sabbath. It was shortly after this second Sabbath that there was so much opposition to what was being done that Paul and Barnabas had to move on.

I am not necessarily recommending Paul's procedure for ourselves. I do think it pays to plan carefully, especially when we have limited resources. But the story suggests that what God does in a situation does not necessarily depend upon us, or the length of time, or the preparation, or the study, or the expertise we may have.

The Word of the Lord

As we saw in the last chapter, when Paul began the work in Antioch he preached a sermon on the person and work of Christ preceded by a review of what God had done in the Old Testament period leading up to it. Then he cited a number of texts that were fulfilled by Christ's ministry. This sermon would have been longer than the words actually recorded in Acts, but what Luke has given is certainly the gist of it, and it is significant that at the end of the preaching those who had heard Paul invited him to come back the next week. During the week that intervened between the first Sabbath and the second, this new gospel circulated the town.

When we come to Acts 13:44, we discover that almost "the whole city gathered to hear the word of the Lord."

Antioch was chiefly a Gentile city, but like many Gentile cities in those days it had a Jewish community. The Jews had a synagogue, and that is where Paul preached first. However, the Word of God spread quickly among the Gentiles. When Paul and Barnabas came to the synagogue on the second Sabbath to preach again, the place was packed by Gentiles—people who probably had not set foot inside the door of the synagogue previously.

Why did they come? In our day, people are overwhelmed with information. We have radio, television, newspapers, magazines. People did not have any of this in that day. So when somebody came through from another city, the person was a source of precious information and people naturally thronged about him. The missionaries were proclaiming something new. So there must have been the same kind of curiosity for their message as there was among the Athenians when Paul and his companions arrived there later.

Yet this is not what the text itself says. It does not suggest that the interest of the people was in the novelty of these men.

Nor was it in their eloquence or their dramatic presentation of the gospel. Today some religious figures get attention by saying outlandish things. Newspapers, magazines, television, and radio sometimes pick up on the outlandish, and for a short time at least, religious news is in vogue. Everybody pays attention, but it is only because what is being said is bizarre. If these same people had been saying anything sensible, no one would have paid any attention.

Paul and Barnabas did not have anything entertaining to say, nor did they make some new or striking presentation. According to the text, the curiosity of the people of Antioch was provoked by "the Word of God." That is said four times in this short section.

> Verse 44: "On the next Sabbath almost the whole city gathered to hear *the word of the Lord*" (italics mine). You might say, "Well, they gathered to hear the word of Paul or Barnabas." Perhaps so, but it doesn't say that. They gathered to hear what these men had preached earlier. It is what they had come to preach, and it is what they preached again. It was the Word of the Lord that stimulated the interest of these people.
>
> Verse 46: "Paul and Barnabas answered them boldly: 'We had to speak *the word of God* to you first'" (italics mine). Paul and Barnabas were conscious of the fact that this is what they had come to deliver.
>
> Verse 48: "When the Gentiles heard this, they were glad and honored *the word of the Lord*" (italics mine). Not the word of Paul. Not the word of Barnabas, but the Word of the Lord.
>
> Verse 49: *"The word of the Lord* spread through the whole region" (italics mine). What stimulated the interest of the people was the Word of the Lord as the Holy Spirit blessed it.

Much preaching in our day is directed to what we call "felt needs," including the "need" for entertainment. It is designed to stimulate interest by using the world's methods and devices. It succeeds, at least in the world's way. It draws crowds. Paul and Barnabas did not use any of these devices. I am aware that there are times when the gospel seems to fall on deaf ears. Sometimes it is possible to do the right thing and not see visible results. There have been people who have preached the Word of God faithfully for long periods of time and so far as we can tell there has been minimal response. Yet that is no excuse for abandoning one's true commission. The commission is to take the Word of God into all the world.

Paul and Barnabas did this. Sometimes when they took the gospel to a new city they were well received and a church was established. At other times, the Word they preached was rejected. But whether it was received or rejected, they persisted in their God-appointed task. Usually people found their curiosity stimulated and were drawn to the preaching.

So the first new reality associated with the preaching of the gospel in Antioch was interest on the part of the Gentiles as God blessed the preaching of the Word.

We have had an account of the preaching of the Word of God in Jerusalem, which the Holy Spirit blessed. Many Jews responded. We have been told of Philip witnessing to the Ethiopian along the desert road. We saw how the church was established in Antioch of Syria and how there was a mixture of races in the leadership and how the teaching there progressed. We saw the missionary trip to Cyprus. All that time, there was preaching and response, but there had not been anything quite like this. Here, for the first time, there was an overwhelming response to the gospel among Gentiles.

A Pattern of Jewish Rejection

What about the Jews among whom Paul first began his preaching? They "were filled with jealousy and talked abusively against what Paul was saying" (v. 45). Why? There were a number of reasons. For one thing, the way the gospel was presented had indicated to these Jews that their leaders in Jerusalem had rejected Jesus. Paul said that Jesus was the Messiah but that the leaders in Jerusalem had not responded positively to this claim. This statement would not be lost on the Jews in Antioch.

Again, Paul had said something about the law that they would have disagreed with. Jews were committed to the Old Testament law. It was their life: learning the law, trying to figure out what the law meant, obeying the law. Paul had said in his sermon on the previous Sabbath, "Through him [Jesus] everyone who believes is justified from everything you could not be justified from by the law of Moses" (v. 39).

That is simple truth, of course. All law can do is condemn those who have broken it. We all have. If a person is trying to get to heaven by obeying the law, well . . . he or she is destined to fail in the attempt. Paul knew this from his own experience. Paul was trying to point out, as he did on every occasion and as he does in his epistles, that we are justified by the work of Christ and through faith in him only. The Jews who were listening must have construed that as preaching against the law of Moses.

The leaders in Jerusalem had said as much about Jesus too. Jesus said, "Do not think that I have come to abolish the Law or the Prophets; I have not come to abolish them but to fulfill them" (Matt. 5:17). But the very fact he had to defend himself shows what the Jews were thinking. They were thinking, He has come to tear down our traditions. It must have been exactly the same in Antioch when Paul preached. They would have reacted negatively just because he had exposed the limitations of "their" law.

All that aside, it seems to me that what bothered the Jews of Antioch most was not so much that their leaders in Jerusalem had rejected Jesus or that Paul had said something that they might have construed as a negative comment on their law, but rather that the Gentiles were responding to the preaching of Paul in large numbers. It is why the text uses the word "jealousy," saying, "They were filled with jealousy and talked abusively against what Paul was saying" (v. 45). That had been the problem all along. They had not cared if the Gentiles sat in the back of their synagogues, paid attention, and perhaps in time became good Jews through circumcision. That was all right. They were glad to have that, just as Christians are glad to have people sit in their pews and eventually become good Presbyterians or Baptists or Episcopalians or whatever. But they did not want the Gentiles coming as Gentiles and being received by God in exactly the same way they thought they themselves should be received since they were Jews.

We are told that at the end of the first Sabbath "many of the Jews and devout converts to Judaism followed Paul and Barnabas" (v. 43). They would have asked how a person could be saved, what the grounds for salvation were, what a person had to do to qualify. Paul, who certainly preached a gospel of salvation by grace through faith alone, did not tell the Gentiles that they had to become Jews first before God would receive them. To the Jews this would have been seen as a betrayal of their religious heritage.

Turning to the Gentiles

Paul made an important decision, establishing a principle that he was to follow from this time on in virtually every city where he preached. He said to the Jews who were resisting him, "We had to speak the word of God to you first. Since you reject it and do not consider yourselves worthy of eternal life, we now turn to the Gentiles. For this is what the Lord has commanded us: 'I have made you a light for the Gentiles, that you may bring salvation to the ends of the earth'" (vv. 46–47).

The reason Paul felt he had to speak to the Jews first was because he was a Jew himself and because when the Lord gave the Great Commission, particularly the one we have recorded in the Book of Acts, he said to begin in Jerusalem, that is, with Jews. Our equivalent if we are Gentiles is beginning where we are. I do not think Jesus' words mean that if we are Gentiles we are to begin with Jews. We are to begin where we are and go on from there. But Paul was a Jew. The gospel had started in Jerusalem. So when Paul went about preaching the gospel, he went to the synagogues first.

Yet what is significant about the decision recorded in Acts 13 is that Paul went on to say, "Since you reject it and do not consider yourselves worthy of eternal life, we now turn to the Gentiles" (v. 46). Why did he say this? Obviously, because the gospel, although proclaimed to the Jews first, is not a Jewish gospel exclusively. It is a gospel for the whole world. And that is why Jesus, although he told his Jewish apostles, "You will be my witnesses in Jerusalem," nevertheless also went on to say, "... and in all Judea and Samaria, and to the ends of the earth" (Acts 1:8). Paul supported his statement with a text from the Jews' own Scripture: Isaiah 49:6. "I have made you a light for the Gentiles, that you may bring salvation to the ends of the earth." The Jews themselves were to be the Gentiles' light. But if the Jews would not believe and then propagate the gospel, the Word would not be bound. Paul, a Jew himself, would carry it.

The first part of that verse, "I have made you a light for the Gentiles," is something the elderly Simeon quoted in Jerusalem when he saw the infant Jesus at the time of his nativity. He took the child in his arms, then praised God, saying:

> Now dismiss your servant in peace.
> For my eyes have seen your salvation,
>   which you have prepared in the sight of all people,
> a light for revelation to the Gentiles
>   and for glory to your people Israel.
>   Luke 2:29–32

Simeon applied "a light for . . . the Gentiles" to Jesus. But now Paul is saying that the Jews themselves were to be that light in the sense that they were commissioned to carry the gospel of the light of Christ to the world's communities.

Gentile Belief

The wonderful thing about this passage is that when the gospel was proclaimed to the Gentiles, they believed it. We are told a number of important things about their response.

First, when the Gentiles heard Paul's announcement "they were glad and honored the word of the Lord" (v. 48). I think that means that they believed and obeyed it. The fifth of the Ten Commandments says, "Honor your father and your mother" (Exod. 20:12). One thing "honor" means is to obey them. When we are told that these Gentiles honored the Word of the Lord, this must mean at the very least that they obeyed it. The Word called for faith in Christ. So they obeyed God and believed on Jesus.

Second, we are told that "the word of the Lord spread through the whole region" (v. 49). The believers became witnesses as soon as they were converted. Since most of those converted were Gentiles, this became a largely Gentile mission.

When Luke says, "The word of the Lord spread through the whole *region*" (italics mine), he is being quite accurate in describing this community. William Ramsay has pointed out that an inscription was discovered in Antioch describing a centurion who was assigned to this city as a "regional centurion." Ramsay shows that this word does not just denote a general area, as if we were saying "the neighborhood." Rather, it was a technical term, the "Region of Antioch." The centurion was appointed to be in control of this region and was therefore called a "regional centurion." So when Luke says, "The word of the Lord spread through the whole region," it shows that he knew what he was talking about and was getting his terms exactly right.[1] This is where the gospel spread, and it spread by those who came to believe on Jesus during these first few weeks of Paul's preaching.

In the middle of those two statements, between the words that say they "honored the word of the Lord" and the words that imply that they took that Word to others, we read, "and all who were appointed for eternal life believed." This is the doctrine of election: that those who believe are those who are appointed to eternal life by God. Isn't it interesting that we should have this statement of the doctrine of election right in the middle of this great evangelistic story? There are people who cannot imagine how anybody can be an evangelist if God decides who will be saved and then saves them. The argument goes, "If God is going to save certain people, God will save them regardless. What I do doesn't matter. Or, if it depends on me, then it depends on me and you must not talk about election."

Actually, those who have had the greatest faith in God's electing power are also those who, by the grace of God, have proved to be the most effective evangelists. Virtually all the famous missionary pioneers were believers in election.

"Why did they go out to evangelize, then, if they believed God was going to save people anyway?"

That isn't quite the way to put it. If God is going to save someone, God will save them. That is true. But it is not quite correct to say that God will save them *anyway*, because when we say, "God will save them anyway," we mean that God will save them apart from our (or another's) witness, and that is not true. The God who appoints the ends also appoints the means, and the means he has appointed in the evangelization of other people is our witness.

We are to take the gospel into all the world. But as we go we are to know that God will work through that witness to bring to faith those he has appointed.

I sometimes say I do not know how you can evangelize any other way, at least not in a thinking manner. Suppose it does not depend on God; suppose it depends on you. Suppose people are saved because you are eloquent or because you have the right answers or because you happen to be in the right place at just the right time—entirely apart from God's election. If that is true, it means that if you do not have the right answers, if you are not in the right place, if you do not present the gospel in just the right way, then these people will perish and it will be your fault. I do not know how anybody can live with that.

On the other hand, if you believe that God has appointed some for eternal life and that as you testify God will use that testimony to bring those persons to faith, the burden is removed and witnessing becomes what it was meant to be: a joy, as it obviously was for Paul and Barnabas. Persecution? Yes, they had that. But in spite of the persecution a church was founded and it was not subdued. On the contrary, it prevailed and went on to become one of the strongest churches of the ancient world.

29

A Tale of Three Cities

Acts 14:1–28

At Iconium Paul and Barnabas went as usual into the Jewish synagogue. There they spoke so effectively that a great number of Jews and Gentiles believed. But the Jews who refused to believe stirred up the Gentiles and poisoned their minds against the brothers. . . .

In Lystra there sat a man crippled in his feet, who was lame from birth and had never walked. He listened to Paul as he was speaking. Paul looked directly at him, saw that he had faith to be healed and called out, "Stand up on your feet!" At that, the man jumped up and began to walk. . . .

Then some Jews came from Antioch and Iconium and won the crowd over. They stoned Paul and dragged him outside the city, thinking he was dead. But after the disciples had gathered around him, he got up and went back into the city. The next day he and Barnabas left for Derbe.

Acts 14:1–20

The fourteenth chapter of Acts tells about Paul's ministry in an area of Turkey called Galatia. There has been a great deal of debate about how the term Galatia is used in the New Testament. The debate does not affect where Paul traveled, of course; Luke, who became

250

Paul's traveling companion later in the journey, makes clear that Paul went to Antioch in Pisidia, then to the cities of Iconium, Lystra, and Derbe.

The question is: When Paul later wrote his letter to the Galatians, was he using the word Galatia to refer to the old ethnic area of Turkey, where the Gauls had settled and from which the name Galatia comes (a more northern area), or was he referring to the newer Roman district, which embraced a larger area to the south? If it was the former, then we have no information about these people or Paul's ministry among them in Acts. If it was the latter, then Acts 14 tells of Paul's work in three of the cities of this region. If that is the case, then the letter to the Galatians gives valuable information about this area.

This debate has raged back and forth, and there are strong arguments on each side. I hold to a southern Galatian view, because I think that Acts 14 relates closely to what we find in Paul's Galatian letter.

If we take the two sources together we get more than just a sketch of these people. We find that they had difficulties. But even more important, we find that although they were on their own for many years and had been bombarded with much false teaching, they nevertheless were a true church and remained strong for many centuries. In the ancient church, Asia Minor was a fortress of authentic Christianity.

The Pattern of the Ministries

Acts 14 contains a repetition of what became each ministry's pattern. We have already seen this pattern worked out at Antioch. Now we see it in each of these three cities of Galatia. First the apostles preached, then as a result there was division, persecution, and growth.

1. *Preaching.* Today people are so interested in things that are spectacular that some insist that if Christians are to be effective in their evangelistic work, the one thing they must do in a targeted community is miracles. Then, after they have gotten the attention of people by doing miracles and have an open door, they can preach the gospel. From time to time in these early days, God did work miracles through the apostles. But the apostles did not go into these cities to do miracles, and then preach. Rather it was the other way around: They went to preach; then sometimes there were healings.

The miracles proved that the apostles were God's true messengers. It was how God authenticated them when there was no New Testament. Verse 3 says, "The Lord . . . confirmed the message of his grace by enabling them to do miraculous signs and wonders." Paul in another place speaks of "signs, wonders and miracles" as "the things that mark an apostle" (2 Cor. 12:12).

2. *Division.* When the Word is preached it always produces a division. Division happened from Jesus' and Paul's ministries, and it happens when the gospel is preached today. When the Word of God comes into a dark area, whether a dark human heart or a darkened environment, it does what light always does. It causes things to grow; in the case of the gospel it produces a

warming of the heart and a bringing forth of the fruit of the spiritual life God has already put there. And it causes the creatures of the dark to scatter; Jesus said that some people would not come to the light "because their deeds were evil" (John 3:19).

3. *Persecution.* On the side of the rejection of the message, there is a quickly developing opposition that becomes so intense that it results at last in the persecution of the messengers. We find this case again and again. Gentiles from this or that area (or Jews from this or that city) got so stirred up that they moved against Paul and his associates. He had to flee from city to city, but they even pursued him to new cities to create opposition there.

4. *Growth.* In spite of the division and consequent persecution, the apostles always left a growing church behind. We know it was growing in this area because after Paul and Barnabas had visited and been thrown out of the cities of Iconium, Lystra, and Derbe the first time, when they went back to visit those they had left, in each case they found the church prospering.

How can that be? The apostles had left behind only a tiny core of believers, and these had hardly been taught anything, since the apostles had been there at best for only a few weeks. How could this little group survive? It survived because the work was actually being done by God. The church was his church. Therefore, years later, in spite of persecution (and perhaps even neglect, since there were not many workers in those days), we still find these churches thriving.

The Work in Iconium

What is emphasized chiefly in the story of Paul's work in Iconium is division, which ends in persecution. The division is explained carefully: "The Jews who refused to believe stirred up the Gentiles and poisoned their minds against the brothers" (v. 2).

The Lord himself said that many would reject the preaching of God's Word but that some would believe. He told about a farmer and the four different kinds of ground on which his seed fell. He said that when the gospel is thrown out like seed, sometimes it falls upon a hard path where it simply lies on the surface and the birds of the air swoop down and snatch it up. At other times, it falls on rocky soil where there is not much earth. It springs up quickly under those conditions. But as soon as the sun comes out, the sun scorches it and the plant dries up. At still other times, the Word falls upon good ground. It grows and does well. But the ground also contains weeds, and these grow up alongside the plant and eventually choke it out. There is no fruit under any of these conditions. It is only when the Word falls on good soil that it bears fruit. Sometimes it multiplies itself thirty times, sometimes sixty times, and sometimes one hundred times (Matt. 13:1–9, 18–23).

When our Lord told that story the disciples did not understand it. So he explained it to them. He said that when the Word falls on the path and the birds swoop down and eat it, that is like Satan snatching the Word away from people before it has a chance to affect them. That is characteristic of the preaching of the gospel in our day. The gospel is preached. People hear it all the time. It is on the radio and television, in books, pamphlets, and newspapers. Churches are everywhere. Yet there is so much of the devil's work around that no sooner does it begin to be known to people than the devil snatches it away, and other things come in and take its place.

Sometimes people receive the Word, but for them it is like seed falling on rocky soil. It springs up. But as soon as life gets tough, as soon as some of the persecutions that accompany the Christian life or the hardships that accompany Christian living come, the one who has made the profession fades away and is no longer seen following after Christ.

Sometimes there are thorns, which Jesus identified as the cares of this world. They choke out the new life.

It is only in the fourth of these four cases, twenty-five percent of the time, that the Word actually falls upon good soil and is fruitful. But notice: When it falls upon good soil, soil that God has prepared, then it does spring up. It does bear fruit, and the fruit it bears lasts to the glory of God.

That is what happened in Iconium. Although there was much persecution and undoubtedly some who at the beginning seemed to respond later fell away, nevertheless some of the seed fell upon soil that God had previously prepared. It took root, grew, and there was life and fruit. As a result, when they came back later, the apostles found a church established in Iconium.

Standing on the Rock

Acts 14:6 was an important verse in the life of Sir William Ramsay, whom I have mentioned several times in this book. Together with a few other verses, verse 6 produced a change in his thinking that brought him to a strong trust in the reliability of Scripture.

Ramsay was a classical scholar, somewhat like Heinrich Schliemann, who discovered the ancient city of Troy. He came from Scotland, and because classical scholars liked to visit the countries they were studying, Ramsay, who was studying Acts, set out for Asia Minor, what is now Turkey. Nobody knew much about Turkey in those days. Travel was difficult. Many of the ancient sites, which particularly interested Ramsay, had been lost for centuries.

Ramsay began his research, and one of the things he investigated was the boundary line between the ancient Roman territories of Pisidia and Lycaonia that seemed according to an ancient boundary marker to have been between the cities of Lystra and Derbe. That could have been an incidental and somewhat unimportant matter in itself. Boundaries can be anywhere at all. Why should it matter? But there was a puzzle in the case of this boundary in respect to what Luke had written in Acts. When Luke wrote Acts 14, he said that the apostles left Iconium and fled to "the Lycaonian cities of Lystra and Derbe," thereby putting Lystra and Derbe in the same province. In other words, Luke differed from the apparent evidence and was therefore assumed to be wrong.

Ramsay had been brought up on the liberalism of the nineteenth century. He did not doubt that Luke had made a mistake. He was retracing Paul's steps, studying the cities he visited and the roads he walked, trying to understand not only where Paul went but also why he went where he did. When Ramsay got to Lystra and Derbe, he discovered that the ancient boundary stone between the two cities suggested they had been in different provinces. But he also discovered that the stone had been moved. It wasn't where it had been originally. He began to investigate the matter more carefully.

Today, if you read his book *St. Paul the Traveler and the Roman Citizen* and get to his account of Paul's ministry in these cities, you will find him pointing out that once again Luke is remarkably accurate. This is because Ramsay discovered Lystra and Derbe were in the same province, the province of Lycaonia, between the years A.D. 37 and 72, but not before those dates and not afterward. That is, they were in the same province in the very years Paul was there, as Luke accurately reports.[1]

We find situations like this frequently in serious studies of the Bible. If you want to seem very wise and popular today, you can gain attention by making a career of criticizing the Bible. Show all the places where modern scholarship "proves" that it is wrong—if you are not afraid of looking very foolish about thirty years from now, and perhaps much sooner, when the explanation of the apparent difficulty is found. However, if you want to look wise in the future, though you may be thought foolish now, you should take your stand on the integrity and complete accuracy of this Book. If you do, you will find the same sort of things Ramsay and others discovered.

The Work in Lystra

The account of the work in Lystra contains the report of a miracle (Acts 14:8–10). Someone may say, "But isn't that contrary to what you said earlier? You said that when Paul and Barnabas went into a city, they always preached first and did the miracles (if any) afterward. Here we start with the healing of a lame man."

Actually this is no exception, because when we come to verse 9, we read: "He [that is, the man who is going to be healed] listened to Paul as he was speaking." In telling the story, Luke begins with a reference to this man since he wants to tell about the healing. But the work of the apostles did not begin with the healing. It began with their speaking. In other words, in Lystra Paul did the same thing he always did: He went into the city and began to preach. While he was preaching he noticed the lame man, who was giving great attention to what he was saying. Paul perceived that he had faith to be healed and so healed him.

When Paul passed to this area, he must have passed into an area where he no longer understood the language. In the ancient world, almost everyone spoke Greek, even if it wasn't their native language. Greek seems to have been the dominant language at Antioch in Pisidia. But here in Lycaonia the people seem to have been more at home in their native tribal language. For when the miracle took place and the people began to babble to themselves about it, Paul and Barnabas did not understand at first what was going on. They noticed that the people were impressed. But when the people said in their own language, "The gods have come down to us in human form" (v. 11), Paul and Barnabas did not understand what they were saying.

So the apostles were proceeding on their way, not really understanding what was going on, when they came upon a procession moving out of the city toward them. A priest was leading an animal that had been made ready for sacrifice. The apostles must have said to themselves, "We must have come here on a feast day, a religious day. They are practicing their pagan rites. We will have to speak to them about this in due time." But then they discovered to their horror that the people were coming to sacrifice to them. And why to them? Because they believed, as we discover, that Barnabas was Zeus in human form. Zeus was the greatest of the gods. And Paul, who was the chief speaker, was presumed to be Hermes or Mercury, the gods' spokesman.

It is not surprising that they did this. This could have happened in any ancient city, of course, but we know something very interesting and relevant about this area because of Ovid's book *Metamorphoses*. In *Metamorphoses* Ovid collected the mythological stories that have to do with people being changed into one thing or another, which is what metamorphosis refers to, and at one place he told a story about this very area. According to Ovid's story, Zeus and Hermes had once visited a valley near Lystra. They went from door to door, but the people refused to take them in. Finally, they came to a poor house occupied by a man named Philemon (the same name as that of the runaway slave of Paul's acquaintance) and his wife Baucis. These elderly people received Zeus and Hermes. So they stayed the night. In the morning the gods took the couple up out of the city to a mountain, and when they looked back on the valley they saw that the gods had flooded it, drowning everyone. Then, while they were looking on, Philemon and Baucis saw that the gods had transformed their poor hovel into a great temple with a glittering gold roof.[2]

This story must have been known in Lystra. So when Paul and Barnabas did a miracle, the people inevitably thought that Zeus and Hermes had returned. And if they had returned, the last thing in the world they wanted to do was offend them. They remembered what had happened the first time around.

Paul and Barnabas discovered what was going on and were aghast. "When the apostles Barnabas and Paul heard of this, they tore their clothes and rushed out into the crowd, shouting: 'Men, why are you doing this? We too are only men, human like you. We are bringing you good news, telling you to turn from these worthless things to the living God'" (vv. 14–15). Then Paul began to preach.

Preaching to a Pagan Audience

We ought to compare this sermon with the one in chapter 13, which was spoken to a largely Jewish audience. In that chapter Paul quotes the Old Testament frequently, rehearsing God's great acts in the Old Testament and in Jesus Christ. That is not the case here. Here Paul is speaking to a Gentile or pagan audience that had no knowledge of the Scriptures whatever. He couldn't have told these people about God's great acts in the Old Testament period, because they would not have known what he was talking about. So he started at the point at which they did have understanding and spoke of God as *the Creator:* "the living God, who made heaven and earth and sea and everything in them" (v. 15); and *the God of providence:* "He has shown kindness by giving you rain from heaven and crops in their seasons; he provides you with plenty of food and fills your hearts with joy" (v. 17).

I do not know, because the sermon breaks off at this point, whether Luke is shortening it and Paul actually went on to preach the gospel, or whether the situation got so out of hand that he had to stop. Luke seems to indicate it was the latter, since he says in verse 18, "Even with these words, they had difficulty keeping the crowd from sacrificing to them." But whether Paul preached the full gospel on that occasion or later, he certainly got to the gospel at some point, because the people began to believe it. Then the same divisions and persecutions happened here as elsewhere.

As a result of trouble caused by Jews who had traveled to Lystra from Antioch and Iconium, the crowd was drawn away. The same crowd that days before was ready to worship Barnabas as Zeus and Paul as Hermes stoned Paul, dragged him outside the city, and left him for dead. What fickle people these were! Yet they were no different from people in our time. People are always fickle until God brings true stability into their lives through the gospel. If anything of any permanence is to happen, if lives are to be changed, if the seed of the Word is to fall into good soil and bear fruit, and do it year after year—it is only going to be by the grace of God.

They thought Paul was dead, but he wasn't. He could have been. Others have died under such circumstances. But God had more for Paul to do, and so he did not die. In the same way, if God has more work for you to do, you won't die either. God will keep you living until you do it, because the God who has ordained your salvation has also at the same time ordained good works for you to do (Eph. 2:10).

The Work at Derbe

It was a good time to leave Lystra. The missionaries went on to Derbe. Luke does not tell us much about the ministry there, saying only in verse 21: "They preached the good news in that city and won a large number of disciples." If in the earlier story the emphasis was upon division and the resulting persecution, here it is on results.

There is no church in Derbe today. This city, like many ancient cities, is a ruin. The tide of history has swept over it, and the church that was there is gone. But this was a great church for a very long time. We are going to find out more about it later on in Acts. When we read in chapter 20 about the delegation that went with Paul with the offering from the Gentile churches to Jerusalem, we find that the church at Derbe sent a representative along. The church was strong enough to have taken a sizeable collection for this fund, and it had resulted from the very short ministry that Paul had with them.

Yet the work was not quite over. In the very last section of chapter 14 we find Paul and Barnabas retracing their steps, going back through the cities where they had been persecuted and from which they had been ejected. They went to strengthen those left behind. They did a number of things.

1. *They gave encouragement.* It was a hostile, pagan community in which citizens of these cities were called to live for Jesus Christ, and they didn't even know much about him. So the apostles went back to encourage them.

2. *They taught the believers.* Paul taught that "we must go through many hardships to enter the kingdom of God" (v. 22). He taught other things as well.

3. *They organized the church.* Here for the first time in the Book of Acts we find the appointing of elders (v. 23), which we learn later was to become Paul's natural pattern of church organization. I do not know how "elderly" these elders were, but I know they had not been Christians very long, since the gospel itself had not been known to them very long. Was that any way to establish a church? Most Presbyterians wouldn't do it that way. We want to be slow, careful, dull, and (maybe) ineffective. But Paul had faith in what God was doing, and if there were to be churches in these cities, they obviously needed sound organization. So Paul appointed elders, more than one, and the churches thrived.

4. *They prayed.* The last thing Paul did (and possibly the first thing too) is that he prayed for them (v. 23). We should be praying too, praying for those to whom we witness and for the church.

When we get to the very end of this chapter we find something marvelous. Verse 26 says, "From Attalia, they sailed back to Antioch, where they had been committed to the grace of God for *the work they had now completed*" (italics mine). This was only one stage in Paul's lifelong ministry, the end of the first missionary journey. There were going to be two more, but this was the first stage. It had been clearly defined, they were commissioned to do it, and they completed it. So they went home, reporting, "The task is done."

That is a great thing to be able to say. How many Christians have started out in some work but have not finished it! Many have been given a task to do, but because of the hardships, divisions, persecutions, and such things they have said, "I think I had better quit." The victory is not to those who start. It is to those who finish. That is what Jesus said: "He who stands firm to the end will be saved" (Matt. 10:22). Paul did it, not only here but also throughout his entire life. When he came to the end he was able to write to Timothy, "I have fought the good fight, I have finished the race, I have kept the faith" (2 Tim. 4:7). Paul raced the whole way to the finish line, and when he reached the finish line he passed over into glory.

30

The First Church Council

Acts 15:1-35

The whole assembly became silent as they listened to Barnabas and Paul telling about the miraculous signs and wonders God had done among the Gentiles through them. When they finished, James spoke up: "Brothers, listen to me. Simon has described to us how God at first showed his concern by taking from the Gentiles a people for himself. The words of the prophets are in agreement with this. . . .

"It is my judgment, therefore, that we should not make it difficult for the Gentiles who are turning to God. Instead we should write to them, telling them to abstain from food polluted by idols, from sexual immorality, from the meat of strangled animals and from blood."

Acts 15:12–20

The hardest of all ideas for human beings to grasp is the doctrine of salvation by grace alone. This is because we all always want to add something to it. If a person is trying to add anything to the work of Christ for salvation, that person is not saved and is operating under a fatal misunderstanding. People will say, "Of course you need the grace of God to be saved. No one can save himself. But you still have to do something." Some would say that this extra something is baptism. Some would

259

say that this extra something is belonging to a particular church. Others want to add good works or some ecstatic spiritual experience.

In the early years of the church the details of this controversy were different, but the issue was the same. The first believers were Jews. They had grown up in Judaism and were attached to their traditions. They thought that there were certain things that you just had to do to be saved. These early Christians would have said that it is indeed wonderful that Jesus, the Messiah, has come. It was what Jews had been looking to for centuries. They would even have confessed that Jesus died for their sin. Yet they would also have said that no one can be saved without being a Jew first of all. What is more, they believed that the door to Jewishness is circumcision.

In the early days the convictions of these Jewish traditionalists was not so serious a problem, because there were not many Gentiles. But as the size of the Gentile church grew it became increasingly problematic for those in the Jewish tradition that these Gentiles were not rejecting their Gentile background in order to become Jews but rather were continuing in the church as Gentiles. And nobody was telling them that in order to be Christians they had to keep the law of Moses.

Jewish believers became increasingly troubled about what was happening, and Gentile believers were not resolving the problem by taking on the yoke of Judaism.

The Thesis to Be Argued

Acts 15 tells us what the Christians did to solve this mounting difficulty. They called a council. The Protestant Reformers wisely and insistently pointed out that councils have erred and do err. They have erred throughout history, and they continue to err today. As a matter of fact, probably even this council made mistakes. But God blessed it nevertheless, as he has often done with the formal meetings of sinful human beings who nevertheless gather to seek God's will in a matter. The leaders of the church realized that they were dealing with an important matter. So they must have said, "Since this affects the very essence of the gospel we should not decide it by 'political clout.' We need to discuss this matter with great care. We need to pray about it and seek the mind of God." Among the representatives from the various churches that were called to meet together were Paul and Barnabas, who represented the church at Antioch.

The thesis to be argued is stated very clearly by Luke because he wanted his readers to understand precisely what the issue was. It is presented twice. Acts 15:1, part of the introduction to the chapter, states: "Unless you are circumcised, according to the custom taught by Moses, you cannot be saved." The second statement is in verse 5: "The Gentiles must be circumcised and required to obey the law of Moses."

The issue was not whether Gentiles could be saved. I have made this point several times before (see chapter 20). But in each of the cases I have mentioned, those who were saved were saved through formal, or at least symbolic, incorporation into the nation of Israel.

You might say, "But Naaman the Syrian was an exception. He never became a Jew." True. He never moved to Israel and settled there, as Ruth did. But do you remember the story in which he took dirt from Israel and brought it back to his homeland? Do you remember how, whenever he prayed, he knelt down on that Jewish dirt? Naaman was not in a position to move to Israel. His standing in the Syrian court prevented it. But he acknowledged the Jewish God who had healed him, and when he came to God, he came not as a Syrian, who had no right to approach him, but as a Jew on Jewish soil.

The focal point of the debate before the Jerusalem council was circumcision. The rite signified incorporation into the covenant people of Israel and so the taking upon oneself the observance of the law. Every Jew understood the keeping of the law to be his divine responsibility. Peter refers to it as "a yoke" put upon one's neck (v. 10). To argue that the Gentiles had to be circumcised to be saved meant that they had to take on the burden of the law as the Jews understood it. They had to observe the Jewish feasts, dietary and other laws, and the pharisaic interpretation of the Decalogue (Ten Commandments).

Many of the "circumcision party" were no doubt honest and even spiritual men. Paul was not so charitable when he spoke of them in Galatians. He regarded their view as heresy—as indeed it is—and he considered those who were advancing it to be subverters of the church and God's enemies. He pronounces an anathema upon them. But this does not mean that these people were all consciously trying to do the church harm. If you had asked them, "Do you believe that Jesus died for your sin?" they would have said, "Of course, we do. That is why he came." But then they would have asked us, "Don't you believe that God has given us the law and that it is essential for everyone to keep it? We believe God gave a special revelation through Moses, and that what God says in the law is true and eternally binding. God has told us that we must be circumcised. If you disobey the commandment of God at that point, how can you say that you are a saved person?"

When you put the argument that way it begins to carry some weight. And you may even find yourself saying, as people undoubtedly did in these early days, "Perhaps the circumcision party is right. Perhaps the Gentiles are not saved. Maybe they need to assume the law's yoke." But think what was at stake.

First, if it was necessary for the Gentiles to keep the law of Moses to be saved, *then Paul and Barnabas were false teachers.* This is because Paul and Barnabas were on the other side. Paul taught that the Gentiles did not have to keep the law of Moses to be saved. They were to be saved by the work of Christ received by faith alone.

Paul was the first to admit that all who profess the name of Christ must live a righteous life. He said that anybody who says, "Let us sin that grace may abound" doesn't understand the faith at all. A person like that deserves to be condemned. He would say, as the theologians of the Reformation did, We are saved by faith alone, but not by a faith that is alone. True faith results in good deeds, including adherence to the moral law of God. Nevertheless, Paul insisted just as strongly that nothing, absolutely nothing, is a prerequisite to faith. So if you say, "You must be circumcised and believe" or "You must be baptized and believe" or "You must go to this or that church and believe" or "You must belong to this or that denomination and believe," yours is a false gospel.

The legalizing party was diametrically opposed to Paul's teaching. If their understanding of the Old Testament was right and circumcision and a legal adherence to the law were requirements for all Christian people, then Paul and Barnabas were not true apostles and the books that we have in the New Testament from the pen of the apostle Paul are not divine revelation. If that is the case, it would reduce the bulk of our New Testament by a considerable amount.

Second, if it was necessary for the Gentiles to keep the law of Moses to be saved, *then faith is not enough.* In other words, we must reject the Reformation. We cannot affirm *sola fide,* justification by "faith alone." We might still say that faith is important. But it will not be true to say that people are saved by faith *alone,* since we must also have something else, the Jewish legal system. With this thinking, only when we submit to the Jewish legal system, even though we may also believe on Jesus Christ, will we find salvation.

Third, if it was necessary for the Gentiles to keep the law of Moses to be saved, then *Gentiles throughout the whole world, both in the past and today, are not saved.* They are not Christians. No? Then what was it that was happening out there in places like Antioch, Iconium, Lystra, and Derbe? And later in Macedonia, Athens, Corinth, and Rome? In fact, around the world? Apparently a false religion was advancing everywhere.

The Flow of Debate

Luke introduces the debate in verse 6, saying, "The apostles and elders met to consider this question." I do not know if Luke was deliberately understating what went on, but he was at least presenting the public side of the debate in contrast to what we know from Paul's letter to the Galatians to have gone on behind the scenes. What Luke does not tell us is that when Paul went to Jerusalem to meet with the council, he took Titus along. Titus was a Gentile and therefore a representative of the many Gentiles who were uncircumcised and yet had believed the gospel. Paul refused to have Titus circumcised (Gal. 2:3), even though many important people—Paul calls them "those who seemed to be important"—tried to persuade him to change his position.

If you have ever been in church circles, you know how it is. There is an issue to be decided. But there are people who are afraid of offending those who are on the wrong side. These therefore always try to work out a compromise that will satisfy everyone but actually satisfies no one. That must have happened in Jerusalem when Paul brought Titus there.

The leaders must have said to him, "Paul, you are a giant of the faith. You are the church's chief theologian. You outshine all of us. But you don't know Jerusalem the way we do. If you insist on exempting the Gentiles from circumcision as a matter of principle, you are going to divide the church. That must not happen. You are right in your position, of course. But what we recommend is that you show a gracious spirit and have this young Gentile believer, Titus, circumcised. From your point of view that can mean whatever you want it to mean. You can say, 'It is just to keep peace in the church.' But from the viewpoint of our weaker brethren you will be signifying that we are all anxious to uphold the law of Moses."

In Galatians Paul tells how he responded. He says, "We did not give in to them for a moment, so that the truth of the gospel might remain with you" (Gal. 2:5). In other words, Paul understood that forcing circumcision on the Gentiles involved the very essence of the gospel. And if the choice was to be between the truth of the gospel and harmony in the church, then he was for the truth of the gospel. The church can live with disharmony. It is unfortunate when it occurs, of course. We do not want it. We try to avoid it when we can, but we can live with it. What we cannot live with is the destruction of the gospel. So Paul made every effort to preserve it.

There is one other thing Paul says that is worth adding to what Luke communicates in Acts. It is the way Paul speaks of the Jerusalem leaders. He calls them "those *reputed* to be pillars" (Gal. 2:9, italics mine), referring to James, Peter, and John specifically. Earlier he wrote of "those who *seemed* to be leaders" (v. 2, italics mine), and in one place he says, "As for those who *seemed* to be important—whatever they were makes no difference to me; God does not judge by external appearance—those men added nothing to my message" (v. 6, italics mine).

These statements suggest that Paul was pressured to compromise by the very people who should have been most concerned to uphold the truth of Christianity, namely James, the Lord's brother, the chairman of the council; Peter, the "rock"; and John, the beloved disciple. And if that is so, then the danger to the gospel was actually much greater than Luke suggests in his rather formal report of the proceedings. The gospel was in danger of being lost, and for a time at least only Paul and his companions stood in the breech defending it.

Someone might think that Luke was misrepresenting the council in the way he presents it if what Paul writes in Galatians is true. But Luke tells us not what went on behind the scenes but what went on in public. The wonderful thing, the thing he emphasizes, is that in spite of the weakness of these "pillar" apostles in private (if what I have suggested was the case), in public, after they had discussed the matter in council and had prayed for God's guidance and blessing in their deliberations, God led them to stand together and preserve the gospel.

The Public Proceedings

Luke reports the speeches of three people—four, if we count Paul and Barnabas separately. The first whose words he reports is Peter, but there were many who had spoken before him. Acts 15:7 says that it was "after much discussion" that Peter made his speech. This means that there were pros and cons and that Peter, Paul, Barnabas, James, and the others let people air their positions.

I have had to learn the importance of this myself. I like to get things done. I know the agenda meetings have, and I watch the clock. But I have discovered that the more complex the issue is and the larger the body discussing it, the more time a leader has to take to let people express their opinions. Moreover, if opinions need to change, as they obviously do if the group is to approach consensus, then you have to let people express themselves several times. The first time they have to say what they think. The second time they have to react to the views of the other side. Then you hope you get to the point where people change their views, begin to think more or less along the same lines, and begin to express their cohering views together.

After this discussion, Peter gave his testimony: "Brothers, you know that some time ago God made a choice among you that the Gentiles might hear from my lips the message of the gospel and believe" (v. 7). Peter was not trying to speak *ex cathedra* ("from [his] throne") at this point, as some think he could have done. One branch of the church regards Peter as the first pope and believes that a pope speaking *ex cathedra,* that is, officially, is authoritative and inerrant. Peter did not speak that way. He did not pull rank. Instead, he simply rehearsed what God had done (see chapters 20 and 21).

Peter does not use the word "circumcision" here. He talks about God's giving the Holy Spirit instead. But what he was saying is that God saved the Gentiles of Cornelius's household apart from circumcision: "He made no distinction between us and them" (v. 9). The conclusion is obvious. If God had not made a distinction between Jew and Gentile, giving Gentiles the Spirit just as he gave the Spirit to the Jews, then the Gentiles can be saved apart from becoming Jewish people.

Peter's second point was also important for the Jews to hear. He said, "Why do you try to test God by putting on the necks of the disciples a yoke that neither we nor our fathers have been able to bear?" (v. 10). Peter was acknowledging that Jews had not been able to keep the law of Moses. They had tried but failed. Therefore, if they were to be saved, it would have to be by grace, even in their case, and not by law keeping.

I think that of all the surviving words of Peter, those in verse 11 are perhaps the most gracious. Peter says, "We believe it is through the grace of our Lord Jesus Christ that *we are saved, just as they are"* (italics mine). Why is that so gracious? It is because Peter, the Jew, would normally have said it the other way around. He would have said, "We believe that they can be saved by grace through faith, *just like us."* That is, *they can be like us.* But that was the issue. Did they have to become "like us" or not? Because he knew the answer to that question Peter turned it around, saying, "We believe that by grace even we Jews can be saved, *just like the Gentiles."*

Do you ever think that other people have to become like you to be saved? If so, you are probably far from truly understanding the gospel.

The second ones to speak were Paul and Barnabas. The text says, "The whole assembly became silent as they listened to Barnabas and Paul telling about the miraculous signs and wonders God had done among the Gentiles through them" (v. 12). It had probably been difficult for Paul to keep silent until now. He thought in terms of ideas, probably because much of his education had been received in a Gentile environment. The others at the council did not think this way. They thought in terms of God's great acts and deeds. Paul probably wanted to jump up and clarify the gospel for them.

But Paul was a wise man, and he showed his wisdom by what he did. He understood his audiences. When he spoke to Jews, he spoke as a Jew. When he spoke to Gentiles, he spoke as a Gentile. Here he was speaking to Jews, and he understood how the wind was blowing. Peter had shown how God had worked through him. So when Paul and Barnabas began, they picked up on that and did virtually the same thing. They did not argue theology. Rather, they told about all the miraculous signs that God had done among the Gentiles through them. The argument was: "God is working. Who are we to stand against God?"

Finally, James gave a speech. Interestingly enough, James was the chairman of the council, not Peter. James did not think like Paul. He was the most Jewish of all the Jewish leaders. He even seems to have been somewhat of a legalist. But building on what Peter recounted, he now said virtually the same thing: "It is my judgment, therefore, that we should not make it difficult for the Gentiles who are turning to God" (v. 19).

James was wise too, in his own way. He understood that the people to be won over to the right position were not the Gentiles. Probably not many of them were present at the meeting. It was the Jews who needed to be persuaded. So James began by referring not to Paul, who was the apostle to the Gentiles—that may have been a sticking point in itself—but by referring to Peter. And he refers to him not as "Peter," that is, by his Greek name (*petros* means "stone" in Greek), but by his Jewish name, "Simon." And by the most Jewish form of his Jewish name, not "Simon" merely, but "Simeon"[1]: "Simeon has described to us how God at first showed his concern by taking from the Gentiles a people for himself."

Then James did what we have missed thus far in the debate: he quoted Scripture. He quoted from Amos, one of the minor prophets. Amos is a book of judgment. There are only a few verses at the very end that speak of blessing in the last days, but these are the verses James chose.

> "After this I will return
>   and rebuild David's fallen tent.
> Its ruins I will rebuild,
>   and I will restore it,
> that the remnant of men may seek the Lord,
>   and all the Gentiles who bear my name,
> says the Lord, who does these things"
>   that have been known for ages.
>
>   Acts 15:16–18 (see Amos 9:11–12)

James was, in effect, saying, "God has spoken on this matter. God said he would save the Gentiles. Now he has done it. Therefore, in my judgment we must not oppose God or the Scriptures by making it difficult for the Gentiles to turn to God."

The Letter to the Gentiles

James then proposed writing a letter to the Gentiles, telling of the council's decision but encouraging the Gentiles "to abstain from food polluted by idols, from sexual immorality, from the meat of strangled animals, and from blood" (v. 20).

I suggested at the beginning of this chapter that even the Jerusalem council may have made some errors, and when I come to this letter I sense that the letter was at least a weakness if not an error. Commentators have pointed out that in the conclusion brought by James and in the letter written to the Gentile churches, the one thing that is not mentioned is the matter that began the whole controversy: circumcision. James does not mention it, and the letter to the Gentiles does not mention it. All the letter says is that "it seemed good to the Holy Spirit and to us not to burden you with anything beyond the following requirements" (v. 28). I think it would have been better to have mentioned circumcision and to have said nothing about the other matters.

Yet I wasn't there. Who am I to say that the council of Jerusalem erred? Certainly the letter was statesmanlike, and maybe to be statesmanlike was the right course to be taken, once the real battle had been won. Besides, the other matters would certainly be dealt with in time.

How hard it is to know the difference between a principle that involves the very essence of the gospel, which to yield on is to betray Christ, and a mere statesmanlike position. Hard? Yes, but not impossible! Guided by the Holy Spirit, this seems to be what this first great council of the church achieved. Certainly as Paul and Barnabas went back to the Gentiles with this letter, they went back saying the Gentiles were not compelled to be circumcised. Paul tells us about it in Galatians.

Everett F. Harrison has one of the best commentaries on Acts that I have found, and he says that the council accomplished five important things:

1. The gospel of divine grace was reaffirmed.
2. The unity of the church was safeguarded.
3. The evangelism of the Gentiles could proceed without hindrance. Most of Paul's churches were founded after the council and they were Gentile churches.
4. The Gentile churches that had already been established were given encouragement (Acts 16:4–5).
5. The future of the church as a whole was guaranteed.[2]

It would have been a great thing if in every age of the church, in every conciliar debate, just those five things were accomplished.

31

"Come Over and Help Us"

Acts 15:36–16:15

Paul and his companions traveled throughout the region of Phrygia and Galatia, having been kept by the Holy Spirit from preaching the word in the province of Asia. When they came to the border of Mysia, they tried to enter Bithynia, but the Spirit of Jesus would not allow them to. So they passed by Mysia and went down to Troas. During the night Paul had a vision of a man of Macedonia standing and begging him, "Come over to Macedonia and help us." After Paul had seen the vision, we got ready at once to leave for Macedonia, concluding that God had called us to preach the gospel to them.

Acts 15:6–11

When summer comes most of us begin to think about vacations. But have you ever considered that there is hardly a reference in the Bible to vacations? I cannot think of any vacations in the Old Testament, and in the New Testament the only thing that comes close is the example of the Lord, who from time to time would go aside with his disciples and spend time praying, which was not actually what we mean by a vacation. These times corresponded to what we would call retreats. Actually, throughout human history most people never had a vacation, and for good reasons. Nobody had the money or leisure to enjoy one. Most people had to struggle hard daily just to make a living and stay alive.

Vacations come to my mind when I reach this point in Acts. In these verses the apostle Paul sets off on a second missionary journey, and he seems to have done it almost immediately on the heels of his earlier work. He had just finished his first effort, followed by a trip to Jerusalem for the first church council. These had not been easy times for him. Yet at this point, after he returned to Syrian Antioch and apparently with very little break, if any, he decided that it was time to start out again.

Paul's example suggests that in a Christian's life there really are no *absolute* vacations. I believe in vacations. I take them. They are necessary to refresh us for future work, particularly if our work is strenuous or demands great creativity. But in the Christian life itself, in the ultimate sense, there are no vacations, since we are called to serve Christ in all things and be ready *"always* . . . to give an answer to everyone who asks you to give the reason for the hope that you have" (1 Peter 3:15, italics mine).

Not all of us would be able to maintain the rigorous missionary life of the apostle Paul. He was an extraordinary man. But we are called to live for Christ and bear a faithful witness to him daily.

The Second Missionary Journey

The account of the second missionary journey begins at Acts 15:36 with the report of a disagreement between Paul and Barnabas. These two men had traveled together on the first trip, taking Barnabas's relative John Mark with them. It had been the first official missionary journey in which a church actually supported a team of workers, and it had taken the workers themselves to previously untouched areas. The second journey was to prove even greater. On the second trip, Paul got to several of the major cities of the ancient world, among them Philippi, Thessalonica, Athens, Corinth, and Ephesus.

Some have traced this disagreement to the fact that it was Paul who introduced the idea of setting out to visit the churches founded on the first trip. He said to Barnabas, "Let us go back and visit the brothers in all the towns where we preached the word of the Lord and see how they are doing" (Acts 15:36). The people I am referring to contrast this modest beginning with the call in Acts 13 in which the Holy Spirit said, "Set apart for me Barnabas and Saul for the work to which I have called them" (v. 2). Because that earlier call is said to have come from the Holy Spirit, these people argue, wrongly I think, that the second journey was something Paul himself dreamed up and that it was not of God. This was why they began to have troubles.

Actually, the reason why Paul and Barnabas did not receive a second calling of the Holy Spirit at this point is that they did not need one. They had been called to be missionaries, and once a person is called to a task, he or she does not need to be called and called again. To be missionaries was their work. They had completed their first missionary journey but they had not accomplished all God had for them to do. Now in fulfillment of exactly the same mission, Paul wanted to start off again. He says in effect, "We founded quite a few churches on our first journey. Let's go back now and see how the brothers are doing. Our task isn't finished just because we have visited an area once."

American Christians need a challenge of this kind. We think that if we agree to teach a Sunday school class for nine or ten months, we have done a great deal; we are then ready to have somebody else do it. Or if we are elected to a church board, we serve for a short time, but then as soon as we can we get off the board and back to more leisurely times. We need to see that when God calls us to something it is for a lifetime—or at least until God himself clearly moves us in another direction.

Yet this journey was quite different from the first. There were four new things: a new alignment of missionaries, a new worker, a new vision, and a new church.

A New Alignment of Missionaries

The new alignment came about as a result of the disagreement between Paul and Barnabas. On the first journey the two missionaries had taken John Mark with them. When they got into difficulty (so we must suppose), Mark decided that this was not his calling. So he turned around and went back. We do not have any recorded words of Paul about it, but we can assume from what happened later that he was bitterly disappointed. Paul must have regarded Mark's defection almost as a betrayal of Christ, because when he proposed the next journey and Barnabas wanted to take Mark with them again, Paul reacted so negatively that the two ended up going in different directions.

Paul must have said, "Mark failed us once. He quit. This is no game for quitters. This is for those who will hang in there through thick and thin, regardless of the difficulties. I will not agree to John Mark's presence on this journey."

Barnabas must have said, "Paul, that is not right. Mark is young. Young men make mistakes. He failed once; that is true. But it wasn't a terrible mistake. He just got tired or worried about the difficulties. I think we should give him another chance."

"No," Paul said.

"Yes," said Barnabas.

The text says they got into "such a sharp disagreement" (15:39) about it that the only way out of it was for them to part company. Imagine that! Paul and Barnabas—these two extraordinary missionaries, apostles, the kind of people you might bring into a pulpit on a missionary Sunday and say to the people, "This is what you should be like"—disagreed so violently that they actually went separate ways. Barnabas took Mark and went to Cyprus, where the missionaries had gone first on the first journey. We do not hear any more about Barnabas and Mark on Cyprus, but tradition says that Barnabas stayed on Cyprus and died there as an old man. Mark eventually was called by Paul to go to Rome. As far as the other missionary team was concerned, Paul took Silas, another leader in the church at Antioch, in place of Barnabas, and the two of them set out overland to visit the churches of Asia Minor.

Who was right in this dispute? Was Barnabas right to insist on taking John Mark, or was Paul right to say no? I ask the question only to point out that the Bible does not give an answer. There is nothing in these verses to suggest that Paul was right or that Barnabas was right. No doubt we feel a certain amount of sadness that they split up, but even that is not condemned in Scripture. This is just something that happened. Besides, whatever the motivation of the missionaries may have been, there were two good results.

First, John Mark got another chance and did prove himself faithful in the end. Even Paul acknowledged it. In 2 Timothy Paul wrote of John Mark, "He is helpful to me in my ministry" (2 Tim. 4:11). He wanted Timothy to bring Mark with him to Paul in Rome. The second good result was that now, instead of there being only one missionary team, there were two.

That may not be the best of all ways of getting the work done, but in the providence and grace of God the result is sometimes beneficial. You can have a First Baptist Church or a First Presbyterian Church. The church can have an argument and split, and the result is the Second Baptist Church or Second Presbyterian Church. So there are two churches. As I say, this may not be the best of all possible ways to start churches, but it is one way and God does often seem to bless the two churches. That is what happened here. So it was Paul and Silas, rather than Paul and Barnabas, who started overland on this second journey.

The last verse of chapter 15 says that the missionaries "went through Syria and Cilicia, strengthening the churches" (v. 41). Syria was the province in which Antioch was located; these churches would have been to the immediate north of Antioch. Cilicia was the southeastern area of what we call Turkey, where Tarsus was and where Paul had come from.

Paul and Barnabas had not been in these areas on their first journey. They had come into Asia Minor from the southwest, had gone into central Turkey as far as Derbe, and then had retraced their steps. How did the churches in Syria and Cilicia get founded? We do not know, but the fact that there were churches to the north of Antioch indicates that there was other missionary work going on, work that Luke does not tell us about in his history. It may be, since Paul was from Tarsus and there was a time when he lived there before being called to Antioch, that he had himself founded these churches, but we do not know if he did. If he did, he must have been greatly encouraged as he started out on this journey, since the churches he had founded were still there and were growing.

Some ministers, like myself, spend most of their life in one church. Others travel around and start churches or minister to churches here and there. It must be a great blessing to those who have ministered in a variety of places to visit those places from time to time and find that the work is still going forward. I have had one experience like that. When I was doing graduate work in Switzerland, my wife and I started an English-speaking church in Basel. Over the years, as I have had opportunity to go back to Basel, I have visited the church and have found that it is still strong. It has been a great encouragement.

A New Worker

In the first paragraph of chapter 16, we find a new worker coming on the scene. There is already one new worker, Silas, whom Paul took in place of Barnabas. Here we find one whom Paul and Silas discovered on their journey and invited to go along. His name was Timothy. This is the first place in the New Testament that Timothy is mentioned.

Timothy, whom we know largely through Paul's letters to him, must have been a bit uncertain of his abilities. I suppose that he was somewhat overshadowed by Paul, who had a brilliant mind and forceful personality and who was always ready to speak. Timothy was chiefly a pastor, as opposed to Paul, who was chiefly an evangelist. Timothy was gifted to minister to those Paul had first reached through his preaching. He must have acquired wisdom for building up churches, handling disputes, and counseling those in the churches who had difficulties.

We might think that Paul, being such a strong character, might have looked down on Timothy, thinking, Timothy is all right, you know, but he has limitations. He isn't quite like me. Actually, Paul did just the opposite. He thought highly of Timothy and spoke well of him. He speaks well of him in his letters to Timothy, though we might discount these since when you write to someone you generally say nice things. What is more significant is the way Paul wrote about Timothy when he was addressing other people.

There is a superb endorsement of Timothy in Philippians. Paul wrote:

> I hope in the Lord Jesus to send Timothy to you soon, that I also may be cheered when I receive news about you. I have no one else like him, who takes a genuine interest in your welfare. For everyone looks out for his own interests, not those of Jesus Christ. But you know that Timothy has proved himself, because as a son with his father he has served with me in the work of the gospel. I hope, therefore, to send him as soon as I see how things go with me. And I am confident in the Lord that I myself will come soon.
>
> Philippians 2:19–24

In that brief paragraph Paul says a number of interesting things about his young coworker.

1. *Timothy was unique.* Some of our versions say that Timothy was "like-minded," meaning that Timothy thought like Paul. He did not have an identical personality or the same gifts. He had a different work assignment. But so far as the missionary enterprise and the building up of the churches was concerned, Timothy was an individual uniquely like-minded with Paul.

2. *Timothy was concerned for other people.* Isn't it wonderful to have someone around who is concerned for other people? Paul was speaking from his own experience, but it seems to me that he was also speaking perceptively of our

time when he said, "For everyone looks out for his own interests, not those of Jesus Christ." Paul could be describing our country, our city, or our town, because this is what most people are like, today as then. But here was someone who was so under the influence of Jesus Christ, so filled with the Holy Spirit, that he was concerned about others. He put their interests before his own.

3. *Timothy looked out for the interests of Jesus Christ.* This is also important, since it is possible to have someone who is interested in other people but not within a true Christian framework. A good non-Christian counselor can be interested in other people and help them—but not for the sake of Christ. Timothy had his spiritual priorities right.

4. *Timothy worked well with other people.* Have you known people who can't seem to work with anybody? They are the Lone Rangers of the world. They do a good job, but it is all by themselves. They know nothing about teamwork. Well, says Paul, Timothy is not like that. Timothy might not have been the best of all pioneer missionaries—he may have been too timid for it—but he was certainly a good pastor, because he could work with others within the fellowship of a local church. That is why Paul gave him responsibility for churches he had founded.

Acts 16:3 tells us that Paul wanted to take Timothy along on this second journey, "so he circumcised him because of the Jews who lived in that area." This might seem inconsistent in view of Paul's stand against the legalizers at the Jerusalem council, but it was not. Paul's concern was for the defense and propagation of the gospel. When the essence of the gospel was at stake, Paul refused any compromise whatever. However, when the gospel was not at stake, as was the case here, Paul was willing to compromise many things in order to win others to Jesus Christ.

A New Vision

With a new missionary team and new workers, Paul received a new vision for his service. In Troas he received a vision of a man of Macedonia, who challenged Paul to "Come over to Macedonia and help us" (16:9).

After leaving Antioch Paul had pursued a generally westward direction, passing through Cilicia and then through the towns of Derbe, Lystra (where he picked up Timothy), and Iconium in the southern portion of Galatia. Taking that western road, he would have proceeded eventually into the Roman province of Asia, where Ephesus is located, but God stopped him from doing this, though he did reach Ephesus later from the west.

Since the Holy Spirit kept him from going west Paul tried to make his way north, passing by the edge of Asia, to Bithynia. But when he tried to go into Bithynia, the Spirit forbid him from doing that as well (v. 7). The missionaries were cut off from the west and south and from the north and east. The only thing they could do was press on more or less between the two forbidden territories in a direction that eventually brought them to Troas on the coast of the Aegean Sea. There Paul waited to see what God was going to do with him.

This is a good example of negative guidance. The guidance we get in our lives is often like it. We speak of this as "closed doors." Generally we do not like closed doors. We find closed doors frustrating. We pray, "God, what do you want me to do?" But when we look in what we think is a rather promising direction, God closes the door. We ask again, "God, what do you want me to do?" We look in another direction, and God closes that door too. Then we get depressed. We think God is not answering us and that he doesn't care what we do. Sometimes if this goes on long enough, we even get angry at God.

We need to understand that "closed doors," though they are a type of negative guidance, are nevertheless true guidance. If we can learn anything from the apostle Paul here, we learn that negative guidance merely keeps us from where we are not called in order that in God's time we might come to where God is calling us and will provide blessing.

When God closes doors, it is not because he has nothing for us to do. He does not want us to take a vacation. It is to keep us from getting into a work to which we are not called in order that we might be saved for a work to which we are.

The positive leading came at last, and it was the vision to which I referred. This call of God to Paul and his missionary team teaches some important lessons about missions. Why do we engage in world missions? There are a number of reasons.

1. *Jesus Christ has told us to do it.* We call this "The Great Commission," and we find it five times in the New Testament—once in each of the four Gospels, toward the end, and once at the beginning of Acts.[1] If God says something once, we should pay attention. If he repeats it, we should give rapt attention. How, then, if he says it three, four, five, or more times? Obviously, it is something we dare not overlook and to which we must give the most intent, sustained, and obedient scrutiny. Somebody once spoke to the Duke of Wellington about missions. He said, "The Great Commission is Jesus' marching orders for the church."

2. *Christ's love constrains us.* Paul talks about this explicitly in 2 Corinthians 5:14, saying, "Christ's love compels us." It would be important for us to go into all the world with the gospel if for no other reason than Jesus has told us to do it. But it would be sad if the only motivation we had were mere obedience. We would be saying, "I am here to preach the gospel. I don't want to be here, but I have to be. Jesus told me to do it. So here I am." Paul, who understood the marching orders of Jesus Christ, also understood the compulsion of Christ's love, saying, "Christ's love compels me."

Christ's love involves the love of Christ for the lost; he loves them. But it also involves our love, as the love of Christ works its way out through those who know him. Paul loved those to whom he was sent. So must we. In fact, there is nothing that so commends the gospel to the lost as love for them by the one who proclaims it.

3. *The world is in need.* The world is perishing in its sin apart from the gospel of Jesus Christ, and it also has other needs—social and physical. I find it significant that it is largely in these terms that the call to come to Macedonia was given. The man of Macedonia did not say, "Paul, God tells you to come over here." Nor did he ask, "Paul, don't you love us as much as you love those who are in Asia?" No. He said, "Come over to Macedonia and help us." That is, *We* need help and *you* are the one who can help us.

I wonder if you have thought of your church's missionary effort or your witnessing to a neighbor in those terms. You say, "It is difficult to witness today because so many people in our day don't want the gospel." That is true. They don't. They very seldom do. Most people today are self-satisfied. They do not want anything that might upset their life-style. But if that is the case, why not refocus your witnessing for a time at least on those who *are* hurting and *do* have needs. In the past the gospel has spread best among the masses of humankind who have had crying social, intellectual, medical, and other needs. They have been open to the gospel because they needed help. Christians helped them and brought the gospel too. Maybe one reason why the Protestant churches in this country in particular are not prospering is that they are going to those who are prospering when they ought to go to those who have known needs.

After Paul received the vision he must have shared it with his traveling companions, for the result was they all immediately got ready and crossed over the sea to Macedonia. It was the official opening of Europe to Christianity, and with it the gospel began the long westward march that eventually brought it to us.

Now for the first time in Acts we have an occurrence of the first person plural pronoun "we," indicating that the narrator, Luke, has joined the party. Luke will continue to use "we" throughout chapter 16. But he changes to "they" at the end (v. 40), indicating that he remained behind in Philippi when Paul and the others left to go south to Thessalonica. "We" does not occur again until chapter 20, where Paul has returned to Philippi (v. 6). So clearly, Luke joined the travelers again at that time and accompanied Paul and the others to Jerusalem. "We" stops in chapter 21 but then appears again in chapter 27, which contains the account of Paul's being taken on a ship to Rome. There is little question that Luke traveled with Paul at those times.

A New Church Is Founded

A new alignment of the missionaries, a new worker in the person of Timothy, and a new vision issued in the founding of a new church, the church at Philippi. There was no synagogue at Philippi, so Paul could not follow the pattern he usually followed. But down by the river Paul found a group of women under the leadership of a businesswoman named Lydia. They were worshiping God together. Paul recognized this as a proper place to start. So he began to teach them, and they responded to his message. Lydia, who apparently was a very able woman, invited Paul and the others into her home, and that home became a church, the first church of this first Christian community in Europe.

This is what life is about. It is about God's calling out a people to himself, a people who will know him. His purpose for us is to assist in that great call and work.

32

A Straight Question
and a Straight Answer

Acts 16:16–40

About midnight Paul and Silas were praying and singing hymns to God, and the other prisoners were listening to them. Suddenly there was such a violent earthquake that the foundations of the prison were shaken. At once all the prison doors flew open, and everybody's chains came loose. The jailer woke up, and when he saw the prison doors open, he drew his sword and was about to kill himself because he thought the prisoners had escaped. But Paul shouted, "Don't harm yourself! We are all here!"

The jailer called for lights, rushed in and fell trembling before Paul and Silas. He then brought them out and asked, "Sirs, what must I do to be saved?"

They replied, "Believe in the Lord Jesus, and you will be saved—you and your household." Then they spoke the word of the Lord to him and to all the others in the house.

Acts 16:25–32

When Paul knew that God was directing him to Europe, he responded at once by taking his small missionary party across the Hellespont from Asia into Macedonia. The party included Paul and Silas, who had started out together; Timothy, who had been added along the way; and Luke, who indicates his presence by use of the word "we."

The first convert the missionary party had in Macedonia was a Jewish woman of Philippi whose name was Lydia. Someone has said, "Often the best man for the job is a woman." Others, no doubt picking up on that slogan,

277

have added facetiously that in this case the "*man* of Macedonia" turned out to be a woman. However, as the story unfolds, we find that God had at least two other people in Philippi whom he also wanted to bring to faith in Jesus: another woman, who was a slave, and a Roman jailer.

Acts 16:16–40 falls into four well-defined sections: the story of the slave girl (vv. 16–18), the attack on Paul and Silas (vv. 19–21), Paul's imprisonment (vv. 22–34), and the wrapping up of the affairs of the new church (vv. 35–40).

The Deliverance of the Slave Girl

Because of our particular place in history and because of our western experience, the story of a woman who was able to tell fortunes and earn money for her masters by fortune-telling seems almost unreal to us. But this sort of thing was not at all unusual in antiquity. We tend to discount such stories, but they were not discounted then, either by the unevangelized pagans or by the early Christians. In fact, when we read of this slave girl following after the missionaries, shouting, "These men are servants of the Most High God, who are telling you the way to be saved" (16:17), it seems to be a replay of what happened many times in the ministry of Jesus Christ. Those possessed by demons would follow him, and the demons within them would shout out who Jesus was. "I know who you are—the Holy One of God," they would say in effect (Mark 1:24; see also Matt. 8:29; Mark 5:7; Luke 4:34; 8:28).

When the slave girl is introduced to us in this passage, it is as one who had a "spirit" (v. 16). That does not quite do justice to what the Greek text says. It actually says, "She had a spirit of Pythona." That does not mean much to most of us, which is why it is not translated literally. But "pythona" was a certain kind of snake—a python. It is used here because the python was associated with the god Apollo. You have perhaps heard of the Pythian Apollo, that is, the Apollo god who was associated with the snake.

The stories behind the linking of Apollo and the snake vary. One story has it that Apollo killed a great python. Others have it that the python was an animal particularly sacred to Apollo and that he often spoke to people through it. The important thing is that not far from Philippi, in this very area of Europe, there was a shrine to the Pythian Apollo. So this slave girl was identified with that particular manifestation of the Greek god and seems to have told the future by means of her relationship to him. That is, she had been possessed by a demonic spirit associated with that cult.

We are given another clue to how she operated by the word "fortune-telling" that occurs at the end of verse 16. The English words do not tell us a great deal, but the Greek word is based on the word "manic," which indicates an unnatural, frenetic behavior that frequently appeared when one was in a trance under a spirit's influence. Apparently that is the way she got her messages. She would go into a trance, behave in an erratic fashion, and the demon would speak through her.

There are a number of names for God in Scripture. He is the Almighty, the Sovereign One, the Merciful, the Alpha and Omega, the Beginning and the End, the Shepherd, the Lord. I have a book in my library that contains one biblical name of God for every day of the year, 365 of them. The name the girl used, "the Most High God," is important because of two texts from the Old Testament.

The first is Genesis 14:18, which contains the first mention of this name in the Bible. Abraham had just defeated the kings of the east who had overthrown the cities of the plain and carried off Abraham's nephew Lot and his family. He had defeated them by a secret night attack and had recovered all the people and spoils. Then, when he was returning, he was met by Melchizedek, who is identified as "priest of God Most High." This text specifies the sense in which that name is given, adding to that specific name of God the words "Creator (or Possessor) of heaven and earth" (v. 19). It is as the Creator or Possessor of the cosmos that God is called the Most High.

I make that point because later on in the Old Testament in Isaiah 14, which describes the thoughts that went on in Satan's mind when he rebelled against God and brought sin into the universe, the title occurs again. There Satan is quoted as saying, "I will make myself like the Most High" (v. 14). That means when Satan aspired to be like God, it was not to be like God in his most loving or gracious aspects. He did not want to be like God in love or mercy or even wisdom. He wanted to be like God in respect to his possession of the heaven and the earth. That is, Satan wanted to take over the universe.

I go into that background because the name "Most High God" is especially appropriate on the lips of this woman, since the demon, who was associated with Satan in his rebellion, spoke through her. The demons call God "the Most High" because that is what they want to be. They want to possess heaven and earth. But they cannot. In fact, the opposite is the case. What was happening here was that God through the word of the missionaries had come to challenge them and begin to take away from them even that tiny bit of earthly dominion they had.

I suppose that in a certain sense the second part of the slave girl's cry was not surprising either, though we would not necessarily expect one of Satan's followers to say, "These men . . . are telling you the way to be saved." The demons did not want the people of Philippi to be saved, of course. Perhaps some form of divine compulsion came upon them. Yet for whatever reason, they did identify the missionaries accurately, just as the demons identified Jesus and his purposes accurately when he was on earth.

As Luke tells the story, there seems to have been a period when Paul tried to ignore the interruption. We sense that he was trying not to do anything. Why didn't he stop immediately and cast the demon out? I do not know the answer to that, but it may be that he anticipated the problems that eventually erupted. He had been in other cities where due to disruptions of one kind or another he had not been able to stay long. Perhaps he thought, If I do anything now, it will disrupt the work. I need more time to teach about God. At any rate, a period of time went by, which Luke indicates by saying, "She kept this up for many days" (v. 18).

At last Paul became troubled and turning around said to the spirit, "In the name of Jesus Christ I command you to come out of her!" (v. 18).

And the demon did, just as the spirits did when Jesus issued such commands! The girl was delivered in that instant, and we are to understand that Paul then began to teach her about Jesus Christ. She became the second member of the church at Philippi that we know of, right after Lydia. Isn't that interesting? The church began with two women—a Jewess, who was undoubtedly looked down on by those of this very Roman community, and a slave girl, who had been used by her masters to make money.

The Attack on Paul and Silas

The girl's owners were upset by Paul's actions because they had now lost their means of making money. They were so upset by it that they went to the authorities, saying, "These men are Jews, and are throwing our city into an uproar by advocating customs unlawful for us Romans to accept or practice" (vv. 20–21). The accusation they made was not the real reason for their upset. They were angry that Paul had damaged their business.

Today too people are willing to tolerate Christian testimony and worship as long as Christianity doesn't hurt their business. But if we begin to apply biblical principles to the business world—how money is spent and how it is made—then the world is up in arms against Christianity.

These men knew they would not get far before the magistrates by pleading only a loss of income. So they devised an accusation that would appeal to the emotions of this very patriotic community. Philippi had been settled by retired Roman soldiers. The citizens had Roman citizenship and were extremely conscious of their citizenship. They were the most loyal of Romans. It was by appealing to this loyalty that the owners of the slave girl got Paul and Silas beaten and imprisoned.

They also accused Paul and Silas of being Jewish and of having as their bad Jewish purpose the disrupting of Roman traditions.

That is almost funny, because we know from what has been said already that there were not very many Jews in Philippi. Usually when Paul went into one of these Greek or Roman cities, he began by going to the synagogue because he could be sure of finding godly Jews and Gentiles in those places. When he came to Philippi there was not even a synagogue. There had to be ten Jewish men to have a synagogue. So apparently in Philippi there were not even ten Jewish men. Moreover, when he went down to the river, where he eventually found people worshiping, he did not find even one man. All were women.

The Jewish presence was not a very big threat to the Romans of Philippi then. But when you are in the wrong and angry you reach for any scapegoat you can find. It served the purpose of the slave girl's owners to say in essence, "These men are Jews and, well, everybody knows what Jews are like. They go around stirring things up. They are trying to get us to do things that are unlawful for us to do, being Romans." That was utter misrepresentation, of course. Jews did not go around stirring things up. Besides, Romans were allowed to convert to Judaism. Romans were tolerant of a variety of religions. These men were playing on the prejudice of the crowd, and they succeeded, humanly speaking.

There was an uproar. Luke does not mention either himself or Timothy, so apparently the two of them were overlooked. The rulers stripped Paul and Silas, beat them, and threw them into prison. This is one of three times Paul was beaten with rods (2 Cor. 11:25).

God's Work in the Prison

What did Paul and Silas do in the prison? If they were like many normal Christians, they would have said, "We should never have started out on this journey. It is just too hard to bring the gospel to Europe." If they had been more theological, they might have said, "I suppose these people are just not among the elect. As soon as we can, we had better get out of here and go somewhere God is going to bless." If they were like many of our contemporaries, they would have said, "God wants us to be happy, and we're not happy here sitting in these stocks. Let's find a place where we can be happy." They did not say any of those things. Instead, they spent the night hours praying and singing praises to God.

As Paul and Silas sang and praised God, the other prisoners who might have been complaining beforehand became quiet, just as the believing thief who was crucified on the cross next to Jesus did. As they listened, they began to learn something about the God who had sent Paul and Silas to their city.

Later when Paul wrote to the church at Philippi, his dominant note was rejoicing. Paul said to these Christians, some of whom had perhaps even been in the prison that evening, "Rejoice in the Lord always. I will say it again: Rejoice!" (Phil. 4:4).

It has been pointed out that Paul speaks of rejoicing more in the short letter to the Philippians than in any other of his epistles. In view of what had happened, we can see that these were no mere platitudes on Paul's part. Rather, we see that the man who told others to rejoice had learned to rejoice himself because his heart and mind were so filled with what God was doing and with the blessing of God in his life. Paul regarded the privilege of taking the gospel to areas of the world where it was not known as being so great that it blotted out the discomfort from the beating.

We would have said, "Things are so bad that nothing good will ever come of this." Yet it was in Paul and Silas's extremity that God seemed to act. God made this a wonderful opportunity.

When the earthquake came and the chains fell off the prisoners so that Paul and the others could have escaped if they had wished to do so, the jailer, who had been awakened by the earthquake, rushed toward the prison thinking that the prisoners were all gone. He was ready to kill himself because he was a Roman jailer and knew that the penalty for a Roman soldier who allowed a prisoner to escape was death. Therefore, a Roman guard even under the severest enemy attack would not leave his post. If he did, he would be executed afterward. Paul's guards had similar concerns during the shipwreck later when Paul was being taken to Rome (Acts 27:42–43).

Someone has commented on the Philippian jailer's near suicide by saying, "It shows what a violent type of person he was." I do not think that was it at all. I think he was rightfully afraid and was about to do what under the circumstances and by Roman military code was the proper action.

Paul shouted out, "Don't harm yourself! We are all here" (Acts 16:28).

The jailer replied with what is one of the greatest and most profitable questions of all time, "Sirs, what must I do to be saved?" (v. 30).

I heard a sermon on this text once in which the preacher wrestled with the meaning of that question for a long time. "What did the jailer mean?" he asked. "Obviously he was fearing for his life. Did he mean, 'What must I do to attain to eternal salvation?' Or did he mean, by contrast, 'What must I do to be safe?'" The preacher sided with the latter possibility. He said, "The context indicates that what the jailer was afraid of was that he was going to lose his life. He wanted Paul to tell him how he might be able to be safe physically and not die."

It is pertinent to this question, I think, that earlier in the story the slave girl used the same word the Philippian jailer used when he said, "What must I do to be saved?" Our translation has him using the verb form; she used a noun. But it was the same word when she declared by the power of the demon, "These men . . . are telling you the way of *salvation*" (italics mine). Did the jailer know the earlier testimony of this woman? Undoubtedly he did. This was a small town, the kind of town in which stories like this would spread rapidly. Besides, these men had been put in his custody. He must have asked why, and he would have been told that the slave girl had said that these men knew the way of salvation and that they had acted as messengers of salvation when they had cast the demon out of her. When the jailer came in the dark hours of this night, trembling before Paul and Silas in the posture of a suppliant, asking, "What must I do to be saved?" I think it is clear that he was thinking of eternal salvation.

Regardless of how the jailer intended the question, Paul answered in the right way. The jailer might have been confused about a lot of things. He might have mixed up his physical salvation and his spiritual salvation. However, when Paul answered the question he answered it in spiritual terms, stressing the salvation of his soul, which was of greatest importance.

Furthermore, he answered it clearly. He said to the man, "Believe in the Lord Jesus, and you will be saved—you and your household."

I am glad he answered so directly.

Charles Haddon Spurgeon preached a sermon once in which he referred to the cities of refuge in Israel in Old Testament times. When the Jews conquered Canaan they were told to establish cities of refuge to which a person who had accidentally killed somebody and who was therefore subject to the law of *lex talionis*—"an eye for an eye, a tooth for a tooth," or revenge on the part of the relatives of the person who had been killed—could run to and be safe. Spurgeon indicated how the law told the Jews to make sure these roads were well cared for and were unobstructed. If any stones had fallen into these roads, they were to be removed. If any bridges had fallen down, they were to rebuild the bridges. Furthermore, they were to set up signs to mark the way, so that under the stringent pressure of the moment, a fleeing fugitive, pursued perhaps by an avenger, might by these signs actually make it to the city safely. Spurgeon said that this is exactly what the apostle Paul was doing here. He was making the way to the city of refuge plain to the jailer.

Notice that Paul did not suggest counseling. He did not say to this jailer, "I realize you are asking a very important question, but before I answer, it is important first of all to understand yourself so you will know the terms by which you are asking the question. You have to begin with yourself, and after you have done that, we will talk about the gospel."

He did not give a lecture on theology.

He did not explore the significance of the jailer's religious terms.

He did not talk about the sacraments.

He did not even talk about the church. Those things could be dealt with in time, but this was not the time. The man was asking about salvation, and the apostle replied directly: "Believe in the Lord Jesus, and you will be saved—you and your household."

Did the jailer understand what that meant? He must have understood some of it, because he believed and was baptized. Did he understand all of what it meant? Probably not. I am not sure we do, even with all the teaching we have received. But what he did know he believed, and Jesus saved him. Besides, not only was *he* converted; in the course of the evening his entire family was converted too.

This was the third of three striking conversions that Luke records as having taken place at Philippi, those with Lydia, the businesswoman; the unnamed slave girl; and the Philippian jailer. John Stott calls attention to the fact that

> the head of a Jewish household would use the same prayer every morning, giving thanks that God had not made him a Gentile, a woman or a slave. But here were representatives of these three despised categories redeemed and united in Christ. For truly, as Paul had recently written to the Galatians: "There is neither Jew nor Greek, slave nor free, male nor female, for you are all one in Christ Jesus."[1]

When Paul said to this jailer, "Believe in the Lord Jesus, and you will be saved—you and your household," was he promising what has come to be called in some circles "household salvation"? Was he promising that whenever one person in a household believes everybody else in that household will inevitably believe also? Can you count on that invariably? No, I do not think the Bible teaches "household salvation," though Paul was saying that this is what would follow in this instance. However, if it happened in this instance, it is probably what we should expect under comparable conditions. It is what we do see frequently. When God calls one of a family, it is often the means by which he draws others into the gospel net.

Vindication and Encouragement

The next morning the magistrates gave orders for the two missionaries to be released. We do not know why, perhaps because being Romans and being particularly sensitive to matters of legal justice they realized that there was no real charge against them. Whatever the reason, we know how Paul answered. He said, Nothing doing. We are not just going to come out of the prison and then slip away quietly. They have condemned us unjustly, and they have beaten and imprisoned us without a trial; that is criminal conduct against one who is a Roman citizen.

This was a Roman town. These people were concerned about observing Roman laws. Unknown to them but nevertheless, they had broken these laws, and as a result they were frightened. So when Paul demanded that the magistrates not only release them but also actually come and lead them out, they did.

Why did Paul insist on that? I think he had in mind the safety of the church he was to leave behind. He wanted to do everything he could to establish and protect it. And perhaps that is even why he did not declare that he was a Roman citizen when they were about to beat him earlier. He declared so in a later incident in Jerusalem. It may be that he did not do it here in order to place the magistrates in a difficult position and so provide a basis for the future protection of the church. However, when the magistrates requested that the missionaries leave the city, Paul did not insist on his rights but obeyed their wishes.

The story ends by saying that after they had been brought out of prison Paul and Silas went back to Lydia's house, where they met with the brothers "and encouraged them" (v. 40). We might think under those circumstances that Lydia and the others should have encouraged Paul and Silas, but it was the other way around. They were the leaders God had sent to Philippi. So they encouraged the little church they left behind.

Luke decided to stay behind. We know this because at this point Luke drops the use of "we" that he began to use in verse 10, and starts to use "they." He says, "Then *they* left" (v. 40). I do not know why Luke stayed behind. It may be that he was from Philippi, as some have suggested. But perhaps he stayed just to pastor this flock. It was not a prestigious assignment. It had elements of danger. If this is why he stayed, it indicates that Luke had a pastor's heart.

33

Two More Cities

Acts 17:1-15

When they had passed through Amphipolis and Apollonia, they came to Thessalonica, where there was a Jewish synagogue. As his custom was, Paul went into the synagogue, and on three Sabbath days he reasoned with them from the Scriptures, explaining and proving that the Christ had to suffer and rise from the dead. "This Jesus I am proclaiming to you is the Christ," he said. Some of the Jews were persuaded and joined Paul and Silas, as did a large number of God-fearing Greeks and not a few prominent women. . . .

As soon as it was night, the brothers sent Paul and Silas away to Berea. On arriving there, they went to the Jewish synagogue. Now the Bereans were of more noble character than the Thessalonians, for they received the message with great eagerness and examined the Scriptures every day to see if what Paul said was true.

Acts 17:1–11

The seventeenth chapter of Acts is best known for the sermon Paul preached on Mars Hill in Athens. But that is only in the second half of the chapter. In the first half of chapter 17 we find Paul not in Athens but in two other Greek cities: Thessalonica in the north, and Berea on the way from Thessalonica south toward Athens.

People who have studied cities in the Bible have pointed out that there are more than fourteen hundred references to cities and more than twenty-five careful studies of a mission to a particular city. Acts is a great example. Acts begins in Jerusalem, that most important of all biblical cities, and progresses through scores of cities until toward the end of the book we find Paul and his friends in Rome. Thus, Acts moves from the most important biblical city to the most important secular city of that day.

City Mission Goals

Paul and his fellow missionaries had been commissioned by a city church, the church of Antioch. It was the first mission-minded church of the New Testament era. It was cosmopolitan because Antioch was a cosmopolitan city, and it was out of the particular sensitivities of the Christians in that city that the missionary enterprise developed. From Antioch on, we find Paul in Athens, an intellectual center; Corinth, a commercial center; and finally Ephesus, the political center for the region, where some of his most significant work was done.

Paul's mission goals were to preach in a city, to plant a church there, and to use the church for further outreach. Paul was not unconcerned for other areas. But he knew that if he planted strong Christian churches in cities, the gospel (like everything else) would eventually spread from those centers to the outlying regions. In this chapter we see how Paul worked out his goals in Thessalonica and Berea.

The Mission in Thessalonica

The first example is Thessalonica. Thessalonica was an important city. It was a port, first of all. It was not as great a commercial city as Corinth, which was in a more direct line of commerce, sitting astride the isthmus linking northern and southern Greece. Nevertheless, Thessalonica was the chief city of Macedonia. Much of the produce of Macedonia left from Thessalonica and many of the items imported into Macedonia passed through it. It is there today, though it has a slightly different name, Salonika. Paul's mission strategy to achieve his goals in Thessalonica was to establish contact and teach the people.

Establish Contact

The first thing Paul did was establish contact with the city's residents. Paul's pattern was to go to the synagogue first. His chief contact point was the synagogue because he had a hearing there. He found godly Jews and God-fearing Gentiles who were already interested in religious things and familiar with the Word of God. They did not know about Jesus Christ to whom the Scriptures pointed. But on the basis of their prior knowledge Paul had an open door for announcing Christ to them.

I suggest that to reach today's world we also should focus on the cities. That is where a majority of the people are, and more people are moving to the cities all the time. I would also suggest that when we focus on the cities we should look for points of contact.

What are those points? Are they synagogues? No. In most places that would not be an effective point of contact today. What then? My experience in Philadelphia, where I work, suggests that today the greatest point of contact for sharing the gospel is those areas of city life where Christians can be of service to city people. City people are conscious of their needs. Some are single but have children. They need to work. They wonder what they are going to do with their young children. A good point of contact with such people is a pre-school. We established one at Tenth Presbyterian Church years ago, and I suppose that over the years we had more fruitful contacts with city people through that means than perhaps anything else we did up to that time.

In more recent years we have established a high school, and for the same reason—not necessarily because we think we know how to run a high school better than anyone else, but because there is a tremendous need for one of our type. We are trying to provide quality pre-college education at a price most city families can afford. This is because in our judgment the public schools seem to become ineffective at the high school level while ironically most of the Christian schools tend to stop at grade eight.

The same thing is true of direct service ministries. We have a ministry to street people known as ACTS. It stands for "Active Compassion Through Service." Another ministry is to homosexuals. It is called Harvest. We have a ministry to people who have AIDS. It is called Hope. We have a service for those who are having crisis pregnancies. It is called Alpha Pregnancy Services.

I do not think these ministries are at all original or comprehensive. In fact, I would say that in Philadelphia we have perhaps only begun to scratch the surface. There is a great deal more that needs to be done, but these have at least been places to begin. It has been out of these services that our most effective contacts have come.

Another thing we have learned to stress is Christians' living in the cities, thereby establishing a Christian presence in them. This does not mean that Christians are not to establish a Christian presence elsewhere. We are to go into all the world with the gospel. But if most people in America live in cities and we are trying to reach these people, then obviously the majority of us should live in the cities where the people are.

Our model in this respect is E. V. Hill of Los Angeles. When he became pastor of Mount Zion Baptist Church some years ago, he made it a goal to establish a Christian presence in every block of Los Angeles. He had been a ward leader for the Democratic party in Texas before he went to Los Angeles. As ward leader his job was to have a block captain for every block of his ward so that when election day came his block captains could get out the vote. When he became a Christian and went to Los Angeles, Hill said to himself, If I could organize a city for the Democrats, I can do it for God. So he began to establish Christian block captains for every block of that great city. That sounds like an overwhelming task, but it is not as impossible as it sounds. How many blocks do you suppose there are in Los Angeles? The answer is about nine thousand. The last I heard—and that was quite a few years ago—Hill had block captains in nineteen hundred blocks of Los Angeles. If he can do it there, it can be done in other large cities.

Teach the People

The second thing I notice about Paul's method is that having made contact with people through the synagogue he then taught them. Philippians 4:16 says that Paul received more than one gift from the Philippians while he was in Thessalonica. So he must have taught the Scriptures in Thessalonica for some time. How did he go about it?

First, Paul began with the *Scriptures*. The Scriptures are the Word of God, and God has promised to bless his Word. He has said that he will not allow it to return to him empty (Isa. 55:11). So for theological as well as very practical reasons Paul began with the Word, knowing theologically that God would bless it and judging that if such was the case he would be more effective preaching the Scriptures than doing anything else.

Second, he *"reasoned . . .* from the Scriptures" (v. 2). That Paul "reasoned" is something the evangelical church especially needs to hear today since we have a tendency to denigrate reason. We say, sometimes on supposedly theological grounds, "If the Holy Spirit is the one who has to bring men and women to faith, then it doesn't matter whether we give them reasons for what they are supposed to believe. The only thing we have to do is proclaim the Scriptures, that is, just quote Bible verses to them." It is better to quote Bible verses than do nothing at all, and it is better to quote Bible verses than the sayings of mere men, however valuable they may be. But quoting is not all Paul did. He told people to think about a verse, think about what it says, think about what it implies, think what it says about Jesus.

Third, Paul also *explained* the Scriptures, proving from them that "Christ had to suffer and rise from the dead" (v. 3). Paul helped them understand the gospel by explaining the Bible to them.

At this point it is helpful to think negatively about Paul's approach. What did he not do?

He did not try to coerce them. He did not hit them over the head with the Bible. Sometimes we think that in order to witness effectively all we have to do is shout louder. Sometimes we even try to compel people by threats. Paul did not do any of those things. He reasoned with them, winsomely I presume. He tried to win them to his side.

He did not entertain them. We need to hear that fact today especially since we live in an entertainment age and evangelical Christianity is caught up in the entertainment business.

Have you noticed the way people are talking about so-called Christian "ministries" today? The Bible teaches that we all have a ministry. But we do not use the word "ministry" that way very much today. When we speak of a ministry, what we usually mean is a business wrapped around an individual. I have noticed in the media recently that there is much talk about various television "ministries" and whether some of the people who are no longer in a television "ministry" are going to establish another "ministry." What they mean is a business, and what those businesses often largely consist of is entertainment.

Paul did not go to Thessalonica to entertain the people or to start a business. He went to teach the Word of God. If you decide to entertain, whether you do it on a large scale with millions of dollars or on a small scale, you will get results because people like to be entertained. But the results will not be what we find from Paul's work in Thessalonica, a communion of Christian people called into being by God and blessed by him. Rather, you will have a business. You will have a ministry wrapped around you that when you are gone will fade away. Why is it that Bible-teaching churches thrive from generation to generation while "ministries," in our sense of the word, do not? It is because the "ministries" center on an individual and are largely entertainment. Paul's work flourished because he focused on explaining the Scriptures rather than on advancing his own ideas.

Finally, he *preached Christ*. There are other important things Paul could have talked about, and I am sure that as he explained who Christ was, what he came to do, and the implications of both, he touched on many other doctrines also. When Luke writes the condensed form of this story he does not mention these other matters, important as they may have been, but only Jesus. Paul came to preach Christ, that he had to suffer and die and rise again from the dead, and he proclaimed Jesus of Nazareth as that Christ.

In this passage we have a restatement of the *kerygma*—the good news that Jesus is the Son of God, that he died for our sins according to the Scriptures, that he was buried, that he rose again on the third day according to the Scriptures, that he was seen alive by chosen witnesses and is now proclaimed throughout the world as our only Savior from sin and the Messiah. Any teaching that leaves out this core leaves out the very thing God blesses, the only thing that results in the salvation of sinful men and women like ourselves (see the discussion of *kerygma* in chapters 5 and 12).

A Sound Church Established

The result of Paul's method is what I have been speaking of all along, namely, that a church was established in these cities. In Thessalonica we are told that "some of the Jews . . . joined Paul and Silas, as did a large number of God-fearing Greeks and not a few prominent women" (v. 4). The next paragraph tells us that the name of one of the believers was Jason.

This church soon experienced persecution. Those who did not believe were jealous, rounded up certain bad characters—the kind you find hanging around on street corners everywhere—and started a riot in the city. They went to Jason's house because that is where Paul and Silas were staying. They did not find them. They found Jason and a few other brothers instead. So they dragged them before the city officials, shouting, "These men who have caused trouble all over the world have now come here, and Jason has welcomed them into his house. They are all defying Caesar's decrees, saying that there is another king, one called Jesus" (vv. 6–7).

Interestingly, in our translation the people in charge of Thessalonica are called "the city officials," translating the Greek word *politarch*. This is the only place in ancient literature where this word is found, and there was a time when the liberal scholars were saying that it was proof that Luke didn't know what he was writing about and could not be trusted as a historian. They assumed that Luke made up the word because he didn't know the proper title.

However, as is often the case in such matters, it is the liberal critics rather than Luke who have been proved wrong, because today this term has been found. And remarkably, it has been found not scattered throughout the Roman world as we might expect but in this very city of Thessalonica. In fact, there are sixteen inscriptions of this very word. It was even found on an arch that was once above one of the gates to the city.[1] Since the inscriptions are not found elsewhere it seems that this was a term unique to Thessalonica. Thus, far from its being evidence of inaccuracy on Luke's part, it is actually proof of his extraordinary power of observation and of his reliability as a historian.

When they came to the city officials, the leaders of the riot made a two-part accusation: (1) that Paul and Silas, who had been upsetting people elsewhere, had come there; and (2) that they were teaching people to defy Caesar's decrees. The second half of the accusation was untrue, though it was a wise move for them to have raised it. If they could get people thinking that the disciples were teaching rebellion against Caesar, they had a point in their favor. But although that part of their accusation was untrue, the first part, which claimed that they were upsetting the world, was accurate.

This is another place where we have lost something in translation. The New International Version says, "These men who have caused trouble all over the world have now come here" (v. 6). Well, they were and they had. But the text is actually stronger than this. It says literally, "These men . . . have turned the world upside down."

There is an ancient letter in which a teenager is writing to his mother to complain that his father wouldn't let him go to Alexandria. He says, "Father has upset me." That word "upset" or "turn upside down" is the word Luke uses.[2] Paul and Silas had been upsetting the world. But that wasn't a bad thing for them to do. It was a good thing, because the world had already been turned upside down by sin. So by turning it upside down again, they were actually setting it right.

I wish all Christians would upset the world that way. A lot are upsetting other people, but not like that. They should be upsetting the world by bringing the grace of God to it through the preaching of his Word. This alone is able to bring the world back to its senses and bring blessing.

A Later Assessment

In the first two chapters of 1 Thessalonians Paul reflects on what happened in Thessalonica as the result of his preaching.[3]

1. *The preaching was blessed by God.* Paul says that when he preached at Thessalonica the gospel came "with power," that is, by the Holy Spirit (1 Thess. 1:5). The way Paul writes makes us think that there were times in his ministry when, at least so far as he could tell, the gospel did not come in such power. He preached the same gospel. But for reasons known only to God, not as many responded and the results were not as firm or long lasting. In Thessalonica God had blessed the preaching powerfully.

2. *The people received God's Word eagerly.* Paul says that when he preached the gospel the words he spoke were received by the Thessalonians "not as the word of men, but as it actually is, the word of God" (1 Thess. 2:13). Paul often referred to his teaching in that way, saying that what he taught was God's direct teaching, since he taught as an apostle of the Lord. People did not always receive Paul's teaching as God's Word. Often they rejected it completely. But in Thessalonica they received it as given by the Holy Spirit and were blessed accordingly.

3. *The believers tried to model their Christian lives after Paul.* Paul wrote that those who received the gospel became "imitators" of Paul and his companions (1 Thess. 1:6). There was no New Testament in those days. It had not been written yet. There was no Sermon on the Mount for the disciples to place before them and say, "This is our model." What they had was Paul, Silas, and Timothy, and they tried to model their Christian life after them.

4. *They became models themselves.* Having imitated Paul, these new Christians then became models themselves, not only to one another but "to all the believers" in the area (1 Thess. 1:7). Their faith and way of life became known everywhere.

5. *The church at Thessalonica became a missionary church.* Finally, as a result of all those things, the church at Thessalonica became a center through which the gospel "rang out" everywhere (1 Thess. 1:8). That is, they became missionaries. What we need today are churches in the major cities of America that have received the Scriptures as the very Word of God, in which individuals are trying to imitate Jesus Christ and have a strong missionary vision, and from which the gospel therefore spreads to others.

The Church in Berea

Because of the trouble in Thessalonica, Paul and Silas left the city by night and made their way to Berea. Thus, we come to the second of these two examples of city ministry.

Of all the stories from Acts that I was taught in my childhood, the one I have most remembered over the years is about the Bereans, that "these were more noble than those in Thessalonica" (KJV) because they "searched the

292 The Witness to the World

Scriptures daily" to see whether what Paul had been teaching them was so. The sentence is translated differently in the New International Version: "the Bereans were of more noble character than the Thessalonians, for they received the message with great eagerness and examined the Scriptures every day to see if what Paul said was true" (v. 11).

Three things are said of the Bereans. First, they received the message eagerly; second, they examined the Scriptures; and third, they examined the Scriptures *daily*.

When verse 11 says that they received the message with great eagerness, it does not mean that they were naive and simply believed everything they heard. It means that unlike those in some of the other cities these people were open to the gospel and had not prejudged it. In other cities the people tended to regard the gospel as something to be rejected out-of-hand, just because it was new. The Bereans instead said: This sounds good. We'd like to hear more about it. Let's listen.

Then, having heard the good news, they went to the Scriptures themselves to see if the things Paul was teaching really were in them. Moreover, they did it daily—not just on Sunday mornings for an hour, but daily, because these teachings were matters of life and death. They wanted to spend all their available time studying them. There are preachers who want people to accept what they say just because they say it. They do not want to be challenged. Good preachers want a congregation that hears the Word, receives it eagerly, and then goes to the Scriptures daily to see if what is being taught is really true.

What were the results? They are in verse 12: "Many of the Jews believed, as did also a number of prominent Greek women and many Greek men." That means that in Berea as in Thessalonica (and Philippi before that) a church was established that grew strong and itself eventually sent missionaries to other places.

I have already mentioned that Luke stayed behind in Philippi. Here we find that Paul's company is reduced still further. Silas and Timothy stayed on at Berea while Paul went on alone to Athens.

We know the reason. The early churches needed leaders to strengthen them. That is why Paul allowed his coworkers to stay on. But if we look at it from a human point of view, it seems that what Paul was doing was dividing what was already a pitifully small force. Paul had set out to overturn the entire Roman world with just four workers: himself, Silas, Timothy, and Luke, who had joined them along the way. And what does he do? He leaves Luke in Philippi, Silas and Timothy in Berea, and then he goes on by himself to Athens. Later they rejoin him. But after that he will dispatch them again: Timothy back to Thessalonica and Silas somewhere else—we do not know where. What an inadequate force! Yet what a revolution as men and women everywhere—Jews and Greeks, young and old, slaves and free—were led to Jesus as their Savior.

34

The Sermon on
"The Unknown God"

Acts 17:16–34

Paul then stood up in the meeting of the Areopagus and said: "Men of Athens! I see that in every way you are very religious. For as I walked around and looked carefully at your objects of worship, I even found an altar with this inscription: TO AN UNKNOWN GOD. Now what you worship as something unknown I am going to proclaim to you."

Acts 17:22–23

Paul's late missionary efforts centered on the cities of his world. At the beginning, when he first set out with Barnabas, he passed through Cyprus from one end to the other, and we are told almost nothing about any specific ministry in towns. But after he went to Asia Minor (Turkey) he worked in some cities there, small ones at first, then larger. At last, when he came to Europe, his ministry was focused almost entirely on the major cities: Philippi, Thessalonica, Berea, and now, in this chapter, on Athens, the greatest city of them all.

The Glory That Was Greece

New Zealand Bible teacher and commentator E. M. Blaiklock comments that in Paul's day Athens was in the "late afternoon of her glory."[1] Athens

293

had experienced a golden age. Few cities, even few nations, have equaled the splendor of Athens in the fifth century B.C.

To begin with, the city had achieved a series of military victories that had brought it to the height of world power. Herodotus writes about them in his histories. The Persian empire had been expanding westward from the area we know as Iraq and Iran, and the Persians had tried to push into Europe, crossing the Hellespont near the modern city of Constantinople. They did this twice, and they were repulsed by the Greeks on both occasions.

The Greeks defeated the Persians first at Marathon, where a small army of Greeks (no more than one hundred thousand) withstood a Persian army in excess of a million men, according to Herodotus. At the same time, the Greeks thoroughly routed the Persian navy at Salamis. Later the Greeks defeated a second Persian invasion, famous for the stand of the Spartans at Thermopylae.

In the years that followed these victories, Athens rose to its pinnacle of greatness. The Persians had occupied Athens for a short time, destroying the city thoroughly, but the Greeks rebuilt it gloriously. They rebuilt their homes and constructed their grand temples, topped by the magnificent Parthenon. More importantly, they also rebuilt their civilization, creating the first example of a democracy in human history at Athens: a city-state run by elected officials who were responsible to the citizens.

It was an age of literature. The classical Greek plays were written during this period.

It was an age of philosophy, of Socrates and Plato.

It was an age of art. Praxiteles developed the classical forms of human sculpture that were imitated in Europe throughout the succeeding ages down to and including the time of Michelangelo.

Yet this golden age of Greek history passed rapidly away. The Greeks of Athens got into a disastrous war with Sparta that dragged on for twenty-seven years and resulted in the destruction of Greek power and much of Greek civilization. Athens never again regained its former glory. Although it remained an intellectual center and although its reputation for intellectual excellence persisted, even intellectually it declined from the levels of the fifth century B.C. The master philosophers of that age were succeeded by men of lesser ability and finally by those who were only imitators of the giants of the past.

The Apostle Paul in Athens

It was hundreds of years after Athens' golden age that Paul visited the city and preached the sermon recorded in Acts 17, but the city was still a strikingly beautiful city as well as the intellectual capital of the ancient world.

What do you suppose the reactions of Paul were as he came to Athens on this second missionary journey? We remember that he had been trained in one of the prestigious university centers himself, Tarsus, where he had been born and grew up. He reflects his privileged education in this sermon by quoting from two of the Greek poets, Aratus and Cleanthes, both of whom seem to have said, "We are his offspring" (17:28). Paul seemed at home in the intellectual setting of Athens. It was as if a graduate of Harvard or Yale were to visit Cambridge or Oxford. There would be respect for a university that was older and yet was much the same.

Paul was also disturbed as he began to talk with the prominent Athenian philosophers. Luke tells us that they were Epicureans and Stoics. The Epicureans and Stoics were two leading schools of philosophy in Paul's day.

The Epicureans

Epicureans derived their worldview from Epicurus, who had lived in the second and third centuries B.C. According to Epicurus, the chief goal in life is to attain the maximum amount of pleasure and the minimum amount of pain. We use the word "Epicurean" to refer to a person who is a mere hedonist, but the Epicureans were not quite hedonists in our sense. Hedonists abandon themselves to pleasure. The Epicureans did not do that exactly; they sought a balance between pain and pleasure. Nevertheless, they were pure materialists. They said in effect, "This life is all there is; you only go around once. So if it feels good, do it. If it doesn't feel good, stay away from it. Avoid what hurts." They tried to create a lifestyle that would achieve the maximum good based upon their philosophy.

Do you know anyone like that today? You probably know hundreds of such people. We live in an age dominated by a pleasure-first, do-what-pleases-me, avoid-the-pain philosophy. "Above all," say our contemporaries, "do not take any responsibility that might prove difficult. Enjoy yourself, because this life is all there is."

Can you imagine what Paul, steeped in the Old Testament and with his sound knowledge of the true God, must have thought of that philosophy? We read that when he saw the Athenian idols he was bothered by them, but he must have been bothered by Athenian philosophy too. Are we similarly bothered by the faulty philosophies around us? Does it bother us that people are living for the present moment only and do not seem to have the faintest idea that they are eternal beings and must one day face God?

The Stoics

The second group of philosophers were Stoics. Their school had been founded by a man named Zeno. There were two Zenos. This one had come from Cyprus and had taught that life is filled with both good and bad, that you cannot really avoid the bad so what you have to do is "grin and bear it."

That is stoicism. It says, "I can't control everything that is going on out there, and things are going to happen to me that I will not like. But I am still in charge of myself. Therefore, I am going to stand tall, stick out my chin, and take it—whatever comes." The Stoics were not ignoble. Epictetus was a stoic, and he was one of the bright lights of Greek thought. The second-century Roman emperor Marcus Aurelius was also influenced by Stoic thought. These people were willing to endure hardship for some good, and they contributed much to society, as the Epicureans for the most part did not. Yet theirs was still a rather sad philosophy.

There are many Stoics around us. They are people who have no sense of a divine presence or of divine guidance in their lives. They just do the best they can. If bad things come, well, they think they just have to be strong and endure it. I think that Paul must have been bothered by this faulty philosophy as well, just as much as by the Epicurean.

Luke tells us that what bothered Paul most was the Greeks' idolatry. Their idolatry was father to their philosophy. Our idea of God (or denial of God) will always give shape to what we think. If we have a high idea of God, if we know the true God, then we will have a godly, uplifting, helpful, positive philosophy. But if we do not have a knowledge of the true God, if instead we have a god who is made merely in the image of men or, as was the case in those days, of things less than God intended man to be, then our idea of man will descend to that level and our philosophy will become as degenerate, negative, and despairing as the philosophies of the Stoics and Epicureans.

When Paul looked around the city, he saw idols everywhere. One of the ancients said that in Athens it was easier to find a god than a man, meaning that the city was filled with idols. Paul realized that idolatry was the fundamental problem with that society.

I wonder if we share his insight today. Idolatry is the basic problem of our society. We read in the papers about a breakdown in moral values; lack of commitment by people to people, causes, or standards; dishonesty in many forms; irresponsibility. But do we realize that the reason for the breakdown is spiritual? If people have a concept of God that is noble, they will find it ennobling and will do better. But if we lose sight of God, as America has in our day, then we lose sight of the only thing that can lift up ours or any other civilization.

When Paul got to Athens he was not excessively awed with it, as we might expect him to have been. Rather, he analyzed it rightly and responded to it as a Christian. We need Christians today who have proper respect for the achievements of our time, who do not despise what has been done in science and other intellectual pursuits, but who are not too awed by these achievements, are able to see the limits of our predominantly secular culture, and respond to it helpfully with the Word of God.

The "Address" on Mars Hill

Paul's address begins in verse 22. It is a classic. When you write a formal address or sermon, you generally begin with an introduction, have three or four main points, and then a good conclusion. This is exactly what Paul does here. He has a short but brilliant introduction, followed by four clear points:

(1) God is the Creator of all things; (2) God is the sustainer of all things; (3) God is the ordainer of all things; and (4) we should seek him. Paul concludes that we should repent since we have not sought God as we should. To this he appends several sharp inducements.

The Introduction

Paul began by reminding the Greeks of something he had noticed as he walked through the city. He said: "I even found an altar with this inscription: TO AN UNKNOWN GOD. Now what you worship as something unknown I am going to proclaim to you" (v. 23).[2] Nobody has found this altar, but there are references to similar inscriptions in ancient writings. A number of ancient visitors to Athens saw altars or statues that bore such writing.

Paul does not say why the true God was unknown to the Athenians, though we know the answer from his teaching in Romans 1. The reason men and women do not know God is that they do not want to know him. God has made himself known; they reject the revelation. They do not like the God who is there. Paul does not explain this here. Instead, he cites the Greeks' ignorance, proposing to correct it by his proclamation.

Sometimes people ask how to deal with people who seem blind to Christian truth. These are difficult questions for me because I really do not know the answers in each case. Sometimes as we talk with people the Lord gives us answers that seem to speak directly to their hearts. And certainly, if the person we are speaking to has intellectual questions, he needs to have thoughtful answers. Peter wrote, "Always be prepared to give an answer to everyone who asks you to give the reason for the hope that you have" (1 Peter 3:15). We want to be able to do that. But generally the problem is not in the nature of our reasoning or explanation but rather in the rebellion of the human heart. The problem is the hearer. Paul's solution—indeed, the solution of Christian preaching generally—is proclamation. It is declaring who God is and what he has done and allowing God to bless the declaration. What happens is that God takes the truth of his Word and by the power of his Holy Spirit carries it to the heart and brings conviction.

God the Creator

Paul's first point after his introduction is that God is the Creator of all things. Verse 24 says, "The God who made the world and everything in it is the Lord of heaven and earth and does not live in temples built by hands." The doctrine of creation, in addition to teaching man's responsibility to seek and serve him (which Paul develops later), means that God has not left himself without a witness. It is true that not all peoples have had the Scriptures. In the Old Testament period God gave the Bible only to the Jews. But all people at all times have nevertheless had a witness to God in creation, in the heavens, and on earth. No one can claim utter ignorance of the true God.

298 The Witness to the World

God the Sustainer

Paul's second point is that God is the sustainer of all things. Verse 25 says, "He [God] is not served by human hands, as if he needed anything, because he himself gives all men life and breath and everything else." God sustains his creation. It is not that we provide for him; he provides for us.

There is debate as to whether creation was made once for all, after which God let it go, or whether God sustains it constantly by what might be called "moment by moment creation" or "continuous creation." Did God create the world and then just continue to preserve and guide it? Or does he constantly re-create it in the sense that if God stopped creating it for even a single instant everything we know would disappear? I do not have the answer, and I am not sure anyone else does either. But I know that in the first chapter of Colossians Paul says that "in him [that is, Christ] all things hold together" (v. 17). That seems to suggest that if the Lord Jesus Christ were not holding all things together everything would fly apart.

I think Paul proclaimed in Athens a God who not only created all things but who also sustains them, perhaps not by a "moment by moment" creation, but at least by continuing to give the universe and world stability. The very fact that we and the world are here, that we are alive, and that we can think about both it and ourselves are all due to the sustaining activity of God.

God the Ordainer

Third, Paul says that God not only sustains the universe but also guides the affairs of men. Verse 26 says, "From one man he made every nation of men, that they should inhabit the whole earth; and he determined the times set for them and the exact places where they should live."

Theologians refer to this guidance as "the hidden counsels" of God. The word "hidden" means that God has not revealed these eternal counsels to us in Scripture as he has other things. So we do not know the future; we do not know what God has determined to do in national affairs. Nevertheless, God is in control of what happens. He has made plans and thus also determines whatever comes to pass. This is the true God, not a weak God, not a God we must beg in order to get him to change his mind about something. He determined, for example, that the Greeks would be Greeks; the Athenians, Athenians; and the Americans, Americans. None of these things are accidents.

We Should Seek God

If God has revealed himself to us in creation, as he has, and if God sustains creation (including ourselves), and if God has determined the bounds of our habitations and our destiny, which Paul declares to be the case, it follows that we have an obligation to seek God out and find him. Indeed, such is the purpose of the general revelation: God has revealed himself so that we might seek him out. Paul states clearly and emphatically in verse 27, "God did this so that men would seek him and perhaps reach out for him and find him, though he is not far from each one of us."

Paul uses a word here for "reaching out for [or 'feeling after'] God and finding him" that the Greek poet Homer used in the well-known story of the Cyclops. The giant one-eyed Cyclops had captured Odysseus and his men, and Odysseus had gotten him drunk and then blinded him with a sharp stake. The epic's hero then wanted to sneak out of the cave where he and his men were being held. But it was difficult because the Cyclops was groping around, feeling after Odysseus so that he might find him and kill him. That is the very word Paul uses. So it is as if he is saying: In our sin we are as blind as the blinded Cyclops. Nevertheless, because creation is still there, we have an obligation to feel after God and find him, even though we cannot see him.

The Conclusion

Verses 29–30 say, "Therefore since we are God's offspring, we should not think that the divine being is like gold or silver or stone—an image made by man's design and skill. In the past God overlooked such ignorance, but now he commands all people everywhere to repent."

We can see why Paul calls for repentance. He has not spoken of the gross immorality of the Athenians, though he could have. He has not spoken of the intellectual arrogance of the philosophers, though he could have. There was a sense in which the Greeks did not know any better in these areas. Not so with the revelation of God in nature. In this area they did know better, just as we do, regardless of our disclaimers. Consequently, being guilty in this area, they needed to repent of their sin and turn from it.

We need the message of repentance for our generation too, though we are far guiltier than the Greeks. Besides, we need it for ourselves, if we have not yet repented. Christianity does not begin by saying, "You're a very good fellow" and "everything is going to be nice for you if you will just get in touch with God." Christianity says, "You have failed to seek after God. You have gone your own way. You are willfully ignorant. Therefore, God commands that you repent of that ignorance." As we repent, God holds out the gospel of salvation through Jesus Christ.

Three Reasons to Repent

Paul ended with three inducements to repentance:

God has been patient, overlooking ignorance for a time (v. 30). God's patience should encourage us as well as having encouraged the Athenians. Our land is as corrupt as theirs, even though we have known the gospel for hundreds of years, which they had not. God has not yet destroyed America for its sins. Why? It is because God is patient. He has also been patient with you. He has overlooked your ignorance for a time. Pay attention, and let God's patience lead you to repentance.

God commands repentance. If God tells us to do something, we had better do it. It is no small matter.

God has appointed a final day of reckoning when Jesus shall be the final judge. Paul's exact words were, "He [God] has set a day when he will judge the world with justice by the man he has appointed. He has given proof of this to all men by raising him from the dead" (v. 31).

Did Paul Succeed in Athens?

The audience interrupted Paul at that point, for his sophisticated hearers did not believe in resurrections. This was one point on which the Stoics and Epicureans agreed. All Greeks thought that man was composed of spirit (or mind), which was good, and matter (or body), which was bad. If there was to be a life to come, the one thing they certainly did not want it cluttered up with was a body. They did not believe in and did not want a resurrection. As a matter of fact, there could not even *be* a resurrection, according to Greek philosophy.

Was Paul disappointed with the results of his address to the Greek philosophers? He may have been. In the other Greek cities, particularly where he had worked for a time, Paul had left a church behind him and this did not seem to have happened at Athens. This fact has caused some commentators to suggest that Paul made a mistake in teaching as he did. William Ramsay was one such commentator. He said that Paul abandoned preaching for philosophy and that, as a result, there were no converts.[3] There may be something to that, especially since Paul says that he changed his approach when he got to Corinth (1 Cor. 2:1–5). Acts also offers justification for this view. Just a few verses farther on in chapter 18 Luke, in an almost uncharacteristic way, says, "When Silas and Timothy came [to Corinth] from Macedonia, Paul devoted himself exclusively to preaching" (v. 5). Maybe that is a way of saying that Paul realized that the type of address he had given in Athens was not right.

Yet this judgment may be unfair. Earlier in Acts 17 we are told that Paul "reasoned in the synagogue with the Jews and the God-fearing Greeks" (v. 17). When it says he reasoned with them it means he reasoned from the Scriptures. So he must have been doing the same thing in Athens that he had done in other Greek cities. He was teaching the Bible. What about the invitation to address the philosophers? All he did was speak to people in terms they could understand. Moreover, he taught biblical theology. I do not know whether it is proper for scholars to criticize the apostle Paul at that point or not, but I know that I am not going to criticize him.

But if you ask, "Was he discouraged?" well, he may have been. Athens was a great city. He had worked hard, and when he finished he did not have much to show for it.

Yet he had something, didn't he? We read at the end: "A few men became followers of Paul and believed. Among them was Dionysius, a member of the Areopagus [that is, one of the leading philosophers], also a woman named

Damaris, and a number of others" (v. 34). "Others" means two at least. So there were at least four, and maybe a few more. Later there was a church in Athens, though it did not seem to have gotten established until after Paul's day.

Whether or not Paul was discouraged, he had a hard time in Athens. It is hard to speak to intellectuals, even harder to speak to people who are basking in the glory of a former age. It is hard for us too. Yet Paul did try to reach such people for Christ, and so should we. Suppose our results are meager. Well, so were Paul's. On the other hand, we should not be profoundly disheartened, because God always allows his Word to bear fruit in one form or another. There will be some who sneer. There will be some who postpone their decision, perhaps indefinitely. But there will always be some who believe. They are the sheep Jesus is calling into his one fold. It is our joy to be used by him in calling them.

35

Many People in This City

Acts 18:1–17

After this, Paul left Athens and went to Corinth. There he met a Jew named Aquila, a native of Pontus, who had recently come from Italy with his wife Priscilla, because Claudius had ordered all the Jews to leave Rome. Paul went to see them, and because he was a tent-maker as they were, he stayed and worked with them. Every Sabbath he reasoned in the synagogue, trying to persuade Jews and Greeks. . . .

One night the Lord spoke to Paul in a vision: "Do not be afraid; keep on speaking, do not be silent. For I am with you, and no one is going to attack and harm you, because I have many people in this city." So Paul stayed for a year and a half, teaching them the word of God.

Acts 18:1–11

I n the eighteenth chapter of Acts, we find Paul working for a year and a half in Corinth. Corinth was not like Athens. In fact, it was different from most other cities Paul had visited. Yet it was receptive to the gospel, and Paul spent the first long period of his missionary career in this city. Later he would spend a similarly long time in Ephesus.

A Contemporary City

Here are three words to help remember what Corinth was like. They are easy to remember, because Corinth begins with the letter C and each of these words also begins with the letter C.

302

1. *Cosmopolitan.* Corinth contained a mixture of people and races. This was not strikingly true of all the cities Paul had visited, though in the Roman world of that day all cities had some mixture. Antioch in Syria, from which Paul started out, was an amazingly cosmopolitan city. But Philippi was a Roman colony; it had been settled by retired Roman soldiers and was almost entirely Roman. Athens was a center for intellectuals. Other cities also tended to be more or less homogeneous. Not so Corinth. Corinth had a tremendous mixture of people because it was a seaport and its work was commerce. As a result, people came to Corinth from all over the Roman world. I like Corinth in that respect, because it was a lot like the cities we know. Our cities also have great mixtures of people, classes, and races—people from around the world studying in our universities, people of various races each trying to maintain their own ethnic traditions, people from different classes of society living together.

2. *Commercial.* Every city has its commercial aspects, of course. Generally, cities are where they are because their location is convenient for the exchange of goods. Corinth was uniquely such a place.

It was situated on the narrow isthmus between the upper and main part of Greece and the area of the Peloponnese to the south. Because the isthmus was narrow, traffic crossed Corinth in two directions. It crossed from north to south and from south to north along the land—that is, from the Peloponnese up into the mainland and the reverse. But it also crossed Corinth east to west and west to east across the isthmus. To us that seems like a difficult way to ship goods. It seems that it would be easier to sail them around the Peloponnese. That is because we have modern boats and modern means of navigation. In ancient times, sea voyages were hazardous. So it was common for ships to dock at Corinth on the Adriatic side and have their cargo unloaded and then carried by slaves up over the isthmus to the other side, where it would then be reloaded onto other ships that would sail into the Aegean Sea and points east. It was the same in reverse.

In the days of the emperor Nero there was an attempt to cut a canal across the isthmus, but it was not successful. It was only in the last century that a canal was built. It is there today. I sailed through it once on a trip from Istanbul to Venice.

3. *Corrupt.* In the ancient world, the name "Corinthian" was synonymous for the most perverted behavior. Corinth was a center of the cult of the love goddess Aphrodite. Aphrodite was the same as Venus; Venus was the Roman name, and Aphrodite was the Greek name. The temple of Aphrodite in Corinth was one of the architectural wonders of the ancient world, and at one time there were ten thousand temple prostitutes. They did business with the sailors and other commercial people who passed through the town. If you were called a "Corinthian" in the ancient world (and were not actually from Corinth), you would regard that name as an insult.

Was Paul Discouraged?

As I read this chapter, I find myself wondering about Paul's frame of mind as he arrived in this very contemporary city. I ask whether Paul, strong man of God that he was, was discouraged. I tend to think he was. Not a great deal is said about it. But I think, as I look at what had happened in the days leading up to his arrival and also at the way he conducted himself when he got to Corinth, that he was probably very discouraged.

Great Difficulties

Paul had had a rough time on both the first and second missionary journeys. He had been opposed virtually everywhere he went, and instead of decreasing, the opposition actually seemed to be increasing. At the very beginning when he crossed Cyprus there is no mention of any real trials or persecution. When he went into Pamphylia and came to Antioch in Pisidia, he was opposed so strongly that he had to leave the city after being there only a very short time. The same thing happened in Iconium. At Lystra, the opposition that had been dogging his footsteps became outright physical abuse, and he was stoned.

Stoning was meant to kill the victim. When those who were with Paul saw him fall under the barrage of missiles, they must have thought that the missionary journey was over and Paul was dead. But we are told that after his assailants had left and gone back into the city, Paul rose up and went back into the city with the brethren. This may mean that God healed Paul miraculously, though the text does not say that explicitly.

Then, on the second missionary journey when Paul went to Philippi he was flogged. This was the first of several experiences of that particularly cruel form of Roman punishment. He and Silas were thrown into prison. This was the first time Paul was imprisoned for the faith, and it was fresh from that experience that he had passed down the coast from Philippi to Thessalonica, Berea, Athens, and finally Corinth.

I am sure Paul did not say this, but if you and I had been through those experiences, we might have said, "Who needs this? I had a perfectly good life in Jerusalem. There I was somebody. I set out to serve Jesus Christ. He said, 'Lo, I am with you always, even to the end of the age.' Yet here I am abused, hounded from city to city, stoned, beaten, and imprisoned. I can do without this." As I say, I am sure Paul did not say that; I am sure he did not even think it. But knowing human nature as I do, I think the abuse had an effect upon him personally.

Meager Results in Athens

When we studied the account of his time in Athens in the last chapter, I said that we have to be careful how we evaluate it. The academic address Paul gave to the intellectuals of that city was a marvel of sharp communication. It shows his keen mind at work, including his extraordinary ability to adapt to any situation. Only somebody of Paul's training and acumen could have given an address as brilliant as that. Yet the results were still meager.

When we come to the end of the story, we find that a few believed. Nothing is said about the founding of a church in Athens. We know that in time a church was founded. It endured for many years. But when Paul left Athens and went on to Corinth, as we find him doing in this chapter, it must have been with a sense, if not of failure, at least of disappointment that what he had done in Athens had not borne any special evidence of the blessing of God.

I think too that Paul may have been disappointed with the address he gave on that occasion. When he wrote to the Corinthians later and in retrospect recalled his ministry among them, he said, "When I came to you, brothers, I did not come with eloquence or superior wisdom as I proclaimed to you the testimony about God. For I resolved to know nothing while I was with you except Jesus Christ and him crucified" (1 Cor. 2:1–2). We find the same thing in Acts 18:5.

Paul Was Alone

Paul had left his coworkers in Macedonia, with very good reason. He had founded churches there; he had to leave; and he had not been able to teach the converts very long. Obviously, they needed teaching. So Silas and Timothy were left to teach them. It was the right thing to do. Nevertheless, having left Silas and Timothy and having gone on, as he felt called to do, Paul was alone. Some people apparently do well alone; we call them "loners." But it is hard to be alone, and it is especially hard when you are trying to accomplish some important work or tackle some particularly difficult assignment. Paul must have been just a bit down because of it.

Lack of Funds

Not only the experiences that he had before he came to Corinth must have weighed upon him, but also the difficulties once he was there. We can learn a great deal about Paul's condition if we read the chapter carefully.

The first thing we are told in this chapter, right away in verse 2, is that Paul "met a Jew named Aquila, a native of Pontus, who had recently come from Italy with his wife Priscilla" and that he teamed up with this Jewish couple because they were tentmakers. He worked with them, helping them in their business, no doubt in order to support himself.

In evangelical missionary circles we often hear the term "tentmaker." It refers to somebody who goes abroad to be a missionary but who instead of being supported by people from back home supports himself or herself by working in the economy of the local country. The missionary then does his or her missionary work "on the side." I think that is the direction mission work is moving today for a number of reasons. To begin with, it is the only way one can get into some countries. Also, the world's economy is changing

so adversely to the American economy that it is becoming increasingly expensive to support an ever-growing roster of missionaries. There are places where
missionaries need full support. It should be done and no doubt will continue
to be done. Yet the situation is changing.

However, although "tentmaking" may be common with us, this is the first
time in the missionary journeys of the apostle Paul, so far as we can tell, that
he found it necessary to support himself by making tents.

How had he managed before? No doubt those who sent him had given
him sufficient money. He had been sent from the church in Antioch in Syria,
and that church in that prosperous city undoubtedly had the means to support him. Then again, other churches supported him. We know this because
he writes about it in his letters, thanking them for their help. When he got
to Corinth apparently his money had run out. There is not much doubt that
he was in need, since he says in his second letter to the Corinthians that he
was kept from being a burden to them only by supplies eventually sent by
the Christians in Macedonia (2 Cor. 11:9). He does not complain. But even
though he talks about this condition positively, he does indicate that there
was a period when he lacked funds.

There are Christian works like that today. I would go so far as to say the
best Christian works I know seem to lack funds. I often say—sometimes
humorously, except I do not think it is very funny—that when I get to heaven
I am *not* going to ask, "What is the correct outline for eschatology?" or "What
is the proper mode of baptism?" I am going to say, "Lord, why is it that when
we were trying to do your work, so many solid evangelical efforts operated
hand-to-mouth while others that seemed to offer only the chaff of religion
thrived? The hucksters raked in millions of dollars, which they wasted, while
faithful workers struggled."

I do not know the answer to that question. But I know that the apostle
Paul was at least for a time in financial need at Corinth. This first missionary
and prince of apostles, this great man of faith had to work at tentmaking to
feed himself and carry on the ministry.

Rejection at the Synagogues

Paul had other difficulties. We read that when he went to the synagogue
he had little success. Verse 4 says, "Every Sabbath he reasoned in the synagogue, trying to persuade Jews and Greeks." Verse 5 adds, "Paul devoted himself exclusively to preaching, testifying to the Jews that Jesus was the Christ."
The next verse shows the discouraging result: "The Jews opposed Paul and
became abusive," so much so that he eventually shook out his clothes in a
symbolic protest, saying, "Your blood be on your own heads! I am clear of
my responsibility. From now on I will go to the Gentiles."

Paul's policy had been to go to the synagogues: "first for the Jew, then for
the Gentiles" (Rom. 1:16). He had a special concern for his people. He prayed
for them. Yet in spite of his prayers, in spite of his ministry, in spite of his

knowledge of the Scriptures and his ability to expound them clearly, very few believed. Initially, perhaps none at all believed.

Abuse from the Jews

Finally, not only did Paul fail to have success in his approach to the Jews through the synagogue, he actually got abuse from his people. If Paul had not had enough of an excuse earlier to say, "I have had enough of this; I am going home," certainly he had a good enough excuse to say it now. He could have said, "Look, not only am I rejected by my people, not only do they turn away from Christ, but they are even abusive to me. I have been through this before. I know how it works. Here it is starting all over again. The next thing they are going to do is stir up the Greeks against me. Then I'll be hauled into court. After that I'll be beaten and thrown in jail. I had enough of that at Philippi. I'm going to quit."

If Paul had fears like that, they were not idle fears, because the latter half of the story tells us that this is precisely what his opponents in Corinth tried to do.

Encouragement for God's Servant

Paul had ample cause to be discouraged and no doubt was, just as we have causes to be discouraged and are. But now comes the good news. At this very point, when Paul was most discouraged, God intervened in several important ways to encourage him.

God Sent Silas and Timothy

Paul had tried to carry on alone in Athens. Now he was trying to carry on alone in Corinth. That gets to you after a while. Sometimes we think we can carry on alone. But we cannot, at least not for very long. We need one another. That is one reason God has given us the church, and it is why he has established a plurality of leadership in the church. Christian work is supposed to be a team effort. Although for perfectly good reasons Paul had gone on alone and had begun the work in Corinth alone, God knew that he did need help and therefore saw to it that Silas and Timothy came south from Macedonia to help him.

When you see somebody who seems to be doing a good work but who is perhaps carrying on without a great deal of encouragement, do what you can to encourage or help that person. There is a sense in which anyone who is doing anything worthwhile is in a lonely position. Seek out such people. Speak a good word.

God Helped Paul Financially

When Silas and Timothy came from Macedonia they brought help from the Macedonian churches. In 2 Corinthians Paul says, "The brothers who came from Macedonia supplied what I needed." The churches at Philippi,

Thessalonica, and perhaps at Berea too must have said, "Paul is out there on his own now. I wonder how he is getting on. What if he doesn't have enough money to live on, if he can't even buy food to feed himself? He'll have to go to work if that's the case, and that will take time away from his preaching. Let's take a collection and have Silas and Timothy take it to him." So they sent Paul money.

I think that is the way Acts 18:9 should be taken. Now he no longer had to work at tentmaking. Their financial help released him to do what he was particularly called by God to do.

God Blessed the Missionary Activity

Although Paul had not had great success through his initial preaching in the synagogue, God now began to give him fruit for his efforts. We are told about Crispus: "Crispus, the synagogue ruler, and his entire household believed in the Lord" (v. 8). Here was a Jewish believer. Crispus is not a Jewish name, but he must have been a Jew since he was the leader of the synagogue. Then in the same verse we are told, "and many of the Corinthians who heard him believed and were baptized." Titius Justus, a Gentile, must have believed too (v. 7). It had been a slow start. But now the Word of God was beginning to take effect, the Holy Spirit was blessing, and men and women—one here, two there, another one here—were beginning to place their faith in Jesus Christ.

God Spoke to Paul

The last thing God did to encourage Paul was to speak to him, saying that there would be great blessing on the work in Corinth. Each part of what God said deserves special attention.

1. *"Do not be afraid"* (v. 9). What? Paul afraid? Could Paul, who stood up to a stoning, who had allowed himself to be beaten, who sang songs of praise while in the stocks in prison in Philippi, be afraid? Yes. He must have been afraid, because God does not waste words and God was telling him not to be. Paul must have been afraid because of the hostility of the Jews and because of what might happen to him again.

2. *"Keep on speaking, do not be silent"* (v. 9). Why these words? Speaking is what Paul did, after all. That was his calling. How could Paul do anything but keep on speaking? Obviously, he must have been tempted to stop. In his situation today, we might think, I have been preaching and teaching. It is not bearing fruit. Perhaps I should seek out a different methodology. Liturgical dance perhaps. Maybe I should get into popular music. A rock concert. Maybe I should go on television and have a talk show. Something different has to be tried. But God did not tell Paul to change his methods. The results had been meager. But God said, "Keep speaking. Keep teaching." Why? Because God has chosen to bring men and women to Christ through his

Word. Romans 10:17 says, "Faith comes from hearing the message, and the message is heard through the word of Christ."

3. *"I am with you"* (v. 10). This was a virtual repetition of what Jesus had said to the disciples in the Great Commission, and I am sure Paul recognized it as such: "Surely I am with you always, to the very end of the age" (Matt. 28:20).

Did Paul ever find himself wondering if God really was with him? I think probably he never did. He knew that God was with him, just like you and I know that God is with us. God says, "Never will I leave you; never will I forsake you" (Deut. 31:6; Heb. 13:5). If he says it, it's true. At the same time, I wonder if in his discouragement Paul did not also *feel* abandoned, just as we do.

Do you ever find yourself trying to be a witness in your office, live morally when faced with temptation, or whatever you think God wants you to do and have so much trouble that you begin to think, Is God really with me? Is it worth it? Should I just give up? If so, you need to hear what God said to Paul. God said, "I am with you" after he had first said, "Do not be afraid" and "Keep on speaking."

4. *"No one is going to attack and harm you"* (v. 10). The same sort of trouble as Paul had experienced earlier was brewing here. We read about it in the next verse: "The Jews made a united attack on Paul and brought him into court" (v. 12). They tried to hurt him, but they failed. Gallio was the proconsul in Corinth. He was a wise administrator and recognized that this was not a matter for civil jurisdiction. It was a dispute about religion. So he wisely and properly threw the case out of court.[1]

5. *"I have many people in this city"* (v. 10). Of all the things God said to Paul in this vision undoubtedly this was the most important. What people was God talking about? It was not the ones to whom Paul had already spoken, who had already believed, because there were not many of them, only a few. If God said, "I have many people in this city," it must have been because God, who alone is able to see the future and determine it, was looking ahead, saying that by the preaching of the Word through Paul's ministry he would bring many people to faith in Jesus Christ. They were his people and they would stand together as a church and bear a witness in this most corrupt city.

Immediately after having received this word from heaven, we read, "So Paul stayed for a year and a half, teaching them the Word of God" (v. 11). Before this Paul had been moving from place to place. He spent a week here, three weeks there, a month somewhere else. Then he moved on. But as soon as God spoke to him Paul changed his tactics and stayed on. And do you know what happened? People believed and came to Jesus Christ. Moreover, his experience in Corinth was such a turning point that it affected everything Paul did from this point on.

The next major city he visited was Ephesus; he stayed there two years. Then he was imprisoned in Caesarea for two years. Eventually he got to Rome, and he spent several years there. Paul was no longer a missionary gadfly, even though he recognized that he still had the same call to take the gospel throughout the Roman world. It is as if he now put down roots and began to teach in-depth over a period of time in order that those who were being won to Christ might be faithfully grounded in the Bible.

We cannot take a text like this and simply transfer it to ourselves, as if God is saying the identical things to us: Nobody will ever attack you; nobody will harm you; I have many people in the city. However, I cannot help but think that if God has placed us in a particular place, it is because he has a work for us to do there, and for that very reason we should be encouraged and stay on and do it to the best of our ability. It is not because he does not have many people in our neighborhoods or cities but because he does. Our job is to keep on keeping on, knowing that God is with us.

36

More Laborers for the Harvest

Acts 18:18–28

Meanwhile a Jew named Apollos, a native of Alexandria, came to Ephesus. He was a learned man, with a thorough knowledge of the Scriptures. He had been instructed in the way of the Lord, and he spoke with great fervor and taught about Jesus accurately, though he knew only the baptism of John. He began to speak boldly in the synagogue. When Priscilla and Aquila heard him, they invited him to their home and explained to him the way of God more adequately.

When Apollos wanted to go to Achaia, the brothers encouraged him and wrote to the disciples there to welcome him. On arriving, he was a great help to those who by grace had believed. For he vigorously refuted the Jews in public debate, proving from the Scriptures that Jesus was the Christ.

Acts 18:24–28

One of the great things about closed doors is that they are not always closed forever. Sometimes God uses a closed door to send us in a contrary direction. But then, as we go on in the Christian life, we find that God later opens that very door. We have an example of this in Acts 18.

Acts 16 reported how Paul had wanted to go into Asia, but the Holy Spirit forbade it. So he kept on and eventually ended up carrying the gospel into

311

Europe. But that did not mean that God had forgotten Asia. It might have seemed so. Yet in the province of Asia there was the major city of Ephesus, and as Paul wrapped up his second great journey and headed home, he and his companions finally arrived in Ephesus and planted the seeds of what was to become a significant work. Ephesus was the second city, after Corinth, in which Paul invested a considerable period of time. Luke seems to have been particularly aware of the importance of this city because now and for the rest of the next two chapters of Acts he concentrates his account on Ephesus.

The Blending of Two Journeys

Luke's concentration on Ephesus leads him to do something that has always been confusing to Sunday school teachers. Those who teach Acts know that Paul made three great missionary journeys followed by his final trip to Jerusalem and Rome. It is easy to see where the first missionary journey begins and ends. It begins in Acts 13:2, where the Holy Spirit said to the church in Antioch, "Set apart for me Barnabas and Paul." It ends at the close of Acts 14 with the account of the missionaries' return to Antioch to report to the church about the work that had been done. It is also easy to see where the second journey begins (Acts 15:36) and where the third journey ends (Acts 21). But here is the problem: It is not easy to see where the second journey ends and the third journey begins.

Because the ending of the second journey and beginning of the third journey are run together in Acts 18, it is easy to read past them and not understand what is happening. Nevertheless, there is a division. It is found between verses 22 and 23. Verse 22 says that Paul "landed at Caesarea" and "went up" (the verse does not specify where he went up, but it means Jerusalem) and "greeted the church and then went down to Antioch." In Antioch Paul would have reported on his second missionary journey, as he had reported on the first. Then verse 23 says, "After spending some time in Antioch, Paul set out from there and traveled from place to place throughout the region of Galatia and Phrygia, strengthening all the disciples." These words mark the beginning of the third and final journey.

Why isn't the division between these two great efforts by Paul more clearly marked? The reason, I think, is that Luke's interest shifts from the journeys themselves to the establishing of the very solid church at Ephesus. At the end of the second journey, which we are dealing with now, Paul passed through Ephesus (though briefly) and met with some success. Therefore, on the third journey he returned to Ephesus again and spent two years there. This period of service became the longest period of ministry in any place Paul visited.

A Husband and Wife Team

We have a new mission field, then, beginning with Acts 18:18–19. As we study it, the first thing we notice is that new workers are provided for this field. Several are mentioned in this chapter. First, there are Priscilla and Aquila, who were already introduced to us at the start of Acts 18. Paul met them in Corinth, and they traveled with him to Ephesus and ended up hosting a church there. Second, we are told of Apollos, an interesting and eloquent man who came to Asia from Alexandria in North Africa. God was providing people to help Paul in the work. He helps us in the same way today.

Priscilla and Aquila were working people. They were tentmakers, which probably means that they worked in leather since tents were usually made of skins. They were not from the upper classes certainly. They were probably not particularly well educated. They were Jews. They had been living in Rome. But when the Emperor Claudius issued his well-known edict banishing the Jews from Rome, Priscilla and Aquila left the capital of the empire and went to Corinth.[1]

When Paul wrote to the Romans, which he did from Corinth on the second missionary journey, he said that he wanted those at Rome to greet Priscilla and Aquila (Rom. 16:3). Sometime during the year and a half he spent in Corinth, Priscilla and Aquila must have left Corinth and gone back to Rome, probably because the edict of Claudius had been lifted. Maybe all they did was to wrap up their affairs in Rome; they apparently came back to Corinth rather quickly, since in the passage we are studying they were present to accompany Paul to Ephesus when he left Corinth at the end of his ministry there.

Here was a couple who, though they had no particular status in the Roman world and no exceptional education, were nevertheless active Christian people. And they were mobile! They traveled with Paul and were helpful to him in his ministry—not only now but also later, as we will see. They seem to have been willing to relocate for the sake of the infant, growing church.

We learn some interesting things about this couple from the scattered references to them in the New Testament. Already in this chapter (v. 3) we have found that Paul lived with them when he was at Corinth. He had come to Corinth from Macedonia and at that point had run out of money. So this couple opened their house to Paul and labored with him, not only in their mutual trade of tentmaking, but also in the gospel. Undoubtedly they learned a great deal from him during the time they lived together in that city.

In Romans 16 Paul says: "They risked their lives for me" (v. 4). We do not know how or for what reason. Nothing in Acts relates to it, but since Paul wrote Romans from Corinth, we presume he is referring to something that happened in Corinth. There must have been an occasion on which the Jews tried to make trouble, though it did not seem to have affected Paul directly. How wonderful that when Paul was perhaps a bit down and discouraged, being in financial need and having left his coworkers, God provided a wonderful couple, who were willing even to risk their lives for him.

When they got to Ephesus, Priscilla and Aquila apparently established themselves in a home where they would have conducted their business and where eventually the church met. In 1 Corinthians 16:19, Paul says that Aquila and Priscilla send greetings, adding "and so does the church that meets at their house." So we have an indication that this remarkable couple were not only coworkers with Paul but also hosted the church and were thus serviceable in the ministry.

A New Worker from Alexandria

These verses also tell about Apollos. Apollos was quite different from Aquila and Priscilla. Aquila and Priscilla were Jews; he was a Gentile. They were a married couple; he was single. They were working people; he was an intellectual. They came from Rome, the capital of the empire; he came from Alexandria in Egypt. Alexandria was a center of learning, like Athens, but more serious in its scholarship. Alexandria was the city of Philo, the famous Jewish philosopher who was well-versed not only in the Greek philosophy of the day but also in the Old Testament and who interpreted much of the Old Testament in Greek terms. Since Apollos had been educated in Alexandria, it is tempting to think that he probably knew Philo, though nothing in the New Testament tells us that directly.

Acts 18 tells us several facts about Apollos.

1. *Apollos was "a learned man"* (v. 24). That is, he had acquired the learning of his day. He had gone through what we would call university and graduate school. His credentials were impressive.

2. *Apollos had "a thorough knowledge of the Scriptures"* (v. 24). The reference is not to the New Testament Scriptures, of course, because they were only coming into existence at this time and had not been widely circulated, certainly not in Egypt. The reference is rather to the Old Testament. Here again, it is hard not to think of Philo, because Philo was a master at handling the Old Testament in contemporary terms. If Apollos knew the Scriptures well, it is probable that he had been in touch with and perhaps even have studied under Philo and would therefore probably have adopted his approach to the Scriptures.

3. *Apollos "had been instructed in the way of the Lord"* (v. 25). It is hard to know how to take this sentence. When we read "the Lord" we think naturally of Jesus Christ, which may be the case. Later on the verse says that Apollos "taught about Jesus accurately." He knew something about Jesus. On the other hand, "the Lord" often also refers to Jehovah, the God of the Old Testament. Considering his knowledge of the Old Testament, the statement probably means that he knew the ways of Jehovah. At the very least, it means he knew the Old Testament law and tried to follow it.

4. *Apollos "spoke with great fervor"* (v. 25). He did not merely know the Old Testament with detached intellectual or academic awareness. On the contrary, its teachings were important to him. So when he spoke about them and taught them, he did so fervently. We would say, "with energy and conviction." No doubt that is one reason why Apollos was so effective as an orator. He would have had all the skills of Greek oratory. He knew how to hold an audience,

how to develop his points, how to use language to win and persuade his hearers. But what is mentioned here is "fervor," and this means not merely skill on his part but conviction based on something deeply embedded in his heart.

5. Apollos *"taught about Jesus accurately"* (v. 25). That is an important thing for Apollos to have done. But in order to understand it we need to add, as the text itself does, that although Apollos had this very important asset, he also had a great liability: "he knew only the baptism of John" (v. 25). What does that mean?

It can mean one of two things. It can mean that he knew only a baptism marking repentance, which is the way John baptized, not a baptism associated with the work of the Holy Spirit in enlightening a person, producing repentance in him or her, and drawing that person to Christ. This would mean that Apollos was strong in his knowledge of the First Person of the Trinity and even to a certain extent in his knowledge of the Second Person of the Trinity but that he knew nothing about the Third Person of the Trinity. In the next chapter we are introduced to people who also knew only the baptism of John and who, it is explained, needed to believe on Jesus and be baptized in his name.

On the other hand, the fact that Apollos knew "only the baptism of John" could mean that Apollos knew the unfolding of God's plan up to and including the ministry of John the Baptist but that he did not know that the Messiah, whom John the Baptist announced, had now come. I'm inclined to accept this point of view for several reasons, primarily because of the way in which Priscilla and Aquila explained the gospel to him.

Apollos was a well-educated and also a well-traveled man. We can imagine that in his youth he had gone to Jerusalem, especially if he had an interest in the Old Testament, and while there had come under the influence of the preaching of John the Baptist. If he had a sensitive, spiritual heart, as he seems to have had, he would have responded to John's preaching. John was telling people to prepare for the coming of the Messiah. He would have done so on the basis of the Old Testament Scriptures. Perhaps Apollos soaked up these truths and came to believe, no doubt rightly, that the time for the Messiah to come was near. Perhaps he had even taken it upon himself to internationalize John's message.

If this is the case, here was a man who knew the Old Testament, understood what the Messiah was to do, and then said, "The time is here. The Messiah is about to come." I think that is what it means when it says that Apollos taught about Jesus "accurately." It means that Apollos knew what Jesus was to do, though he did not know that Jesus had come.

Instructing a Learned Man

What do you do with someone like that? Here was a man of eloquence and ability, apparently even being mightily used by God, since he went to the synagogues and argued effectively with the Jews and other people. Should he have been rebuked? Opposed? Refuted? What actually happened was quite different.

Let me introduce what happened by a parallel story from church history. At the time of the Reformation in England there was a man just like Apollos whose name was Hugh Latimer (1490–1555). He was a very learned man. He had a thorough knowledge of the Bible and could speak with eloquence. He even had considerable influence in the church because he was a bishop. Latimer was eventually martyred for his faith by being burnt at the stake along with Nicholas Ridley. This was the occasion on which he spoke those heroic words that are so often quoted in church history courses: "Be brave, Master Ridley, and play the man. We shall this day, by the grace of God, light such a candle in England as, I trust, shall never be put out." That was the dying testimony of Hugh Latimer.

However, at the time when the following story took place Latimer was not yet a Christian, though he was in the church and knew the Scriptures well. He knew Jesus Christ; that is, he knew who Jesus was and much about him. But he did not know what it was to be born again. He did not know the gospel. Like many in his day, he thought that the way to get to heaven was by good works.

There was a young monk who knew Latimer and admired him. This monk was known as "Little Bilney" because he was short. He did not have much education. No one thought very much of him. But Bilney was converted, and he wondered how it might be possible for him to bring the gospel to Hugh Latimer. Bilney thought that Latimer would be a tremendous force for the Reformation in England if he could just hear the gospel. So Bilney prayed about this and finally hit upon an idea.

Priests were required to hear those who wanted to confess their sins. So one day when Latimer was serving in the church, Bilney went up to him, tugged at his sleeve, and asked Latimer to hear his confession. Latimer said he would. So they went into the confessional, and Bilney confessed the gospel to him. He told how he was a sinner, how he was unable to save himself by his own good works, how Jesus had died for him, and how now, by faith, the righteousness of Jesus had been imputed to him apart from good works. That is what he confessed to Hugh Latimer, and in that way Latimer heard the gospel for the very first time and was converted. It was an important moment in the English Reformation.

Something like that happened in the case of Apollos. I can imagine that when Apollos came to Ephesus, Priscilla and Aquila, who were there at the time, must have said to each other, "This is a very able man. Let's go hear him." Apollos was teaching in the synagogue. So they went to the synagogue and had the same kind of reaction many Christians have when they visit some so-called Christian churches. They hear a minister who is learned and eloquent but does not know the gospel. They must have said to themselves, "This man certainly knows the Bible. He can quote the Old Testament effectively. But he does not know that Jesus has already died for our sin, was raised from the dead, and is now ascended into heaven."

After the service when they were standing in the vestibule, they must have said to each other, "What do you suppose we can do?"

Priscilla suggested, "Let's invite him to dinner."

Aquila replied, "That's a good idea. Maybe we'll have an opportunity to talk to him."

So they did. Apollos came to dinner, and after he had enjoyed their hospitality they began to tell him about Jesus. They must have said, "We were very moved by your teaching from the Old Testament last Saturday. You know it well, and it was a great blessing to our hearts. But we wondered whether you have heard that the One you were speaking about has come."

Apollos would have said, "What do you mean, 'has come'? John came only to announce the way."

They would have replied, "That is true. John the Baptist was the forerunner of the Messiah. But the Messiah came. As a matter of fact, John pointed him out. He baptized him. Then he said, 'Look, the Lamb of God, who takes away the sin of the world!'" (John 1:29).

Apollos would have wondered, "Is that really true? Can I believe that? What are the evidences?" So they began to explain "the way of God more adequately" (v. 26), telling Apollos all that Jesus had said and done.

I must say that Apollos was more receptive to teaching than many members of the clergy I have known, for he received the Word of God humbly, believed it, and assimilated it with the knowledge he already had. It completely transformed his ministry. We know that because later he went on to Corinth, where he was again used of God. The very last verses of the chapter say, "When Apollos wanted to go to Achaia, the brothers encouraged him and wrote to the disciples there to welcome him. On arriving, he was a great help to those who by grace had believed. For he vigorously refuted the Jews in public debate, proving from the Scriptures that Jesus was the Christ" (vv. 27–28).

Practical Application

Apollos's story is a fascinating glimpse into the life and history of the early church, and it is rich with practical spiritual lessons. Here are three of them.

1. *Learning and fervor, though valuable gifts, are not in themselves enough for Christian workers.* We must know Jesus Christ. Even knowledge of the Scriptures and skill in presenting them are not enough. I emphasize this truth because there are always people in churches who are not saved but who know a great deal. They know not only the Old Testament but the New Testament as well. If you ask them to tell the Bible stories, they are able to tell them. They can even teach them to others. But they do not know Jesus. They do not know that he died for them and that he rose again for their justification. They know his name, but they do not know him personally as their Savior and Lord. They are not his disciples.

It may be true of you. Although you may have gone to church for many years and may know a great deal about the Scriptures, the mere learning and even fervent teaching of these things is not enough. You must know Jesus Christ. To know the other is good, but you can know all that and still be lost.

2. *Different kinds of people are needed in Christ's work.* Aquila and Priscilla were different from Apollos, and Apollos was different from Paul. Paul was a feisty Jewish rabbi. Apollos was a man of polish, erudition, and learning. Later on and quite apart from anything Apollos or Paul did, these differences produced divisions at Corinth, where some people were attracted to Apollos and his gifts, saying, "I follow Apollos," while others were more attracted to Paul and said, "I follow Paul" (1 Corinthians 3).

Aquila and Priscilla, Apollos, and Paul were all needed in the church. How do we know? We know because God called them: Paul, with his energetic missionary fervor; Apollos, who watered the seed that Paul had sown; Priscilla and Aquila, who settled down, opened their home, and were hosts to the developing church. Each one was necessary.

So are you, if you are Christ's disciple. The Bible says that the Holy Spirit imparts gifts to Christians as it pleases him. God has given you a distinct spiritual gift. That gift is needed where you are. If you choose not to use your gift, if you think, I am not needed, because someone else is more eloquent or someone else is more hospitable or someone else has more energy or is a better evangelist than I am, you are making a great mistake. If you neglect to use your gift, the church will be impoverished.

If you do not know what your gift is or how to use it, you need to pray about it. Say, "Lord Jesus Christ, show me what I can do. Show me why I am here, why you have brought me to faith, why you have made me the way I am. Teach me to use what I am where I am in order to advance Christ's gospel."

3. *If you lack workers for Christ where you are and feel the need, you should pray about it, asking God for help.* I am sure Paul did this. He must have been acutely aware of the need, having left so many of his coworkers to care for the other newly founded churches. Paul must have been praying strongly for these churches, and knowing that he was unable to do all that needed to be done himself, he must have been asking God to send new workers into the missionary field. And God did.

The Lord Jesus Christ said, "The harvest is plentiful but the workers are few. Ask the Lord of the harvest, therefore, to send out workers into his harvest field" (Matt. 9:37–38).

Those words are as true for us as they were in Paul's day or in the day of our Lord. The harvest is plenteous. Just outside our doors are many people who need to hear the gospel. They are resistant. No one left to himself or herself is going to come to God. But if God told the apostle, "I have many people in this city" in the city of Corinth, then certainly in our cities God has many people as well. We need to reach out to them. And we need workers. That is why you must pray for God to send more workers into his vineyard. It is by many that God works to save some.

37

The Church in Ephesus

Acts 19:1–22

Paul entered the synagogue and spoke boldly there for three months, arguing persuasively about the kingdom of God. But some of them became obstinate; they refused to believe and publicly maligned the Way. So Paul left them. He took the disciples with him and had discussions daily in the lecture hall of Tyrannus. This went on for two years, so that all the Jews and Greeks who lived in the province of Asia heard the word of the Lord.

Acts 19:8–10

In 1978 Roger S. Greenway, a professor and former missionary to various parts of the world, published *Apostles to the City: Biblical Strategies for Urban Missions.*[1] This book considers the shift of the world's populations to the cities in our time, and it is helpful for studying Acts because toward the end of the book the author rightly focuses on the strategy of Paul in reaching cities. I say "rightly" because of all the people in the Bible who worked in cities and had a strategy for urban evangelization the apostle Paul heads the list.

As I study Acts, I sense that at the beginning Paul probably had not carefully worked out his urban strategy. He had some ideas about reaching major cities. But when he started out he seemed simply to be visiting one community after another and not to be particularly focused on cities. However, as time went

319

on Paul came to recognize that if the world was going to be reached effectively, it would have to be through ministry to the major cities of the empire.

Today, even more than then, we live in a world of cities. And the task we face in bringing the gospel of the supernatural redemption of humanity through the work of Christ to secular people is the challenge that faced Paul.

Paul's Overall Goals

Greenway points out that Paul had certain basic goals. We saw these goals in chapter 33.

1. *To preach a message, one that demanded personal repentance and conversion.* Sometimes when people think of advancing into new areas, they think of changing their message to accommodate the new audience or situation. Are we going into the cities? If so, we think we will have to say what city people want to hear. Are we going on television? If we are, we think we imagine that we will have to do what the television audience has been programmed to expect. The apostle Paul never changed his message. He taught the nature of sin, the need for repentance, the saving work of God in Christ, and the necessity of conversion. Paul always kept personal repentance and conversion before his mind. We have already seen it in the accounts of these missionary journeys.

2. *To plant churches.* Paul was not just an evangelist who somehow was removed from the task of planting churches. When he went into a new area, church planting was a goal. If he settled in Corinth, he wanted to leave a church in Corinth when he passed on to other cities, and he wanted to leave Corinthians in charge of it.

When we enter an area, we need to spread the gospel, which we can do through books, tracts, radio, television, and other forms of mass communication. Books will explain Christian doctrine. Tracts will popularize the gospel and attract new people. Radio and television will break new ground. But proclamation alone is not enough. It must be followed by actualization. There must be living communities of believers present, so people living in the cities will be able to look at them and say, "Not only are these Christians speaking the gospel to us, but they are living it too."

I notice that much of Paul's work was done in what we today would call "house churches." Sometimes, as in Ephesus, Paul had a formal lecture hall. What he did there would correspond closely to what we do in our churches on Sundays. We use them as places to teach. Teaching was an important part of Paul's strategy. But where he succeeded, churches were established, and these it would seem were in the homes of the people. So here and there throughout these cities were little communities of believers who met together regularly to worship God and model the gospel by their obedience to Jesus Christ.

3. *To use his churches as bases for reaching out into adjoining areas.* Once Paul had established churches he also drew them into his missionary strategy by using them as bases for the extension of the gospel into the surrounding neighborhoods and the world.[2]

The City of Ephesus

Ephesus was so strategic that it is surprising that Paul had not gone there before, especially since he had already been in the Roman province of Asia, where Ephesus was located. The reason, as we have already seen, is that the Holy Spirit had stopped him from doing so, having had other work for him to do first (see chapter 31).

Ephesus was a port city. Today the port is silted up and Ephesus is located three or four miles inland from the present coastline. When the port silted up, Ephesus lost its commercial advantage. But at the time Paul was there, the city was at the height of its glory. It had about one-third of a million people, which for an ancient city was a large population. It had a theater, which has been excavated and which I have seen. The theater seated twenty-five thousand people. The Rosebowl in Los Angeles seats about one hundred thousand people, so this was about one fourth of that size.

Then, too, Ephesus was noted for its magnificent temple of Diana, or Artemis. The temple of Diana was known as one of the wonders of the ancient world. It was lost to history for a time, twenty-five feet beneath the surface of the ground because of destruction and rebuilding at that site over the centuries. But in Paul's day it was in full beauty and at the height of its influence. It was as extensive as a football field, and it was the center of much superstitious religion and cult prostitution, which was common at such temples.

Ephesus is mentioned first among the seven churches of Revelation. Its leading position probably means that among the seven important cities addressed—all of which were outstanding for one reason or another—Ephesus was of first rank.

Paul's goals were to preach, establish churches, and use the churches for further outreach. In achieving these goals in Ephesus we see Paul's typical urban strategy at work, just as previously in other cities. He made initial contact, worked with others, taught, and followed up.

Initial Contact

The first thing Paul did was establish initial contact with the people. This initial contact is not described in chapter 19, which we are studying, but in chapter 18, verses 19–20. Paul had been at Corinth for a year and a half and was now on his way back to Jerusalem and Antioch to report on his second missionary journey. On the way he touched down at Ephesus and began to teach there. The text says, "He . . . went into the synagogue and reasoned with the Jews" (v. 19). When he had to go on, he left Priscilla and Aquila behind.

I do not know exactly what Paul's motives were in this initial contact with the city, but I suspect in view of the way his visit is described that he was conducting a reconnaissance. He went to Ephesus to see what the city was like and to explore the potential for establishing a church as a base for proclaiming the gospel throughout Asia.

Acts 18:20 tells us that as a result of this initial teaching the Jews of Ephesus asked him to spend more time with them. In other words, he had a fairly decent reception in the synagogue. That would be significant to Paul because in other places, in a very short amount of time, he provoked such opposition that he had to leave and in some cases was driven out of the city. So although when they wanted him to stay he said, No, this is just a brief visit; I'm on my way to Jerusalem, he nevertheless promised to come back later (v. 21).

I think we are also to surmise that Paul was doing a reconnaissance by the fact that he left Priscilla and Aquila behind. If the situation had not been promising, we would have expected him to say, Oh, well, nothing seems to be happening here. Come with me. We'll go to Jerusalem and then we'll start out again and find another place to labor. Instead he said, Why don't you stay here? I have to go, but I'll be back, and in the meantime, why don't you see what you can do? That is exactly what they did.

Moreover, Aquila and Priscilla were helped by Apollos (see chapter 36). Apollos taught in the synagogue, and the ground was thereby prepared for what Paul came to do later.

Working with Others

A second element in Paul's strategy is that he worked with other Christians. He had what we would call a multiple or pluralistic ministry. We have already seen that Paul followed this strategy on his missionary journeys in general, always taking along two or more additional workers. Acts 19 fails to mention Paul's two helpers, Timothy and Erastus at the beginning, but we discover at the end that they were there. Verse 22 tells us that Paul sent them to Macedonia after the work in Ephesus had gotten under way, while he stayed a bit longer.

Working with others is an important feature of city work. I find that in most city work (in fact, in most gospel work wherever done) we are seldom called to work alone. Working alone is not impossible, and sometimes we have to do it when there is no one else to call on. I think of Saint Patrick. He was captured by pirates and carried off to Ireland when he was just a boy. He was very much alone, but he witnessed there and was greatly blessed by God. That happens. But often when we are called to a work, we find that the area to which we are called has been prepared by God already—not only in the sense that the hearts of the people have been prepared, but in the sense that other laborers have been sent to work with us.

I myself found that to be true at the time I first came to Philadelphia, in 1968. My wife and I discovered in those days that about the same time we had come to the city, the Lord also brought in a large number of other young couples like ourselves who were committed to the city, wanted to raise their children in the city, and wanted to bear a witness—not just for a short period of time, but for years. It was an encouragement to see what God was doing. We reasoned that if God was leading other people to Philadelphia, obviously

God was about to do something important, and it was a privilege to be part of that kind of promising urban outreach.

Teaching the People

The third element in Paul's urban strategy is teaching the people. Paul taught the Bible, he taught all kinds of people, and in Ephesus he taught over a long period of time.

Paul Taught the Bible

Did the apostle Paul have a rock concert or something of that nature? Obviously, he did nothing of the sort. Paul had one method only, and that was to teach the Word of God. And he really did it. He did it everywhere. In every town he went to, he went into the synagogues and taught from the Scriptures that Jesus was the Messiah. He taught that this one, who had come in his own lifetime, who had lived, taught, died, and then been raised from the dead, this Jesus of Nazareth, was the fulfillment of the Old Testament Scriptures. He took the Old Testament, showed what God had said his Messiah would do, and then told how Jesus had done it.

He Taught All Kinds of People

Paul dealt with all kinds of people at Ephesus.

There were *disciples of John the Baptist*. Their situation was similar to that of Apollos. These men had heard of John's teaching. They knew that people were to repent of sin and prepare for the coming of the Messiah. But like Apollos, they had not heard that Jesus had come. So when Paul arrived in the city and began to teach, here were these disciples whose hearts had been prepared but who had not yet heard the full gospel. Paul conducted a special ministry with them. And when he began to explain to them that Jesus had come, well, their hearts were ready for the message and they believed at once. The Holy Spirit came upon them just as he had come upon the disciples in Samaria when the gospel first came to them.

Paul also taught the *Jews*. He had been in their synagogue before on his first visit. When he got back to Ephesus, he returned to the synagogue and began to teach them again. The text says, "Paul . . . spoke boldly there for three months" (Acts 19:8). Three months was a long time compared with some other places he had visited, where he had been put out after only a few weeks. So there must have been a genuinely receptive audience. However, as time went on the attitudes of the unbelievers hardened and Paul was forced to leave. We are not told what the results of the three months of teaching were, but we can assume that some actually did believe as a result of this ministry.

Paul taught *Gentiles*. They were the large majority of those who lived in Ephesus, and Paul began a specially directed ministry to them after he had been forced to leave the Jews' synagogue. We are told that when he left the synagogue, he went to the lecture hall of a man named Tyrannus. Tyrannus was a Greek, a philosopher no doubt; we know he was a teacher, because he had a school. The word translated "hall," as in "the lecture hall of Tyrannus," is literally the word "school." Since there were times when his building was not being used, he leased it to Paul for Paul's courses. Paul taught in this lecture hall, and the hall became a base for his ministry to whatever Gentiles would come.

At Ephesus Paul seems to have started a new ministry to *those involved in the occult.* Probably most of the Ephesians were involved in the occult in one way or another, because when the Spirit of God began to move in a really big way all seem to have turned from their occult practices.

Finally toward the end of the chapter we find the impact of the gospel on *the business class.* One of the major businesses of this city was making statues and other votary objects for the temple of Diana, and this business was hurt by the "revival" that took place. No doubt there were other groups of people who were affected. But here in this very short account Luke indicates what Paul accomplished by the impact of his teaching on these five groups of people.

Paul Taught for a Considerable Length of Time

Paul also taught for a long period of time. He had been staying longer and longer in the cities. When he was at Corinth, he was there for a year and a half. Now we are told that he stayed in Ephesus for two years. For a man who was an itinerant missionary, who felt his calling to be the advancing of the gospel throughout the entire Roman world, that was a major commitment of time. It would be the equivalent of many more years—perhaps a lifetime—for you or me.

There is a note in some of the Greek texts of Acts at this point. It is not in the majority of manuscripts, so it is not included in our translations, no doubt rightly so. But in some texts in the margin there is a note saying that when Paul lectured daily in the hall of Tyrannus, he did so from "eleven o'clock in the morning until four in the afternoon" (from the fifth to the tenth hour). The hours were in the middle of the day. This was the hot time of the day when presumably the hall was not being used by Tyrannus. Tyrannus would be there in the morning and perhaps in the evening as well. Paul would have said, "Could I use your hall in the middle of the day?" Using the hall was convenient, creative, and effective.

Five hours a day add up to a lot of teaching. In terms of that culture, daily meant every day. No one took vacations then. No one had ever heard of a five-day work week or a forty-hour work week. So Paul would have taught five hours a day, seven or at least six days a week, if he took time off for different kinds of work on Sunday. In two years that adds up to fifteen to eighteen hundred hours of teaching—more solid teaching than most seminarians receive in a three-year academic program preparing them for the pastorate.

In chapter 20 where Paul is speaking to the Ephesian elders, he says that he supported himself while he was in Ephesus. This must mean that in the morning, when other people were working, Paul was working at his tents. Then at eleven o'clock, when others knocked off for lunch and a rest, he went over to the hall of Tyrannus and began to lecture. Paul also said in speaking to the Ephesian elders that he went from house to house instructing them in the things of God. So we may suppose that when the hall was taken over again by the owner, at four o'clock, Paul started off to teach in homes, doing what is called in some forms of church polity "catechizing"—that is, teaching the mothers, fathers, and children the things of God.

Following Up

The fourth thing Paul did was follow up. He had done follow-up visits with other churches already. As a matter of fact, it was on such a follow-up journey that he first stopped at Ephesus. He had trouble getting back to Ephesus after he left the final time. In fact, he only got as far as Miletus, a city nearby, where he called the Ephesian elders to him because of the shortness of time available on his return journey to Jerusalem. He was arrested there and sent to Rome. As far as we know, he never got back again. Nevertheless, his strategy was to return to where he had been, to see how people were doing, and where possible to help correct any problems.

Part of Paul's follow-up was written communication. That is, he wrote letters, providing written lessons for the people. In this case, he wrote the Ephesians a six-chapter (or six-lesson) course on what it means to be a Christian. Ephesians talks about the sovereignty of God in salvation, rebirth, the fact that we are ordained by God to do good works, the nature and function of the church, relationships between people—husbands and wives, slaves and masters, children and parents—and finally, the nature of our spiritual warfare and our weapons for it. Paul must have realized how important that last point was for this particular community.[3]

Did Paul's Strategy Work?

After an investment of time like that, what were the results? In contemporary terms we would say that we have examined Paul's goals and studied his strategy; now we want a period of evaluation. What happened? There were many blessings.

1. *A church was established.* This has been Paul's strategy from the beginning, not only here but in every city he visited. He had worked for this from early in his missionary travels: first, fixing Ephesus in his mind as a promising place for a church; second, conducting a preliminary study, a reconnaissance; then, third, actually launching and continuing the work. And he succeeded. The church was established and continued strong for centuries, long after Paul had left.

2. *There were miracles as the power of God was seen.* The miracles were not done first to attract people, which is what some are saying should be done today.

Rather, the preaching of the Word came first, God blessed the Word, and then the miracles followed—in this case through Paul, as God authenticated his message.

3. *There were changes in the lives of the believers.* Many of them had been involved in the occult, as I indicated. But as the gospel was preached and the lordship of Jesus Christ emphasized, the believers saw that it was not possible for them to confess Jesus as Lord and still cling to their occult practices. They could not keep one foot in the church and the other in the world. So they repented of that sin (v. 18) and then brought their occult objects together and had them destroyed, particularly the magic scrolls that contained incantations.

Luke puts the value of the objects at fifty thousand drachmas. A drachma was a day's wage. So if we can assume that a day's wage in the United States in our time is roughly a hundred dollars (annual income $25,000), the equivalent of fifty thousand drachmas would be about five million dollars in our currency. That may be a high estimate, but by any estimate it was a large sum of money. What these Christians did as they heard the gospel and came to understand what they owed to Jesus Christ was to "lay it on the line," as we would say. Anything in their lives that was holding them back or indicated a divided allegiance was rejected.

If you have something in your life like that, it is important that you get rid of it. If there is something you are hanging on to and do not want to give up but you know is inconsistent with your following after Jesus Christ, you need to get rid of it, as these Ephesian Christians did.

4. *"The word of the Lord spread widely and grew in power"* (v. 20). I link that verse with verse 10, which says that as a result of Paul's teaching in the lecture hall of Tyrannus for two years, "all the Jews and Greeks who lived in the province of Asia heard the word of the Lord." There is a difference between those two sentences. As a result of Paul's consistent teaching, everybody heard the gospel. But that is not the same thing as saying that the people who heard believed. However, verse 20 tells us that when the Christians really "laid it on the line," the Word of the Lord not only spread widely but also "grew in power." It was at this point that the people of Asia not only heard the gospel but also believed it and began to follow Christ. What happened in Ephesus should be a challenge for Christians in cities everywhere.

38

The Riot in Ephesus

Acts 19:23-41

About that time there arose a great disturbance about the Way. A silver-smith named Demetrius, who made silver shrines of Artemis, brought in no little business for the crafts-men. He called them together, along with the workmen in related trades, and said: "Men, you know we receive a good income from this business. And you see and hear how this fellow Paul has convinced and led astray large numbers of people here in Ephesus and in practically the whole province of Asia. He says that man-made gods are no gods at all. There is danger not only that our trade will lose its good name, but also that the temple of the great goddess Artemis will be discredited, and the goddess herself, who is worshiped throughout the province of Asia and the world, will be robbed of her divine majesty."

When they heard this, they were furious and began shouting: "Great is Artemis of the Ephesians!"

Acts 19:23–28

In the last chapter we saw the remarkable success Paul's preaching had at Ephesus. He stayed there for two years, and he taught every day. As a result of this effort, the Word of God spread from Ephesus throughout the entire Roman province of Asia.

But it was not without opposition. In the second half of Acts 19, we see how opposition developed in Ephesus because of all that was being accomplished through Paul's preaching. Strikingly, it developed among the mem-

327

bers of the silversmith guild, whose income was threatened by the changed lifestyles of those who were being converted to Jesus Christ.

This is a marvelous section. William Ramsay, whom I have referred to on other occasions because of his insights into the time and conditions in which Paul worked, wrote of the second half of this chapter that it is "the most instructive picture of society in an Asian city at this period that has come down to us."[1]

Some readers have been so impressed with this story that they have concluded Luke must have been present in Ephesus as an eyewitness. He probably was not. We saw earlier that Luke indicates his presence in the events he is narrating by using the word "we." When he was not present, he uses "they." This section is narrated in the third person, so Luke probably was not in Ephesus. Still he must have had firsthand information, because this is a dramatic and stirring picture.

Idolatry in the Ancient World

What emerges here aside from the incidental details that are of such interest to historians is the intensity with which the ancients worshiped false gods. We hardly have a sense of that today. We go to museums and see the sculptures that represent the ancient gods. But we do not have any real sense of how intense or how pervasive the worship of these idols was. Everywhere in the ancient world there were temples and shrines—in the cities, in the countryside, even in the homes. The manufacture of these shrines was big business. In a city like Ephesus, it was an extremely big business. It was the basis of the city's economy.

Ephesus was the center of the cult of Artemis (or Diana, as the Romans called her). In Roman lore, Diana was goddess of the hunt. She symbolized virginity. But in the ancient metropolis of Ephesus, Artemis symbolized sexual fertility. The idols that represent Artemis and have been found today show a rather grotesque, multi-breasted female figure. In Ephesus, as in other Greek and Roman temples, a great deal of the so-called worship of the goddess was actually cult prostitution. Sex worship had a hold on the people, as it does on many of our contemporaries though in a different form. Their condition was typical of the world at the time of Christ.

Remarkably, within three hundred years as Christianity advanced, idolatry in the ancient world virtually disappeared. This is not the same thing as saying that the world became truly Christian, because it did not. But idolatry vanished. It just ended. This was not a period in which philosophy or education or any of the other things that we look to as evidences of the sophistication of our civilization advanced; none of these things was happening. But Christianity was moving forward.

This is what we should expect, of course, because the Bible itself says, "The unfolding of your words gives light" (Ps. 119:130). Where Christians go forward with the message of the gospel and the Scriptures, the light of God that shines from the pages bursts into the darkness. And even though people are not in every case—perhaps not even in the majority of cases—regenerated or born again, the light of the gospel penetrates so forcefully that many dark practices, like those at Ephesus, simply disappear.

Proof of Paul's Success

The riot in Ephesus, described in Acts 19:23–41, was a proof of Paul's success. If Paul had come to the city and had simply made a tiny, little beginning, with only a few people meeting perhaps somewhere in a home, the riot would not have happened. Such a movement would have had no impact on Ephesian society. But the fact that there was a riot and so many people got stirred up in defense of Artemis is proof of how successful the preaching of the gospel had been.

There had been a strengthening of the Christian community, first of all. That is, not only had the gospel spread so that many had become Christians, but the Christians had become serious about being Christians. Maybe that is where we ought to start when we think in terms of social reform today: with the transformation of Christians. These Christians had come under the power of the Spirit of God through the preaching of the Word so thoroughly that they were convicted of sin, confessed it, and then actually brought out and destroyed the things that were opposed to Christianity. These things were magic scrolls in which incantations were written, and they were very valuable (see discussion of these scrolls in chapter 37).

What followed after the Christians got serious was an impact on the society so strong that the riot described in this chapter was the inevitable reaction by those who resented it. Christianity had impacted their business. That is where people are hurt most, in their pocketbooks. Christians certainly and perhaps other people too simply lost interest in the pagan temples.

There was a guild of silversmiths in Ephesus, just as in the Middle Ages. A guild is an organization of artisans, and in the Middle Ages there were guilds of leather workers, who made shoes; guilds of tailors, who made clothes; guilds of people who worked with wood and fine metals, and so forth. Guilds were like trade unions, only in the ancient world guilds were more important than our trade unions. The Ephesian silversmiths obviously had the power of a union, but theirs was a social grouping as well. I think that probably the closest contemporary parallel to the silversmith guild at Ephesus are the mummers of Philadelphia. The mummers, who parade up Broad Street on New Year's Day, get together not only for the purpose of this parade but for social reasons too. In fact, they have almost as much fun throughout the year as on January 1.

The Ephesus guild had great enthusiasm and certainly also great concern for their own well-being, particularly their financial well-being. Christianity had caused people to lose interest in the temple and therefore naturally in buying the kind of things that were sold at the temple for use in worship. Formerly people would buy these cult objects, little statues of Artemis or of the temple, and would take them to the temple, where they would offer them as part of their worship. None of these silver objects have been found, but the reason is probably that the priests would melt them down and make hard currency of them. Of course, people would sometimes take these objects home as souvenirs, just as today when you visit a foreign country you might buy a little silver spoon.

Demetrius and the others in his trade noticed that their profits were slipping. Last year they had made . . . well, so much money. This year they discovered that they were down . . . well, 18 percent perhaps. What was worse, the way things were going, it looked as if they would be down even more next year. Since they were interested in their profits more than anything else, they started a riot to see if they could get Paul to leave Ephesus.

Demetrius was clever in the way he went about it. He talked to the silversmiths about money because that is what concerned them. But when he talked to the population, not all of whom were silversmiths and not all of whom naturally would be harmed by the decline in the silversmiths' business, he talked not about financial matters but about civic pride. Everybody knows how important Ephesus is because of the great temple of Artemis, he said. These people have come to take away the glory of our great Artemis.

Similar problems would continue throughout the days of the Roman Empire. To give one example, seventy years after this incident, in the province of Bithynia there was a Roman governor named Pliny. The emperor was Trajan. Pliny wrote a number of letters to Trajan to ask him how he was to handle problems that were coming up in his province. Some of these letters concerned Christianity. Pliny had examined a number of Christians personally, he said, and as far as he could tell they did not seem to have done anything wrong. They were not subversive; they were not immoral. The only thing he could see is that they had some queer ideas about religion. "But it has had this bad effect," he said. "The people have stopped going to the shrines."

We might wonder why Pliny would care about that, until we remember that the shrines were big business. They were places where priests, prostitutes, and artists were employed. When people stopped going to the temples, a large block of the population of an ancient town were unable to support themselves. Pliny didn't know what to do about this, so he asked Trajan if he should drive the Christians out so the people would come back to the temples, start giving money, and take this problem off his hands.

Pliny indicates that the butchers (rather than the priests, prostitutes, or artists) had been having the greatest problems. They sold meat that had been offered to idols. When an animal was sacrificed to an idol the meat was not just thrown away, it was sold later in the stalls. The Christians, who were becoming careful about that sort of thing at this time, weren't buying it. Perhaps they were beginning to eat fish, which wasn't sacrificed. Or perhaps they were becoming vegetarians. Trajan advised him to go easy on the Christians and not press the matter but to prosecute them if specific charges were made.

A similar impact was happening in Ephesus as a result of Paul's strong preaching. Let me suggest that if our Christianity is not affecting the economy of our world, we do not have much Christianity. I know we do not like to hear that, because we tend to think that our economy is the product of our Christianity. We think of the Western world as being Christian and therefore capitalistic, and there is some truth to that. At the same time, when Christians live as Christians, it will affect how they use their money, there will be an impact on the economy (negatively for some), and inevitably there will be hostility toward Christians, as there was here.

The Defense of Artemis

There are two spirited defenses of Artemis in this chapter. Demetrius gave the first. We have his speech in verses 23–27. Then, beginning in verse 35, the city clerk takes over. By this time he was already quieting the uproar, but he uses many of the same defenses Demetrius used, though in different language.

How did they defend Artemis, the goddess who was worshiped so intently? First, they both appealed to numbers. Demetrius said Artemis "is worshiped throughout the province of Asia and the world" (v. 27). In other words, "Everyone's doing it." That is exactly what the city clerk says later: "Men of Ephesus, doesn't all the world know that the city of Ephesus is the guardian of the temple of the great Artemis and of her image, which fell from heaven?" (v. 35).

Second, Demetrius appealed to emotion. The crowd, which had been stirred up by Demetrius and the others, stormed into the amphitheater, a place seating about twenty-five thousand people, and for the space of two hours (almost as if they were at a football or a baseball game) shouted with one voice again and again,

"Great is Artemis of the Ephesians!
"Great is Artemis of the Ephesians!
"Great is Artemis of the Ephesians!"

Those were emotional moments. As the energies of the crowd were beginning to be drained away the city clerk, a wise man who had probably waited for the moment, came forward, told them to quiet down, and then dismissed the assembly.

These are the ways wrongdoing is defended in our day too. We know the appeal to numbers. It is the classic and characteristic defense of our time, though we call it "statistics." If you can prove that enough people believe something, then obviously their belief must be true. I am always astounded when I see this rationale on television, especially in newscasts. It used to be that on the newscasts, especially newscasts by the major networks, what you got was real news—things that were really happening. I am sure you have noticed how the results of opinion polls are being increasingly reported as if they were news. It goes like this: "NBC conducted an opinion poll this week, and

68 percent of the people think that the President is lying." Or, "Two percent of the people think the President is lying; 98 percent think that he is telling the truth." My response is always, "Who cares?" The point is not how many people *think* a government figure is lying (or doing anything else), but rather, *is* he lying? People generally think as they think only because of what they see on television anyway, which is largely inevitable. How would they know to form an opinion otherwise? They do not know the individuals involved. They have no way of investigating the details.

The pressure of numbers is often harmful to young believers. A student goes away to college and wants to live as a Christian, but what he is told is: "Nobody holds those old values anymore." That is not true, of course. *He* holds them, for one thing; and unless he is nobody, which he is not, he ought to be able to say, "Well, I don't know about everybody else, but there is at least one who thinks that way, and that's me." But, of course, when people say, "Nobody thinks that way anymore," what they really mean is: "The majority think differently today." If you press the point, they might say, "Only a little core of narrow, uninstructed fundamentalists hold to that old-fashioned morality. If you want to get on with us, you had better abandon that old way of thinking and join the 'in' crowd."

At Ephesus Demetrius said, Everybody worships Artemis. Not everybody did, of course. Paul and the other Christians did not. But even if everybody did, that alone did not make Artemis a true goddess nor her worshipers right.

Sometimes the argument is put like this: "I know you want to have standards, but you have to recognize that everything is relative. There is no such thing as truth today. That's just your truth. You have your truth; I have my truth; everybody has his or her truth."

Sometimes the argument goes: "Science has proved that men and women are just slightly advanced animals. What they do, we do. And that's all right, because we are all evolving upward anyway."

Or there is this argument: "Right now is all there is. Don't think about tomorrow. Above all, don't think about a life to come. Nobody knows anything about a life to come. Don't live for some far-off day. Enjoy yourself now."

Or how about this one: "If it feels right, do it. It can't be wrong." Or "It can't be wrong if it feels so good." But of course it can be wrong, and many things that are defended in that way are evil. Numbers and feelings will not make them right.

The other argument advanced by Demetrius and his friends was a defense by emotion. If you can't carry the day by argument, at least you can call the people together, stir them up, and get them to repeat for two hours, "Great is Artemis of the Ephesians!" We have that kind of argument in our day too. It is what most modern advertising does. It does not give us reasons. It appeals to our emotions and uses a similar process of repetition. If you listen to it critically, think as you are watching it, and begin to ask questions, you will discover that the reasoning is absurd.

In an old commercial for Ivory soap, the slogan said: "99 and 44/100 percent pure; it floats." That suggested to almost everyone that Ivory soap floated
because it is purer than other soaps. The slogan did not say that, of course,
but it implied it. The problem was that the implication was not true. Ivory
soap did not float because it was pure; it floated because it was filled with air
bubbles. Many of today's commercials are like that, except that they are even
more emotional. Sex is the chief selling tool, but images of success are used
too. These images tell us that people will think well of us if we have certain
necessary possessions. What they are really saying is: "Great is Artemis of the
Ephesians! Great is the American economy! Great is materialism! Look at
her benefits! Look at her pleasures! Worship at this shrine!"

It takes a lot of courage (and sound thinking) to stand firm when the
majority are going the other way. But it is only the people who stand up against
the crowd who make a difference. The world is never changed by the majority;
the world is changed by a minority who "hear a different drummer."
Christians listen to a different Spirit and go in the Holy Spirit's way.

Who Has the Victory?

What was the outcome at Ephesus? For one thing, the Christians were vindicated. Paul was not attacked, and he was able eventually and seemingly without any trouble to leave Ephesus. Luke records in detail (as he did at Corinth
where Gallio would not listen to the accusations brought against Paul) how
Paul and the Christians were vindicated. Those who were in charge said they
had done nothing wrong.

Luke reports the clerk's speech. The clerk made four points: (1) Everyone
knows that Ephesus is the guardian of the temple of Artemis. Since this is so
and no one can deny it, there is no point to this disturbance. (2) These men
(Gaius and Aristarchus, who had been dragged into the great amphitheater)
are guilty neither of sacrilege nor blasphemy. They are innocent. (3) If there
is a case to be made, Demetrius and his colleagues in the silversmith guild
know the proper legal way to make it. They are not behaving properly. Finally,
(4) we are in danger of being charged with civil disorder because of this riot.
If we are charged, we will not be able to justify today's conduct.

If we look ahead to the end of Acts, we find that the apostle Paul is not
dead, though we might have expected that this would be the way the book
would end. Rather, Paul is in prison in Rome, awaiting trial. Given those circumstances, one of the purposes Luke had in writing Acts must have been
to provide an apologetic for his friend. So he records very carefully that Paul
had repeatedly been declared to be innocent. He did so probably "to establish
legal precedent" by examples from around the Roman world. Moreover,
Christianity had been recognized by various officials to be no threat to Rome.

Christians were not always vindicated. Many died for their profession. But
they were willing to die precisely for the reason we have been studying, namely
that they looked beyond this life to the life that is to come. They judged that

what was going to happen to them in the life to come was far more important than anything that could happen to them here. So they were willing to suffer here for that surpassing weight of glory. Because they were willing to suffer, Christianity triumphed.

And Artemis? Well, it is no exaggeration to say there is not a soul living in the world today who worships "Artemis of the Ephesians," while there are millions who worship Jesus Christ and would willingly die for him.

How did Christianity triumph? How did Christians win the day? It was not by appealing to numbers. It was not by a play on the emotions. The Christians did not circulate a petition to see if they could get 51 percent of the Ephesians to sign it, a petition saying, "Artemis is no goddess, and the God of the Old Testament is the true God." The Christians did not have a mass rally. They did not send Christians into the amphitheater to do their thing, the way Demetrius and his crew had gotten people together to do his thing. They didn't sing emotional songs. They did exactly what Jesus Christ had done and what he had sent them into the world to do: They preached the gospel so that men and women got converted, and once they were converted they taught them how to live for Jesus Christ.

Do you want to make an impact on the world today? Do you want to turn this economy of ours upside down? That is the way. It is by teaching the Word and by following hard after Jesus Christ. It does not take large numbers; a small group can do it. Many small groups have.

39

Going Home

Acts 20:1-12

When the uproar had ended, Paul sent for the disciples and, after encouraging them, said good-by and set out for Macedonia. He traveled through that area, speaking many words of encouragement to the people, and finally arrived in Greece, where he stayed three months. Because the Jews made a plot against him just as he was about to sail for Syria, he decided to go back through Macedonia. He was accompanied by Sopater son of Pyrrhus from Berea, Aristarchus and Secundus from Thessalonica, Gaius from Derbe, Timothy also, Tychicus and Trophimus from the province of Asia. These men went on ahead and waited for us at Troas.

Acts 20:1–5

It is not always easy to determine where one section of Acts ends and a new section of Acts begins. This is because Luke's purpose in writing was not strictly historical but theological, and sometimes his theological concerns override the historical ones. There is an example of this difficulty in the verses we come to now. Starting at Acts 20, we have a new section of the book in some ways. Yet we also have a wrap-up of what has happened before. There is a shift in Paul's ministry. It is noticeable at the beginning of this chapter, but it becomes more noticeable as we advance toward the conclusion of the book.

Up to this point, Paul has been engaged primarily in pioneer work. He has been going into new areas and has founded churches. In Acts 20, by contrast, he is visiting for the last time churches he has already founded, giving them final teaching and encouragement.

A New Set of Concerns

There is a new concern manifested by Paul. Paul had a plan to reconcile to the Jewish church the Gentile churches he had been instrumental in establishing. The plan involved collecting a large offering from the Gentile churches for the Jerusalem church. His plan did not work very well, but its purpose was good and its intent spiritual.

We notice another shift too. Up to this point, Luke has focused on the places Paul visited and on what happened there. Now there seems to be a greater emphasis upon Paul's speeches. In this chapter we are going to find some important farewell words to the elders of the church at Ephesus. Later on, as Paul is hauled before one secular authority after the other, we find him giving addresses in defense both of himself and Christianity. There are new emphases in these speeches.

There is also more autobiographical data than we have seen before. For example, Paul tells of his conversion in detail, explains why he had come to Jerusalem, and so on.

There is also a renewed emphasis upon the resurrection of Jesus. This may be because as the early preachers were beginning to bring the gospel to non-Jewish communities, they went back to the resurrection as evidence for their claims. We also hear about the call of God to Paul to go to Gentiles and therefore hear about the expansion of the church into Gentile areas.

These final chapters tell of Paul's imprisonment, and that was a great change too. Paul was arrested in Jerusalem. Then he was imprisoned, first in Caesarea for two years and then, after he appealed to the emperor, for two more years in Rome. This was not an easy time for him. Yet during these years we also find new opportunities for Paul to be a witness. Paul was bound but the gospel was not bound, and God continued to bless Paul's ministry.

A Final Tour of the Field

The first verses of Acts 20 give details of Paul's final tour of the mission field. They tell how he went back to the churches of Macedonia and Greece, no doubt strengthening them, teaching them, dealing with problems, training their leadership, and establishing them so that they might prosper when he was no longer able to come to them.

Luke begins the chapter by telling us that Paul left Ephesus and went to Macedonia. He does not give much detail. But when we read what Paul has written in his letters, we find that this was a period of great agony on Paul's part. His chief concern at this time was the situation in the church at Corinth.

At some time during his two-year ministry at Ephesus, word had come to him of problems in the Corinthian church. His letters to the church reflect the problems. There were factions in the church. Some were claiming to be followers of Apollos; they formed an "Apollos party." Others were claiming to be followers of Peter; they were a "Peter party." Some were even claiming to be followers of Paul; they were a "Paul party." And then there were the spiritual ones who said, "We don't follow any earthly leaders. We are followers of Christ." So there was a "Christ party" too.

There was immorality in the church. One church member was sleeping with his father's wife, presumably his step-mother. There were lawsuits among the Christians. The communion service was not well observed, and it was contributing to disunion among the congregation rather than to union. The well-to-do were feasting by themselves while ignoring their poorer brethren.

All these problems troubled Paul, because among other reasons he had spent a good bit of time in Corinth. He had been there a year and a half, pouring much energy into the church in this great cosmopolitan center. After he had written to them he was understandably anxious to find out how the church was doing. Paul had left Titus in Corinth. Titus had been given the responsibility of dealing with the problems and then reporting back to Paul. He was supposed to meet Paul at Troas. But when Paul left Ephesus, arrived at Troas, and waited for Titus there, Titus did not come. Paul says in his second Corinthian letter that he was so upset by what he imagined was happening in Corinth that he passed over into Europe, probably intending to go directly to Corinth himself. However, there in Macedonia he did at last fortunately meet his coworker, who informed him that his anxiety had been unnecessary. The Corinthians had responded to his letter and had dealt with the problems (2 Cor. 2:12–13; 7:5–16). Paul says that he was greatly comforted by the coming of Titus.

I suppose that is why Paul spent as much time in Macedonia as he did, ministering further. It is also why he wrote 2 Corinthians. Perhaps in Philippi, but certainly while he was in Macedonia, Paul must have said to himself, God is certainly blessing the church at Corinth. The problems that bothered me seem to have been resolved. If that is happening, well, I can leave things in the hands of the local leadership. Instead of going to Corinth at once, I'll check up on the churches in Macedonia. Then I'll move on down to Corinth for the winter. Paul spent the summer traveling around Macedonia. He refers to this work in Romans 15:19, saying that "from Jerusalem all the way around to Illyricum, I have fully proclaimed the gospel of Christ." He then spent the winter in Corinth, where he wrote the letter to the Romans in preparation for the trip he planned to make there later.

During the months of December, January, and February the seas were too rough for boats to travel. But Paul had made up his mind that if possible he was going to get to Jerusalem for Passover that spring.

As it turned out, he did not get there for Passover. When he was about to leave Corinth to sail to Jerusalem, word came that the Jews of Corinth were plotting to kill him. Not much is said about this plot, but it is not hard to imagine what was involved. Jews going to Jerusalem would sail on a "pilgrim ship." It would carry cargo, but it would take as many passengers as possible. It would be crowded to make a lot of money, and it would be quite possible in such crowded conditions for someone who had been hired by Paul's enemies to sneak up on him and kill him some dark night at sea, perhaps pushing him overboard so people would assume he had simply fallen over the side and been lost. Word came to Paul that something like this had been planned. So rather than going by sea, Paul decided to return overland through Macedonia. This took longer than a trip by sea and delayed his timetable. However, he would be able to visit the Macedonian churches again, and then later from another port make his way to Jerusalem.

The Traveling Party

We are told here about a team of church workers who joined Paul to go together with him to Jerusalem. Not a great deal is said about their mission, but we know from Paul's letters that he had been traveling through the Gentile areas in order to take up an offering that he was going to bring to Jerusalem to help the Jerusalem Christians. Famine followed by poverty had come upon the church in Jerusalem, and Paul, although he does not say this in so many words, undoubtedly hoped by this tangible act of concern for the Jewish Christians to bridge the gap that had developed between the Jewish and Gentile branches of the church. Perhaps he would even be able to demonstrate something of the love of the Gentile Christians to all Jews. If they could see an act of love and compassion for Jews by Gentiles, it might be a step in winning some of them to Jesus Christ.

Paul may have gotten a little heavy-handed about this at times. Some people think that he almost ordered the Gentiles to give to this collection. But whether he was a bit out of line or not, the Gentiles did give and the money was collected. It was the purpose of this traveling party to convey it to Jerusalem. Verse 4 lists those who went along. "These men," Luke says, "went on ahead and waited for us at Troas" (v. 5). There is that plural pronoun again. Luke himself once more joined the company. It is worth reflecting on these men and their cities.

Sopater from Berea was one. Berea was the town where the citizens were "of more noble character than the Thessalonians" because they "examined the Scriptures every day to see if what Paul said was true" (Acts 17:11). These were real Bible students. It was to be expected that out of people like that a strong church was established. Sopater was one of their leaders.

Aristarchus and Secundus came from Thessalonica, a city on the north Aegean coast. I do not know if this was intentional or not, but the combination of names is important. Aristarchus means what it seems to mean in English, "aristocrat" or "aristocracy." The first part of it is a word meaning "best"; the second part means "rule." An aristocracy is a form of government in which rule is by the best possible people. (Of course, that generally means those who are in positions of power and who regard themselves as the best.) If the name means anything in this context, it would suggest that the person bearing it was from what we would call the upper levels of society.

The second name is exactly the opposite, "Secundus." It is a Latin word, and it means "second" or "number two." Why would anybody be named "second"? Names like these were frequently given to slaves who would not be called by their real names. Rather, in a prosperous Latin or Greek household, there would be a slave who was the Number One slave, in charge of all the other slaves. He would be called Primus, "Number One." Then you would have his understudy, who worked for him and actually carried out many of Number One's responsibilities. He would be called Secundus.

We do not know for sure if Aristarchus really was from the aristocracy or Secundus was a slave, but it would seem so. And if that was the case, then this great church at Thessalonica must have said, "Let's send men with Paul who are truly representative of our church. Let's send someone who can represent the upper classes, because we have a few like that here, and let's send Secundus to represent those of our number who are slaves." If this is an accurate picture, it is an illustration of the remarkable change that had come about in ancient culture as a result of the revolutionary impact of Christianity.

Gaius represented Derbe, one of the cities of Galatia.

Timothy we know about. He traveled with Paul. He was from Lystra.

Then, from the province of Asia there were Tychicus and Trophimus.

Some people ask, "If these were supposed to be representatives from all the great Gentile churches, where in this list are the representatives from Philippi (one of the strongest churches of Macedonia) and Corinth (where Paul spent a year and six months)?" That is a good question. Derbe and Lystra, smaller towns in Galatia, are represented. Thessalonica represents Macedonia. Berea represents a lower section of Greece. Where is Philippi? Where is Corinth?

It may be that Luke represented Philippi. He stayed behind to work there on one occasion. It would be characteristic of Luke not to mention that fact about himself.

What about Corinth? One commentator suggests that we have a clue here that things had not worked out very well at Corinth. According to this view, Corinth was alienated from Paul. Paul had written about the offering, but the people had resisted his suggestions. Consequently, when the time came for them to send a representative and an offering, they had no offering and therefore sent no one. That may be possible. Yet to judge from Paul's letters, particularly from his second one to the Corinthians, in which he is encouraged by the resolution of their problems, it is possible that something else happened. Paul had been among them that winter. When the time came for him to leave and they were to send their offering, they might have said something like this: "Paul, you are such a beloved pastor among us that we would really like you to represent our church. Why don't you become one of the party and carry the offering from the church here in Corinth?" We do not know if this was the case, but it would account for what seems to have been a serious omission otherwise.

Early Christian Worship

Before Luke describes the departure of this group for Jerusalem, he gives a glimpse into a normal day of worship of the church at Troas. Paul was delayed there seven days, probably because the winds were unfavorable or the ship was taking on cargo and couldn't go. Whatever the reason, during those seven days the first day of the week, Sunday, rolled around, and the Christians got together. I find in the account of this day not only a glimpse into the worship of the people of this city, but also an indication of the importance of this day and of the elements that should generally be present in all Christian worship.

Sunday Worship

It is significant that the first day of the week is mentioned. It had been and continues to be the tradition of the Jews to worship on the seventh day of the week, the Sabbath. This is mandated in the Old Testament, and it is part of what one would expect Old Testament believers to do. But significantly when we come to the New Testament, we find that almost automatically—it would seem almost without any real thought—the Christians, most of whom (at least in the early days) were Jews and who were used to worshiping at least once a week, switched their normal day of worship to Sunday.

The switch must have happened as a result of the resurrection of Jesus Christ, which had occurred on the first day of the week. Here was a new beginning. When Christ rose from the dead old things really had passed away. A new era had begun. Christians began to worship not on the old day, the Sabbath, but on the new "Lord's Day," which is what they called it.

This change is a proof of the resurrection. There are many evidences: the empty tomb, the graveclothes, the changed character of the disciples, and so on—all these and other historical facts are powerful evidences for the fact of the resurrection of Christ. But among these many evidences, there is the change of the day of worship to Sunday. Why would that happen? Particularly, why would that happen among Jews, who mostly made up the early Christian congregations and who were trained by centuries of tradition to worship on the seventh day? There is only one explanation: Jesus rose from the dead on that day.

Much Bible Teaching

We cannot fail to notice how much time was given to teaching on this particular Lord's Day, in this case teaching by the apostle Paul. He delivered what we would call a sermon or exposition of the Word of God. From the very beginning this had been the prime element in the Christian services.

Not everybody can (or should) preach as long as Paul did. We do not know when he began. I guess it would be after the end of the normal work day, after everybody had gotten together in this upper room of the house—perhaps seven o'clock at night, maybe later. But he was still going strong at midnight. That is a message of four or five hours.

Should preachers preach that long today? Probably not. People are not trained to listen for that long. We would quickly lose them if we tried. But the fact that Paul had so much to say reminds us of the importance of the gospel message for Christianity. Whenever Christians have lost that emphasis, whenever they have begun to think of worship chiefly as entertainment, or that what is accomplished in worship is essentially an emotional response that can be worked up by the singing of certain hymns or choruses, or that worship should consist of a series of testimonies of how people were lost in sin (with a great deal of emphasis on the sin) and were then brought to Christ—when they have substituted these other elements for careful Bible exposition in sermons, the church has always been weakened and sometimes has even died.

This is because the power of God is not in our emotions or experience but in the Word of God. His Word is what God has chosen to bless, and that is why in properly conducted Christian services we emphasize it. It is not the eloquence of the preacher or even his authority that blesses, but the Word of God.

The Lord's Supper

The third thing to notice about the worship at Troas is the observance of the Lord's Supper. They had it late in the evening. Paul preached first; then they celebrated the sacrament. The Reformers rightly emphasized the combination, saying that there was to be no observance of the Lord's Supper without preaching.

Supplemental Informal Conversation

After the observance of the Lord's Supper, Paul talked with them in an informal way until daylight (v. 11). The word that is used here for "talking" is different from the words used earlier for Paul's preaching to them. In the earlier instance, the words indicate formal teaching, teaching that is sustained and carefully reasoned. That was the heart of the actual worship service. Toward the end, the word that is used refers to informal conversation. It was what we think of as fellowship.

Luke recorded almost the same thing toward the end of Acts 2. After Pentecost, when the church was established in Jerusalem, "they devoted themselves to the apostles' teaching and to the fellowship, to the breaking of bread and to prayer" (Acts 2:42). That is precisely what we find here. In fact, the only one of the four elements mentioned in Acts 2 that is not mentioned in Acts 20 is prayer, but the fact that the Christians in Troas also prayed is to be assumed.

This format is natural to Christian people. Wherever we go, wherever the gospel has penetrated and churches have been established, we find that Christians come together naturally to hear the Bible taught, pray, observe communion, and enjoy fellowship.

The Man Who Fell Asleep

These verses also contain the story of Eutychus. Christians probably think about Eutychus a lot, particularly when they have to sit in long church services where the preacher is going on and on, the lights are flickering, the air is stale, and they are falling asleep. Eutychus fell asleep and fell out of the window where he was sitting, so that people thought he was dead.

I am glad this story is in the Bible, though not for the reasons most people are glad to know about it. I am happy because it indicates that sometimes people fell asleep even when the apostle Paul was preaching. I am sure Paul was not boring or irrelevant. He did not turn people off with the dullness of the things he was teaching. Paul taught well and deeply. But sometimes, in spite of even the best teaching, human flesh is weak. That was the case with Eutychus.

Was Eutychus dead? There are different opinions. Verse 9 says that he was "picked up dead." But when Paul got to him, he said, "Don't be alarmed. He's alive" (v. 10). People have concluded from Paul's words that the people thought Eutychus was dead but that, when Paul got to him, he discovered he was actually alive. Others believe that Eutychus died and that when Paul got to him he performed a resurrection. I suppose this is a matter we cannot fully resolve. Luke was present. Luke was a physician. If Luke says Eutychus was dead, I am willing to believe that he was dead and that there was a resurrection.[1] On the other hand, not a great deal is made of the event, and maybe that is a way of indicating that the situation was not as serious as the onlookers originally thought.

The significance of the incident may be this. Paul was not going to see these believers again. This is a farewell scene. Moreover, they were observing the Lord's Supper, and it was clear that they would not do that together again until they were together in heaven. Before then they would all die, though they would be raised again. Maybe the story of Eutychus is a picture of our future reunion after physical death. If it is, then it is a picture from which we can take heart. We are alive now and are with other believers, but death will come and with death a parting. If this life were all there is, that would be the end. But it is not the end, because there is a resurrection, and we will meet again.

We also know the end of Paul's story. Paul will go to Jerusalem, be attacked, arrested, beaten, and imprisoned. Then he will be sent to Rome, where eventually he will lose his life, though Luke does not end Acts with Paul's death but rather with his life in Rome spreading the gospel everywhere. But even the death of Paul was not the end. Paul had many trials, but for two thousand years now he has been with Jesus, and so have these faithful believers from Troas. The ending is never bad for Christians. The God who has begun a good work in us keeps on perfecting it until the day of Christ.

40

Paul's Farewell to the Ephesian Elders

Acts 20:13-38

From Miletus, Paul sent to Ephesus for the elders of the church. When they arrived, he said to them: "You know how I lived the whole time I was with you, from the first day I came into the province of Asia. I served the Lord with great humility and with tears, although I was severely tested by the plots of the Jews. You know that I have not hesitated to preach anything that would be helpful to you but have taught you publicly and from house to house. I have declared to both Jews and Greeks that they must turn to God in repentance and have faith in our Lord Jesus." . . .

When he had said this, he knelt down with all of them and prayed. They all wept as they embraced him and kissed him. What grieved them most was his statement that they would never see his face again. Then they accompanied him to the ship.

Acts 20:17-38

To anybody who has an interest in Paul as a person, the twentieth chapter of Acts is a delight. This is because we see him in two different but very important lights. We see him in public at Troas, leading the worship of the church. Then we see him in a private setting, meeting with the Ephesian elders at Miletus, a little town about twenty or thirty miles south of the Asian capital. This section is known as "Paul's farewell to the Ephesian elders," and it has three parts: Paul's personal testimony before the elders, his specific charge to them, and his prayer on their behalf.

343

Paul's Testimony

Paul's personal testimony is found in verses 18–24 and 33–35. It is in two parts because it is interrupted by his charge to the elders. The testimony that precedes and follows this charge is an inspiring passage for any pastor to read.

It is helpful too because we see Paul toward the end of his ministry among these people looking back and pointing out, not in any boastful manner but rather in an honest way, what he considered to have been the important features of his work, those blessed by God and for which he praised God. Clearly, these are characteristics that ought be present in the life of any Christian minister and of all Christians.

Paul tells the elders he served with humility and tears, that he was diligent in preaching, that his priorities were right, and that he served without greed and with hard work.

Serving with Humility

The first thing Paul mentions is his humble approach to Christian work, for he reminds the elders that while he was with them he "served the Lord with great humility" (v. 19). It is interesting he should mention humility, because when he writes about the qualifications of an elder as he does later in 1 Timothy and Titus, two of the pastoral epistles, although he touches on subjects that relate to humility, he does not mention humility. Moreover, he never says, except here, that he was humble himself.

Humility is important, of course, because the opposite of humility is pride, and pride is a great danger for those who are in prominent positions of church leadership. It is a danger for anyone, but it is particularly dangerous for those who stand up and talk, at least if they are effective doing it, because people will always come up afterward to say, no doubt meaning well, "Oh, that was a wonderful message" or "I was greatly blessed by that." The situation is dangerous because the minister may come to believe that he is indeed rather wonderful. After all, he has been a source of such great blessing to so many people. He may forget that any blessing that comes is from the Lord.

A minister has to learn early on how to deal with praise and actually grow in humility rather than in pride. I do not think this means that ministers will always be talking about humility. Paul did not. But humility has to be present in their ministry.

The eighteenth-century evangelist George Whitefield developed a technique for handling such compliments. He was the most popular preacher of his day and probably the most popular of all speakers of whatever type, whether political or otherwise. He was a spellbinder, brilliant. Everybody talked about his mastery of language and his control over the emotions of an audience. Moreover, he lived in a day when there was not the competition among ministers that exists today through television and other media. When Whitefield came to town, everybody streamed out to hear him. The minute they heard Whitefield was coming, people would drop their plows in the fields, their hammers in the blacksmith shops, their shuttles at the looms, and rush off to hear Whitefield. He spoke to thousands upon thousands in his day, as many as 20,000 to 25,000 people at a time.

Today we wonder how he could have done it. Benjamin Franklin, his contemporary, also wondered about it. He thought reports of the size of Whitefield's congregations must be exaggerated. So when Whitefield came to Philadelphia, Franklin went to hear him. He started near the front, then gradually worked his way back, seeing how far he could go and still hear Whitefield's voice. He counted his paces, which allowed him to figure out how many square feet there were in a circle about Whitefield. He allowed so many square feet to a person, and he discovered that Whitefield could indeed be heard by 25,000 or 30,000 people, if they gathered around closely.

You can imagine that if a man like that preached effectively, as he did, and large numbers of people were blessed, when he was finished preaching people would flock around him and say, "Mr. Whitefield, you were wonderful. Your words were eloquent."

Whenever anybody would say that to him Whitefield would reply, "I know it; the devil told me that just as I was stepping down from the pulpit."

I remember a story in a somewhat similar vein. A young Scottish preacher who was quite self-confident literally bounded up the steps into the pulpit one Sunday, filled with self-esteem. Unfortunately, he lost his way in the middle of his address, became quite confounded, and forgot his message. As he came down from the pulpit humiliated, an old Scottish elder who had been present in the church that morning said to him, "Young man, if you had gone up the way you came down, you would have been able to have come down the way you went up."

Paul had obviously gone up and come down properly many times. He had bowed low before God, and as a result he knew that he was no different from anyone else. He was only a sinner saved by grace. If he had gifts that had been used in the ministry, they were gifts that had been given him by God. He had applied to himself what he had said earlier to the Corinthians: "Who makes you different from anyone else? What do you have that you did not receive? And if you did receive it, why do you boast as though you did not?" (1 Cor. 4:7). It would make a great difference in the lives of many workers if they could only learn to think of their gifts like that.

Serving with Tears

The second thing Paul says about himself in his testimony before the Ephesian elders is that as he served among them with humility, he also did so with tears. Paul mentions tears twice in the chapter, in verse 19 and also in verse 31: "Remember that for three years I never stopped warning each of you night and day with tears." Obviously his tears were something of considerable importance to him, though as far as I know this too is not mentioned elsewhere.

I do not think Paul was what we would call a "weepy" person. We know people like that, people who for one reason or another are inclined to be emotional. They tend not to be terribly effective in working with other people. I knew a person like that in high school. He taught romance languages, and he was so moved with compassion for the students that he would literally break into tears. I remember his crying in chapel once, tears running down his cheeks. He cared for us certainly. But he was not very effective either with me or my high school peers. That is not the way you communicate effectively with teenage students or, for that matter, with anybody else.

I think that when Paul says he served the Lord with tears he does not mean that he was given to frequent outbursts of emotion, except perhaps in prayer. He means that he was what we would call a man of great empathy. That is, he learned to identify with those to whom he ministered. We are told in Romans that we are to "rejoice with those who rejoice" and "mourn with those who mourn" (Rom.12:15). Paul obviously did so. If somebody was happy, he was happy with them because he was happy for them. If someone was weeping, Paul could weep with them because he identified with them and to some extent could live what they were going through.

Francis Schaeffer made a great deal of tears. He believed in the need to separate from unbelief, but he always said, "If we separate, it must be with tears. And if we speak truth that hurts, it must be with tears." He was right in that. He meant that we must empathize with others.

Have you ever asked why Paul was so effective as he went through the Greek and Roman world planting churches? Was it his preaching? Yes, of course. His preaching was strong. We are going to come to that in a moment. He taught the whole counsel of God, and God blessed the hearers through his Word. But I sense that Paul's success also had a great deal to do with the empathy he had for other people. He struggled with them in their struggles and grieved with them in their griefs. They remembered this and recognized that in Paul there was something they did not see in the world around them.

Diligence in Preaching

After reminding the elders of the attitude with which he had done his work, Paul spoke of his chief function, which was to teach and preach the Bible. He says a great deal about his preaching, and rightly so, because it is what he was chiefly called to do. I see at least five things that he has to say about his preaching.

1. *He preached publicly* (v. 20). We know that already, because earlier in Acts we saw what he did in Ephesus (see pp. 323–25).

2. *He preached privately* (v. 20). That is, he went from house to house with his message. To use our terms for it, he did house-to-house visitation.

In 1659 an Englishman named Richard Baxter wrote *The Reformed Pastor,* essentially an exposition of Acts 20:28. It is about methodology for ministry. Baxter's chief point in this book was something that he had developed in his own ministry in a rather backward section of England. He said the minister should go from house to house, visiting his parishioners and catechizing them, that is, taking them through the questions of the Westminster Shorter and Longer Catechisms on a regular basis as a family. Under Baxter's ministry the church prospered in that community, and it was reported that there was a time when most of the people of that city would have been known as true Christians and on a Sunday could even be heard singing psalms.

I do not know if that could be done today. Our churches are large. Our communities are scattered. Families are busy. It probably would not work in a large city like Philadelphia or New York or Los Angeles or Washington.

But if this says nothing else to us, it at least says that Paul was not above this sort of work. He did not say to himself, I am a great preacher and scholar. I stand before masses of people. It would be beneath me to take time to visit in somebody's home and try to help them on a one-to-one basis. God's diligent servants have always recognized that what happens on a one-to-one basis or in small groups is often in the providence of God of much greater significance than what happens in large mass meetings.

David Brainerd, a missionary to the American Indians, got tuberculosis and died at a young age. His biography was written by Jonathan Edwards. When he was on his deathbed he worked with a young Indian child, teaching him to read. He said he counted it a blessing that when he was unable to do anything else, he was at least able to teach one of God's children to read the Holy Scriptures. Paul had that attitude, and God blessed it.

3. *Paul preached to everybody* (v. 21). He declared the Word of God to both Jews and Greeks. The Jews gave him a hard time. They gave him a hard time everywhere he went, and they gave him a particularly hard time at Ephesus. Yet he ministered to them. And the Gentiles? Well, they weren't much better. We remember that there was a riot at Ephesus, and it was not the Jews who were rioting in the great amphitheater, shouting, "Great is Artemis of the Ephesians!" The gospel was a universal gospel, and the Savior whom Paul served was a universal Savior. So he spoke about the Lord Jesus Christ to everybody.

4. *Paul spoke pointedly* (v. 21). I add this because his message was that "they must turn to God in repentance and have faith in our Lord Jesus." Repentance means turning from sin. Faith in Jesus means believing in him alone for salvation. That is pointed preaching, and it is the only kind that is any good. Some preaching is so general and some references to sin are so indirect that hardly anyone can be offended. If they cannot be offended, then they can hardly turn from sin, since they have not even recognized that they are guilty of it. Paul did not preach that way. His preaching was pointed, and God blessed it.

5. *Paul's preaching was comprehensive* (v. 27). It was comprehensive in the sense that it embraced not just what we would call "a simple gospel" or "an evangelistic message" but rather "the whole will of God." John Stott called Paul's work an example of "evangelism in depth," noting that "he shared all possible truth with all possible people in all possible ways."[1]

Right Priorities

Paul also had a proper set of priorities (v. 24). He told the elders, "I consider my life worth nothing to me, if only I may finish the race and complete the task the Lord Jesus has given me—the task of testifying to the gospel of God's grace."

When I read that verse I think of Philippians 3:13–14, where Paul gives a similar testimony: "Forgetting what is behind and straining toward what is ahead, I press on toward the goal to win the prize for which God has called me heavenward in Christ Jesus." This is an exposition of what he said to the Ephesian elders, for it tells us that his goals involved forgetting what was behind—the failures, temptations, weaknesses, even the achievements—and pressing forward instead to the things God yet had for him, always having his eye on the prize to which God had called him in Christ Jesus.

One reason why many of us are not more effective in our Christian lives is that we do not have our priorities in order. Isn't it true that most of us value our lives far more than our witness? We value the praise of men far more than the approbation of God.

Without Greed and with Hard Work

The final thing Paul says about himself is that he labored without greed and that he demonstrated his concern for the Ephesians by hard work.

> I have not coveted anyone's silver or gold or clothing. You yourselves know that these hands of mine have supplied my own needs and the needs of my companions. In everything I did, I showed you that by this kind of hard work we must help the weak, remembering the words the Lord Jesus himself said: "It is more blessed to give than to receive."
>
> Acts 20:33–35

It is a scandal to the ministry that so many ministers are lazy. They can be because in most churches they do not have anybody to supervise them, at least not very well. What they do with their time is between them and God. So if the minister is not thinking about God and remembering that he is answerable to him, it is very easy to waste a great deal of time. There are always easy things he can do rather than working hard.

I think it would be a great thing in many cases if those who are in the ministry, in addition to laboring in ministry, would actually work with their hands, the way Paul did, in a secular job. Then, at least they would be working, and out of the work there would come a sense of the value of work and the preciousness of time. Besides, the ministry of the gospel would be commended in the minds of many people.

Paul's Charge to the Elders

The second part of Acts 20:13–38 is Paul's charge to the elders. It is in verses 25–31. He puts it in different ways, but when we analyze what he is saying it boils down to one thing: Keep watch over the flock within your charge. He says this in a variety of ways: Be diligent, Watch out for enemies, Take heed of wolves. But basically he is telling them: "Keep watch over yourselves and all the flock of which the Holy Spirit has made you overseers" (v. 28).

It is interesting that the word Paul uses for the elders in this verse is not the word "elder" (Greek, *presbyteros*), which literally means "older ones," though it occurs in verse 17, but "overseer" (Greek, *episkopos*). *Episkopos* has given us our word "bishop." What is a bishop? A bishop is "an overseer." Here, of course, Paul is not using the word in an ecclesiastical sense to describe a certain order of clergy, even less a person who is singularly responsible for a certain segment of the church. Rather, he is speaking of all the elders of a local church as overseers, that is, as those who have a responsibility for the oversight of Christians in their area.

Episkopos is composed of two parts: *skopos*, which is from the verb *skopio* (meaning "to look") and *epi* (meaning "over"). So an *episkopos* is literally "one who looks over" or "keeps watch over" someone else. Paul is saying, If you are overseers, people who have been elected to this responsible position in the church, then make sure you do the job for which you've been elected. He spells it out.

They are to keep watch over themselves. They are to keep their lives upright. They are to keep their relationships to God strong.

Second, and having done that, *they are to look out for the flock.* The image of a flock and its shepherd is not frequent in Paul's writings, but it is a strong image in the Old Testament, since it was written to people whose lives were mostly pastoral. It was also important in the teaching of Jesus Christ. Jesus spoke about himself as the Shepherd, saying, "I am the good shepherd. The good shepherd lays down his life for the sheep" (John 10:11). So although the image is not frequent in Paul, when he does use it, as here, he is telling the leaders of the church to imitate Jesus. Their task was to take care of the sheep—not to let them wander away, but to watch out for their health, defend them from enemies, and such things. The reason they were to do this is that the flock was not their flock but God's. It is a flock Jesus purchased with his blood. The elders were to be overseers so that no one without and no one within would damage the flock for which Jesus died.

Paul's Prayer for Them

The third part of Paul's farewell to the Ephesian elders is his prayer for them. We do not have it in so many words. We are told only that when he had given them his charge, "he knelt down with all of them and prayed" (v. 36). I suspect that if we look back carefully over the preceding paragraph, probably we have the gist of what he prayed. This is because in verse 32, which introduces a part of the charge, Paul says, "Now I commit you to God and to the word of his grace."

How did he do that? No doubt by praying for them. He would say: Almighty God, I commit into your care these men who are the leaders of the church in Ephesus. Keep them by the power of your Holy Spirit and by the Scriptures, by which alone you speak to the church and through which you have chosen to operate. Keep them from danger. Preserve this church from evil within and without. Grant that it might be strong. Fill it with people who know your Word and because they know your Word live in close fellowship with you. Let them grow in grace and thus instead of succumbing to the temptations of the world, become strong in the knowledge of who you are and by the Holy Spirit determine to obey you and walk after you.

Do you think God heard this prayer? I do. I think God heard it and answered it, because the church in Ephesus was strong and survived to be an effective witness in Asia for many years.

Treasures in Heaven

How do you conclude a study like this—a farewell in which the apostle Paul gave his personal testimony, charged those he was leaving behind, and prayed for them? I think there is a suggestion of a way to conclude in verse 32, where Paul speaks of "an inheritance" that God has prepared for his people. It reminds us that if we are faithful to our task, as Paul was urging the Ephesian elders to be, there will be laid up for us "treasures in heaven, where moth and rust do not destroy, and where thieves do not break in and steal" (Matt. 6:20).

I suppose that is why Paul went on in an unexpected way to speak about himself again. He had already given his testimony; he had spoken directly to the elders. At first glance it seems strange that Paul should then have begun to talk about himself some more, saying, "I have not coveted anyone's silver or gold or clothing" (v. 33).

It may be a bit unexpected, but it is not hard to understand how he got there. He had just urged them to deny themselves for the sake of God's kingdom, concluding, "God [will give you] an inheritance among all those who are sanctified." Then, having said that, he reminded them that what he was urging on them he had himself done. He said in effect, "I have not tried to build an earthly fortune. I have not coveted anyone's gold. I have not been in this religion business to become wealthy. The reason I have not done that is that I have had my eyes set upon the inheritance laid up for me in heaven."

What a difference it would make if we would all learn to think like that. I know it is hard. The world bombards us with its values and with a philosophy that says, "You only go around once. Now is the time to make it. If you do not lay up for yourself now, you'll never have it."

By contrast, the Word of God says, You can lay it up now. But when you die, it will be gone forever; on the other hand, if you live for God now, you will have treasure forever. It is literally true that you cannot take it with you into heaven. But if you are obedient to God and try to serve him whole-heartedly now, spiritual treasures will be waiting for you in heaven when you get there. These treasures are the eternal well-being of the soul, eternal felicity, basking in and enjoying the favor of God forever. Compared with those spiritual treasures the things for which we sell our souls here are worse than trifles. They are nothing. They are literally the refuse of this disintegrating world. Learn to lay up treasures in heaven, as Paul did.

PART FOUR

The Journey to Rome

41

When a Good Man Falls

Acts 21:1-26

After we had torn ourselves away from them, we put out to sea and sailed straight to Cos. The next day we went to Rhodes and from there to Patara. We found a ship crossing over to Phoenicia, went on board and set sail. After sighting Cyprus and passing to the south of it, we sailed on to Syria. We landed at Tyre, where our ship was to unload its cargo. Finding the disciples there, we stayed with them seven days. Through the Spirit they urged Paul not to go on to Jerusalem.

Acts 21:1–4

The missionary journeys are completed. Paul is going to Jerusalem for the last time and arrives there in this chapter. He is arrested and so far as we know never again finds freedom. There is an argument that Paul may have been released from prison and perhaps even traveled to Spain to found more churches, and there is much to be said in its favor. But so far as we know from Acts itself or from any direct testimony in the New Testament, that was not the case. Therefore, what we have here is in all probability the beginning of the final chapter of Paul's long and influential life.

When I was looking for a title for this chapter, my mind ran to a book by Erwin W. Lutzer, the pastor of Chicago's Moody Church, called *When a Good Man Falls*.[1] As you might expect from the title, the book contains studies of

Bible characters who experienced a period of disobedience or sin in their lives. It contains the story of Moses, who began his own private liberation movement by killing an Egyptian. The book also contains the story of Samson, who was so bewitched by Delilah that he gave away the secret of his strength.

The reason I thought of this book in connection with Acts 21 is that in my opinion in this chapter we come to a period of Paul's life that was similar. I say in my opinion because, although the majority of commentators do not take such a view, I hope to show that though Paul was driven by high motives, what he did at this time of his life was wrong. Being wrong, it had unfortunate consequences for him and perhaps also for other people.

God's Warnings to Paul

God had apparently warned Paul not to go to Jerusalem. Paul acknowledged this himself. If we look back to Acts 20, which we have already studied, we find that when Paul was speaking to the Ephesian elders, he said, "I only know that in every city the Holy Spirit warns me that prison and hardships are facing me" (v. 23). It is true that this verse does not say in categorical language, "Do not go to Jerusalem, Paul." But it is a warning, and it carries weight because it was not simply that in every city Paul's friends were warning him not to go to Jerusalem but rather that the Holy Spirit was speaking. Paul does not say how the Holy Spirit spoke in every city. Perhaps he spoke through his friends or in a personal way, but the Holy Spirit was speaking and Paul disregarded the warning and went.

The story continues in chapter 21, where twice, in verses 4 and 11, we find Paul again being warned not to go. If we count the original warnings "in every city" as one warning, though there must actually have been many of them, here we have additional warnings that we can call warnings two and three.

In verse 4 we find: "Through the Spirit they [that is, the disciples in Tyre, whom he was visiting] urged Paul not to go on to Jerusalem." That is a bit stronger than what was said in Acts 20. The disciples are speaking, and it is "through the Spirit." Of even greater importance is the fact that what they say is not only a warning that Paul would be imprisoned if he went to Jerusalem but also a direct statement "through the Spirit" not to go.

Then, in verse 11, there is the warning of the prophet Agabus. This man had come down to the Mediterranean coast from Judea, perhaps from Jerusalem, and when he arrived at Tyre he performed a symbolic act. He took Paul's belt, tied his own hands and feet with it, and said, "The Holy Spirit says, 'In this way the Jews of Jerusalem will bind the owner of this belt and will hand him over to the Gentiles.'" This was an even stronger statement. Yet, in spite of this, Paul was determined to go to Jerusalem.

I want to put one other bit of data with this, though I acknowledge at the start that it is somewhat ambiguous. If we turn a chapter further on, from chapter 21 to chapter 22, we find an account of Paul's speech before the crowd in Jerusalem. In that speech Paul refers to a special revelation God had given him when he was in Jerusalem. He says, "When I returned to Jerusalem and was praying at the temple, I fell into a trance and saw the Lord speaking. 'Quick!' he said to me. 'Leave Jerusalem immediately, because they will not accept your testimony about me'" (22:17).

I consider that ambiguous because Paul had been speaking about his conversion on the Damascus road, and the verses immediately before this tell how Ananias, God's servant in Damascus, was instrumental in restoring Paul's sight. It is after this that Paul says, "When I returned to Jerusalem."

We know that after Paul had been in Damascus there was a brief time when he did go to Jerusalem. So it may be that it is this visit he is speaking of—in other words, something that had happened years before. He would be saying, "I was in Damascus. I was converted there. I came to Jerusalem. While I was in Jerusalem, the Lord spoke to me, saying, 'Go to the Gentiles.'" This may be all the words mean. On the other hand, when we look back to what we have already been told in Acts, we do not find anything that suggests such a warning at that earlier time. So it is far more likely, I would say almost certain, that Paul meant his final visit to Jerusalem, not the earlier one. This second possibility fits the context of these chapters best.

There seems to be a pattern of increasingly intense warnings. God seems to have told Paul not to go to Jerusalem and then when he did go not to linger there but to leave at once and go to the Gentiles. In spite of these warnings, Paul yearned for the salvation of the Jews so much that he disregarded what he had been told and went to Jerusalem and did the things we will consider in this study.[2]

In a Good Man's Defense

I want to say several things in defense of Paul, however, because his actions should not be blown out of proportion.

First, if this is what Paul was doing, then it is at worst merely the exercise of a very strong, obstinate, and determined personality. We often use those words as if to be like that is an extremely bad thing. But we have to remember that if Paul had not had that kind of a personality, he would not have been the kind of aggressive pioneer missionary he was. It took more than a Casper Milquetoast to evangelize the Roman world, and that is what Paul did. Paul was a great man, a man of great determination. When things got tough, he did just what our little saying says: he, the tough, got going. Paul persevered in a difficult job for many long years in spite of opposition, persecution, and even physical abuse. If Paul had not had the kind of personality he had, he would not have achieved what he did achieve in his ministry. God had given him his personality.

Second, Paul certainly had a love of people and particularly of his own people, the Jews. If we doubt that, we need only turn to the ninth chapter of Romans, where he writes of the "great sorrow and unceasing anguish" of his heart caused by Israel's unbelief (v. 1).

Paul was a missionary to the Gentiles; God had called him to be so. But he was still a Jew, and he had a heart for the Jewish people. He even says in Romans 9: "I could wish that I myself were cursed and cut off from Christ for the sake of my brothers, those of my own race, the people of Israel" (vv. 3–4). I do not know that I would say that. I doubt if there are many Christians today who could say and actually mean that they would be willing to be sent to hell for the sake of their own people, whoever those people might be. Yet that is what Paul said. He meant it. He loved his people and was concerned for them. If he had not been concerned for them, he would not have gone to Jerusalem for this final time, particularly after having received the many warnings he did receive against going.

Third, Paul had a great evangelistic plan, a strong strategy for world missions, and this was part of it. Paul knew that there was a growing rupture in the church between its Jewish and Gentile branches. This was probably inevitable, given Jewish prejudices against the Gentile world. But whether it was inevitable or not, Paul wanted to do everything possible to overcome the presence of prejudice in the church. One way he tried to do this was by collecting an offering from the Gentile churches, which he was determined to bring to Jerusalem as a demonstration of the love of Gentile believers for Jews and of the solidarity of the people of God throughout the world.

Luke says very little about this offering. As a matter of fact, it is not mentioned at all in Acts, except in the twenty-fourth chapter in the context of a speech Paul gave before Felix ("After an absence of several years, I came to Jerusalem to bring my people gifts for the poor and to present offerings," v. 17). We do not learn much about this offering from this one reference in Acts, which leads me to suspect that Luke was not as sold on the idea as Paul was. Perhaps he was even unhappy about it.

However, when we turn from Acts to Paul's letters, especially 1 and 2 Corinthians, we find that this collection was a most important matter for Paul. It was part of his strategy for welding the church together. In 1 Corinthians 16 he gives specific instructions as to how the offering was to be collected:

> Do what I told the Galatian churches to do. On the first day of every week, each one of you should set aside a sum of money in keeping with his income, saving it up, so that when I come no collections will have to be made. Then, when I arrive, I will give letters of introduction to the men you approve and send them with your gift to Jerusalem.
>
> 1 Corinthians 16:1–3

In 2 Corinthians, written in part at least because the offering project had not been going very well, he reiterates what he had in mind. In this letter he talks about the offering in one way or another for the better part of chapters 8 and 9.

As I read those chapters, I suspect that the matter may have been getting out of hand. Paul gives a lot of valuable instruction in those chapters about how we are to give of our substance to the Lord's work. I have often referred to them in stewardship sermons. But one nevertheless wonders at times whether the tone is quite right. Isn't Paul being just a little preemptory in his instructions? Isn't he ordering them about just a bit too much, particularly in something that should be voluntary? There is room for disagreement here, and I confess that I may be reading too much into the situation. But, as I said, I suspect that Luke's silence may be indication that the project may have gotten just a bit out of hand.

Paul's intention was good. He wanted to bring this gift to say to the Jews in Jerusalem, "Look how much the Gentiles love you." Still, I do not believe this was God's plan for Paul, however well intentioned, and, as we are going to see, the offering did not accomplish Paul's purpose.

Finally, here is one other thing in Paul's defense. When the Christians in Tyre were pleading with Paul not to go to Jerusalem, he said, "Why are you weeping and breaking my heart? I am ready not only to be bound, but also to die in Jerusalem for the name of the Lord Jesus" (Acts 21:13). This was quite true. Paul was willing to be bound and even die for the sake of Christ, as eventually he did. He was martyred in Rome.

But that was not the point. Paul may have been willing to die for Jesus. But that was not what Jesus was requiring in this matter. Jesus was not asking Paul to die for him. On the contrary, he seems to have been telling him not to die. The issue was not martyrdom but obedience. This is very relevant to us, because we sometimes try to cover up disobedience in our lives by taking what seems to be a high spiritual road. We say, "I am willing to do anything, suffer anything, even die for Jesus." But what we really mean by that is, "I want to do what I want to do regardless." As I read this story, it seems to me that this is what Paul was doing and that this is the main point of the application.

Consequences of Disobedience

Someone may object, "But what's the big deal? What difference did it make that Paul went to Jerusalem, even if he was out of the will of God? Certainly many of us do similar things. Didn't God just say, 'Well, all right, let him do it; I'll get him on the right track later'?"

We find the answer to those questions as we read on in the story, for we learn that Paul's disobedience quickly led to something quite bad, something that almost became a terrible compromise of the gospel.

The church in Jerusalem was composed largely of Jews who wanted to maintain as many of their Jewish traditions as possible. There are ways in which that might be done rightly, at least in part, just as German Christians can retain certain German customs while still being Christians and Asians can retain certain Asian customs, and so on. But it was more complicated than that in this case, because so much of the Jewishness of the church was wrapped up in traditions that had been fulfilled and abolished by Christ's coming. The Jerusalem church was trying to maintain not merely the moral standards of the law of Moses, which are binding upon all men and women, but also the Law's system of ceremonial purifications and observances.

When Paul and the other missionaries began to establish Gentile churches this became an immediate problem because Jewish Christians thought Gentile Christians should follow Jewish law. Paul, the defender of Gentile freedom, argued forcefully that Gentiles were to be allowed to stand fast in their liberty.

This put the Jerusalem church in a difficult position. It was composed almost entirely of Jews, existed in the midst of a surrounding Jewish culture, yet was supposed to be Christian. What was it to do about the traditional Jewish ceremonies? Apparently, the believers tried to walk with one foot in each camp.

It is true that when this issue came to a head at the great council of Jerusalem recorded in Acts 15 the battle was won for the cause of Gentile liberty. But the problem did not go away then, at least not for the Jerusalem believers. In Jerusalem the law was still very important, and anybody who suggested that it was not necessary or even proper to keep the ceremonial law was suspect.

It was against this murky background of compromise that Paul was himself almost trapped into compromise by coming to Jerusalem.

The leaders of the church approached him and said something like this: "Paul, we know that you are right in insisting that no Christian has to keep the ceremonial law. You have stood for Gentile liberty, and you have been right in that. But you have to understand that we have a difficult situation here. We live in a Jewish culture, and there are many people in the church who just do not see it your way. They think that you are trying to destroy their traditions and that you are even harming the cause of religion. We would like to dispel that idea. So what we suggest is this: We have four men who have taken a vow and will be presenting themselves at the temple. We would like you to join them. They are poor people. They are not able to pay for the sacrifice that is part of the ceremonial purification rite. We'd like you to pay for that sacrifice, go through the days of purification yourself, and then join with them as the sacrifice for sin is made in the temple area."

This was what we would call realistic politics. Quite simply, it was a compromise. On an earlier occasion, if something like this had been suggested to Paul, we would have expected Paul to have reacted indignantly, as he did in Antioch when Peter moved away from the Gentiles in order to sit with the Jews and eat kosher food. Paul had been right to oppose Peter. Yet this was far worse than anything Peter had been guilty of. Peter was caught in a hypocritical position. But Paul's error was worse than mere hypocrisy, though it was that too. It was a compromise of the gospel. The same apostle who had written so many New Testament books, the man who had argued so forcefully that we are saved by Jesus Christ alone was about to go to the Jewish temple and in the presence of the very priests who had crucified the Lord, there participate with others in a sacrifice of an animal that was meant to be an atonement for his sin. That is, he was about to turn his back on the only sufficient sacrifice of Christ.

I know that as Paul made his way to Jerusalem on this last journey he was not thinking of these things. Paul did not know that this compromise was going to be suggested. But that was the reason God had been trying to hinder him from going. When he persisted in his own way, he got trapped in the compromise.

It is always that way when we are out of the will of God. Temptation comes, and we do not even recognize that it is temptation. Instead we say, "Well, there's something to be said for that. Maybe that is what I should do." So the stand we should take is undermined, and the gospel we should defend is compromised.

God Will Not Be Compromised

It is interesting to see how God dealt with this problem. There were seven days of purification and at the end of these seven days the offering that would have compromised Paul and his gospel would be made. Paul seems to have proceeded on his way unhindered for six of those seven days. But notice! "When the seven days were nearly over, some Jews from the province of Asia saw Paul at the temple. They stirred up the whole crowd and seized him" (v. 27). Before Paul could participate in the sacrifice there was a riot, and Paul was carried away by the Roman authorities and imprisoned.

God is the God of circumstances. He was certainly active in these circumstances. They were God's way of saying, "This is the point beyond which I will not let Paul go." Paul may have been willing to compromise the gospel, though he wouldn't have called it that, but God will not be compromised. So God would not allow Paul to go to the temple and present a blood sacrifice for his sins when Jesus had already died for his sins and taken them away.

In spite of the fact that this is what we would have to call a low point in Paul's life, it nevertheless did not end Paul's usefulness. Some people have pointed out that if Paul had not been arrested, he would not have had many of the opportunities he did have to testify to the grace of God in Christ. In fact, from this point on we find Paul testifying in one high setting after another: first, in Acts 23 to the Sanhedrin (the Sanhedrin would never have heard him unless he had been arrested); second, in Acts 24 to Governor Felix; third, in Acts 25 to Governor Festus; fourth, in Acts 26 to King Agrippa; and finally, at the end of Acts to the imperial Roman guard. Paul witnessed to soldiers who as we know from Philippians in turn eventually spread the gospel in the palace. Later documents from early church history tell us that even some of the royal family became Christians.

If we look at Acts 23:11, we find that in spite of all that had happened, Paul received a vision one night in which the Lord stood by him and said: "Take courage! As you have testified about me in Jerusalem, so you must also testify in Rome." I love that verse because it shows that in spite of Paul's disobedience the Lord did not throw his failure up to him to taunt him with it, but rather appeared to him to cheer him up and let him know he was still useful.

That takes me back to those other biblical characters I mentioned at the start of this chapter. As in Paul's case, in spite of their sin and failures, most of which were far worse than Paul's, God did not end their service but rather worked again to bless them and those to whom they ministered. Each paid a price for his mistake. Moses spent forty years in the desert as an alien. Samson lost his sight. Jonah was thrown overboard and swallowed by a whale. David's family suffered. Peter was humiliated. But each was also used of God again—mightily. Moses led the people for an additional forty years. Samson destroyed Dagon's temple. Jonah preached to Nineveh. David ruled for years. Peter evangelized widely.

You and I also fall into sin. We are as stubborn, disobedient, and willful as these biblical characters seem to have been. But we should be encouraged by their stories. They teach us that the fact we have sinned does not mean we have been eliminated from God's service or have lost our chance for usefulness. Rather, our failures give renewed opportunity for God to display his great grace.

Whenever we have to deal with others who have been trapped in sin or who have failed for one reason or another, we should not approach them in a spirit of superiority to them. We know that we are not superior in any way. We must approach them in a spirit of humility and helpfulness in order to strengthen them. Paul said in Galatians, "Brothers, if someone is caught in a sin, you who are spiritual should restore him gently. But watch yourself, or you also may be tempted" (Gal. 6:1).

What this verse says to us is that in this business of living the Christian life, we need one another. There are times when one is strong and another is weak, when one is off the path but another is on it. But that can always be reversed. We, like others, can stumble and fall. We need to be humble and realize that we always need each other, just as we also always need the Lord.

42

Gentiles! Gentiles!

Acts 21:27–22:22

"'Lord,' I replied, 'these men know that I went from one synagogue to another to imprison and beat those who believe in you. And when the blood of your martyr Stephen was shed, I stood there giving my approval and guarding the clothes of those who were killing him.'
"Then the Lord said to me, 'Go; I will send you far away to the Gentiles.'"
The crowd listened to Paul until he said this. Then they raised their voices and shouted, "Rid the earth of him! He's not fit to live!"

Acts 22:19–22

Was Paul wrong in going to Jerusalem? There are two sides to the argument. Some commentators have pointed out that in Acts 20, when Paul said that the Holy Spirit had been warning him in every city that prison and hardships awaited him, the first part of the statement also says, "And now, compelled by the Spirit, I am going to Jerusalem" (v. 22). If that means that Paul was being led by the Holy Spirit to go to Jerusalem, it cancels out what I was saying in the last chapter. But it is ambiguous. One might argue that the words "compelled by the Spirit," since they lack the word "Holy" before "Spirit," merely refer to an inner compulsion on Paul's part. I think this is what it does mean.

Nevertheless, for this reason and perhaps for others, one has to be careful not to claim too dogmatically that Paul was disobeying God in going to Jerusalem.

On the other hand, I would insist that what Paul was prepared to do once he got to Jerusalem was unambiguously wrong. He may have been right in going up to the city. However, the leaders of the Jerusalem church proposed he go through the Jewish rites of purification and then offer a sacrifice for sin to demonstrate to the Jews that he was not opposed to Jewish laws and traditions. Paul agreed to do it, and he was in error for a number of reasons.

First, the idea of purification is wrong for Christians. We do not find anything in the New Testament about any rite of purification for Christians. What we do find in the New Testament is the command to confess our sins to God, which is quite a different thing. If we confess our sin to God pleading the blood of Jesus Christ, which has been shed for us, and when we ask forgiveness, we have the promise of God that "he is faithful and just and will forgive us our sins and purify us from all unrighteousness" (1 John 1:9). That is different from a purification rite. The reason Christians are not given rites of purification is that our purification is already provided through the work of Jesus. To go through some system of purification is a virtual repudiation of Christ's completed work.

Second, the rite also involved a sacrifice. It is referred to in Acts 21:26 as "an offering," but it was not what we mean by "an offering." When we say, "Let's receive an offering," we mean, "Let's take a collection, give money." It was an animal sacrifice, brought by the worshiper and handed to the priest. The worshiper confessed his sin over the head of the animal; then the animal was killed as a substitutionary sacrifice for the individual's sins.[1] It is almost inconceivable that Paul could have been prepared to do that. Yet he was.

We might plead that he did it with good motives. He loved the Jewish people, and he did not want a schism in the church between Jewish Christians and Gentile Christians. He wanted to hold the church together as well as show his love for Israel. But right motives do not make a wrong action right. They did not make this right.

What Paul should have done is what he had told the Galatians to do when they were faced with a similar but less serious problem. Legalizers from Jerusalem had come to the Galatian churches, saying that Gentiles could not be saved unless they kept the law of Moses. The focal point of the debate was circumcision. Paul argued in the Book of Galatians that if they were circumcised Christ would profit them nothing. He said, "Stand firm, then, and do not let yourselves be burdened again by a yoke of slavery" (Gal. 5:1). Yet here Paul himself became burdened.

In my opinion, the great proof that Paul was wrong was that God, who is sovereign over the details of our lives, did not allow him to do it. It is good that God intervenes like this. Sometimes you and I act wrongly. We are prepared to do wrong things—perhaps with good motives, but quite often with bad motives—and God simply slams the door on us. He will not let us do it, because what we do matters to God, even if at the moment it does not seem to matter a great deal to us.

Conflicting Forces

Paul was arrested as a result of an attempt by a Jerusalem mob to have him killed. Acts 21:27 says that this mob action began because some Jews from Asia saw Paul at the temple. Asia refers to the Roman province of Asia, what is now Turkey. Its capital city was Ephesus. Paul had spent a long time in Ephesus (see chapter 37 for a discussion of this period).

We are not told that the Jews who began this riot were from Ephesus. Luke only says they were from Asia. But the problems started when they recognized a man named Trophimus, who was from Ephesus. Since the Jews from Asia recognized Trophimus it is likely that they were from Ephesus too, and if they were from Ephesus, then they had undoubtedly been exposed to Paul's teaching and knew where he stood on Gentile observance of the Jewish laws.

Paul had been asked to compromise his position for the sake of Jewish-Gentile harmony, and he seemed to have been willing to assume the ceremonial law of Israel again, contrary to his own teaching and to the point of denying the finished work of Christ. But the Jews from the province of Asia knew him better than that. They had heard Paul teach. They knew where he stood and what he believed. So they said (rightly), We don't care whether or not Paul is going through a purification ceremony. We know perfectly well that what he really believes is that the Gentiles can be saved apart from the law of Moses.

They were wrong about Trophimus, however. The idea got around that because Trophimus was a Gentile and was in the city, and because Paul had gone into the temple area, where only Jews could go, somehow Paul must have brought Trophimus along. Luke makes clear that this was not the case. Nor would Paul have been foolish enough to have done it. Paul was trying to show his concern for the ceremonial laws of Judaism. He would not have violated the temple precincts by bringing in a Gentile.

When the Jews accused Paul, they gave the argument their own special twist, saying that Paul was teaching "all men everywhere against our people and our law and this place" (v. 28). Paul had not been doing that either. He had great respect for the law of Israel. But it was true that he was teaching that the Gentiles could be saved apart from keeping it.

The mob fell upon Paul while he was in the temple area. It dragged him out of the inner area where only Jews could go and into the courtyard of the Gentiles, where the rioters fell upon him in force. They would have killed him in a very short time if it were not that the Roman garrison was stationed next to the temple area. As soon as the riot started, someone must have reported it to the commander. He sent two groups of soldiers, each under a centurion (meaning there would have been about two hundred soldiers), out of the fortress into the courtyard and rescued Paul.

The commander was apparently a very able man, because he handled the situation well. When he had taken Paul into custody, keeping him from being murdered, he tried to find out from the crowd what it was Paul had done. But they were all shouting one thing and another. He was not able to understand them. So he concluded that the best thing was to take Paul inside and interrogate him. As he started to take Paul away the mob followed, shouting, "Away with him! Away with him!"

These were the same words they had used of Jesus Christ at the time of the crucifixion, and they did not mean, "Take him away from the temple area." They meant, "Remove him from the earth." They wanted him dead. This hatred of Paul was so fierce that the soldiers had to protect him forcibly as they worked themselves out of the crowd and into the fortress.

In Acts 23 we have a record of a letter the Roman commander wrote to the Roman Governor Felix, and the letter begins, in good ancient letter-writing style, with his name. His name was Claudius Lysias (v. 26). Although Claudius is a Latin name, Lysias is a Greek name and it indicates that this Roman commander was actually of Greek background. Lysias was his family name, but he had added to it the Latin name Claudius, no doubt because it was the name of the current emperor. This means that he must have spoken Greek as a first language.

As these soldiers were leading Paul into the barracks, Paul spoke to the commander in educated Greek, saying, "May I say something to you?" (21:37). The language of Judah was Aramaic; therefore, when Paul spoke to the commander in Greek, the commander was surprised and immediately said to Paul, "Do you speak Greek?" He didn't just mean, "Do you know the Greek language?" Many people spoke Greek. Because he himself was Greek, he meant, "You speak good Greek. Are you a Greek? I thought you were that Egyptian who was causing trouble around here a little while ago." Because Paul had been raised in Tarsus and spoke good Greek the officer supposed he was dealing with a Greek of good education and bearing.[2]

Paul identified who he was. "I am a Jew, from Tarsus in Cilicia, a citizen of no ordinary city" (v. 39). Then he asked permission to speak to the people. Under other circumstances this Roman commander probably would have said no. But Paul had impressed him as a reasonable, cultured man, and he said yes instead. He thought that there must have been some mistake, and he wanted to solve the problem. If Paul's speaking to them could clear it up, he was willing to have him go ahead.

Paul's Formal Defense

Paul gave a magnificent defense. He actually used the word "defense" (Acts 22:1). In Greek it is the word *apologia,* from which we get our word "apology." It refers to a formal defense of one's past life or actions.

The story of Paul's conversion is found several times in the New Testament, three times in Acts alone. It is in the ninth chapter, where it is presented historically in Luke's words. It is in this twenty-second chapter, where Paul defends himself in Jerusalem. This is a Hebrew version, spoken in Aramaic with Jewish overtones. Finally, it is in chapter 26, where Paul is appearing before the Roman governors Festus and Felix. There it has a Roman slant; it is a Gentile version.

We also find it twice more in Paul's letters. It appears in Philippians 3. This is what I call a theological version. It does not deal with the historical details but rather with the changes in Paul's thinking. Last of all, though much briefer, it is in 1 Timothy 1, where Paul is reminding Timothy of what had happened to him so that Timothy might be encouraged to bear a witness similar to Paul's. This is a hortatory version.

In Acts 22 the story of Paul's conversion has three parts: his past in Judaism (vv. 1–5), the conversion itself (vv. 6–16), and a record of what God said to him (vv. 17–21).

Confidence in the Flesh

When Paul speaks of his past we are reminded that apart from the single fact that he persecuted Christians Paul never thought of his background as something about which he needed to be ashamed. On the contrary, he spoke of it favorably. In Romans 9 he wrote about the advantages of being a Jew, saying, "Theirs is the adoption as sons; theirs the divine glory, the covenants, the receiving of the law, the temple worship and the promises. Theirs are the patriarchs, and from them is traced the human ancestry of Christ" (vv. 4–5). In Philippians he spoke more personally: "If anyone else thinks he has reasons to put confidence in the flesh, I have more: circumcised on the eighth day, of the people of Israel, of the tribe of Benjamin, a Hebrew of the Hebrews; in regard to the law, a Pharisee; as for zeal, persecuting the church; as for legalistic righteousness, faultless" (Phil. 3:4–6).

Paul uses some of the words that appear in Philippians in this account, which means that this must be the way Paul was accustomed to talking about his conversion. He was a pure-blooded Jew, and he was zealous for the traditions of his fathers. He emphasizes this zeal, saying that he was trained by the famous Rabbi Gamaliel. Everybody in Jerusalem would have known who Gamaliel was. Paul was not ashamed of his Jewish background, because God had chosen the Jewish people. Every spiritual advantage in history before the coming of Jesus Christ was with Judaism, and Paul was not afraid to acknowledge it.

There is a story in this respect about the great English politician and prime minister Disraeli. Disraeli was a Jew, and in Parliament he was once chided by an opposition leader for his Jewish background. His opponent said disparagingly, "You, sir, are a Jew."

Disraeli drew himself to his full height, which was not very great, and replied: "Yes, sir, that is true. I am a Jew. But I remind you, sir, that half of Christendom worships a Jew, and the other half a Jewess. And, sir, when your ancestors were gathering acorns in a German forest, my ancestors were giving law and religion to the world." It was a powerful and absolutely justified rebuff.

That is the way Paul thought. Yet, in spite of the fact that he had this heritage, in spite of the fact that he had been trained in the law—the law God gave for our benefit to restrain evil and direct us to the Messiah—Paul had been woefully off base because he had been trying to do as a Jew the same thing the Gentiles had been trying to do with their own non-biblical religions. He had been trying to establish a righteousness of his own that because he was a sinner was no true righteousness. He had been rejecting the salvation God provided.

Paul and Jesus

The second thing Paul talks about is his conversion, when Jesus appeared to him on the road to Damascus. Paul had been consumed by zeal for his religion. It has blinded him to what he was actually doing. But when Jesus appeared to him, he suddenly understood. God had stopped him short. Before this he had thought he was doing God's work. But when Jesus suddenly appeared to him, he learned that in persecuting Christians he had been persecuting the very Son of God, opposing what he was doing in the world.

From a purely human point of view it is remarkable that Paul was converted at all. (See chapter 17 concerning Lord Lyttleton's classic study of the apostle Paul's conversion.) So how was Paul converted? What explains it? The only possible answer: Paul was converted because the Lord Jesus Christ, the Lord of glory, not a myth created by the early Christians, appeared to him on the Damascus road.

Paul's Great Commission

On the Damascus road, when Paul asked what he was to do, Jesus replied that he was to take the gospel to the Gentiles. Paul takes a while to tell this part, because he must have sensed that for his hearers this would be the difficult part of his speech. He tells of going into Damascus, of the visit of Ananias, of receiving his sight again, of his subsequent journey to Jerusalem. At last he gets to the point of his commission, saying: "Then the Lord said to me, 'Go; I will send you far away to the Gentiles'" (v. 21).

That is where the speech stops, but not because Paul himself would have stopped there. It stops at that point because when Paul mentioned the word "Gentiles," those who had been listening quietly up to this point suddenly burst into turmoil, yelling, "Rid the earth of him! He's not fit to live!" (v. 22). The noise was so loud that there was no possibility of carrying the address further. The commander simply ordered the soldiers to bring Paul inside and prepare for an interrogation.

The commander did not understand what was happening, but he must have been impressed when Paul, who a moment earlier had spoken to him in fluent Greek, suddenly addressed the crowd in Aramaic. Besides, Paul did so with such rhetorical skill that he immediately succeeded in quieting the people down. The commander, being Greek and a Roman officer, probably did not understand Aramaic very well, but Paul's rhetorical abilities and initial success must have impressed him. Unfortunately, just when he thought things were under control, suddenly everybody burst out screaming. What in the world has this man said? he must have wondered. What has he done?

The only thing Paul had done was say: "Gentiles."

Why should that have upset them? He had been doing everything possible to stress how Jewish he was. He even gave the story of his conversion a Jewish emphasis: he pointed out that Ananias was a devout Jew. When Ananias came and talked to him, he talked in Jewish terms, according to Paul's account: "The God of our fathers has chosen you to know his will and to see the Righteous One" (v. 14). Paul did not even use the word "Jesus." He had done everything he could to bridge the gap; but as soon as he uttered the word "Gentiles," the mob reacted violently and would have killed him if it could have.

Why did they object to that word? They were objecting to Paul's persuasion that Gentiles could be saved without adhering to the law of Moses, without becoming Jews.

But God saves people his way, and his way is through Christ.

If you are a Gentile, you can come as a Gentile. But it must be through Jesus Christ alone.

If you are a Jew, you can come as a Jew. But you must come through Christ alone.

If you are an Englishman, you can come as an Englishman. But you must come through Christ.

If you are Japanese, you can come as a Japanese. But you must come through Christ.

Why must we come in this way and not in some other way? Why can't we invent our own way? It is because God sent Jesus Christ to be the Savior. This is how God has done it. So when we talk about the gospel today, we are not talking about a religious opinion, though the world would like to make it that. We are talking about reality, about truth. Once I talked to a woman on an airplane about spiritual things, and every time I said something about the gospel, she said, "But that's just your opinion."

I replied, "That's true, it is my opinion. But that's not the point. Whether it is my opinion or not does not matter. What matters is, is it true?"

When I explained something else the same thing happened. "But that's just your opinion," she said.

I replied, "Yes, that is my opinion. But the point is not whether it's my opinion or not. The point is, is it true?" We went on that way for about an hour, and at the end I knew even she was beginning to get it, because she was laughing. She knew what was coming.

Paul had met Jesus on the road to Damascus, and that meeting turned his life around. God sent Jesus Christ to be the Savior. If you rebel against that fact, you are doing exactly what the Jews did. You are not saying you have to become a Jew first, though you may say so if you are Jewish. But you are saying that you have to do something first and you want others to do it your way. If you are thinking like that, it is no wonder you despise and even hate a gospel as humbling as this gospel is.

It may be simple and it may be humbling, but it is still the gospel, and it is the way to be saved. May God give you grace to embrace it wholeheartedly.

43

God's Servant in Roman Hands

Acts 22:23–23:11

As they were shouting and throwing off their cloaks and flinging dust into the air, the commander ordered Paul to be taken into the barracks. He directed that he be flogged and questioned in order to find out why the people were shouting at him like this. As they stretched him out to flog him, Paul said to the centurion standing there, "Is it legal for you to flog a Roman citizen who hasn't even been found guilty?"

When the centurion heard this, he went to the commander and reported it. "What are you going to do?" he asked. "This man is a Roman citizen."

Acts 22:23–26

Paul had been a free ambassador of Jesus Christ for nearly twenty years, but in Acts 22 he passes from being a free man to being a prisoner of the Roman state. We would think that being in Roman hands would be worse than being in Jewish hands. But we soon discover that Paul was better off in the hands of the secular authorities than he would have been in the hands of his own people. They were trying to kill him, after all.

The section we are going to look at in this chapter has three parts. First, we see Paul and the Romans (Acts 22:23–29). Second, we see Paul and the

Jewish authorities, the Sanhedrin, who were the leaders of Paul's people (Acts 22:30–23:10). Third, we see Paul and the Lord (Acts 23:11).

Paul and His Captors

We have already looked at the opening scene of the drama (see chapter 42). Now we find that the commander had a problem. His job was to keep order in the city. To do so, he had to understand what was going on. Based on the crowd's reaction, he must have concluded that there was something Paul was guilty of but had not confessed. So he thought, The only way we're going to get to the bottom of this is by torture. I'll have to force this man to tell us what is causing the trouble, because until we do that, I'll never be able to restore order in the city.

Therefore, they took Paul away and stretched him out to flog him. This was not the normal Jewish flogging, which was bad enough, but the dreaded Roman flagellum. It was a beating so severe that in some cases it resulted in the death of the victim. It was what was done to Jesus before his crucifixion. As they were about to begin this dreaded punishment, Paul asked a question: "Is it legal for you to flog a Roman citizen who hasn't even been found guilty?" (22:25).

It was not lawful, of course, and Paul knew it. In fact, everyone knew it. So when the soldier in charge of the beating heard Paul's question he immediately broke off his preparation for the beating, went to the commander and said, You had better be careful. This man is a Roman citizen.

The officer went to Paul. Is this true? Are you a Roman? he asked.

Yes, I am.

That was not something anyone would lie about, of course. If a person claimed Roman citizenship falsely and was later discovered to have lied, the penalty was death. So if Paul said he was a Roman citizen, it was no doubt true. The officer assumed Paul could prove it.

The commander, now with quite a different attitude, began to converse with Paul, questioning him as to how he had secured his citizenship. He said, I had to pay a great price for mine. To judge by his name, Claudius Lysias, this man was a Greek who had probably purchased his citizenship during the reign of the emperor Claudius and had named himself after him. Claudius's administration had sold citizenships to raise money, and the commander had purchased such a citizenship.

But Paul replied that he had not had to purchase his citizenship. He had been born a Roman citizen.

This meant that Paul's father was a Roman citizen. We do not know how he had become one. He might have been awarded it because of some great service to the state; it might be that his father before him had been a Roman citizen; it might be that Paul's father had purchased his citizenship, in which case, Paul would have come from a family of some means, which we have reason for suspecting on other grounds. But we really do not know. All we know is that Paul was a citizen, and on the basis of that fact he was immediately spared the flogging. It had even been a fault to have bound him, but that was a lesser offense and was forgotten. Certainly Paul was not about to press it.

When we see the Roman government functioning wisely and according to the law as it did in these circumstances, we see the state functioning as it should function.

What is the role of the state? In the Western world, we have fanciful ideas of what we think the state should do for us today. But the role of the state as the Bible speaks about it is just two-fold. The state exists: (1) to establish, maintain, and assure justice; and (2) to provide for the defense of its citizens. Justice and defense. And, of course, that is exactly what this Roman commander, operating on behalf of the Roman government, had done or was in the process of doing. There can be different kinds of disorder. There can be disorder without; then the state must defend its citizens against enemies. There can be disorder within; then it has to defend against internal chaos. In this case, the disorder was within, and the commander had intervened rightly to save Paul and stop the riot.

Moreover, he was concerned with justice. That is, he was operating under the strictures of explicit Roman law. In fact, when he later called the Sanhedrin together to find out what their accusation against Paul may have been, he was trying to push this concern for justice even further.

The problem today is that we look to the state for things the state was never intended to do. And the state, perhaps in part as a result of its mistaken attempt to do these other things, sometimes neglects the two things for which it is chiefly responsible. We have entered into a time in American history when people want the state to provide them with security. They expect the state to care for them from the cradle to the grave. But the state was never meant to do that. As a matter of fact, when we are talking about the care of people, this care is a duty God has given to his people, the church, and to families, which have a moral obligation to care for their own members. This is not something the state should do. Nor can the state do it well, even if it tries.

The tragedy of our day is not only that we look to the state to do things that we are supposed to do ourselves (and can do much better than the state can, if we will do them), but that the state also is failing to do the things God created it to do. Defense from enemies? Yes, if what we are thinking about is enemies without. But no, if we are thinking of dangers and turmoil within the country. And justice? It is in this area that our system fails most. I believe we are going to have to face this fact increasingly in the years to come.

As I look back over the last ten or twenty years, I remember a time when the minorities in our country were saying something like this: "You speak of justice and you think you live in a country that provides for justice, but that is only because you are well off. Minorities don't get justice; the poor don't get justice. Only the rich get justice." I remember thinking then that it was a basically unfair accusation. There may be miscarriages of justice among the poor, I acknowledged, and certainly the poor do not get quite the same attention as the rich, since they are unable to pay for it. But it is not really true to say that only the rich get justice. Certainly we are a nation ruled by law.

However, as the years have gone by, I have become increasingly aware that there was and continues to be much truth in that early accusation—at least, there is more truth to it than we would like to think. Most of us have never been in a legal proceeding and therefore do not know how much money it takes to pursue a case or defend oneself against an accusation. Just get sued, and you will find out how difficult and how expensive it is to defend yourself legally. What I am saying is that today justice is often not at all a matter of right or law but of money. Do you have enough money to sustain your case? That is what it boils down to.

I know of a Christian organization that was sued by another organization for the sole purpose of trying to destroy it because of what it was saying. The discovery phase of the case alone cost the first group $400,000. (A discovery phase is an exploratory period in which the lawyers on both sides try to uncover facts.) This discovery phase took $400,000 because the second organization kept it up for so long, subpoenaing everyone even tangentially related to the case. They did this because they had sufficient funds, and the first organization, the Christian organization, did not. The trial was going to cost an additional $100,000. When the time for the trial came around, the Christian group had run out of money. So all they could do was go into chapter 11 status and declare bankruptcy. The case went to their opponents by default. This is not justice.

When we look at the Roman Empire we tend to exclaim, "What a cruel empire it was." It was capable of great cruelty. But when I look at how the authorities dealt with Paul in this instance I find a state that for all its ignorance of the true God was nevertheless operating quite correctly.

Paul and the Sanhedrin

We move to the second stage of the story, and here we find Paul with his own people, represented by the Sanhedrin. The Roman commander, who recognized that he still did not have the full story and could not understand why the Jews were so incensed against Paul, commanded the Sanhedrin to make a case. The text says, "The commander wanted to find out exactly why Paul was being accused by the Jews" (Acts 22:30). He must have thought that once he had a concrete accusation he would be able to decide what to do.

There is a contrast here between the Romans on the one hand, into whose custody Paul had fallen, and the Sanhedrin, the leaders of God's people, on the other. The Romans were promoting justice and maintaining order, or trying to. But it was entirely different in the Jewish court. Neither a concern for justice nor the maintenance of the public order was present. These men were not interested in justice. They just wanted to get rid of Paul. If one were to seek justice in this situation, he or she would be far more likely to get it from the Romans. The Jews weren't interested in order either! The disorder that had taken place in the courtyard of the temple the day before and was repeated even after Paul's address to the people in Aramaic now burst forth even on the floor of this august assembly.

Paul's Conscience

Paul was brought before the Sanhedrin and was given a chance to speak. He began, "My brothers, I have fulfilled my duty to God in all good conscience to this day . . ." (Acts 23:1). That was undoubtedly only the opening line of an address Paul was prepared to deliver. But he didn't get a chance to make his defense. The presiding high priest, Ananias, a secular and most ungodly man who perished during the Jewish rebellion at the hands of his own people, ordered those standing near Paul to strike Paul on the mouth, so incensed was he that this great apostle to the Gentiles would claim that he possessed a clear conscience.

Paul's claim to have lived "in all good conscience to this day" (v. 1) is a striking and bold statement. People have read that and reacted incredulously, asking, "How in the world could Paul say that? What in the world was he thinking of?" He had been in great error during his days in Judaism, as he himself admits. He had persecuted the church. He was instrumental in the death of some of its most important members, including Stephen, the first martyr. How could Paul say, I have lived all my life up until now in good conscience?

The answer is that Paul had indeed lived in good conscience. He was very wrong, of course; it required the intervention of the Lord Jesus Christ to show him how wrong he was. But in those early days, Paul did not think he was wrong. He fervently believed he was right. That is why he could say, when he summed up his life in Judaism, "As for legalistic righteousness, [I was] faultless" (Phil. 3:6). He wasn't faultless in God's sight. But so far as he knew, he had lived in good conscience.

While conscience is something to which we can and should listen, it is not an infallible guide to right conduct. Conscience will tell you that you should not do what is wrong and that you should do what is right, but conscience alone cannot tell you what is right or what is wrong. It is only the Bible, the written Word of God, that can teach you that. When you have the Bible and when the Holy Spirit is shining on its pages teaching you what you should do, then conscience will tell you that you ought to do it. But if you do not have the Word of God, then even though conscience will tell you to do the right thing, you will not know what the right thing is and you will err, as Paul had done.

Paul and Ananias

To strike an unconvicted person was illegal, of course, as Paul, who was a well instructed Pharisee, knew. He retorted, "God will strike you, you whitewashed wall. You sit there to judge me according to the law, yet you yourself violate the law by commanding that I be struck!" (v. 3).

What commandment of the law was Paul referring to when he claimed that the high priest had caused him to be struck illegally? There is no verse in the Old Testament exactly like this, but Paul may have been thinking of Leviticus 19:15. A contemporary saying ran: "He who strikes the cheek of an Israelite strikes, as it were, the glory of God."[1] Whatever the reasoning was, Paul's point was obviously valid. Until Paul was convicted he could not rightly be punished.

When Paul rebuked the high priest for his illegal action, someone who was standing nearby reproached him for speaking to the high priest disrespectfully. Paul had not known that he was speaking to the high priest. But once he was told this had been the case, he admitted that his remark had been improper. He said, "Brothers, I did not realize that he was the high priest; for it is written: 'Do not speak evil about the ruler of your people'" (v. 5). The reference is to Exodus 22:28.

Why didn't Paul recognize the high priest? After all, he was looking "straight at the Sanhedrin," according to verse 1.

Several answers have been given. Some have suggested that Paul could not see very well. We have reason for suspecting this on other grounds. For example, Galatians 6:11 says, "See what large letters I use as I write to you with my own hand!" This may mean only that Paul was not a good writer; he did not use small, neat letters as a trained scribe would. But the verse might also mean that he could not see to write small and so wrote large and laboriously. If that is the case, Paul had looked toward the Sanhedrin but could not see that it was the high priest who had commanded that he be struck.

The second explanation is that Paul was being sarcastic. That is, when he said, "I did not realize that he was the high priest," he meant that a true high priest would never talk as he had.

The third explanation is probably the best: Paul had simply been away from Jerusalem for twenty years, had never gotten to know Ananias personally, and therefore did not recognize him. We find that a bit hard to imagine today because our leaders have their pictures in the newspapers and we see them on television all the time. But mass media did not exist then, and even though Paul had been in Pharisaic circles twenty years earlier, he would not necessarily have mingled with the higher-ups like Ananias. Whatever the case, Paul did not recognize Ananias on this occasion, and when he was rebuked, he immediately placed himself beneath the law, which he, of course, was anxious to uphold.

The Resurrection

Paul's first attempt at a defense had been turned aside by this exchange, but he was resourceful and did something brilliant. Knowing that some of the rulers were Sadducees—they were the modernists of their day—and others were Pharisees—conservatives—he raised a doctrinal matter that was in dispute among them. "My brothers, I am a Pharisee, the son of a Pharisee. I stand on trial because of my hope in the resurrection of the dead" (v. 6). This was a blatant pitch for the Pharisees' support, and it worked, because the Pharisees immediately began to argue that Paul was all right after all. We don't find anything wrong with him, they said. The Sadducees, being confronted by one who was both politically dangerous and in their view heretical, immediately took issue with the Pharisees and there was a new falling out.

The poor Roman commander did not seem to be getting anywhere.

Some commentators are very unhappy with what Paul did here. For example, W. A. Farrar says that it was unworthy of Paul to have acted in such an unscrupulous manner. It was a case of his stooping to a dirty trick when he threw out something irrelevant merely to divide the assembly.[2]

This was not the case. The riot that led to Paul's arrest had been caused by people claiming that he had brought a Gentile into the temple area. That was against Jewish law. But Paul had not done that, and in fact, the Sanhedrin never accused him of it. The reason is that fundamentally that was not the real problem. The real problem was actually wrapped up in this whole matter of the resurrection.

When we talk about the resurrection (and when Paul talked about it) we are not merely talking about the resurrection of Jesus Christ, though it has bearing on the subject. The resurrection of Jesus proves a general resurrection. Rather, we are talking about resurrection itself. And what that means, to put it in contemporary terms, is that there is a reality beyond what we see and know physically. Our age focuses on what is visible. It only believes in what it can observe. So the great division in our day (as in Paul's) is between those who are willing to be bound only by what they can see, measure, touch, and feel, and those who believe there is something beyond what is tangible, something that is intangible and has to do with God.

Francis Schaeffer, one of the great apologists of our age, described this division as those who are above and those who are below a "line of despair." This line has been drawn through all areas of thought: in philosophy, art, literature, and science. Before that line was drawn people were willing to reason about spiritual things. Dialogue could take place. But once that line was drawn, faith was separated from reason. And now, although a person can still talk about God, for most of our contemporaries spiritual things no longer have any tangible meaning. They are just one's opinion.[3]

People in our world, particularly in our universities, say, "If we cannot observe God, we must discount him. He exists only in some fantasy land of the imagination." Christians do not agree with this. We believe in an unseen world, a world linked metaphysically and rationally to the truth of the resurrection. Therefore, Christians must be able to stand up and say, along lines similar to Paul's speech, "I believe in the resurrection of the dead."

Paul and the Lord

In the last verse of this section (Acts 23:11), we find Paul with the Lord, that is, with the risen Jesus in whom his very skeptical world (and ours) would not and will not believe. It tells us that "the following night the Lord stood near Paul and said, 'Take courage! As you have testified about me in Jerusalem, so you must also testify in Rome.'"

I suppose that when the Lord Jesus Christ spoke those words to Paul, all he was really doing was giving a specific application of what he had said earlier to the disciples in the Great Commission (Matt. 28:18–20).

Jesus did not say, "Well, Paul, you did a very good job. Thank you. Now you're off duty because, after all, you've been arrested." No, he said, I have called you to be a witness, and that is what you shall be. You have witnessed here. You will witness in Rome also. You are to be a witness for me until the day you die.

And Paul was! Paul witnessed to the grace of God in Jesus Christ until the day of his death, and God blessed that witness. Moreover, the Lord Jesus Christ stood with him and strengthened him as he made it.

When I look at the world and think of the way our culture has fallen away not only from spiritual values but even from rationality, I can almost find myself sinking down into despair. I ask myself, How can anyone speak to a culture like ours? How can anyone speak reasonable spiritual words to those who will not reason, or even listen? Humanly speaking, I suppose the task is impossible. But we are not left to merely human resources. Jesus says, Take courage! Don't give up! Keep witnessing! I am with you, and I will bless your witness, even to the end of the age.

When Paul stood before the representatives of Rome, he appealed to his Roman citizenship. When he stood before the Sanhedrin he appealed to his conscience. But over and above that and at all times, Paul appealed to and relied on the Lord. If we rely on the Lord, he will be with us also, give us the words we need to speak, and bless that witness, however uncertain and stammering, to the conversion of other needy individuals.

44

The Plot to Murder Paul

Acts 23:12–35

The next morning the Jews formed a conspiracy and bound themselves with an oath not to eat or drink until they had killed Paul. More than forty men were involved in this plot . . .

But when the son of Paul's sister heard of this plot, he went into the barracks and told Paul.

Acts 23:12–16

Some years ago, I heard a sermon on marriage in which the minister began by saying, "This sermon is for everybody who is married and for those who hope to be." I thought when I heard it that the introduction included just about everybody and so was a good attention getter. Yet what I have to say in this chapter is of even broader application. It is possible that there are people reading this who are not, never have been, and do not even hope to be married. Yet what I say here is for even those people. It is about hardships, about the difficult times in life that come to all.

You may think now, especially if things are going well for you, that there are not going to be any difficulties in your life. But there are going to be, if you have not had them already. The Book of Job says, "Man is born to trouble

379

as surely as sparks fly upward" (Job 5:7). That is a poetic way of saying that hardships are a normal part of life, for Christians as well as others. So hardships will come eventually, just as they came to the apostle Paul. What we are going to see in this chapter is how Paul went through his hard times and how God took care of him.

When God Is Silent

Paul had begun to experience some of these dark days already. Even when he was free, traveling from city to city to preach, he experienced difficult and uncomfortable circumstances. On more than one occasion he was the victim of mob action. He was beaten, stoned. Later he is going to be shipwrecked. Yet during those earlier days he was at least free. Now he has entered into a period of his life in which he is imprisoned. He does not have liberty to travel, and the days of incarceration in Jerusalem, Caesarea, and eventually Rome become quite long. Paul was imprisoned for two years in Caesarea and for another two years in Rome, at a minimum. So, including travel time, Paul was in Roman custody for at least five years, and possibly longer.

After Paul had spoken to the Sanhedrin, Jesus appeared to him to say, "Take courage! As you have testified about me in Jerusalem, so you must also testify in Rome" (23:11). That is a New Testament equivalent of God's appearing to Abraham after he had rescued his nephew Lot from the four kings of the east who had attacked and overthrown Sodom, Gomorrah, Admah, Zeboiim, and Zoar. Abraham had won the battle through a surprise attack. But he was in danger of a full retaliatory assault from the superior force. God told him, "Do not be afraid, Abram. I am your shield, your very great reward" (Gen. 15:1). That must have been a tremendous comfort to Abraham, as God's words on this later occasion must have been to Paul.

But in this story Jesus does not appear to Paul or speak to him, so far as we know from anything mentioned either in Acts or in Paul's letters. Paul has no special revelation, no direct word of comfort during the events that are recorded in this chapter.

In his study of Acts Harry Ironside points to this lack, making it an introduction to what he says about living through dark times. He says that there are days in our lives when not only do things seem dark, but also God does not seem to be speaking to us. He seems silent and remote. Does that mean that God has forgotten us or does not care what is happening? Ironside says quite rightly, "God is never closer to his people than when they cannot see his face."[1] That is gloriously true. But there are still those dark times when we seem merely to be plodding along in some weary path from day to day, and we wish somehow we could break out of it.

What do we do in these times? We live by the words we have received from God earlier. And what that means in our case is that we are to live by the Bible, for that is where God has spoken and continues to speak.

"Do not be afraid," God told Abraham.

"Take courage!" Jesus told Paul. These words were not repeated. But they had been spoken, and they were meant to remain with these men and strengthen them to trust God in the difficulties.

By now you have the drift of where I am heading. What I want to say is that those words were also spoken for you. If you are going through hard times, as many are (or if you are anticipating them), you are to live by faith in these promises and trust God, who gave them.

The Conspiracy against Paul

The story is straightforward. Paul had been attacked by the Jerusalem mob and almost been lynched. Paul was taken into Roman custody, and it would have seemed to all who were in Jerusalem, Jews and Romans alike, that in the keeping of this large military force Paul was now certainly very safe.

Yet there were men in the city known as zealots who were determined that the apostle should not escape their hands. There were about forty of them, and they got together to take an oath that they would not eat or drink until they had killed Paul. They went to the chief priests and elders, said what they had done, and made this suggestion: "Now then, you and the Sanhedrin petition the commander to bring him [Paul] before you on the pretext of wanting more accurate information about his case. We are ready to kill him before he gets here" (vv. 14–15).

The zealots of Paul's day were the equivalent of what we call terrorists. Their cause was the deliverance of their people from Roman occupation and control, and they proceeded exactly the way terrorists do in our time. They were secretive. Nobody could be certain who they were. They operated apart from the law. They were violent. They were ready to do anything they thought necessary to accomplish their political objectives, particularly assassinating people.

It has been suggested that Judas, who was a member of Christ's band of disciples, was in his earlier days one of these zealots. This is because his last name, Iscariot, may be a reference to these men and their activities. Iscariot means "assassin." That it refers to the zealots is uncertain, because Iscariot could also be a place name; it could mean only that Judas came from a place called Iscariot. Yet it seems more likely that in his early days before he met Jesus, Judas was something of a zealot. This might even explain his later betrayal of Christ. If in his early years of following Jesus he was thinking of Jesus as being a Messiah who would accomplish his political goals by driving out the Romans and if along the way he discovered that this was not what Jesus intended to do, then he might well have been disaffected and angry enough to betray him. This theory is uncertain, as I said. But it would be an example of the fierce type of character the zealots had.

Some have questioned whether the zealots could have cooperated with the Sanhedrin, as the zealots seem to have done in this story, since they were not supportive of the Sanhedrin. They were fanatics, and they considered the rulers of the Jews to be compromisers. As a matter of fact, there were times in Jewish history when they were violently and openly opposed to the Sanhedrin's policies. Ananias, the high priest who presided over the Sanhedrin, exemplified a spirit of cooperation with Rome. So at the time of the Jewish rebellion against Rome a decade or so later than this story, when the zealots managed to take over the city of Jerusalem, they murdered Ananias because of his policies. How could men like this cooperate, even for such a limited objective, with those who were their actual enemies?

The answer is that they could, just as terrorists today will cooperate with various governments temporarily for their own, sometimes quite antagonistic, objectives. Terrorists are a threat to their own governments as well as to the external enemies they oppose, but sometimes terrorists are in some ways useful to these governments. Because they are useful the governments shield them and allow them to operate under the blanket of their own political authority. Certain Near Eastern governments do so today. That cooperation was going on in Jerusalem. The Sanhedrin hated Paul for his teaching. If the zealots, for whatever reason, wanted to kill him, the Sanhedrin was willing to cooperate with them to this extent.

We are trying to apply this passage to ourselves, so let me say that I would be very surprised if anyone who reads this has a band of fanatical people literally united against him or her today. For most of us these are very different times.

Still it is worthwhile noting that although we may not have a band of forty terrorists trying to kill us we nevertheless have a far greater enemy than that. Our enemy is Satan, whom the Bible describes as "a roaring lion looking for someone to devour" (1 Peter 5:8). Satan is an extremely fierce foe, and he is all the more dangerous because he is a spiritual being and we cannot see him. Moreover, although Satan is for himself and not others, not even for the world itself in its opposition to God, there is nevertheless a certain cooperation between Satan and the world so that Satan uses it and the world uses him. These two, the world and the devil, are allied against us in much the same way that these Jewish terrorists were allied with the Sanhedrin against Paul.

In fact, Satan and the world have a beachhead for their evil in us. In Christian theology this is spoken of as "the inclination of the flesh," which means a natural inclination toward evil because we are sinful beings. That is why temptation is said to come to us from "the world, the flesh, and the devil." They are a formidable alliance.

Formidable! But not invincible, and destined not to win ultimately. The enemies of the apostle did not succeed in their plan, and neither the world, the flesh, nor the devil will succeed in overthrowing us.

God's Provision for Paul

Paul had a nephew, the son of his sister, who was living in Jerusalem. Up to this point in Acts and in all we may have read from the pen of Paul himself we have been given not the slightest information about Paul's family. All we know is that Paul received his Roman citizenship from his father, who was therefore obviously a Roman before him. There are places in Paul's writings where we might have expected him to write about his family. They were Jewish. How had they reacted to his conversion to Christianity? we might wonder. How did his father take to it? He had invested a great deal in Paul's education. He had sent him to the best universities; he had given him the best religious training. Paul had become a distinguished rabbi. He was on his way up among his people when suddenly he went over to the other side. We may suppose his family disinherited him.

Did Paul have brothers?

Did he make an attempt to see his family during his travels throughout Asia?

Suddenly, in the midst of the story, here is a boy who is Paul's nephew. And not only is this boy present in Jerusalem, perhaps having been sent to Jerusalem to study as Paul had been sent years earlier, but he is also somehow privy to things that are going on in the Sanhedrin. He overhears the plot against Paul and learns of the Sanhedrin's willingness to become involved.

This small fact may indicate, incidentally, that Paul's family was rich and had contacts with the most important people in Judaism. If they had sent Paul's nephew to Jerusalem to study the same way they had sent Paul to Jerusalem years before and if the boy seems to have had access to the Sanhedrin, Paul's may have been a very distinguished family indeed.

When Paul's nephew heard the plan he went to the military barracks and told Paul. For his part, Paul asked the soldier who was guarding him to take the boy to the commander to whom he would tell his story. The soldier did it. The commander heard the story and immediately acted to remove Paul from danger.

The God of Small Things

Here we have another of those startling biblical cases where God, who is able to use the great as well as the little things of life, uses small things to accomplish his purposes.

A woman I have known for a long time once told me something about her background that I had not heard before. She said, "God used a horse to bring me to the Savior." She saw the puzzled look on my face and asked, "Haven't I ever told you that story?"

"No, you haven't."

"Well," she said, "my daughter got interested in horses and joined an equestrian team, where she met a Christian who was one of the other riders and a competitor. He led my daughter to the Lord. Then my daughter helped me to find the Lord too."

I wonder if you have ever thought about this in terms of the Bible's stories. God does not hesitate to use small objects for his purposes. When he made the first man, Adam, in Eden, he made him from the dust of the ground, stooping to collect and form it. He could have used some more noble substance, I suppose. But in order that we might be reminded later, "Dust you are and to dust you will return" (Gen. 3:19), he chose dust.

When God revealed himself to Moses to call him to be the deliverer of his people, he appeared in a burning bush on a hillside in a remote, barren area of the world.

When he sent David to kill the Philistine giant, Goliath, it was with a sling and five small stones.

Samson killed a thousand Philistines with a jawbone of a donkey.

Many of the great people of the Bible were, at least in their early days, hardly great people at all. Abraham, the father of the faith, worshiped idols until God revealed himself to him.

Moses was a son of slave parents, killed an Egyptian, and spent the next forty years in the desert as a shepherd.

David was the youngest son in an obscure family in an obscure town in Judah. Yet God called this nobody to be the greatest king of all.

Most striking, when God was ready to send his own Son to earth, he chose a poor virgin of Nazareth to be his Son's mother.

That is the way God operates. If that is the way God operates, if God delights in using little things, then God can use us, however small or apparently insignificant we may be. Paul states this principle in 1 Corinthians 1:

> Think of what you were when you were called. Not many of you were wise by human standards; not many were influential; not many were of noble birth. But God chose the foolish things of the world to shame the wise; God chose the weak things of the world to shame the strong. He chose the lowly things of this world and the despised things—and the things that are not—to nullify the things that are, so that no one may boast before him.
>
> vv. 26–29

If that is true, then there is hope for each of us.

In this story, God used Paul's nephew to save Paul.

Don't ever say, especially when you go through dark periods, "Things are really bad for me. I am not accomplishing anything. God cannot use somebody like me, especially not in the circumstances in which I find myself now." It is usually people like us in circumstances like ours that God uses.

The God of Circumstances

In this story, not only was the boy in Jerusalem, which was significant in itself, but he also happened to be in the right place at just the right time.

Do you think of circumstances as being things that are against you— something that God cannot control? Have you ever found yourself thinking, If the circumstances of my life were different, perhaps then I could have been somebody or could have done something great for God or could have triumphed in the particular difficulty in which I am now? Do not think that way. Circumstances do not limit God. Circumstances are not independent of God. God creates circumstances. God is the master of circumstances.

Think of the amazing circumstances in Joseph's life that God used to raise him from the pit of slavery to become the prime minister of Egypt: circumstances as small as the fancy coat his father gave him that provoked his brothers' jealousy; the fact that the cistern in Shechem was dry at the season of the year he was thrown into it so that he did not drown but his life was preserved; circumstances that involved the passing of the Midianite caravan at precisely that moment so that his brothers said, Look, here's a caravan on its way to Egypt. Let's not kill him. Let's sell him and make money out of this; circumstances as small as his being purchased, not by a person of little importance in Egypt, but by Potiphar, the captain of Pharaoh's guards; the circumstance of the attachment that Mrs. Potiphar had for him; the accusation that caused him to be thrown into prison—not just any prison either, but the one where the political prisoners were kept; circumstances so small as the chief cupbearer and the chief baker being imprisoned along with him, and their having dreams, and the fact that he was able to interpret their dreams.

When the chief cupbearer was restored to his position in Pharaoh's court he forgot Joseph, who had interpreted his dream favorably. Two years passed—two dark years for Joseph, who was languishing in prison. But one day Pharaoh himself had a dream and the cupbearer was there to remember that Joseph had been able to interpret his dream earlier and so spoke about Joseph to Pharaoh. They sent for Joseph, and he became the second highest power in the land.

Insignificant circumstances? Yes, but circumstances that were created and were being used by God. So do not say, "God cannot deal with my circumstances; they are too complicated, too difficult, too depressing." It is probably in those very circumstances that God wants to work through you. He has a way of using many kinds of circumstances to bring people to faith and glorify his own great name.

The Night Trip to Caesarea

When the commander received word of what was up, he did what he could. It was his job to keep Paul safe; so he prepared an escort for him. It is amusing to read about it:

> He called two of his centurions and ordered them, "Get ready a detachment of two hundred soldiers, seventy horsemen and two hundred spearmen to go to Caesarea at nine tonight. Provide mounts for Paul so that he may be taken safely to Governor Felix."
>
> Acts 23:23–24

Think of it! This man assembled four hundred and seventy of the "crack" troops of the Roman army: foot soldiers, spearmen, even cavalry to escort Paul safely out of town. And Paul had horses (plural) too. He did not even have to walk.

This mighty company took him by night about thirty-five miles downhill from Jerusalem to a staging area for troops that had been built by Herod. It was called Antipatris. There, the greatest danger being behind them, the men on foot left Paul and returned to the Jerusalem garrison while those who were on horseback went on to Caesarea.

The Roman commander in Jerusalem wrote a letter to the Governor, whose name was Felix and who resided in Caesarea. Felix was the corrupt brother of Claudius's freedman Pallas and was at this time married to Drusilla, the daughter of Herod Agrippa I. Felix was the procurator of Judea from A.D. 52 to 59. He was ruthless in quelling Jewish uprisings, and though he was a freedman he seems never to have outgrown his slavish mentality. The Roman historian Tacitus wrote that he wielded "the power of a king with all the instincts of a slave."[2]

The letter is interesting because while it is basically accurate it is nevertheless at the same time rather self-serving, as official correspondence tends to be. The commander wrote, "This man was seized by the Jews and they were about to kill him, but I came with my troops and rescued him . . ." Thus far the letter is absolutely accurate. But it continues, ". . . for I had learned that he is a Roman citizen." It was true that Paul was a Roman citizen and that the commander had learned this. But he had learned it after the rescue, not before. He carefully leaves out that he had already bound Paul and was about to have him flogged before he learned it.

All the same, the letter was generally accurate, and the commander had acted responsibly in dealing with this volatile situation.

When Paul was moved to Caesarea, he was able to speak about Jesus to kings. Twenty years before, the Lord had said that he was to carry his name "before the Gentiles and their kings" (Acts 9:15), and now that promise began to be fulfilled. Paul had not testified before kings when he was free. But now as a prisoner, who we might say was a victim of circumstances, Paul testifies in Acts 24 before Governor Felix, in Acts 25 before Governor Festus, and eventually in Acts 26 before King Agrippa—all before he was taken to Rome.

I cannot tell you what God is doing in your circumstances. I cannot see the future any more than you can. But God *is* doing something in your circumstances. And if you are going through dark times, as Paul was, if you are discouraged, if the way seems dark, if you are weary with the struggle, the message of this chapter is to continue to trust in God and serve him regardless. His purposes for you will be accomplished, the day will brighten, and the will of God will be done.

45

The Trial before Felix

Acts 24:1-27

Five days later the high priest Ananias went down to Caesarea with some of the elders and a lawyer named Tertullus, and they brought their charges against Paul before the governor. When Paul was called in, Tertullus presented his case before Felix: "We have enjoyed a long period of peace under you, and your foresight has brought about reforms in this nation. Everywhere and in every way, most excellent Felix, we acknowledge this with profound gratitude. But in order not to weary you further, I would request that you be kind enough to hear us briefly.

"We have found this man to be a troublemaker, stirring up riots among the Jews all over the world. He is a ringleader of the Nazarene sect and even tried to desecrate the temple; so we seized him. By examining him yourself you will be able to learn the truth about all these charges we are bringing against him."

Acts 24:1-8

In the twenty-fourth chapter of Acts Paul finally testifies before the rulers of the world (see chapter 44 concerning Paul's trip to Caesarea). Paul's appearance before Governor Felix is recounted in some detail and includes in Luke's account the accusation brought against Paul, Paul's defense, and the response of the governor to Paul's presentation of the gospel.

387

The Case against Paul

Felix was the Roman governor. He had status, but his background had not been particularly distinguished. He had been a slave, then became a freedman under Claudius. He pandered to the depravity of the emperor and rose in the court until he was finally awarded the governorship of Judah. He was corrupt in his administration and was hated by the Jews. His time as governor was characterized by graft. His wife was a teenager whom he stole from another king. Finally, the corruption of his rule became so great that Nero, who was no great model of morality himself, recalled him. He would have been executed if his brother, who was in Rome at the time, had not pleaded on his behalf. This was the man before whom Paul now appeared to give an accounting.[1]

Five days had passed. During that time the Sanhedrin had gotten their case together and responded to the invitation to come to Caesarea to press their charges against Paul before the governor. They brought a lawyer with them whose name was Tertullus. Tertullus is a Roman name, but that is all we know about him. People who know the Greek language thoroughly say they detect certain Latinisms in his speech (vv. 2–8).[2] E. M. Blaiklock believes, no doubt rightly, that in Acts we have a Greek translation of a Latin speech. Tertullus was a professional orator, which is what the lawyers of the day tended to be. He had been hired by the Jews to present their case in Caesarea before the Roman governor.

Luke probably gives a condensed form of what was said, just as he has done with other speeches in the book. But if his condensation of Tertullus's speech reflects the proportions of what this man actually said, we can assume that half of his address was given to flattery of the governor. He said, "We have enjoyed a long period of peace under you, and your foresight has brought about reforms in this nation. Everywhere and in every way, most excellent Felix, we acknowledge this with profound gratitude." That was sheer hypocrisy, of course. The Sanhedrin hated this man. And corrupt and vain as he must have been, I suppose that even Felix was shrewd enough to have listened with tongue in cheek. What is it that these Jewish leaders are after that they should come all the way from Caesarea and flatter me in this fashion? he must have wondered.

It soon became clear. They wanted the governor to kill Paul. They had several charges against him, which their lawyer skillfully developed.

1. *He is a troublemaker.* A literal translation of "troublemaker" would be "pest," but it was stronger than what pest usually means for us today. For us "pest" usually means a nuisance. But in earlier days of the English language, "pest" meant "plague," an idea that we preserve in the stronger but somewhat archaic word "pestilence." What they were saying was that Paul was a plague of mammoth proportions. He was an infectious disease. He spread contagion. Tertullus was suggesting that if Paul were set free, he would spread turmoil, disorder, and maybe even rebellion throughout the empire.

This was the charge the Jewish rulers had brought against Jesus Christ at the time of his trial, and for the same reasons. They knew that the Romans were not interested in religious matters but were intensely concerned about anything that might stir up trouble. Before Pilate the Jews accused Jesus of making himself a king to rival Caesar, and here before Felix they accused Paul of causing turmoil.

2. *He is a ringleader of the Nazarene sect.* Each of these words was loaded with strongly negative connotations, as the reader is at once aware. Paul was a follower of Jesus, of course. But even at this early date, the Jews apparently wanted to avoid using Jesus' name. He was just "the Nazarene." Moreover, Tertullus did not even refer to Paul as a follower of the Nazarene. It was the Nazarene "sect" instead. "Sect" has overtones of heresy. Finally, Tertullus called Paul a "ringleader." He could as easily have said "leader," but he didn't. He said ringleader because the word had the same overtones for them as it has for us. They were saying that Paul was whipping up this troublesome heresy that for some unknown reason had grown up within Judaism.

3. *He tried to desecrate the temple.* This third charge was not true; Paul had not tried to desecrate the temple. This was only the mob's accusation. Yet now, in telling the story, Tertullus distorted the truth even further. "So we seized him," he said. He meant, "We arrested him because he had tried to desecrate the temple." But that is not what had happened. The mob had fallen upon Paul and was trying to kill him. The people who had actually arrested Paul were the Romans, and they did it in order to save his life.

Those were the charges. Paul is a troublemaker (we don't need any of those; we've had enough already). He is a ringleader of the sect of the Nazarenes (we all hate heresy). He has tried to desecrate our temple (even Rome acknowledges that to be a sacrilege). Perhaps Tertullus thought he could score points with the last accusation, because Roman law gave special status to the Jewish temple and even prescribed the death penalty for those who violated it.

Tertullus had made his accusation. He sat down. Felix must have nodded to Paul, and Paul, according to the strict procedures of Roman law, had a chance to present his rebuttal.

The Defense before Felix

Paul began his defense in a polite manner. But his words to the governor are restrained, especially when they are compared with those of the professional orator, Tertullus. Tertullus had flattered Felix. Paul would do no such thing. Nevertheless, he pointed out that he knew Felix had been a judge over Israel for a number of years—long enough to know something about the kind of nation it was—and because of that Paul was glad to be able to make his defense before him. Felix would have been aware, Paul points out, of the kind of charges that were being brought and the fact that they were (he implies rather than states this) insubstantial.

After this brief introduction Paul began to answer the charges Tertullus had made. He dealt with each one in order.

1. *I am not a troublemaker.* The first charge had been that Paul was a trouble-maker, and his response was that it just was not so. Moreover, he said, I can prove my assertion, and they are unable to prove theirs. First, it has only been twelve days since I arrived in Jerusalem. Felix was aware that Paul had already been in prison in Caesarea for five days (v. 1). He had been in prison in Jerusalem one day. So six of the twelve days are accounted for. At the most, then, Paul had six days to stir up the kind of trouble they were accusing him of starting. How much trouble can one person stir up in a week? It was not Paul who was stirring up trouble but the Asian instigators and the Jerusalem mob.

If they had been given time for a rebuttal, these men might have replied, "We are not so concerned about the trouble he was stirring up in Jerusalem as we are about the trouble he has been creating all around the world." In fact, Tertullus had referred to worldwide troubles earlier. But these Jewish scribes and priests were not in a position to testify about what had been happening in other places. This was a court of law. It was not a place where second-hand information could be credited. The Jews had to testify to what they knew Paul had done during the six days he was in the Jewish capital.

Then Paul said, I am also clearly no troublemaker, because during the six days I was in Jerusalem I was not even debating with the crowds. I was not lecturing. I have done that in other places; that is my line of work. But in Jerusalem I was not disputing anybody. There were no crowds around me. As a matter of fact, the only reason I was at the temple was that I was trying to worship the very God these men also profess to worship, since I too am a Jew.

2. *I am a follower of the Way.* The second accusation was that Paul was a "ringleader of the Nazarene sect." Paul admits to this accusation, although he phrases it differently. He does not say, "It is true; I am a ringleader." He does not even change it to say, "It is true that I am one of the distinguished leaders of the movement." He does not refer to Christianity as "the sect of the Nazarenes" either. He calls it "the Way." Yet in spite of those qualifications, the apostle nevertheless agrees with the substance of the accusation.

But that was no problem, because the only substantial legal question was whether Paul's following "the Way" was sufficient grounds for a punitive judgment, and this the Jewish leaders had not argued. Was Paul not permitted to practice his religion? Didn't Roman law provide religious freedom? Besides, if "the Way" was a sect within Judaism, as the accusation had tended to admit, and if Judaism was itself protected by the government, as it was, was Paul himself not protected also? If the governor was to rule against Paul for his adherence to Christianity, would he not also have to move against these very leaders of the Sanhedrin who had come to press their case against him? You see how wise a response this was.

Paul also stressed the similarity between his beliefs and those of the men who were accusing him: "I believe everything that agrees with the Law and that is written in the Prophets, and I have the same hope in God as these men, that there will be a resurrection of both the righteous and the wicked" (vv. 14–15). If pressed, Paul would have argued that following Jesus was not a deviation from Judaism but rather true Judaism itself. If anyone had strayed from true Judaism, it was his opponents.

That is the sort of thing Christians can say today when witnessing to Jews. They can claim, especially if they are witnessing to a Jew who hardly practices his or her Judaism, that Christians are more Jewish than Jews. They can claim that they believe everything that is written in the Old Testament, adding that the Old Testament prophecies have been fulfilled in Jesus Christ.

For political purposes Paul did not mention the resurrection in this case. The resurrection was essential to Christian belief and practice. So when he had an opportunity, which he did not have on the earlier occasion but did have here, particularly in his later private conversations with the governor, Paul testified that he believed in the resurrection not only as a matter of doctrine but also as personal experience, since the Lord Jesus Christ, who was raised from the dead, had appeared to him.

3. *I did not desecrate the temple.* The third charge was that Paul had tried to desecrate the temple. Paul emphatically denied it. He had not come to desecrate the temple. In fact, said Paul, that is the last thing on earth I would ever want to do. Why did he come to Jerusalem then? It was on an errand of mercy. He had been establishing churches in Gentile lands, and these churches had taken an offering for the Jerusalem poor, which he had come to the city to deliver.

He said, When they found me in the temple, not only was I not causing trouble, I was submitting to the laws of our religion. I was ceremonially clean. There are people in Jerusalem who know that is true. I had gone through the rites of purification when they fell on me. So it was not I who created the disturbance but themselves.

This was Paul's defense against Tertullus's formal charges.

He adds one other thing. He adds that the trouble that occurred was because of charges raised by certain Jews from Asia. Since this was a court of law, it was the Jews from Asia, not the Sanhedrin, who should have been present to testify against him. The Sanhedrin had not been there when it happened. They were not eyewitnesses. If anyone was to testify, it needed to be those who had been present.

The only thing the Sanhedrin could possibly testify about was that when Paul was before them he had shouted, "It is concerning the resurrection of the dead that I am on trial before you today" (v. 21).

A Political Non-Decision

Felix heard the arguments. What did he do? He did what many men in similar situations have tried to do. He knew Paul was innocent. Caught between what he knew to be right and pressure from people who were demanding that he do wrong, Felix refused to make a decision. He said, I just can't make a decision now. I'll wait until Commander Lysias comes and can tell me what happened.

In itself that was perhaps not so bad. The facts seemed clear. Felix should have released Paul. But he had the right to hear what the commander of the Jerusalem garrison had to say. The difficulty, as Luke shows, is that Felix was not merely postponing his decision until the case was presented to him, hoping to make a judgment at the earliest possible moment. Rather, delay and compromise were characteristic of this man. He habitually postponed what he knew he needed to do.

The real tragedy of his life was not that he postponed making a judgment about Paul in regard to the Sanhedrin's accusations, but that he postponed the far more serious matter of making a decision concerning Jesus Christ.

Luke ends the story by telling us that Felix kept Paul in custody and heard him on more than one occasion. He was interested in what he had to say. Paul told him about Jesus, "righteousness, self-control and the judgment to come" (v. 25). Felix was moved by this testimony. He was afraid; but he did not believe. He said, "That's enough for now! You may leave. When I find it convenient, I will send for you" (v. 25). But the convenient moment never came.

Felix had a great deal going for him. Luke says he was "well acquainted with the Way"—that is, he already knew something about Christianity. He knew Paul was innocent. Most important, he knew he was himself a sinner, because when Paul spoke about righteousness, self-control, and the judgment to come, he trembled. Yet in spite of all that was going for him Felix postponed his decision. It never was convenient to send for Paul. And with these words, Felix passes from the pages of Acts, from history, and from life.

This is where many people find themselves today. They know about Christianity, maybe not a great deal, but enough. Some have learned about it from their parents as they were growing up. They had godly parents who taught them about Jesus. Some learned about it from a friend. They know someone who is a Christian, the Christian explained the gospel to them. Some have read books. Some have heard the gospel on radio. Some have heard it on television. Literally millions of people know about Christianity.

Like Felix, they have no real reason to doubt the character of those who have testified about Jesus. There have been prominent representatives of Christianity whose character has been doubtful, and sometimes they will use the sins of these prominent persons as an excuse for not believing. But generally the people who have told them about Christianity are of good character and strong in faith. They will even say to them things like, "I am glad you have a strong faith. I am happy for you."

Maybe also like Felix they know that they are sinners and that they are in danger of the judgment. When Christians talk to them, when they read Christian books or hear Christian radio broadcasts, they are troubled. They wonder, What will become of me? I do wrong things. What will happen to me if I have to stand before God in the judgment? Yet, although the gospel is known to them, when the need to decide for Christ is urged upon them they say, "Not now; a little later perhaps. I'll have to think about it. I'll decide at a more convenient time."

They say to themselves, "I'll put it off until later." I ask: How much later? and, What is going to happen in the meantime?"

They say, "Well, a little later. I feel too young now. I want to live a bit before I consider such serious things." What are they going to be doing in the meantime? They are going to go on sinning, of course; they can't stop. Is the accumulation of their sin day by day, week by week, year by year going to make them more open to the gospel as time passes? It will be many times harder for them to respond to Christ's offer a year from now, and even harder a year after that and again a year after that. They are not going to become more open to the gospel by delaying. That is why the Bible says, "Now is the time of God's favor, now is the day of salvation" (2 Cor. 6:2). There is never a better time to turn from sin and receive the Lord Jesus Christ as Savior than the present moment.

In his study of Acts, Harry Ironside tells of something that happened to him when he was twelve years old. He had gone to hear Dwight L. Moody in Chicago. Moody was preaching in an old theater that held about ten thousand people, a building that has since been torn down. Because the theater was jammed with people and he was just a boy, Ironside managed to climb up on a rafter above where Moody was speaking. From there he was able to look down upon that vast host of people. There was a point in Moody's address where he said to the people, "I want everybody who knows the Lord Jesus Christ as his or her Savior to stand." From where he was looking down, Ironside saw perhaps six or seven thousand people out of that great host of ten thousand rise to their feet.

Then Moody went on, saying something like this: "I want everybody from this large number who are Christians but who became Christians before the age of fifteen to be seated." Ironside saw that about half of those who had been standing resumed their seats. There were about three thousand left.

Moody said, "I want everybody who became a Christian before the age of twenty to sit down." Another half were seated. Now there were only fifteen hundred standing.

Moody raised the number by tens—thirty, forty, fifty. By the time he got to fifty, there were only about twenty people on their feet in all that vast auditorium.[3] The point had been clearly and dramatically made: It is never easier to believe on Jesus Christ than when you are young, and it is always harder later.

Felix was a judge but he died. And when he died, he appeared before that One who will not postpone his judgments and who does not accept bribes. So far as we know from Scripture, Felix is in hell at this moment. One day we all will stand before that great Judge too. We will have to give an accounting for what we have done and for what our lives have been. How will you stand in that day? Make sure that you are not like Felix. Come to Jesus while there is still time, and help others to do the same.

46

The Trial before Festus

Acts 25:1-12

Festus, wishing to do the Jews a favor, said to Paul, "Are you willing to go up to Jerusalem and stand trial before me on these charges?"

Paul answered: "I am now standing before Caesar's court, where I ought to be tried. I have not done any wrong to the Jews, as you yourself know very well. If, however, I am guilty of anything deserving death, I do not refuse to die. But if the charges brought against me by these Jews are not true, no one has the right to hand me over to them. I appeal to Caesar!"

After Festus had conferred with his council, he declared: "You have appealed to Caesar. To Caesar you will go!"

Acts 25:9–12

Acts 25 tells of the trial of the apostle Paul before Festus. Compared to the account of the trial before Felix, which is given in Acts 24, and the account of the trial before King Agrippa, which follows, this narrative is relatively brief. No doubt what happened here was of less significance for Paul. In some ways, it is only a repetition of the charges and responses, but before another judge.

Yet it is worth looking at the different characters in this trial with some care. There are three individuals or bodies of people: the accusers, the Jews;

the judge, Festus, who was quite different from Felix, who preceded him; and the apostle Paul.

The Jews

The Jews in this setting illustrate what I would call the corrupting effects of religion when it is not actually in contact with God. We tend to look upon religion as a good thing. We say, "Even if a person isn't really born again, even if she or he doesn't really trust God, isn't it at least better to be religious than not be religious?" That is not necessarily the case. It can be. But religion can also be very corrupting. This is because if the life of God is not actually present in the worshiper, then his or her religion can become a mere veneer, hypocrisy, and can be used as an excuse for doing what is obviously evil. History teaches that some of the worst things that have ever been done have been done by people who claimed they were doing the will of God—that is, by religious persons.

These Jewish leaders wanted to have Paul transferred to Jerusalem for trial because they "were preparing an ambush to kill him along the way" (v. 3). Here were religious leaders, the heads of the most enlightened nation in the history of the human race, plotting murder. You would think that the Decalogue alone would have kept them from it. The Ten Commandments say, "You shall not murder" (Exod. 20:13). They might have pled that these were unusual circumstances, that Paul was actually guilty of a crime requiring death, and therefore that they had to act in an unorthodox manner to secure it. But even if this reasoning could be accepted, they were still violating their own criminal laws, which provided rigorous safeguards for anyone accused of a capital offense. We would say they were doing everything possible to avoid due process of law. The irony is that they were supposed to be the upholders of the law.

In the Jewish system, these were not just secular leaders. They were also the religious leaders of the people. The secular law and the religious law were one. Yet here they were, willing to turn their backs on their own laws in order to secure the death of one they obviously hated.

Moreover, we see a growth of corruption. In Acts 23, where the plot to murder Paul was first launched, we find that it was the zealots who were responsible. Now, in Acts 25, we find that the leaders are initiating the very thing they were only tangentially involved in earlier.

This is how wickedness spreads, and it is why we always have to be on guard against it. It is easy for religious people to go astray and then claim God's authority for their disobedience.

Who Was Festus?

The second party to these proceedings was Governor Porcius Festus. The most noticeable characteristic of this man is that unlike Felix he was unwilling to delay decisions.

When Festus arrived in the province, it was only three days before he went from Caesarea to Jerusalem. He would have arrived by ship, which would not have been an easy trip. One would have expected him to have taken time in his capital city of Caesarea to relax and perhaps get things in order there first. But this was not his way. Jerusalem was the center of the nation, though not the Roman capital. So Festus immediately went there to confer with the Jewish leaders. He wanted to know what he was facing. Then, after spending eight or ten days with them, he made his way back down to Caesarea (v. 6). This was a man who was trying to take charge right away. The next day, having brought with him those who were going to accuse Paul, he convened his court and heard Paul's case.

Festus was a good administrator. Yet he had his own serious flaw, and in this respect he was much like his predecessor. He wanted to please the people. He wanted to show the Jews a favor. A person might say, "Well, that is just a part of what it means to rule well. When you're in charge of something you have to get along with those you govern." That is true, of course. But this was a legal matter. Paul was on trial. Any giving of favors in this situation was in reality a perversion of justice and the abuse of an innocent man.

Paul knew what was happening. That is why he exclaimed, "I have not done any wrong to the Jews, as you yourself know very well" (v. 10). If Festus had not been able to discover this on his own, he certainly would have learned it from his predecessor, since Felix had examined Paul on more than one occasion and had concluded that he had done nothing wrong. Yet "wishing to do the Jews a favor" (v. 9), Festus compromised.

How many right actions have been bartered away because those who knew to do right wanted to please someone else or at least not offend people they considered to be important? That is not just something that happens in the world, either. It is done by Christians and the church. Perhaps it has been done by you. If so, it is something of which to repent.

The trial itself is told in very brief language. Verse 7 says, "When Paul appeared, the Jews who had come down from Jerusalem stood around him, bringing many serious charges against him, which they could not prove." Luke does not tell us what those charges were, but we can guess what they were because of what was said in Acts 24 and by the way Paul responds in verse 8: "I have done nothing wrong against the law of the Jews or against the temple or against Caesar." These would have been charges of heresy (something that was contrary to God's law), sacrilege (something done against the temple), and treason (an act against Caesar).

These are close to the charges that were brought against the Lord Jesus Christ: He had violated the law by not observing the Sabbath correctly; he was guilty of sacrilege because he had prophesied the destruction of the temple; and he had made himself a king thus setting himself against Caesar. It was because Pilate feared the Jews would tell Caesar he had released a rival to the imperial throne that he finally consented to Christ's death.

These accusations are made against believers in virtually any country where people feel free to attack them.

1. *They disregard the laws or customs of the nation.* Christians do not see things as those about them do. They do not have the same priorities. Christians are a breed apart. Christians have another Lord. They will try to obey their country's laws, but not when God's law supersedes human law.

2. *They do not adhere to the religion of the people among whom they live.* In the early church Christians were accused of being atheists because they denied the existence of the pagan gods.

3. *They are guilty of treason.* This may not be true in America, at least in an obvious way, but it has happened in other places, as in the former iron curtain countries. Christians will not acknowledge the ultimate sovereignty of any secular state. Only God is absolute for Christians.

In his defense Paul said that he had not done any of these things, at least not in ways that would bring him into danger in a Roman court. John Stott notes that

> if in his trial before Felix Paul had emphasized the continuity of "the Way" with Judaism, in this trial before Festus he stressed his loyalty to Caesar. Caesar is mentioned eight times in this chapter, five times as *Kaisar,* twice as *Sebastos* (21, 25), the Greek equivalent of Augustus, and once as *ho Kyrios,* "the Lord." Paul knew that he had not offended against Caesar (8) and that he stood in Caesar's court (10).[1]

Luke says that although they brought "many serious charges against him" they could not "prove" them (v. 7). They had accused Paul of stirring up trouble all over the Roman Empire, but they did not have any witnesses. They had accused him of sacrilege, but they could not prove it. They accused him of speaking against Caesar, and they could not prove that either. So all Paul had to do in these circumstances was deny the charges. The burden of proof rested with his accusers, and Festus, being a perceptive judge at least in this respect, understood so and knew that there were no grounds for condemning the apostle.

Ah, but Festus wanted "to do the Jews a favor." He said, I don't know how to resolve this, Paul, but it might help the situation if we could transfer your case to Jerusalem and let you be tried there. It is hard to think that Festus could have suggested this with pure motives. For one thing, he must have known the case's previous history. He must have known that Paul had been brought from Jerusalem to Caesarea precisely because of the danger. Paul could never get a fair trial in Jerusalem.

But even more than that, can we believe that Festus hadn't heard of the plot to have Paul assassinated? Hadn't he examined the records? Hadn't he seen the letter written by Claudius Lysias?

One commentator suggests that this crafty Roman governor might have thought that he could solve the dilemma if he could get Paul to concede to go to Jerusalem for trial, and if perhaps along the way Paul might be assassinated. Then the governor could say, "My goodness, that is too bad, but I didn't have anything to do with it. Paul went willingly, and this is really a very sad thing indeed."[2]

With the wisdom God had given him, Paul understood the situation well and knew that the only way he could hope to get his case resolved fairly was to exercise his right as a Roman citizen to appeal from local jurisdiction to the court of Caesar in Rome. That equally suited Festus. It got the sticky matter out of his hands. So he replied, "You have appealed to Caesar. To Caesar you will go" (v. 12).

Paul, the Victor

We have looked at the accusers and the judge. We look finally at the accused, Paul himself. What a contrast! Here were the accusers, who out of hatred were trying to assassinate the prisoner. Here was Festus, who failed to do what he should have done because of his desire for popularity. And Paul? Paul was the prisoner, the accused, the one in danger of his life. Yet he was the only one who actually emerged victorious. He was victorious because he was innocent of these false charges and because he depended on God, whom he trusted in this as in all other circumstances.

Most of us do not live in circumstances where the world's accusations against us are as fierce as these were against Paul, though there are places in the world where they are harsh and Christians do suffer physically. Nevertheless, you and I face a world whose value system is hostile to the standards of the Lord Jesus Christ and in which we are constantly pressured to compromise or deny our faith. How are you and I, weak and sinful human beings as we are, to stand against such pressure? How are we going to stand when the world says, "You have to go along to get along. Nobody who is rigid ever gets ahead. If you tell the truth, your competitor is going to get the edge on you, and pretty soon you'll be broke"?

Let me suggest three things.

Know God Is Sovereign

Knowing God is sovereign over your circumstances gives you great power, because it means that even if things do not go right for you from a human point of view, it will still be right, since God understood and ordained those hard circumstances from the beginning. God knew they were going to come, and they are part of his plan for your life.

This knowledge is what gave power to Shadrach, Meshach, and Abednego when they stood against the most powerful monarch of their day, King Nebuchadnezzar. Nebuchadnezzar had decreed that everyone had to worship a golden statue he had set up on the plain of Dura. It represented the Babylonian empire. To refuse to bow to it was treason. These young men would not bow to it, however, because to them such an act was idolatry.

Nebuchadnezzar hauled them in. He was outraged. He was about to execute them by throwing them into a burning furnace, but they were utterly unafraid. How could that be? Nebuchadnezzar was threatening them with death. Where did their strength come from? It came from their knowledge of God's sovereignty. They said:

> If we are thrown into the blazing furnace, the God we serve is able to save us from it, and he will rescue us from your hand, O king. But even if he does not, we want you to know, O king, that we will not serve your gods or worship the image of gold you have set up.
>
> Daniel 3:17–18

God is sovereign over even the most minute details of your life.

Know the Bible

You have to know your Bible because the situations we face are generally not black or white. If the situation is black and white, we know what to do. But the problems we face are usually gray. It seems that we ought to do one thing, but then again there is another side to it. And if the situation does not seem gray immediately, if you talk to your friends it will become gray soon enough, since everyone will see it from a different point of view. There is only one way to find your way through the gray areas: by studying, meditating on, and seeking to apply the Bible. There are things in it we may not fully understand, but when we do understand them, they are clear. The path is dark because the world is dark. But the Bible illuminates the path and shows us where to go.

Pay Any Price Necessary

You have to be willing to pay any price necessary to stay true to Jesus Christ. Any price? Yes, any. There are times in history when Christians are told, "Bow down or die," as Daniel's three friends were. They have refused to bow down. Many have died. The history of the church is filled with the stories of martyrs. At other times it is not death that is required but such things as loss of reputation, success, advancement, or the good opinion of our friends. We say, "If I acted as a Christian in that situation, my boss would never understand; my wife, my parents, my friends would never understand." We fail to do what is right because we are not willing to pay that high price. We are not ready to surrender everything to follow Jesus.

You can know that God is sovereign. You can know what is right because you study the Bible. Yet you can still fail to do what is right because you value something else more than your obedience to Christ.

In *The Gulag Archipelago* the great Russian writer Aleksandr Solzhenitsyn reflects on why in the notorious prison system of Russia some prisoners seemed to survive the interrogations and maintain their integrity while others collapsed under it and lost their identity entirely. He says that it had to do with whether or not one was willing to pay the price for one's integrity.

At the very threshold, you must say to yourself: "My life is over, a little early to be sure, but there's nothing to be done about it. I shall never return to freedom. I am condemned to die—now or a little later. But later on, in truth, it will be even harder, and so the sooner the better. I no longer have any property whatsoever. For me those I love have died, and for them I have died. From today on, my body is useless and alien to me. Only my spirit and my conscience remain precious to me."

Confronted by such a prisoner, the interrogation will tremble.

Only the man who has renounced everything can gain that victory.[3]

You and I are servants of the Lord Jesus Christ in the midst of a hostile world, and the only way we are going to be able to stand against the world when it pressures us is if we are willing to give up everything to follow him.

"Everything?" you say.

Yes, everything. But why should we be surprised? He gave up everything for us, and it is he who said, "If anyone would come after me, he must deny himself and take up his cross daily and follow me" (Luke 9:23). A cross is a symbol of death. He was teaching that we must be willing to die to be his followers. That is the victory of faith that overcomes the world.

47

The Trial before King Agrippa

Acts 25:13–26:32

At this point Festus interrupted Paul's defense. "You are out of your mind, Paul!" he shouted. "Your great learning is driving you insane."

"I am not insane, most excellent Festus," Paul replied. "What I am saying is true and reasonable. The king is familiar with these things, and I can speak freely to him. I am convinced that none of this has escaped his notice, because it was not done in a corner. King Agrippa, do you believe the prophets? I know you do."

Then Agrippa said to Paul, "Do you think that in such a short time you can persuade me to be a Christian?"

Acts 26:24–28

$$T$$

he account of Paul's appearance before King Herod Agrippa II begins at Acts 25:13 and continues to the end of Acts 26. It is a large section of the book, so large that it would be desirable to divide it were it not so clearly a single story. These verses recount the third of three formal defenses of the apostle Paul before the secular authorities subsequent to his arrest in Jerusalem.

Agrippa was the grandson of Herod the Great and the son of Herod Agrippa I, who had arrested Peter and killed James. This was not an illustrious ancestry, but compared with his two immediate predecessors, he was a pretty good king.

There is not too much to say about him, though the fact that he was not guilty of the atrocities his father and grandfather had been guilty of is significant. True, he was living in an incestuous relationship with his sister, Bernice, which hardly commends him as a model of virtue. But so far as we know he did not go around killing people. And there was at least this in his favor: He understood Paul's situation, which is how he got involved in his trial.

Festus had inherited Paul from his predecessor Felix. He did not understand the ways of the Jews very much, and when the case involving Paul was handed over to him he did not know how to think about it. Festus could not understand what the trouble was about.

Furthermore, as the trial had been drawing to a close, Paul appealed to Caesar, and Festus, somewhat opportunistically, had seized upon his appeal and granted it. It got him out of a fix. But now he had to send Paul to Rome, and he had to say in the formal documentation that would have to accompany Paul why he was sending him. What was Paul accused of? Why should Festus be bothering the emperor with trivialities he could not understand himself?

Furthermore, the testimony of Felix was that Paul had done nothing wrong—nothing that would merit his being put to death. It seemed to him that this was the situation also. So what was he going to do? Did he dare send Paul to the emperor, saying, "There is no real accusation against him, at least none that we can understand, and as far as what we do understand goes, there is nothing that merits either your attention or his death"? That was not a way to be popular with Caesar.

It was at this moment that King Agrippa and Bernice arrived from their capital north of Caesarea to pay respects to the new Roman governor. Festus, recognizing that here was a man who at least understood something about Jewish law and the customs and spirit of the Jews, recognized this as a significant opportunity. Agrippa said he would be glad to hear Paul. So the scene was set for Paul's defense.

There had been an initial defense before the Jews in Jerusalem, recorded in Acts 22, couched in Jewish language. There was also a second defense, recorded in Acts 24, before Felix, and a third, much abbreviated defense before Festus, recorded in Acts 25, both essentially Gentile in character. In Acts 25 we have a unique defense before a man who was on the side of the Jews and yet was obviously on very good terms with Rome. This may be why Luke records the trial so completely.

We have already heard the arguments. Besides, since Paul's defense was essentially his testimony, we have heard the parts that concern his early life and conversion even more than what is given in these formal defenses. We might say at this point, "Why are we getting this all over again? Haven't we heard these things enough?" Apparently Luke thought they were worth repeating. And if he was right, as he must be, then the testimony that Paul gave on this occasion is something that we need to hear again too.

The Pomp of Yesterday

Beginning in Acts 25:23, we are told that a number of very important people had gathered. They were important in terms of their position and power, and they came together with great pomp or pageantry. Luke calls our attention to the people, their positions, the pomp, the power, and the pageantry.

Agrippa and Bernice, the Jewish king and his queen, were there. Festus the governor was there. The high-ranking officers were present. (These would be the commanders in charge of the Roman military divisions stationed in Caesarea. There were five of them at any given time. So there would have been at least five present.) There were also the leading men of the city, perhaps some of them retired military personnel, but most of them merchants—those who would have money and be in positions of influence.

Here are the important people of the world with all their power and pageantry arrayed on one side, and here on the other side, brought out perhaps without even much warning or opportunity to prepare a special defense, is this little Jew from Tarsus, the apostle Paul. If he had bad eyesight, which we discussed as a possibility earlier, he may even have been squinting as he looked up into the faces of these important persons. What a lopsided contest: all these great people, with their positions, power, pomp, and pageantry on one side. And on the other side, Paul, a poor prisoner.

You do not have to know Hebrew or Greek to understand the Bible, but sometimes knowing the biblical languages contributes important insights to one's study, and that is the case here. In Greek the word "pomp" is *fantasia*. It is the word from which we get our words "fantasy" and "fantastic." It refers to something light, fleeting, or passing, something of momentary interest only. In the context of this great public display by Agrippa, Festus, and the others, the word was probably chosen carefully to suggest that these seemingly important things are only passing fantasies. I wonder if we understand that. We need to.

When we see the impressive things of this world they usually seem to be what is lasting or stable. Indeed, what could be more stable, more impressive, more weighty than the Roman Empire in the person of those who represented it? Yet Luke is suggesting it was all fantasy, all even then in the process of passing away. The pomp and pageantry passed away first. They did not even last out the day. The servants removed the flags, and it was all over. In time the people also passed away. They died. Eventually, even the Roman Empire passed away. It was overrun by the barbarians.

But the gospel of Jesus Christ to which the apostle Paul was called to bear witness prevailed. It prevailed, not only on that day because it was the truth and it was spoken, but it also prevailed in the decade to come and the decade after that and the century that followed that and the millennium after that. So it is that the gospel of Jesus Christ is with us in power even today, when Rome is just a memory.

I think of a verse in Rudyard Kipling's great "Recessional" poem of 1897.

> The tumult and the shouting dies;
> The captains and the kings depart:
> Still stands thine ancient sacrifice,
> An humble and a contrite heart.
> Lord God of Hosts, be with us yet,
> Lest we forget—lest we forget!

Kipling wrote that at the time of the great Jubilee honoring Queen Victoria, and the English people did not like what he wrote. The prevailing opinion is that the poem kept him from becoming poet laureate. But Kipling was right to warn about forgetting. We all need to be warned. The scene in Acts 25 has been written to help keep us from forgetting things we also need to remember.

The Last Defense

The apostle Paul was not about to forget. He had been called by God, and he knew it. He had been given a commission, and he understood his commission. He was not about to be overpowered by the display.

Paul's story has generally been told in three parts.

Paul's Life in Judaism

Paul begins by talking about his life in Judaism, and what he stresses here is that he was a faithful Jew. He had been raised a Jew, having received the traditions of the Jews from his fathers. He knew the law. So far as he knew and understood the law, he had lived by it.

He had lived according to the strictest sect of his day. He was a Pharisee. We have a bad view of the Pharisees because Jesus called them "hypocrites, . . . whitewashed tombs, which look beautiful on the outside but on the inside are full of dead men's bones." That was right. Many of them were exactly that. As a matter of fact, it is a proper description of the entire human race. We are all hypocrites. Yet in their day the Pharisees had a good reputation because they were what we would call "fundamentalists." They were the conservatives of their day. They said, "We believe in the inerrancy of the Bible. We believe everything that is written there." They really did, at least so far as they understood it.

Paul's defense was that the only things he was proclaiming were what was in the law, things well understood by the Jews—at least those who believed the Old Testament Scriptures, as the Pharisees did.

Paul's chief point was the promise of the resurrection. He interrupted his address at this point to ask wisely, "Why should any of you consider it incredible that God raises the dead?" (26:8). We are going to see, as the story continues, that his Gentile hearers did consider the resurrection to be incredible, just as people consider it incredible today. But Paul was a Jew, raised on the

Scriptures, and the Jews as a whole (and the Pharisees in particular) believed in the supernatural.

Paul's Conversion and Commission

The second part of Paul's address concerns his conversion and the commission God gave him. There have been a number of attempts by unbelievers to explain what happened to the apostle Paul on the road to Damascus, eliminating the fact that the Second Person of the Trinity, incarnate and now risen from the dead, actually appeared to him. Some have said, quite seriously, that Paul probably had epilepsy. His experience on the road to Damascus was actually an epileptic fit.

Some have imagined that he had heatstroke. The sun was bright. It was hot. No doubt, these conditions overcame him.

When I think of these far-out, desperate arguments, I remember what Harry Ironside said when he dealt with them in his collection of sermons on the Book of Acts. He quoted Spurgeon as saying, "Oh, blessed epilepsy that made such a wonderful change in this man! Would God that all who oppose the name of Jesus Christ might become epileptics in the same sense." After referring to the sunstroke idea, Ironside wrote: "Would God that all modernists could be so sunstruck that they might begin to preach Christ, and so come back to the grand old gospel of redemption by the blood of Jesus!" Then, in what I suppose was a bit of whimsy, Ironside said, "And yet . . . I am quite in agreement with the modernists save for one letter. It was a Sonstroke, not a sun-stroke! It was the light of the glory of God in the face of Christ Jesus that struck home to the very heart of that man and gave him to see the One he had been persecuting—the Savior of sinners."[1]

The apostle Paul was turned around. He could testify to the grace of God in his transformation. If the Lord Jesus Christ has stopped you and turned you around, then you can testify too. If you are not testifying to God's grace or if you feel you cannot, you need to examine yourself to see whether you have really met Jesus. Has Jesus turned you from sin? Has he revealed himself to you? Have you come to trust him?

Paul's Witness

The third part of Paul's defense before King Agrippa had to do with his service for Christ following his conversion.

The first thing he stresses is his obedience, though he couches it in negative form: "So then, King Agrippa, I was not disobedient to the vision from heaven" (26:19). One of the first marks of our conversion is that we obey Jesus Christ. We might even call it the first mark, except that faith itself is the first evidence. Are you obeying Jesus? Jesus said, "Why do you call me, 'Lord, Lord,' and do not do what I say?" (Luke 6:46). If you are disobeying Jesus, you are not his disciple. If you are not his disciple, you are not saved. People who have heard the voice of Jesus Christ just do not ignore it.

Second, Paul talks about the scope of his ministry, indicating that it widened more and more as God worked through him to reach others (26:20). I find it interesting that here in the twenty-sixth chapter of this book, after we have been through all the history that Luke has recorded concerning the expansion of the gospel, we find the apostle Paul describing the sphere of his ministry in almost the same terms as the Lord Jesus Christ used when he gave his missionary charge to the disciples before Pentecost (Acts 1:8). Paul had been doing what Jesus described. Why? Because he was obedient to the Lord, and that is what Jesus had said his people were to do.

The third thing Paul says when he talks about his service following his conversion is that he preached the gospel. He proclaimed "nothing beyond what the prophets and Moses said would happen" (26:22). What was that?

First, that "Christ would suffer"—that is, die. This was a testimony to the atonement.

Second, that Jesus would "rise from the dead."

Third, that being raised from the dead, he "would proclaim light to his own people and to the Gentiles" (26:23). This happened through witnesses like Paul.

What should our response to such a gospel be? Paul gives this as well, no doubt for the explicit benefit of King Agrippa, Festus, and the others. He says that the Gentiles should "repent," "turn to God," and "prove their repentance by their deeds" (26:20).

To repent means "to turn around." If you are going in one direction and repent, you turn around and go another direction. It is the equivalent of conversion, which means the same thing. It is what had happened to Paul on the road to Damascus. He was going one way, but God turned him around so that he went in a different way entirely. That needs to happen to everyone who would find salvation in Christ.

Turning from sin and going in another way also means "turning to God." Christianity is not just negative. It is not just "sin not" or "abandon your current lifestyle." Christianity is positive. It means finding righteousness and a new life in Christ. This new life is not only different but better. It is a life lived in and with God.

Then, lest there be anything like cheap grace, easy repentance, or a mere verbal profession, Paul also said that Gentiles need to "prove their repentance by their deeds." How do you know if you are a Christian or not? Do you know it simply because you can mouth the right words? Hardly. We can fool ourselves into mouthing just about anything. We know we are Christians when our lives are changed and we begin to do good works. That is the proof—when we begin to follow after Jesus Christ and obey him.

If this is what the gospel really is, then it is the most radical thing that could possibly be proclaimed. If Paul had been speaking here merely of his own religious experience, Agrippa and Festus might have regarded his views merely as "religious ideas" or, as Festus did say, "philosophy." They wouldn't have mattered much. Who cares about philosophy? Ah, but if you are talking about a gospel centered in a risen Lord, someone who lived in history, who was crucified, who rose from the dead and now commands all people everywhere to turn from sin to God and to do works of righteousness, that is a radical message. It cannot be ignored.

The Responses of Festus and Agrippa

It stirred up opposition on this occasion. Paul did not even get to finish, though he seems to have been near the end of his address. Festus, who had been listening all this time, interrupted, "You are out of your mind, Paul! Your great learning is driving you insane" (26:24). He had never heard anything as crazy as the Christian gospel in his life.

Festus might have been willing to hear Paul talk about some future resurrection, particularly if it could be thought of metaphorically. Most people are at least willing to consider the possibility of some future state in which we will all possibly have to answer for our misdeeds. But that was not what Paul was talking about. He was talking about a literal, bodily resurrection that had happened in history and that had made all the difference in his life and in the lives of others who had met Jesus Christ. It was this resurrection that was incredible and intolerable to Festus. "You must be crazy," was Festus's response. He perished because of it.

Paul, who all along had chiefly been addressing Agrippa, turned to him, making a neat little transition in which he began by replying to Festus but quickly switching over to Agrippa, saying, "The king [that is, Agrippa] is familiar with these things, and I can speak freely to him. I am convinced that none of this has escaped his notice, because it was not done in a corner. King Agrippa, do you believe the prophets? I know you do" (26:26–27). Agrippa was no Roman. He would have had some acquaintance with what Moses and the prophets had written. He may even have had considerable understanding of the Jews' religious books. Paul was accurate when he referred to the events surrounding the life of Jesus of Nazareth by saying that they were "not done in a corner." Agrippa would have known something of these events too. Yes, but Agrippa still had his position in life to think about, and he perished because of that.

Festus probably perished through the pride of intellect. How could a Roman governor believe anything as crazy as a literal resurrection? That was not the case with Agrippa. Agrippa probably believed in the resurrection. But he had his position, and he just could not humble himself, acknowledging himself to be a sinner like anybody else, and receive Jesus Christ as his Savior. He was put on the spot—embarrassed, no doubt, before the governor. So he dodged the question, saying, "Do you think that in such a short time you can persuade me to be a Christian?"

This is precisely what men and women do today. When the supernatural gospel of a crucified but risen Savior is proclaimed, a gospel that demands that we turn from sin and begin to show our conversion by good works, the world puts up barriers and rejects it for precisely these reasons: pride of intellect and pride of position. If you are not a Christian, isn't it true that when you look into your heart you find that those are the things that keep you from bowing to Jesus Christ? Think how foolish that is, since both intellect and position will eventually pass away. Jesus said, "What good will it be for a man if he gains the whole world, yet forfeits his soul?" (Matt. 16:26).

48

Peril at Sea

Acts 27:1-44

When it was decided that we would sail for Italy, Paul and some other prisoners were handed over to a centurion named Julius, who belonged to the Imperial Regiment. We boarded a ship from Adramyttium about to sail for ports along the coast of the province of Asia, and we put out to sea.

Acts 27:1-2

Acts 27 contains the account of a great storm on the Mediterranean that overtook the ship that was bearing Paul to Rome. It was a literal storm, but it can also be a symbol of the storms that come into the lives of Christian people. The idea of being overtaken by life's storms has appealed to poets, among them many of our hymn writers. If you think of the hymns you know, it will not take very long before you come up with some that use this image, for example, this hymn by W. C. Martin:

> Though the angry surges roll
> On my tempest-driven soul,
> I am peaceful, for I know,
> Wildly though the winds may blow,
> I've an anchor safe and sure,
> That can evermore endure.

Or this one by Vernon Charlesworth (1880), revised by Ira Sankey (1885):

> The Lord's our rock, in him we hide,
> A shelter in the time of storm.
> Secure whatever ill betide,
> A shelter in the time of storm.

Often when things are going well we persuade ourselves that we are exempt from storms or that they will not affect us. But we are not, and they will. Then the question will be: Are you anchored to the Rock? Do you trust the One who is able to pilot you through those tempestuous seas? This was Paul's experience. As we look at the story, I want us to see how he prevailed so we can too.

A Unique Narrative

This chapter is one of those rare glimpses into a part of ancient life that you just do not find anywhere else.[1] It is amazingly accurate. James Smith was a Scotsman who lived in various parts of the Mediterranean world and investigated its weather patterns and geography. He recorded the results of his investigations in *The Voyage and Shipwreck of St. Paul.* He concluded that the account in Acts 27 was the product of an eyewitness who was not himself a sailor: "No sailor would have written in a style so little like that of a sailor; no man not a sailor could have written a narrative of a sea voyage so consistent in all its parts, unless from actual observation."[2] Luke's words are accurate in terms of the route the ship took, ancient navigating skills, details of the ship's physical construction, and the way in which the sailors tried to cope with the storm.

Smith was right about Luke's presence on the voyage, since Luke himself indicates that he had come along. This is the last of the three sections of the book where he indicates his presence by use of the plural pronoun "we." The first was in Acts 16, the second in Acts 20, and the third beginning with Acts 27 to the end of the book.

Aristarchus (see Acts 20:4) came along too. He is introduced as a Macedonian from Thessalonica. He was probably Luke's friend, since Luke had been working in Macedonia before this.

The Voyage to Rome

The soldiers transporting Paul used several ships. They set out in the first one in order to work their way up the Mediterranean's eastern coast, around the edge of what we call Turkey, gradually making their way west. They had difficulty because at this time of year sailing west was hard. The fast mentioned in verse 9 was in October, and the prevailing winds were from the west. Besides, the storm season came on in early November, and at that time sailing on the Mediterranean usually ceased for the winter. Sailors simply pulled their boats up on the shore and did not launch them again until spring.

The little company did the best they could, eventually making their way around the coast to the town of Myra in Lycia. Yet this was still on the southern edge of Asia and not very far along at all. They changed ships there, switching to a larger Alexandrian ship. The smaller ship would presumably continue on around the coast of Asia while the larger ship moved more directly westward over the open sea.

The travelers got to Cnidus after many days, but the wind would not allow them to follow the most direct route west. So they went with the wind and were driven south toward the island of Crete, which they hoped to round and then be able to sail west along the southern sheltered shore. After much effort they got as far as a port called Fair Havens, about halfway along the island.

Fair Havens was not a "fair" place. It must have been named by the Chamber of Commerce to try to get people to visit it, which they normally tried to avoid doing. It was now late in the sailing season. The sailors knew they would not be able to reach Rome before winter. They would have to winter somewhere. "But not Fair Havens," they must have said. "Anywhere but Fair Havens. There is nothing to do here at all. If we get stuck in Fair Havens, it's going to be a long, hard winter." They knew there was a nicer port further along the coast, a place called Phoenix. So when a gentle south wind began to blow they decided to take a chance and go for it.

Paul warned them not to go (27:21). Probably God had warned him what would happen, just as he later revealed that no lives would be lost when the ship floundered (vv. 23–25). But sailors don't listen to landlubbers—certainly not preachers. "What does Paul know?" they must have said. "We can do it." So they started out.

The story tells how the originally gentle breeze turned into a great Mediterranean storm that caused the winds and waves to rage day after day in a terrifying fashion. As Luke tells the story, there was a period of fourteen days in which the men did not see the sun or even the stars. Luke says, "When neither sun nor stars appeared for many days and the storm continued raging, we finally gave up all hope of being saved" (v. 20).

Hopeless or Hopeful

Now notice the words that follow. Paul said:

Men, you should have taken my advice not to sail from Crete; then you would have spared yourselves this damage and loss. But now I urge you to keep up your courage, because not one of you will be lost; only the ship will be destroyed. Last night an angel of the God whose I am and whom I serve stood beside me and said, "Do not be afraid, Paul. You must stand trial before Caesar; and God has graciously given you the lives of all who sail with you." So keep up your courage men, for I have faith in God that it will happen just as he told me. Nevertheless, we must run aground on some island.

Acts 27:21–25

Isn't that an interesting contrast? The men are in a terrible storm. The mariners, who know how to sail in storms, are so frightened that they have given up all hope of being saved. But this Jewish preacher, who presumably knew very little about ships or storms, said, "Keep up your courage. . . . Do not be afraid."

Paul's words contain several principles by which you and I can keep up our courage and be fearless in the midst of life's storms. We may not be in the midst of a literal storm like this, but we do experience storms. Storms come into our lives, and sometimes they come quite suddenly and are fierce. One day we are in perfect health. Suddenly we experience pain, and within a matter of hours we find ourselves in the hospital and the diagnosis is grim. "We'll have to operate at once," the doctor says. A storm has descended on our lives.

One day we are sitting at home eating. The telephone rings, and someone on the other end says, "I'm sorry, but I have bad news for you. Your son has been killed in a tragic accident." Or perhaps it is your daughter or wife or husband. The storm has descended.

How are we to stand up in life's storms?

This is how Paul responded to the storm that had overtaken him.

Paul Knew God Was with Him

The first thing is that Paul knew that God was with him. On this occasion an angel of the Lord appeared to him to reassure him of God's presence. That was a powerful evidence. Yet Paul was aware of this truth at other times too, just as we should be aware of it. The Lord Jesus Christ, when he was about to leave this world for the final time, said to his disciples, "Surely *I am with you always,* to the very end of the age" (Matt. 28:20, italics mine).

The message is the same for us as it was for Paul: "Surely I am with you always." Christians have found Jesus with them as they have gone through life's storms. They testify to it again and again.

Christians testify that God has been with them in a way that is supernatural. God has quieted their hearts. He has made himself known in small ways that turned out to be so significant the individuals could testify afterward that God did what he did just to reassure them. He taught them that he had a purpose in it all. Do you know that God is with you? Are you aware of his presence? When the storms come, that will make a great difference.

Paul Knew He Belonged to God

The second principle is that Paul knew that he belonged to God. When Paul mentioned God he identified him as "the God *whose I am*" (italics mine). That is, I am not my own; I am bought with a price; I belong to him.

In one of his published sermons Donald Grey Barnhouse dealt with this passage by exploring the ways in which we belong to God, using some of the great images of Scripture. He noted that we belong to God as the bride belongs to the bridegroom, since we the church are the bride of Christ. This is a precious, beautiful picture. Nothing is going to tear the bride from the arms of Jesus Christ.

We also belong to God as a child belongs to his or her father, since we are God's children. What would you think of a father who sees something happening to his child and simply walks off in another direction? We recognize a basic human duty to care for our children. If a father sees his child being hurt or taken advantage of or persecuted in some way, any decent father comes to its rescue. If we think that way, even though we respond imperfectly, we can be certain that God also does.

Third, we belong to God as sheep belong to the shepherd. Recall Jesus' story of the shepherd who loses one of his sheep. Although he still has the other ninety-nine, he goes to find the lost sheep and searches until he brings that sheep back.[3]

I think of a man who whenever temptation came to him or people were giving him trouble used to look up to heaven and say, "God, do you know that they are attacking your property?"

Paul Was in the Lord's Service

The third truth is that Paul knew he was in God's service, about God's business. Verse 23 speaks of "an angel of the God whose I am and *whom I serve . . .*" (italics mine). God had told him what he was to do: He was to bear witness in Rome. But he had not gotten to Rome yet, and it does not take an Einstein to figure out the implication of those two facts. If God had told him that he was going to serve him in Rome, bearing a witness there, and if he had not yet gotten to Rome, then the storm that was battering the ship on which he was sailing was not going to take his life. God was going to preserve him.

You and I do not have special revelations of that nature, to be sure. God has not revealed to us any specific length of service or specific future place of service. But we can know that as long as God has work for us to do, God will preserve us to do it. God will not be frustrated; and if God is not frustrated, we do not need to be frustrated either. If God has work for us to do, then God will keep us alive to do it. And if you have finished the work that God has given you to do, why should you want to linger around here any longer? We may want to go to heaven as soon as possible, but until then we need to get on with our Father's business.

Paul Trusted God in All Circumstances

The final principle comes just a bit later in Paul's speech, where he says, "For I have faith in God that it will happen just as he told me" (v. 25). Paul knew God. So it was not only a case of God's being with him or his belonging to God or God's having work for him to do. He also knew God as the God of all circumstances and was able to trust him for life's details.

When I lose my job? Yes, when I lose my job.

When I have cancer? Yes, that too.

When someone I love has died? Yes, even then.

These things are not insurmountable to God. They are merely circumstances that he brings into our lives for his glory and our good. Romans 8:28 says, "We know that in all things God works for the good of those who love him, who have been called according to his purpose."

Encouragement to Others

Because of the faith Paul had and because of what he knew of God, Paul was able to encourage others. Jonah was running away from God. So when the storm came to batter the ship that was trying to carry him to Tarshish, Jonah was not on the deck helping others. He was in the hold of the ship asleep, like so many Christians. Others were in danger, but he was of no use to them.

By contrast, Paul was obeying God. So when the storm broke, he emerged as the real leader in the situation. Paul said, "For the last fourteen days you have been in constant suspense and have gone without food—you haven't eaten anything. Now I urge you to take some food. You need it to survive. Not one of you will lose a single hair from his head" (vv. 33–34). Then he "took some bread and gave thanks to God in front of them all . . . broke it and began to eat" (v. 35). That was practical Christianity.

Sometimes people say of Christians, "They're so heavenly minded, they're of no earthly use." But that gets it backward. It is the heavenly-minded people who are of earthly use. People who are earthly minded are of no use whatever when the real storms come.

I do not think the world has any awareness of how much it owes to the presence of Christians in its midst. Here were soldiers, sailors, prisoners—276 of them. All of them were spared because of Paul. Yet afterward, when it was over, I am sure that most of them went away and never thought of their deliverance again. They did not thank God.

God was willing to spare Sodom and Gomorrah if just ten righteous persons could have been found there. But there were not ten righteous persons, and those cities perished.

What about America? I am sure that for all our sin, evil, materialism, blasphemy, and determination to eliminate any vestige of God from national life, God is sparing our country because of the remnant of believers.

The Lord Jesus, not long before his arrest and crucifixion, gave a sermon on the Mount of Olives. He spoke of wars and rumors of wars. It was a way of saying, "Life is filled with trouble, and you will experience your share of it." But he added, "See to it that you are not alarmed" (Matt. 24:6).

Not alarmed by war with its calamities?

Not alarmed by life's storms, as difficult as they can be?
Not alarmed by sickness, disease, persecution, loss of jobs?
No. "See to it that you are not alarmed."

Why? Because God is the God of circumstances, and he is able to and indeed does preserve us in the midst of them. It is our task to trust him at all times and bear witness to him. It is our task as long as God permits us to remain in this world.

49

All Roads Lead to Rome

Acts 28:1–16

After three months we put out to sea in a ship that had wintered in the island. It was an Alexandrian ship with the figurehead of the twin gods Castor and Pollux. We put in at Syracuse and stayed there three days. From there we set sail and arrived at Rhegium. The next day the south wind came up, and on the following day we reached Puteoli. There we found some brothers who invited us to spend a week with them. And so we went to Rome. The brothers there had heard that we were coming, and they traveled as far as the Forum of Appius and the Three Taverns to meet us. At the sight of these men Paul thanked God and was encouraged. When we got to Rome, Paul was allowed to live by himself, with a soldier to guard him.

Acts 28:11–16

As we come to the last chapter of Acts and the arrival of the apostle Paul in Rome, I cannot help remembering the first time I saw Rome. It was during my college years. I was traveling alone in Europe, and I had come from the north, where I had been visiting London, Paris, Geneva, and other cities. My arrival in Rome was extremely moving. Rome is a great city even today. Yet a person cannot help feeling, particularly if he or she knows anything about antiquity and has any understanding of the ruins, that it must have been an amazing city at its height—when Paul arrived as a prisoner.

416

There has probably never been another city quite like Rome. It was the capital of the Roman Empire for nearly one thousand years, and during that entire time it was literally the focal point of the civilized world. I am aware that there was also an impressive culture in the Far East of which the West was mostly unaware. But our culture comes from the West, and during those very important years Rome was its capital.

An Inevitable Movement

Paul had been thinking of Rome a long time himself. He recognized that if the gospel was to become a world religion then the time would come when it would have to be proclaimed in the capital. Paul's procedure had been to move from one major metropolitan area to another, establishing churches and then using the cities as platforms from which the gospel could reach out to the lesser communities. He had followed this pattern at Ephesus, Philippi, Thessalonica, Corinth, and Athens. Yet he seemed always to have had his mind set on reaching Rome.

Earlier, when Paul was in Ephesus, he said, "I must visit Rome" (Acts 19:21). We might think this was only a desire of Paul's, not necessarily one that was seconded or ordained by God. Yet when we come to Acts 23, we find Jesus speaking to Paul personally, saying, "As you have testified about me in Jerusalem, so you must also testify in Rome" (v. 11). The angel reinforced this message while Paul was on ship in the storm: "You must stand trial before Caesar" (Acts 27:24). Finally this much-longed-for event happens.

This has been the direction Acts has been moving in all along, of course. We saw this focus at the very beginning in the outline provided by the words of our Lord's Great Commission: "You will receive power when the Holy Spirit comes on you; and you will be my witnesses in Jerusalem, in Judea and Samaria, and to the ends of the earth" (Acts 1:8). That is the outline Luke has been following throughout.

The first seven chapters of Acts focused on the earliest witness of the believers in Jerusalem. It was a wonderful witness. Miracles were done. The gospel was proclaimed. The church was established. Deacons were chosen. They were formative days for the infant church.

Acts 8–12 chronicles the spread of the gospel to the outlying regions of Judea and Samaria. This was the result of persecution following the death of Stephen. Persecution forced the Christians to scatter into more secluded areas.

Acts 13 tells of the beginning of the great missionary expansion of the church to the rest of the world. Paul and Barnabas began to travel, and the missionary journeys eventually took Paul throughout Asia into Europe. Important churches were established in Thessalonica, Philippi, Corinth, and Ephesus. Now, at the very end of the book, the apostle comes to Rome. Thus Jesus' prophecy that his disciples would be his witnesses "to the ends of the earth" is fulfilled.

Christians were in Rome already, which shows that a church could be established without an apostle. And not only were they there, they were there in considerable numbers. Nevertheless, with the coming of the apostle Paul to Rome the first great missionary movement chronicled by Acts is completed. The empire has been reached with the gospel.

The Months on Malta

We are going to look at two portions of Acts 28 in this chapter. The first has to do with Paul's arrival on Malta. The second concerns his arrival in Rome itself.

When the ship was wrecked, all on board got to shore, as the Lord had revealed to Paul they would. Paul had explained this to the centurion who was in charge of the prisoners. This man, who had certainly developed great respect for Paul during the time Paul had been in his custody, made sure Paul and the other prisoners were spared when the soldiers in conformity with Roman custom wanted to kill them lest any should escape. The text says, "He ordered those who could swim to jump overboard first and get to land. The rest were to get there on planks or on pieces of the ship. In this way everyone reached land in safety" (Acts 27:43–44).

When the castaways arrived safely on shore they discovered they were on the island of Malta and were pleased to find that the islanders showed them kindness. The residents built a fire, and as the stragglers came in out of the water they tried to comfort them as well as they could. Paul was not one to sit around, so he began to help out. He went around gathering sticks for the fire. Apparently in the middle of the sticks was a snake, described here as a "viper," which had become stiff with the cold and was therefore mistaken for a stick itself. When the wood was placed by the fire, the fire warmed the snake, which then bit Paul.

T. E. Lawrence, better known as Lawrence of Arabia, described something like this in his book *Revolt in the Desert* about the desert campaign in World War I.[1] It was cold. The Arabs had gathered sticks for a fire. One of the sticks turned out to be a snake that was revived by the fire's warmth and slithered away into the dark night, in this case without biting anybody.

The snake of Acts 28 bit Paul. The islanders, who were looking on and did not know anything about Paul except that he was one of the prisoners, jumped to an immediate conclusion and said to themselves, "This man must be a murderer; for though he escaped from the sea, Justice has not allowed him to live" (v. 4). However, after several minutes, when they discovered that Paul did not swell up, fall over, and die, they jumped to another conclusion and assumed that he must be a god. Of course, they were wrong on both counts.

It is hard to say why people jump to conclusions so easily, but we may remember that even the disciples of Jesus did it on one occasion. The story is told in John 9. When the disciples were leaving the temple with Jesus they saw a man who had been born blind, and they jumped to the conclusion that his affliction must have been the direct result of sin in his life or the sin of his parents. They thought they had worked this through rather carefully and that all they needed was a little bit of divine revelation to carry them over what they could observe or figure out. Jesus explained that they were wrong in their conclusions since neither explanation was valid.

A Christian Answer to Suffering

I have frequently heard people do this in regard to someone else's suffering. If something bad has come into a person's life they say, "Well, obviously, he (or she) has done something wrong. God must be trying to teach the person a lesson." That may be true sometimes. That is why when bad things come into our lives one of the questions we have to ask is whether God is trying to teach us a lesson by it. But we need to understand that this is not necessarily the case. In the case of suffering, we must never make the easy one-to-one equation of suffering and sin.

The Bible gives a number of explanations why believers suffer. It speaks of common suffering, corrective suffering, constructive suffering, Christ-glorifying suffering, and cosmic suffering.

1. *Common suffering.* One thing the Bible says is that suffering is often just the common experience of human beings living in a fallen world. Perhaps Job said it best, observing,

> Hardship does not spring from the soil,
>   nor does trouble sprout from the ground.
> Yet man is born to trouble
>   as surely as sparks fly upward.
>
> Job 5:6–7

Years ago one of the deacons of Tenth Presbyterian Church was sold on the value of health foods. His living room was filled with books on health and health diets. There were hundreds and hundreds of books, and they spilled out of the living room into the other rooms of the house. There was hardly a place to sit down. This man thought that if you ate right, drank the right herbal teas, and took the right vitamins, you would probably live forever.

He lived to his middle eighties. As he got older things began to go wrong with him physically. His body didn't function as well as it had done when he was forty, sixty, or even seventy. I remember visiting him on one occasion, and he said to me, somewhat plaintively, "I just can't understand what's gone wrong."

I had to explain that as you get older, your health just declines. It is not because you have neglected to take care of yourself. It is not because you have sinned. It is just the natural course of life.

2. *Corrective suffering.* When we go astray God sometimes brings hard things into our lives to bring us to our senses. We must ask ourselves whether we

have done wrong and whether God is bringing the hardship into our lives to draw us up short so we will get off the wrong path and back onto the right one. Hebrews 12:5–11 describes it.

You have forgotten that word of encouragement that addresses you as sons:

> "My son, do not make light of the Lord's discipline,
>   and do not lose heart when he rebukes you,
> because the Lord disciplines those he loves,
>   and he punishes everyone he accepts as a son."

Endure hardship as discipline; God is treating you as sons. For what son is not disciplined by his father? If you are not disciplined (and everyone undergoes discipline), then you are illegitimate children and not true sons. Moreover, we have all had human fathers who disciplined us and we respected them for it. How much more should we submit to the Father of our spirits and live! Our fathers disciplined us for a little while as they thought best; but God disciplines us for our good, that we may share in his holiness. No discipline seems pleasant at the time, but painful. Later on, however, it produces a harvest of righteousness and peace for those who have been trained by it.

3. *Constructive suffering.* The third kind of suffering the Bible talks about is constructive. That is, God develops character by what we suffer. Romans 5:3–4 says, "Suffering produces perseverance; perseverance, character; and character, hope." The hard things that come into our lives build character.

4. *Christ-glorifying suffering.* This is what Jesus pointed to when the disciples asked about the man who had been born blind. Jesus told the disciples, "Neither this man nor his parents sinned, but this happened so that the work of God might be displayed in his life" (John 9:3). In other words, some suffering is simply that the glory of God might be displayed in Christians. In most situations it would be presumptuous to assume that this is what God is doing with us. We suffer for other reasons far more often. Nevertheless, it is sometimes the case.

Did God let that man be born blind and sit there all those years without sight just so Jesus Christ could come along at that moment and heal him and thus bring glory to God? Yes, that is what Jesus was teaching. We focus on the thirty-eight years of the man's life while God focuses on eternity, and in the light of eternity the short span of our lives fades into relative insignificance.

5. *Cosmic suffering.* Job is the greatest story in the Bible about suffering. In Job's case God was demonstrating before Satan and all the fallen and unfallen angels that a man will worship and serve God for who God is and not merely because God takes care of him and prospers him.

Even when we get to the very end of Job's story, we find that the meaning of his suffering has not been explained to Job. The only reason we understand it is because at the beginning of the book, we are shown a scene in heaven

in which God calls Satan's attention to Job, saying, You think he worships
me only because of the things I give him; but you can take those things away,
and he will still love and praise me. God permits Satan to afflict Job, and Job
comes through triumphantly—though not without a great deal of puzzlement
and anguish.

Paul's snakebite was a small incident, but it showed how Paul was loving
and serving God regardless of his difficult circumstances: captivity, shipwreck,
hunger, cold, and snakebite. The people took note of the miracle, and later
there were other healings. One who was healed was the father of the "chief
official" of Malta.

"Chief official" is the exact technical term for the person who represented
Rome in that place; it is another example of Luke's extraordinary accuracy.
There is another accurate detail as well. Luke says that the father of the chief
official was suffering from fever and dysentery. It was probably a sickness common to this area of the world, known as Malta fever. It is caused by a bacterium
carried by the goats of Malta and produces symptoms that last four months
on the average but can sometimes last for years. It was identified in 1887.[2]

Rome at Last

At last the party moved on to Rome. They had spent three months on Malta
because they were unable to sail further during the winter months. The shipwreck had taken place in November. That month had to pass, then all of
December and January. So it was certainly well into February, perhaps even
March, when the weather began to clear up sufficiently for ships to sail again.
Another grain ship from Alexandria was wintering on the island, so the soldier
in charge took space on that ship, and the prisoners were carried forward
on the next stage of their journey.

When we read the paragraph beginning at verse 11, it seems almost as if
Luke had a notebook in which he kept a log. His notes say that they put in
first at Syracuse, the capital city of Sicily and the point of land that would
have been closest to them if they were sailing north from Malta toward Rome.
Syracuse had been founded as a Corinthian colony in 734 B.C., but it had
passed to Roman rule in 212 B.C. It was a port city, with a good double harbor.
The traveling party stayed there for three days. Next the ship went to
Rhegium, on the very tip of the toe of the boot of Italy. From there, helped
forward by a strong southerly wind, it passed through the straits of Sicily with
the island on the left and Italy on the right. The wind must have been a very
good one, because by the next day they had covered the nearly two hundred
miles from Rhegium to Puteoli, Rome's southern port. The long, tiring, and
nearly fatal journey by sea was over, and Luke records with a masterful under-
statement: "And so we came to Rome" (v. 14).

When they arrived on the mainland word quickly spread that Paul had
come. We remember that Paul had written to the Romans quite a few years
before, saying that it was his intention to come to Rome. He seemed to have

been preparing for his visit, asking for a good reception and carefully suggesting that the Roman Christians might help him with his plans to plant
churches farther to the west in Spain. Tired from his long sea voyage, Paul
must have been anxious about how these believers would receive him. Would
they even know that he had come? Immediately, it would seem, Christians
from Rome set off down the Appian Way to meet him. Luke says that some
made it as far as the Three Taverns, others as far as the Forum of Appius.
There was a distance of about ten miles separating them. There they greeted
Paul, and Paul was encouraged.

I am sure the greetings of these Christian brothers and sisters meant a great
deal to him. He did not know what he was coming to, perhaps to martyrdom
for Christ's sake. He knew people who were in Rome, but he must have had
doubts as to how he would be received. So when some Christians of Rome
came out to meet him, thereby showing how they loved him and cared for
him, his spirits must have perked up and he must have gone forward joyfully.

Still, when I read of this show of encouragement, I remember that some
years later when Paul was writing to the Philippians from his Roman prison,
he spoke of trouble among the Christians in Rome, noting that some of it
was due to "envy" of himself (Phil. 1:15–17). And later, when he wrote
2 Timothy, the last of his letters, he referred to a man named Onesiphorus
who came to visit him but who was at first unable to find where Paul was. Paul
wrote of him: "When he was in Rome, he searched hard for me until he found
me" (2 Tim. 1:17). This suggests that although the Christians of Rome greeted
Paul warmly when he first arrived they soon lost track of him and were therefore unable to tell Onesiphorus where Paul was when he inquired.

When Paul first arrived he was a celebrity. Paul, the great missionary! The
Christians streamed out to see him. But then this great missionary was imprisoned. First, he was placed under house arrest where he had some freedom
of motion and could meet with his friends and those interested in Christianity.
He would have been chained by his wrist to a Roman guard. Later, Paul seems
to have lost his freedom, perhaps during a second imprisonment, and was
locked away. As time went by, the Christians in Rome seem to have forgotten
about him, as people do.

People run hot and cold. We need to remember that. But we also need
to remember how important encouragement can be when we can give it.

Three Great Contrasts

There are many contrasts in the story of the voyage by ship from Caesarea,
the arrival on Malta, and then finally the arrival at Rome.

1. *Turmoil versus inner peace.* One contrast is between the turmoil without
and Paul's quite evident peace within. These were tumultuous times. The
storm was a literal tumult. But there was also the tumult of the crowd in
Jerusalem. There was tumult in the empire, things going from bad to worse.
Yet through it all Paul seems to have been at complete peace in the Lord.

2. *Vacillation versus consistency and steady progress.* A second contrast is between the vacillation of others and the consistency and steady progress of Paul. When Paul fell into the hands of the Roman authorities, they hardly knew what to do with him. One ruler after another tried to decide what to do and kept vacillating. Even the voyage to Rome illustrates the uncertainty. There were three ships, delays, and a shipwreck.

What impresses us if we take our eyes off these external matters and look at Paul is that God was working with him steadily to bring him to Rome, where he was to bear a witness.

3. *Fear versus faith in God.* The third contrast is between fear on the part of many and faith in God on the part of the apostle. There were all kinds of fears. Fear of what people would say, fear of what the Jewish leaders would do, fear of what Caesar might think. And there was fear of ridicule, fear of being thought ridiculous, not to mention fear of the storm and the death it threatened. Many kinds of fears were expressed. But throughout it all Paul, who had his mind not on others but on God, was strong in faith and remained calm.

What made the difference was that Paul was aware that God was with him. He knew God had a purpose for him. If God said that he would bear a witness for Jesus in Rome, then Paul would most certainly bear witness in Rome. Paul was willing to rest on that.

Perhaps that is where the story should end and where the application should be most evidently made for us. We also live in a vacillating world, a world of dangers, and we live among people who are filled with fear. We are called to be as Paul was in the midst of it: counting on God, resting in him, and moving forward steadily to do the work he has called us to do.

Can we do it? Will we?

We can and will, if we know that God is with us and that he is leading us each step of the way.

50

Preaching Christ
without Hindrance

Acts 28:17–31

From morning till evening he explained and declared to them the kingdom of God and tried to convince them about Jesus from the Law of Moses and from the Prophets. Some were convinced by what he said, but others would not believe. . . .

For two whole years Paul stayed there in his own rented house and welcomed all who came to see him. Boldly and without hindrance he preached the kingdom of God and taught about the Lord Jesus Christ.

Acts 28:23–31

We come in this chapter to the end of Acts, the end of what is by any measurement a most remarkable book. F. F. Bruce points out that in Luke and Acts, Luke set out to chronicle the expansion of Christianity from a small beginning in Judea, a distant province of the Roman Empire, to its being a world religion and a force in many cities. This was a considerable task.

In documenting this expansion, Luke succeeded in relating it to the events and personalities of the time. That is, he did not write a story that merely stands by itself but rather one that constantly brings in those many people

424

who would be known to his contemporaries. For example, he is the only one of the New Testament writers to mention a Roman emperor; none of the others do. And he mentions not only one emperor, he mentions three of them. He even alludes to a fourth—Nero, the emperor to whom the apostle Paul appealed when being tried by Festus. Luke refers to other personalities too. In almost every city Paul visited, Luke mentions the person who was the magistrate in charge. What is even more significant, not only does he allude to them by name and get their names right, he even gets their titles right, in spite of the fact that these varied from place to place and changed from time to time.

Luke shows accurately and in a way that would commend it to the readers of his time the power of the gospel of Jesus Christ to infuse and eventually to transform the world.[1]

A Remarkable Ending

This remarkable Book of Acts also has a remarkable ending. Have you ever come across a book that ended as this book does? It has been chiefly concerned with the apostle Paul: his ministry, persecutions, successes, and imprisonment. But then, at the very end, when we are expecting to learn how it all turned out, the story of Paul's life is abandoned and all we read is that "for two whole years Paul stayed there in his own rented house and welcomed all who came to see him. Boldly and without hindrance he preached the kingdom of God and taught about the Lord Jesus Christ" (vv. 30–31).

It is not an ending that Luke merely threw in without thought. It is exactly the way Luke wanted his history to end, because no matter how fascinating we may find the histories of Peter, Philip, Paul, or any of those strong personalities who dominate the book, the subject of Luke's narrative is not the lives of these servants of God but the gospel. Luke is concerned with how the gospel grew and expanded. So when we get to the very end of Acts, we find that this is happening. Christianity had begun in Jerusalem with the commissioning of the disciples by Jesus Christ, and now in the very heart of the capital of the Roman Empire Paul is preaching. Luke tells us that in those days, for a period of time at least, the gospel was preached without hindrance.

There were all sorts of hindrances if we look at the situation only from a human point of view, and more would come. Persecution is a hindrance, and Paul had experienced plenty of that. He had been beaten, stoned, falsely accused, and arrested. Now he was in prison. He could not move about as he might have wished. There was opposition from Paul's own people, the Jews. There was indifference on the part of the Roman authorities. But in spite of these external hindrances, which were great, the gospel was not hindered because the Word of God cannot be bound.

Isn't that a wonderful thing? When you and I talk to people about Jesus Christ we are often conscious of the hindrances in us. We do not seem to have the answers to their questions, for example. We wish we could present the gospel more clearly and wisely. We wish we had more experience to draw from. And there are hindrances in the people too: They are hostile, out of touch, or indifferent. People do not want the gospel today any more than they wanted it in the days of Jesus Christ or Paul. Yet, in spite of these hindrances, the Word of God itself is not hindered. Our task is merely to make it known, knowing that the God for whom all things are possible will bless it, since he has promised to do so.

God says of the Word that goes out from his mouth:

> It will not return to me empty,
> but will accomplish what I desire
> and achieve the purposes for which I sent it.
> Isaiah 55:11

The First Meeting with the Jewish Leaders

The last verses of Acts describe two meetings the apostle Paul had with people in Rome. Three days after he arrived and got settled he called the leaders of the various Jewish communities in the city together. There were a number of synagogues in Rome at the time. The remains of some of them exist even today, so we know that there were at least three and probably more than that. Paul got in touch with the leaders of these synagogues because he wanted to explain why he was in Rome, what he had been charged with, and why the accusations had been false.

He made three points in his meeting with these leaders.

1. *He was not guilty of any offense against Israel* (v. 17). Paul wanted that to be clear. It was true that charges had been brought against him by the Jewish leaders in Jerusalem, but he was not guilty of these or any other offenses.

2. *The Romans had been ready to release him and actually wanted to release him* (v. 18). Here he is talking about what the Romans would have considered a crime. In other words, he is making two points. He had done nothing against his people, and in addition to that he had done nothing that could offend the Romans. As a matter of fact, the Romans would have released him were it not for the objections of the Jewish leaders.

3. *He had not brought a counter charge against the Jewish leaders* (v. 19). We can understand how that might have been done since it is a standard legal maneuver today. If somebody sues you, you counter sue immediately because you want to show that the other party is the guilty one, rather than yourself. Paul says that he did not do this. He had not brought any charges against his own people.

After Paul had made this presentation to the leading Jews of Rome, the leaders were most discreet. On the one hand, they denied that they had heard anything about his case. It is hard to believe that this was true, but it must have been since they would have had no reason for lying. It may have been that the Jerusalem authorities, assuming that Paul would probably be released by the Romans in Rome and being content that at least he was now out of their hair, simply did not pursue him with their charges. But whatever the explanation may be, the Jewish leaders in Rome maintained, no doubt honestly, that they did not know anything about Paul's case.

On the other hand, they said, "We have heard something about the sect of the Nazarene, and we must tell you, quite frankly, that what we have heard is not good."

"Well," said Paul in effect, since this is what he was leading up to anyway, "why don't we all get together sometime, and I will explain my teaching?" These men agreed to do so. They were serious. They were responsible as well as distinguished leaders, and they recognized that it was their duty to hear, examine, and make a judgment about Christianity. They gave proof of their sincerity by fixing a date for the larger meeting.

The Second Meeting

More people came to this second meeting: that is, not only the leaders themselves but others who were distinguished in some way, or perhaps even laypeople from the various synagogues and Jewish communities in the city who were interested.

At this second meeting, Paul preached the gospel and did it all day long (v. 23). He began in the morning and went on until evening, declaring the kingdom of God and preaching Jesus. That is a sermon I would like to have heard or have had recorded or videotaped. I do not think this would have been a monologue. Paul would have taught, as he did in other places. But in this company, he would have been questioned by the rabbis, who would have known the Old Testament well and would have had very astute minds. If Paul gave a uniquely Christian interpretation of an Old Testament prophecy, they would have challenged it and pursued it as only rabbis can do. This went on all day.

As I say, I wish we had a recording of this day's debate or knew what Paul preached. Nevertheless, although we do not have a record of it, I think it is not all that difficult to surmise what might have been said since the very next book in the Bible is Romans, which Paul had written just three years earlier to explain the gospel to this very community. We may suppose that he followed the general outline of Romans more or less.

He would have begun by speaking of our obligation to know God and worship him, to love him with all our hearts, minds, souls, and strength. This would have been a point of contact with his Jewish hearers because these obligations are what the Scriptures teach.

Paul would also have pointed out that we have all fallen short of God's standard. He would have explained why, much like he did in the early chapters of Romans. "Gentiles have rejected the knowledge of God," he would have said. "But we Jews have missed it, too. We have substituted our own righteousness for God's righteousness, forgetting the matters of faith and trust, which are so prominent in the Old Testament. We have substituted ceremonies for a heart relationship with God."

I do not know the hearts of those to whom he was speaking. But if they were sensitive men, as we have every right to suppose they were, something in them may have acknowledged that this was true. Which of us, if we have any sensitivity at all, even after we come to know God through Jesus Christ, is not aware of a coldness of heart toward Almighty God? We know we should love him, but we find that we do not. We find barriers between ourselves and God. Even our prayers seem to be unheard. These Jews may have acknowledged that to themselves quietly.

Paul must have continued by saying, "So you see, it is not a question of being a Jew or a Gentile. We are sinners, all of us. 'There is no one righteous, not even one; there is no one who understands, no one who seeks God'" (Rom. 3:10–11). Those words are not only in Romans; they are found twice in Psalms (Pss. 14:3; 53:3). His hearers would have known these texts, and the words would have found an echo in their hearts.

Then Paul would have gone on to talk about Jesus, the hope of Israel. The Messiah has come, he would have argued. This is the point at which he would have gotten opposition. "We are expecting the Messiah, to be sure, but not the despised Nazarene," they would have said. Paul would have gone to the many Old Testament prophecies about him and would have shown how Jesus fulfilled these prophecies. The Jews were looking for a day when God would reestablish Israel as the dominant, chosen nation. Paul would have shown that before that happened it was necessary for the Messiah to sacrifice himself to provide salvation for all people. God does not show favoritism. He does not show concern for one nation rather than another. He cares for all peoples equally.

At this point the Jews began to disagree among themselves (v. 25). Some of them believed Paul, apparently convinced by his reasoning. Most did not. The negative reaction was so strong that Paul was led to cite this text from Isaiah.

> Go to this people and say,
> "You will be ever hearing but never understanding;
>   you will be ever seeing but never perceiving."
> For this people's heart has become calloused;
>   they hardly hear with their ears,
>   and they have closed their eyes.
> Otherwise they might see with their eyes,
>   hear with their ears,
>   understand with their hearts
> and turn, and I would heal them.
>
> Acts 28:26–27 (cf. Isa. 6:9–10)

Paul concluded, "Therefore I want you to know that God's salvation has been sent to the Gentiles, and they will listen!" (v. 28).

John Stott points out that Paul was accustomed to this reaction and had done the same thing before:

> Three times before, stubborn Jewish opposition has led Paul to turn to the Gentiles—in Pisidian Antioch (13:46), in Corinth (18:6), and in Ephesus (19:8, 9). Now for the fourth time, in the world's capital city, and in a yet more decisive manner, he does it again (v. 28).[2]

Response to Unbelief

For Paul this must have been an enormous problem. He was a Jew himself. Jesus was the Jews' Messiah. Jesus had done what was prophesied about him in the Jewish Scriptures. The apostles had proclaimed the gospel, but for the most part the Jews were rejecting the message. How could that be? How could it be that the Messiah of Israel should be rejected by Israel? Did it mean that God had cast off his people? Did Jewish unbelief show that God was being unfaithful to the promises he had made to the Jewish nation? In Romans 9–11 Paul carefully worked out the answer to this problem.

First, he says that no one is ever saved except by the electing grace of God (Rom. 9:6–18). The choice is always with God. So if God elects many Jews at one period of history but not at another and many Gentiles at still a different period of history, well, that is God's business. Salvation is never guaranteed simply by being Jewish or by any other line of descent.

Second, the rejection of the Messiah by a large portion of Israel had been prophesied in the Old Testament (Rom. 9:19–29). This meant that Jewish unbelief should not have been unexpected. Paul quotes from Isaiah 10:22–23 and 1:9 to show that only a remnant of the nation would be saved.

Third, although it had been prophesied that a majority would reject the Messiah when he came, the rejection nevertheless would be the unbelievers' fault (Rom. 9:30–10:21). Why? Because they would pursue salvation without faith and by means of their own righteousness, rejecting the righteousness of God. In other words, the Jews of Paul's day wanted God to praise them for how well they were doing. That is exactly the error people of all ethnic backgrounds also make today. They do not want grace from God. They want to achieve salvation by themselves.

Fourth, although most of the Jews were rejecting Jesus, not all were doing so (Rom. 11:1). Some had believed. Paul cites himself as an example. "I am an Israelite myself," he says.

Fifth, this is not new. It has always been this way. Even in the days of Elijah, only seven thousand Jews remained faithful to God. The rest had become apostate (Rom. 11:2–10).

Sixth, although God is moving primarily among Gentiles in this age, even this is for Israel's good (Rom. 11:11–24). Paul speaks of the conversion of the Gentiles as provoking Jews to jealousy. This was intended to lead some of them to consider the case for Jesus being the Messiah and thus eventually to believe on him.

Seventh, in the end "all Israel will be saved" (Rom. 11:22–32). That means that there will yet be a future time of great national blessing for Israel when the masses of the Jewish people will turn to their Messiah.

Someone has said that God never closes one door in our lives but that he opens another one. I do not know how one could prove that to be true. We would have to examine all the closed and open doors in all Christians' lives to do it. Still in a general way we all sense that this is accurate. It has been our experience. God closes one door, but he opens another.

This happened here. The door to the Jewish community was closing. Not many Jews believed. But the door was opening to the Gentiles. Paul himself said, "I want you to know that God's salvation has been sent to the Gentiles, *and they will listen*" (italics mine). It is with the recognition of this truth that Acts ends.

That new door to the Gentiles (and perhaps now in a new way also a new door to the Jews) is open today. Acts ends as it does because throughout this age until Jesus Christ returns the gospel door is open. As long as that door was open Paul was going to preach through it to the Gentile community. If he did it, then we must do it too. It is our opportunity. If God opens a door to the Jews for you, walk through it. If God opens a door to the Gentiles, walk through it. If God opens a door to your neighbor, walk through it. Wherever you go, if people will listen, tell them about Jesus, because this is the day of Christian proclamation. It is by the preaching, teaching, and sharing of the Word of God that people are brought to Jesus.

God's Gospel and God's Plan

I want you to notice a few last points as we end this study of the Acts of the Apostles.

1. *The gospel Paul preached in the twenty-eighth chapter of Acts is the same gospel preached by Peter in the second.* It was not a different gospel because it was being preached to different people, by a different person, or in a different setting. No matter who is preaching or where, it is always the same gospel. It is the gospel of salvation through Jesus Christ. It is our gospel today.

2. *The results of the preaching of that gospel are the same.* Some reject it, and some respond to it. It was that way when Peter preached at Pentecost. It was that way when Paul preached at Rome. It is that way when we teach about Jesus Christ today. We are not to think that if we experience rejection or resistance we are any different from those who have preceded us.

3. *Christ's plan for the expansion of the gospel and the founding of his church has not altered.* As Acts closes the Great Commission is being fulfilled. We may be frustrated by what we regard as the slow progress of the gospel but Jesus is not frustrated. His plans are not sidetracked.

What happened to the apostle Paul? Historians are divided. The general opinion today is that Paul was released after two years. Luke does not write about it, because he was not with Paul then and because he wants the book to close on this open optimistic note. Paul may have traveled to other places. The last books he wrote were the pastoral epistles, 2 Timothy especially, and he seems to refer to things in those books that may not have happened in the historical time frame Luke presents in Acts. Paul may have traveled to the west. He may have gotten to Spain. He seems to have gone to Crete.

The tradition in the church is that Paul returned to Rome after the great fire of A.D. 64. There was such an outcry from the people because of this fire that Nero blamed it on the Christians. Eusebius says that Paul came back shortly after that, in a time of hostility toward Christians, was arrested, and eventually was martyred.

But from God's perspective and from the perspective of the Book of Acts, there is a sense in which it does not really matter. What happens to his servants does matter to God, of course. The Bible says, "Precious in the sight of the LORD is the death of his saints" (Ps. 116:15). What happens to you matters to him. But there is a sense also in which what happens to us is incidental to the greater story, which is the expansion of the gospel. At one period of history there may be a great moving of God's Spirit, and everything will seem to be going well. At other times, times more like our own, the response to spiritual things will be superficial or people will be hostile. But, in a sense, it does not matter.

What does matter is whether we are faithful in the calling to which God has called us. The Lord Jesus Christ told his disciples, "This gospel of the kingdom will be preached in the whole world as a testimony to all nations, and then the end will come" (Matt. 24:14). That end has not yet come. So you and I still have the task of preaching it.

Will we? Will we be found faithful?

That is the final question for us from Acts. The Word is not hindered. We are its messengers. Will we take the gospel to the ends of the earth beginning with our Jerusalem, as we have been instructed to do? If we will, God will bless it to the praise of the glory of his great grace.

Notes

Preface

1. John Stott notes that no fewer than nineteen significant Christian speeches occur in Acts. "There are eight by Peter (in chapters 1, 2, 3, 4, 5, 10, 11 and 15), one each by Stephen and James (in chapters 7 and 15), and nine by Paul (five sermons in chapters 13, 14, 17, 20 and 28, and four defense speeches in chapters 22 to 26). Approximately 20% of Luke's text is devoted to addresses by Peter and Paul; if Stephen's speech is added, the percentage rises to about 25%." See John R. W. Stott, *The Message of Acts: To the Ends of the Earth* (Leicester, England: InterVarsity, 1990), 69.

Chapter 1: *The First Forty Days*

1. F. F. Bruce, *The New Testament Documents: Are They Reliable?* (1943; reprint, Downers Grove, Ill.: InterVarsity, 1992).

2. Stott, *The Message of Acts*, 34.

3. For a fuller treatment of Reimarus's work and its significance see James Montgomery Boice, *Foundations of the Christian Faith* (Downers Grove, Ill.: InterVarsity, 1986), 81–82.

4. Stott, *The Message of Acts*, 41.

Chapter 2: *World Christians*

1. Tertullian, "Apology," in *The Ante-Nicene Fathers*, vol. 3, Alexander Roberts and James Donaldson, eds. (Grand Rapids: Eerdmans, 1963), 45.

2. Adolf Harnack, *The Mission and Expansion of Christianity in the First Three Centuries* (New York: Harper & Brothers, 1961), 368.

3. See James Montgomery Boice, *The Gospel of John*, 5 vols. in 1 (Grand Rapids: Zondervan, 1985), 988–91.

Chapter 3: *Preparing for Growth*

1. F. F. Bruce has the interesting observation that on this last occasion of a legitimate historical reference to Mary, Jesus' mother, we find her with the

other followers of Jesus engaged in worship. See his *Commentary on the Book of Acts* (Grand Rapids: Eerdmans, 1975), 44.

2. For example, in E. M. Blaiklock, *The Acts of the Apostles* (Grand Rapids: Eerdmans, 1963), 53.

Chapter 4: *That Incendiary Fellowship*

1. Stott, *The Message of Acts*, 60.

2. There is also a story of the creation of man in Genesis 1, but there the emphasis is different. It is upon man being made in the image of God. This is stressed by being repeated three times over. In Genesis 2 the emphasis is upon man being created from the dust of the earth.

3. John R. W. Stott, *The Baptism and Fullness of the Holy Spirit* (Downers Grove, Ill.: InterVarsity, 1964), 28.

4. The references are: 2:4; 4:8, 31; 6:3; 7:55; 9:17; 11:24; 13:9, 52. The other New Testament references are Luke 1:15, 41, 67; 4:1; and Ephesians 5:18.

5. Elton Trueblood, *The Incendiary Fellowship* (New York: Harper & Row, 1967).

Chapter 5: *The Sermon that Won Three Thousand Souls*

1. C. H. Dodd, *The Apostolic Preaching and Its Developments* (New York: Harper & Brothers, 1935).

Chapter 6: *A Model Church*

1. John R. W. Stott, "The Sovereign God and the Church," in *Our Sovereign God: Addresses Presented to the Philadelphia Conference on Reformed Theology 1974–1976*, ed. James M. Boice (Grand Rapids: Baker, 1977), 160.

2. Stott, *The Message of Acts*, 87.

Chapter 7: *The First Miracle*

1. The story is told by a medieval writer named Cornelius. See Bruce, *Commentary on the Book of Acts*, 84.

Chapter 8: *No Other Name*

1. Everett F. Harrison, *Acts: The Expanding Church* (Chicago: Moody, 1975), 84.

Chapter 9: *Civil Disobedience*

1. Francis A. Schaeffer, *A Christian Manifesto* (Westchester, Ill.: Crossways, 1981).

2. For a fuller treatment of these four options see Boice, *Foundations of the Christian Faith*, 688–99.

Chapter 10: *The Church at Worship and at Work*

1. Stott, *The Message of Acts*, 99.

Chapter 11: *Two Whom God Struck Dead*

1. It is possible that Barnabas owned property in Jerusalem, of course, and that he sold that property. But Barnabas was a Levite, and Levites were not supposed to own property in Israel. Besides, Luke's identification of him as a citizen of Cyprus is most likely intended to suggest that the land he owned was there.

2. C. S. Lewis, *Mere Christianity* (New York: Macmillan, 1958), 72.

Chapter 12: *Suffering Disgrace for Christ's Name*

1. Although Gamaliel was well known and rightly praised for his gentleness and moderation, Paul (Saul) who studied under him was of a different stamp entirely. Paul concluded that the way to deal with Christianity was to kill Christians.

Chapter 13: *The First Deacons*

1. There is a lesson here for our own relationship to civil government. Today's church is all too ready to have the civil government take care of social problems that are rightly its own responsibility. We would be better off (and more biblical) if we took care of them ourselves.

Chapter 15: *Samaria: The Widening Stream*

1. Later we get back to Judea, though this is not quite the order we expect. We expect (1) Jerusalem, (2) Judea, (3) Samaria, and (4) Rome. Instead we have (1) Jerusalem, (2) Samaria, and (3) Judea. This also suggests that Judea and Samaria are to be taken together as one region.

2. For example, Bruce, in his *Commentary on the Book of Acts,* says on page 179, "The nature of his belief must remain uncertain. No doubt it was sincere as far as it went, but [it] was very superficial and unsatisfactory."

Chapter 16: *Philip and the Ethiopian*

1. Blaiklock notes rightly that "the story sets the seal of New Testament authority on the interpretation of Isaiah 53 and the associated 'servant' passages as prophecies of Christ." See *The Acts of the Apostles,* 81–82. If the New Testament interprets an Old Testament passage one way, we are not at liberty to give it some other contradictory interpretation.

2. Stott, *The Message of Acts,* 163.

Chapter 17: *The Conversion of Saul*

1. My version, an old one, has West's and Lyttleton's books bound together: *Lord Lyttleton on the Conversion of St. Paul and Gilbert West on the Resurrection of Jesus Christ* (New York: The American Tract Society, 1929). In some editions the flyleaf contains the words: "Blame not until thou hast examined the truth." The story of these two men is told in R. A. Torrey, *The Bible and Its Christ* (New York: Revell, 1904–1906), 98–100.

2. Frank Morison, *Who Moved the Stone?* (1930; reprint, Downers Grove, Ill.: InterVarsity, 1969).

3. Lord Lyttleton, *The Conversion of St. Paul*, 487.

Chapter 18: *Saul's First Preaching*

1. Christopher Pike's story is told by Edward E. Plowman in *The Underground Church* (Elgin, Ill.: David C. Cook, 1971), 13–16.

2. Charles W. Colson tells his story in two early books: *Born Again* (Lincoln, Va.: Chosen Books, 1976) and *Life Sentence* (Lincoln, Va.: Chosen Books, 1979).

3. Stott, *The Message of Acts*, 179.

Chapter 20: *No Favorites with God*

1. John Stott also takes this position. "We have already watched [Peter] use these keys effectively, opening the kingdom to the Jews on the Day of Pentecost and then to the Sanhedrin soon afterwards. Now he is to use them again to open the kingdom to Gentiles; by evangelizing and baptizing Cornelius, the first Gentile convert." See *The Acts of the Apostles*, 184.

2. The details of this division are in Leviticus 11, forty-seven verses that distinguish "between the unclean and the clean, between living creatures that may be eaten and those that may not be eaten" (v. 47).

3. H. A. Ironside, *Lectures on the Book of Acts* (New York: Loizeaux Brothers, 1945), 250.

Chapter 21: *Even Gentiles*

1. Blaiklock, *The Acts of the Apostles*, 96. The quoted second half of the citation is from a work by R. J. Knowling.

2. In some commentaries this chapter is therefore appropriately called "The Gentile Pentecost."

Chapter 22: *No Further Objections*

1. Blaiklock, *The Acts of the Apostles*, 97–98.

2. John Stott speaks of God's leading in terms of "four successive hammer blows" of revelation: the divine vision (vv. 4–10), the divine command (vv. 11–12), the divine preparation (vv. 13–14), and the divine action (vv. 15–17). See *The Message of Acts*, 194–95.

Chapter 23: *Christians First at Antioch*

1. This is one evidence of the veracity of Luke as a historian. For an excellent description of the local color and atmosphere of the major cities of the eastern Mediterranean as Luke presents them see F. F. Bruce, *The New Testament Documents: Are They Reliable?*, 88–89.

2. Ironside, *Lectures on the Book of Acts*, 282.

3. Ibid., 284.

Chapter 24: *Victory in Spite of Unbelief*

1. R. A. Torrey, *The Power of Prayer and the Prayer of Power* (Grand Rapids: Zondervan, 1955), 77.

Chapter 25: *The Death of Herod*

1. Details of the Herodian dynasty may be found in many places. I have taken these from *A Dictionary of the Bible*, ed. James Hastings, vol. 2 (1899; reprint, Edinburgh: T. & T. Clark, 1958), 353–62.

2. Josephus, *Josephus*, vol. 9, *Jewish Antiquities*, trans. Louis H. Feldman (Cambridge: Harvard University Press; London: William Heinemann, 1965), 377–81. The early church historian Eusebius, whose material is obviously taken from Josephus, says that it was an angel (no doubt the angel of Acts 12:23) and not an owl that Herod saw prior to his being smitten (*The Ecclesiastical History*).

3. Stott, *The Message of Acts*, 213.

Chapter 26: *The Start of the Missionary Era*

1. See Bruce, *The New Testament Documents*, 82.
2. Stott, *The Message of Acts*, 220.

Chapter 27: *One Sabbath in Antioch*

1. W. M. Ramsay, *St. Paul the Traveler and the Roman Citizen* (London: Hodder and Stoughton, 1895). The discussion of Paul's illness, the "thorn in the flesh," is on 94–97.

2. G. Ernest Wright, *God Who Acts: Biblical Theology as Recital*, Studies in Biblical Theology, no. 8 (London: SCM Press, 1952).

Chapter 28: *Another Sabbath in Antioch*

1. Ramsay, *St. Paul the Traveler and the Roman Citizen*, 102–4.

Chapter 29: *A Tale of Three Cities*

1. Ramsay, *St. Paul the Traveler and the Roman Citizen*, 110–13.
2. Ovid, *Metamorphoses* (New York: The Heritage Press, 1961), 267–72.

Chapter 30: *The First Church Council*

1. See the footnote in the New International Version.
2. Everett F. Harrison, *Acts: The Expanding Church* (Chicago: Moody, 1975), 239.

Chapter 31: **"Come Over and Help Us"**

1. Matthew 28:18–20; Mark 16:15–18; Luke 24:46–49; John 17:18; Acts 1:7–8.

Chapter 32: *A Straight Question and a Straight Answer*

1. Stott, *The Message of Acts*, 269.

Chapter 33: *Two More Cities*

1. See Blaiklock, *The Acts of the Apostles*, 129.
2. Ibid.
3. As we go on from this point we will be dealing with more churches to whom the apostle Paul wrote letters. He goes to Corinth in Acts 18, and he wrote two letters to Corinth. In chapter 19 he visits Ephesus, and he wrote a very important letter to Ephesus. At the end of the book he gets to Rome, to which he wrote the most important of all his letters, the Book of Romans. We have already studied his work in Philippi to which Paul wrote Philippians.

Chapter 34: *The Sermon on "The Unknown God"*

1. Blaiklock, *The Acts of the Apostles*, 132. There is an excellent summary of Athens' rise to greatness and rapid decline on 132–36.
2. Because of the nature of the Greek language, the inscription, which lacks the definite article, can be rendered either "to *an* unknown god" (NIV) or "to *the* unknown god" (KJV and other texts).
3. Ramsay, *St. Paul the Traveler and the Roman Citizen*, 252.

Chapter 35: *Many People in This City*

1. This case was important for Luke's underlying purpose of providing a political apology for Christianity. As John Stott says, "Gallio's refusal to take seriously the Jewish case against Paul or to adjudicate was immensely important for the future of the gospel. In effect, he passed a favorable verdict on the Christian faith and thus established a significant precedent. The gospel could not now be charged with illegality, for its freedom as a *religio licita* had been secured as the imperial policy" (*The Message of Acts*, 300).

Chapter 36: *More Laborers for the Harvest*

1. The edict of Claudius is the first reference in non-biblical literature of the presence of Christians in Rome. Suetonius, the Roman historian, says in reporting on the activities of Claudius, "Since the Jews constantly made disturbances at the instigation of Chrestus, he expelled them from Rome" (*Suetonius*, Loeb Classical Library [1965], 53). Who was Chrestus? Chrestus could be somebody we have never heard of and do not know anything about. But the general feeling among scholars is that Suetonius probably confused the name Chrestus with Christ. If that is the case, the words of Suetonius seem to indicate he knew at this time there was trouble in the Jewish community in Rome centered around this person. When Paul himself got to Rome, he tells us that he experienced mistreatment as a result of similar disturbances (Phil. 1:15–18).

Chapter 37: *The Church in Ephesus*

1. Roger S. Greenway, *Apostles to the City: Biblical Strategies for Urban Missions* (Grand Rapids: Baker, 1978).
2. Ibid., 96.
3. Greenway develops these five points in *Apostles to the City*, 87–95.

Chapter 38: *The Riot in Ephesus*

1. Ramsay, *St. Paul the Traveler and the Roman Citizen*, 277.

Chapter 39: *Going Home*

1. This is John Stott's argument: "Luke declares that he was dead; as a doctor he could vouch for it" (*The Message of Acts*, 320).

Chapter 40: *Paul's Farewell to the Ephesian Elders*

1. Stott, *The Message of Acts*, 328.

Chapter 41: *When a Good Man Falls*

1. Erwin W. Lutzer, *When a Good Man Falls* (Wheaton, Ill.: Victor Books/SP Publications, 1986).
2. John Stott believes that Paul was right to go on to Jerusalem, or at least that Luke thought he was right. As far as Agabus is concerned, Stott draws a distinction between "a prediction and a prohibition" (*The Message of Acts*, 333). Everett Harrison says, "To picture Paul as willfully disobedient through this drawn-out experience is a serious charge, for which there is no justification" (*Acts: The Expanding Church*, 322). Blaiklock considers the matter an open question: "He [Paul] was moving forward under a deep inner compulsion, and it is not for anyone lightly to question the honest convictions of such a man. At the same time great men are not beyond the possibility of error, and Scripture is habitually frank in reporting faults and failings" (*The Acts of the Apostles*, 168).

Chapter 42: *Gentiles! Gentiles!*

1. Bruce points out that the offering "consisted of one he-lamb, one ewe-lamb, one ram, and accompanying cereal and drink offerings (cf. Num. 6:14f.; Mishnah, *Nazir*, vi., 6ff.)" (*Commentary on the Book of Acts*, 431).
2. Blaiklock notes how Paul was perfectly at home in three cultures. "His Greek first caught the tribune's attention. He addressed the crowd in their Hebrew dialect. He was soon to claim his Roman privileges" (*The Acts of the Apostles*, 173).

Chapter 43: *God's Servant in Roman Hands*

1. Harrison, *Acts: The Expanding Church*, 345.
2. W. A. Farrar, *The Life and Work of St. Paul* (London: Cassel, 1879), 541, cited in Blaiklock, *The Acts of the Apostles*, 175.

3. Francis A. Schaeffer, *Escape from Reason* (Chicago: InterVarsity, 1967); *The God Who Is There* (Chicago: InterVarsity, 1968).

Chapter 44: *The Plot to Murder Paul*

1. Ironside, *Lectures on the Book of Acts*, 545.
2. Tacitus, *Histories*, trans. Clifford H. Moore (Cambridge: Harvard University Press, 1962), 193.

Chapter 45: *The Trial before Felix*

1. See Harrison, *Acts: The Expanding Church*, 351, 354; and Bruce, *Commentary on the Book of Acts*, 462.
2. Blaiklock, *The Acts of the Apostles*, 179.
3. Ironside, *Lectures on the Book of Acts*, 586–87.

Chapter 46: *The Trial before Festus*

1. Stott, *The Message of Acts*, 367.
2. C. F. D. Moule, *A Chosen Vessel* (London: Lutterworth Press, 1961), 69, 70, cited in Harrison, *Acts: The Expanding Church*, 366.
3. Aleksandr Solzhenitsyn, *The Gulag Archipelago, 1918–1956: An Experiment in Literary Investigation*, I–II (New York: Harper & Row, 1973), 130.

Chapter 47: *The Trial before King Agrippa*

1. Ironside, *Lectures on the Book of Acts*, 610–11.

Chapter 48: *Peril at Sea*

1. Thomas Walker wrote, "There is no such detailed record of the working of an ancient ship in the whole of classical literature." See Thomas Walker, *The Acts of the Apostles* (Chicago: Moody, 1965), 543, cited in Stott, *The Message of Acts*, 385.
2. James Smith, *The Voyage and Shipwreck of St. Paul* (1848; 4th ed. revised by Walter E. Smith; London: Longmans, Green & Co., 1880), cited in Stott, *The Message of Acts*, 386.
3. Donald Grey Barnhouse with Herbert Henry Ehrenstein, *Acts: An Expositional Commentary* (Grand Rapids: Zondervan, 1979), 224.

Chapter 49: *All Roads Lead to Rome*

1. T. E. Lawrence, *Revolt in the Desert* (New York: Garden City Publishing Co., 1926–1927), 75. See Bruce, *Commentary on the Book of Acts*, 521.
2. The details are in Stott, *The Message of Acts*, 395.

Chapter 50: *Preaching Christ without Hindrance*

1. Bruce, *The New Testament Documents: Are They Reliable?*, 80–82.
2. Stott, *The Message of Acts*, 399.

Subject Index

441

Scripture Index

More great **Tools** _for_ **Christian Leaders**
from JAMES MONTGOMERY BOICE

Fill your _library_ with
uncompromised _quality_

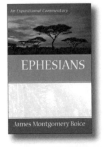

BAKER PUBLISHING GROUP

To purchase, visit your local bookstore or
order online at **www.bakerpublishinggroup.com**.